ENGLISH BLAKE

Also by Bernard Blackstone

The Ferrar Papers, 1938

Virginia Woolf: a Commentary, 1949

The Consecrated Urn: A Study of Keats, 1959

The Lost Travellers: Variations on a Romantic Theme, 1962

Practical English Prosody, 1965

HEAD OF WILLIAM BLAKE

Pencil drawing by John Linnell (1820)

ENGLISH BLAKE

BY

BERNARD BLACKSTONE

M.A., PH.D., LITT.D., CANTAB.

Professor of English Language and Literature in the University College of Rhodesia and Nyasaland; sometime Byron Professor of English Literature, Athens University

I rest not from my great task!
To open the Eternal Worlds, to open the immortal Eyes
Of Man inwards into the Worlds of Thought, into Eternity
Ever expanding in the Bosom of God, the Human Imagination.

ARCHON BOOKS
HAMDEN, CONNECTICUT
1966

para
JUDITH
meu bem

First Published 1949

Reprinted 1966 with the permission of
The Cambridge University Press
with a new foreword by the author

Library of Congress Catalog Card Number: 66-20227
Printed in the United States of America

CONTENTS

PLATES

FOREWORD

THE seventeen years that have passed since this book was first published have brought many advances in Blake scholarship. The unremitting labours of Sir Geoffrey Keynes (*Blake Studies*, 1949, and *The Complete Writings of William Blake*, 1957) have cleared up many textual and biographical problems and have established the canon. Facsimiles of the Prophetic Books appear at intervals: if too expensive for most readers they can be consulted in libraries and open up for the first time since Blake's own day an understanding of his complex genius as poet and painter. On the side of interpretation, we find such investigators as Kathleen Raine and Piloo Nanavutty pointing to his affinities with Neo-Platonism and the metaphysics and cosmology of the Upanishads and the Gita (*The Divine Vision*, 1957). In the historical field David V. Erdman has shown how the Prophetic Books reflect, often in grotesque guise, the social and political currents of Blake's age (*Blake, Prophet against Empire*, 1954).

None of these advances have affected the basic theme of this book however, or made necessary any major modifications in it. One reason for this is that it is a factual survey, a study of Blake's 'Englishness', of the predominantly 'British' rather than alchemical, mystical, or theosophical strands in his thought. Such a survey can be deepened, as indeed it has been in books such as Erdman's, but hardly challenged, since it is rooted in 'the history of ideas'. If I were writing the book now, in 1966, I should give some attention to Blake's reading in the periodical essayists, particularly Addison and Steele, many of whose ideas and attitudes are glanced at in the *Songs of Innocence and Experience*. This is a field which, as far as I know, is still unexplored. And I should have to make a few corrections of fact. H. M. Margoliouth has shown (see Keynes, *The Complete Writings of William Blake*, 1957, p. 884) that the 'Reverend Henry Mathew' who is supposed to have written the Preface to *Poetical Sketches* never existed: Blake's patron was in fact the Reverend Anthony Stephen Matthews, minister of Percy Chapel. The 'sunny Cubes of light and heat' which inspired me to write a somewhat fanciful footnote in the original edition of this book have in the meantime been discovered to be not 'Cubes' at all but 'Orbes'. And there are a few other minor corrections.

As a *survey,* casting back to the Renaissance and taking in the Hermetic as well as the rationalist tradition up to Blake's own time, the book may still serve to correct the over-emphasis on Blake's up-to-dateness, his obsession with the here-and-now of contemporary politics and social problems, which affects such books as Erdman's and Bronowski's (William Blake 1757-1827, *A Man Without a Mask,* 1944). Of course Blake was a man of his time, and a rebel, 'against empire'; but he was also 'not of an age but for all time', a 'prophet' indeed, and a seer. To lose sight of his prophetic mission, to underplay that aspect of his work which is 'doctrinal to a nation' and indeed to the race, and focus attention on the palpable and the limited in him, is to do him—and his readers—the greatest of disservices. The marvellous lines which stand on the title-page of this study, and the Linnell drawing which serves as a frontispiece, will suffice to draw attention once more to what was Blake's true purpose in all he designed or wrote.

B. B. 1966.

PREFACE

THIS study of Blake is concerned chiefly with his position within the tradition of English thought. Many books have been written to trace his sources back to the Cabbala, the alchemists, Jakob Boehme, and Emanuel Swedenborg; many others have sought to fix the exact meanings and relations of his system of symbols. But Blake called himself English Blake, and from first to last he lived and worked within an English context of thought and society. At times he can be almost aggressively patriotic. All the time he is concerned with building Jerusalem in England's green and pleasant land. All the time, too, he is working consciously within an English rationalist tradition which he dislikes, and to which his writings are constantly referring, implicitly and explicitly. And side by side with the rationalist tradition he is conscious of an anti-rationalist tradition within which he feels himself to be at home, and which is just as English: the tradition of Chaucer, Milton, Cowper.

Blake's thought is both constructive and destructive. Error must be cast out before truth can be embraced. Blake saw error working within the process of history, and within every aspect of that process. Politics, philosophy, religion, the social order, education, morality, all were contaminated by the error which springs from division within the human totality.

Now to Blake history was essentially English history. Even the history of the patriarchs, even the narrative of the Fall and the Garden of Eden has reference to Albion. Why this should be so is related at some length in M. Denis Saurat's *Blake and Modern Thought*. Blake was proud of being an Englishman. His mind was soaked in the spirit of English history, in the rhythms of Milton and the Bible, in Chaucer and Shakespeare, and in the sights and sounds of the English countryside and the English metropolis. His art is the expression of a revolt from something peculiarly English towards something even more English—a revolt from the imposing tradition of philosophical thought from Bacon to Hartley, towards the ancient wisdom of the patriarchs who were the first inhabitants of 'Albion's ancient Druid rocky shore'. And he gave the name of

Albion to the ancient primeval Man from whose torn body the earth and the heavens were created, and all the host of them.

To set Blake in his right position within the tradition of English thought I have interspersed my narrative of his life and teachings with discussions of those writers to whom he refers constantly, such as Bacon, Newton, and Locke—his philosophical Trinity of evil—or by whom he has clearly been deeply influenced, such as Milton and Berkeley. This interweaving tends to hold up the narrative but I hope it will be found a help to the understanding in Blake's work—and especially in the longer symbolical books—of some obscure passages. We cannot hope to understand the positive side of a controversial writer like Blake until we are quite clear about what he is attacking, and where he gets his ammunition from. Blake has for too long been regarded as an isolated phenomenon, a literary Melchizedech. For this reason too I have tried to sketch in the social and political background of his age so far as it is relevant to my theme.

Blake is a writer of great significance for our time. His significance is in part absolute and in part historic. He is one of the few Western writers (I can think only of St John of the Cross as a second) who successfully combine poetry and mysticism. For the West, he is a key figure in mystical thought. The writings of Blake stand beside the Gita, the Upanishads and the *Tao Teh Ching* among the spiritual masterpieces of the world. In English literature there is no one to compare him with after the mystical writers of the Middle Ages—Walter Hilton, Richard Rolle, and the author of *The Cloud of Unknowing*. He has no progenitor; and he founded no school. He stands quite alone as a prophet at the close of the materialistic eighteenth century and the opening of the mechanistic nineteenth century, proclaiming in a spiritual wilderness the doctrine of the eternal world.

His significance, I have suggested, is in part historic. The great poets of the past could be great poets in another way than Blake's (and in one sense better poets, since they need be poets and nothing more) because they lived and worked in a religious tradition. The Catholic order was accepted by Chaucer, Malory, and even Shakespeare, as a true system of beliefs. But Milton already finds himself obliged to supply a theodicy, Sir Thomas Browne is a 'fidei defensor', and all important subsequent writers are bound to re-examine and establish the foundations of their belief or unbelief. The eighteenth century is, on the whole, a giving-up of the struggle: it adopts a *laissez-faire* attitude, an acceptance of the doctrine that this world is all we have and we must do our best with our short life while we have it.

> Huddl'd in dirt the reas'ning Engine lies,
> Who was so proud, so witty and so wise,

sneers the Earl of Rochester, at the end of the seventeenth century, with masochistic satisfaction. And we remember the long perverse agony of Jonathan Swift.

Of course that is not the whole story. The names of William Law, Emanuel Swedenborg, Cowper, and Collins remind us that great spiritual forces were at work under the surface. And the succeeding age found in the Romantic revival a reaffirmation of the primacy of the spiritual, a rediscovery of the divine comedy. But these names and these things, as active influences to-day, have passed away. Blake remains, and grows in strength. Why?

The reason lies, I believe, in the singular purity of Blake's personality and doctrine. The continental mystics lost themselves in charlatanry or political embroilments. Cowper and Collins were ineffectual voices tinged with lunacy. Wordsworth bound himself hand and foot, first to the physical world and later (even more lamentably) to Anglicanism. Blake alone kept his soul and his message undefiled. 'He kept the divine vision in time of trouble.'

To give a general account of the life, work and doctrine of William Blake is the purpose of this study. In the main my interpretations must be tentative. The writings of Blake are voluminous and of immense complexity. His thought is difficult, and it is expressed in a mythological form which bears more than one interpretation.

Blake's teaching is a theology, a politics, an aesthetics, a morality, a philosophy, a sociology. Yet in making these divisions—and later on in considering Blake's work, as I must for the sake of order, under these divisions—I am already beginning to falsify the essence of his truth. To divide, to methodise, to analyse, to classify: are not these the very things against which Blake protested? Alas, yes. But the dilemma is unavoidable. To see Blake's truth we must divide it;

but to understand we must again unite. Let it be remembered that these divisions and generalisations are purely technical—indispensable but distorting devices for the discussion of any subject. And let it be remembered too that the essence of Blake's teaching is to be found not only in the long 'prophetic books' but in those brilliant flashes of insight, those 'logoi spermatikoi', which are his lyrics. Above all, I am not trying to make a system, or to 'give the gist' of what Blake said.

The reality to which he bore witness is the existence of the eternal world, and the possibility of each man's attaining to it in this life. 'Eternity on this side of the grave' might be given as Blake's slogan. The power of attaining this reality he called 'vision'. This vision is achieved through the arts, and principally through making life itself an art, i.e. a creative process.

The existence of a spiritual world is of course a postulate of all religions. Techniques of attaining it are inculcated in all systems of devotion. "The kingdom of Heaven is within you", said Christ. Blake did not regard himself as a teacher of any new doctrine. He was an interpreter of Christ to the present age. He was a restorer of the primitive Gospel. Christ was the master, as He must always remain the master of the Western world, however much we may learn from the East. But the original message of Christ has become obscured, Blake thought, by priestcraft. Religion is the enemy of Christ. Mystery, the dark thing at the heart of all religion, and reason, the glaring thing at the perimeter, have destroyed the crystal clarity of the original revelation. Human greed for power has used the gospel of freedom for its own ends; and by a monstrous reversal Christ's teaching has been made a new slavery.

Here again Blake was saying nothing entirely new. All religious reforms have claimed to go back to the original doctrine which lay beneath an accretion of later superstition. This is precisely what the Protestant reformers of the sixteenth century did, what the Franciscans had done, what the Methodists were doing. But, because these movements still clung to the old creeds and sacred books, interpreting them in a literal way and organising new ecclesiastical systems, they in turn sank into the abyss of mystery and power-seeking. Blake knew that if he was to free his belief from the slavery of the past and the danger of corruption in the future, he must devise a new vehicle of revelation; and he must guard against the possibility of systematisation.

In this task Blake had two tremendous advantages; and two disadvantages. In the first place he was a very great original mystic. Even as a child he saw the external world of material forms as the thinnest of veils covering the eternal world of values. His father was angry with him because he insisted that he saw a tree full of angels; and it was perhaps with this memory in mind that he wrote later in the *Proverbs of Hell* 'A fool sees not the same tree that a wise man sees'. Secondly, he was an artist of the first order. He was a very great poet and painter. He had the supreme gift of concentrating a whole vision of life into a few lines which never leave the memory:

> He who binds to himself a joy
> Does the winged life destroy;
> But he who kisses the joy as it flies
> Lives in eternity's sun rise.

Being a mystic he *saw* with absolute clearness. He saw in terms of images; and he used images for the expression of his vision. Here comes the first disadvantage. People are inclined at all times to distrust poetry; they are put off by symbols. And Blake's symbolic framework is particularly complicated. To work one's way into it is more than a difficult task; it is, to begin with at least, a real torture. The processes of Blake's mind are so strange to us, the realms into which he introduces us are so remote from our everyday landscape, that we feel like people who have been taken up unprepared to an impossible altitude, where breathing is difficult and there is a terrifying emptiness. Yet, if we will be patient and courageous, the reward is great. Little by little, as we grow accustomed to the odd personages, events and topography of Blake's apocalyptic kingdom, we become aware of a strange familiarity. Blake is saying something that we know already, though we may never think about it. We may never want to think about it, for there is often a terror in knowledge. Knowledge brings its compulsion and its agony with it. Yes: we know this country already: it is the region of the human mind.

> [For] in the Brain of Man we live & in his circling Nerves...
> Where Urizen & all his Hosts hang their immortal lamps.

Blake's kingdom is the mind of Man: it is the eternal world. For the mind is boundless. It includes all things, and transmutes all things in understanding. And because this message is enormously difficult to convey in words, Blake felt himself compelled to construct a mythology which should have no reference to the Christian mythology as given by the churches.

> I must Create a System or be enslav'd by another Man's.
> I will not Reason & Compare: my business is to Create.

He was compelled to create a system, and so came the second danger, the danger of generalisation. 'The man who generalises is a fool.' Wisdom, as we shall see later on, consists in 'minute particulars', not in systematic generalisation. It is not by collocating particulars, and then deducing from them some general law, as the logicians do, that we attain wisdom. It is by accepting each minute particular in love, and seeing through it to the divine unity, and only thus. This power Blake calls faith or vision. And it could, he believed, be taught. He firmly believed that he was here to teach it.

It was, he knew, a difficult task. The thing itself was immensely simple. It was the recovery of innocence, of that power which the child has, so soon lost and so seldom regained. But to regain the power one has to struggle with terrible accretions of prejudice, blindness, sloth and cruelty. The very difficulty of the task is an essential condition for success. Blake knew that he was not a quack doctor administering an infallible medicine. He was a teacher. He was teaching men to help themselves.

> That which can be made Explicit to the Idiot is not worth my care. The wisest of the Ancients consider'd what is not too Explicit as the fittest for Instruction, because it rouzes the faculties to act,

he says in one of his letters. Hence the 'difficulty' of his symbolic works was, in his eyes, inevitable for two reasons: first, it greatly removed the danger of religious systematisation of his teaching; secondly, it 'roused the faculties to act' for themselves.

Few poets have been so serenely conscious of their vocation as Blake. He burned with 'the desire of raising other men into a perception of the infinite'. He is a teacher. But if we ask 'What does Blake teach?' using the word *teach* to imply the formulated exposition of a body of doctrine, we are approaching him in a wrong way. Blake does not 'teach' as a schoolmaster teaches. His work is accomplished on the level of what Keyserling calls 'creative understanding'. On that plane he can even use, if he pleases, the old names and the old forms, while infusing into them an entirely new meaning. His originality does not lie in any precise system which one can extract from his writings. Piece by piece, we can trace his thought to many sources. It lies in the extraordinary passion and conviction with which he conveys his thought, in the lovely and burning words of his verse.

Far from seeking to set forth abstract doctrine, Blake's aim was purely practical: to embody wisdom in life, to create new personalities, to bring men to the New Birth. His message is that of Christ: "Except ye be born again, ye cannot inherit the Kingdom of God." Blake's appeal was to the young men of the New Age, the modern world which was then dawning. And it is to each individual man and woman that Blake appeals, not to an abstract humanity, but to the 'minute particulars' of the individual. Blake knew that the individual is unique, a precious and ungeneralisable whole; and that it is in the unique and not in the general that the eternal world is revealed. He expected that his teaching would be understood and followed by the young generation; by few at first, but later by many. That expectation was not fulfilled. The emotional forces of the nineteenth century were diverted from wisdom first by the natural animism of Wordsworth, the rhetorical humanism of Byron and the lyrical utopianism of Shelley; and secondly by the nation's growing industrial wealth. The verse of Tennyson at the end of the century represents the very antithesis of what Blake was striving for at the beginning. Blake saw the French Revolution as a cosmic event heralding man's re-entry into Eternity:

> "Till the power and dominion is rent from the pole, sword and scepter from sun and moon,
> The law and gospel from fire and air, and eternal reason and science
> From the deep and the solid, and man lay his faded head down on the rock
> Of eternity, where the eternal lion and eagle remain to devour."

He saw the French Revolution in this light because it was abolishing law and reason, the chief enemies of vision. And he was able to keep his faith in the *meaning* of the French Revolution even after its empirical collapse, because to him all earthly things were images; while Wordsworth, pinning his faith too precisely to the event in time, lost his belief and fell into despair, in the end rejecting man in favour of 'the delusive goddess nature and her laws'. The empirical failure or success of the French Revolution was irrelevant for Blake. That was a mere question of politics; and politics he despised.

> I am really sorry [he says in the *Public Address*] to see my Countrymen trouble themselves about Politics. If Men were Wise, the Most arbitrary Princes could not hurt them. If they are not wise, the Freest Government is compell'd to be a Tyranny. Princes appear to me to be Fools. Houses of Commons & Houses of Lords appear to me to be fools; they seem to me to be something Else besides Human Life.

Something other than human life! In this phrase we have the key to the vast complex of Blake's thought. He will deal with nothing which is not human life in some aspect or other. The vicious generalisations of priests and politicians, in which the precious, unique individuals are sacrificed to the Moloch of political and religious codes, are his sworn enemies. 'One Law for the Lion & Ox is Oppression.' His appeal is to the sacred self—not the ego—in each man: an appeal to return to the source of life and joy and energy in the unity of mankind. For to Blake's vision, Man is all; there is nothing outside the divine humanity.

The cosmic reach of Blake's thought lifts him far above the plane of the religious reformers of his own or any other day; and his great gifts as an artist are an advantage which few other mystics possess. Again, it is possible that the second half of the twentieth century will see a growing interchange of thought between East and West; and here Blake is undoubtedly our representative thinker. 'The philosophy of the east taught the first principles of human perception,' he asserts. In the Hindu scriptures we have, as we have it in Blake, the account of a deity forming the world of matter: prajuana, or the eternally active self-conscious Reason, responsible for the whole realm of change. Lao-Tzu taught: 'The Great Significance was abandoned, so there came to be morality and duty.' In the Upanishads again we have precisely Blake's inner world of the mind.

'Thou art the sheath of Brahman. . . . Whosoever worships another deity, in such a manner as he is another, another "I am", does not know.' And so too with his insistence on returning to the world of eternity. The proper aim of man, the Upanishads say, is the undoing of the causes which lead to finite existence. The supreme misfortune is to dwell contentedly in the world of plurality, staking all on the small self, so subject to disease and suffering. By the cleansing of the senses we may attain to eternal life.

Eternal life is the gospel which Blake preached all his life: eternal life which can be entered into here and now, not a life beyond the grave. Blake knew that there is no death, for each soul by accepting life in the here-and-now creates its own eternity; he believed in the immortality of the spirit. But he did not believe in the immortality of the material body. Nor did he believe that eternal life is achieved by following ceremonies or moral laws. The great sin—the only sin which can shut out from the eternal world—is unbelief, wilful blindness. Here again Blake's thought has much in common with Eastern thought. The Buddha makes unawareness one of the deadly sins. In Blake's own words:

> Men are admitted into Heaven not because they have curbed & govern'd their Passions or have No Passions, but because they have Cultivated their Understandings. The Treasures of Heaven are not Negations of Passion, but Realities of Intellect, from which all the Passions Emanate Uncurbed in their Eternal Glory. The Fool shall not enter into Heaven let him be ever so Holy. Holiness is not The Price of Enterance into Heaven. Those who are cast out are All Those who, having no Passions of their own because No Intellect, Have spent their lives in Curbing & Governing other People's by the Various arts of Poverty & Cruelty of all kinds. Wo, Wo, Wo to you Hypocrites.

Unawareness always induces cruelty, intolerance, and all the vices which are the contrary of energy. The secret of life is vision. We have to cultivate the power of seeing 'not with, but through the eye'. Once this faculty is achieved all the rest will be added unto us.

The whole of Blake's work consists of an attempt to develop this faculty of vision, to set forth what is seen, and to induce his fellow men to follow the same road. To see is to understand; to understand is to forgive, and to act rightly. Vision is not only of the eye. The other senses have their part to play, for they are the doors of perception:

> If the doors of perception were cleansed every thing would appear to man as it is, infinite.
> For man has closed himself up, till he sees all things thro' narrow chinks of his cavern....
> The whole creation will be consumed and appear infinite and holy, whereas it now appears finite & corrupt.
> This will come to pass by an improvement of sensual enjoyment.

These words will make very clear an aspect in which Blake differs not only from Christian mystics but from Indian mystics too: his renunciation of renunciation, his opposition to asceticism of all kinds. It is through an improvement of sensual enjoyment that the eternal world is to become apparent. Blake knew that the doctrine of renunciation is one of the subtlest means by which the power-seekers of this world are able to impose on the good and the humble. To renounce is to lower vitality, to shrink from that fullness of life which Christ expressly said He was come to give to the world. It is easy to renounce, for it is always easy, especially for the timid, to cultivate a negative attitude; much more so when it has the approval of religion. What is the hard thing is to accept: to accept the glorious multifariousness of life as an expression of energy, to accept the necessity of cultivating one's understanding so that one can identify oneself with that energy and so escape for ever from the prison of the self.

This, Blake firmly believed, is to be attained through the senses. Not through the senses as they are now, with their pitiful limitation to a material world. But through the senses which have opened themselves to truth in a childlike faith, senses which are regenerate. And principally this emancipation through sense is achieved through the sense of touch: in other words, through sex. Blake believed that the sense of touch was the one of the five senses unvitiated by the Fall. It is the sense in which we share union with another being, and through which we create new forms of life.

It is, indeed, in this doctrine of energy and the senses that Blake most notably differs from his Oriental brother-mystics; and it is this doctrine which renders him so peculiarly valuable for Western Man.

In his conception of energy as the last significance of things, Blake has anticipated the finding of modern science and philosophy. Not matter, but force, is the ultimate reality in Nature. Matter is energy. For this reason all ideals which are static are erroneous. The admirers of the starry universe, such as Wordsworth and Matthew Arnold, fall under the condemnation of death-worshippers; as do all those who praise perfect serenity or balance in the individual. Life is an interplay of contraries. The philosophy of India, with all its wisdom, conveys to the Western mind an impression of passivity. It does not sufficiently recognise the phenomena of change. But change, for the Western mind, is an indispensable aspect of progress and of life itself. It is for this reason that Blake's interpretation is so valuable. His supreme achievement on the practical plane is the *energising* of Oriental wisdom so as to make it accessible to the Western mind: 'Persian lotus-leaves', as Swinburne has it, 'hardened into the consistency of English oak-timber.'

B. B.

ACKNOWLEDGEMENTS

My thanks are due to the Syndics of the Fitzwilliam Museum, Cambridge, for permission to reproduce the pencil drawing by John Linnell; the photographs for plates I–VII and X were supplied by the British Museum; plate VIII is taken from Laurence Binyon, *Engravings of William Blake* (1926).

B. B.

ABBREVIATIONS

A.	*America* (1793).
B.A.	*The Book of Ahania* (1795).
B.E.	*Annotations to Bacon's 'Essays'* (*c.* 1798).
B.L.	*The Book of Los* (1795).
B.S.	*Annotations to Berkeley's 'Siris'* (*c.* 1820).
B.Th.	*The Book of Thel* (1789).
B.U.	*The Book of Urizen* (1794).
D.C.	*A Descriptive Catalogue* (1809).
Did.	*Didactic and Symbolical Works* (1788—1822).
E.G.	*The Everlasting Gospel* (*c.* 1818).
Ep.	*Epigrams, Verses and Fragments* (*c.* 1808—1811).
Eu.	*Europe* (1794).
F.R.	*The French Revolution* (1791).
F.Z.	*The Four Zoas* (1795—1804).
G.A.	*The Ghost of Abel* (1822).
G.P.	*The Gates of Paradise* (1793, 1818).
I.M.	*An Island in the Moon* (*c.* 1788).
J.	*Jerusalem* (1804—1820).
L.	*Letters* (1791—1827).
L.A.	*Annotations to Lavater's 'Aphorisms'* (*c.* 1788).
L.G.	*The Laocoon Group* (*c.* 1820).
M.	*Milton* (1804—1808).
M.H.H.	*The Marriage of Heaven and Hell* (*c.* 1793).
M.P.	*Miscellaneous Poems and Fragments* (1787—1818).
M.Pr.	*Miscellaneous Prose* (1773—1827).
P.A.	*A Public Address* (*c.* 1810).
P.S.	*Poetical Sketches* (1783).
R.D.	*Annotations to Reynolds' 'Discourses'* (*c.* 1808).
S.D.L.	*Annotations to Swedenborg's 'Divine Love'* (*c.* 1788).
S.D.P.	*Annotations to Swedenborg's 'Divine Providence'* (*c.* 1790).
S.E.	*Songs of Experience* (1794).
S.I.	*Songs of Innocence* (1789).
S.L.	*The Song of Los* (1795).
T.	*Tiriel* (*c.* 1789).
T.L.P.	*Annotations to Thornton's 'Lord's Prayer'* (1827).
V.D.A.	*Visions of the Daughters of Albion* (1793).
V.L.J.	*A Vision of the Last Judgment* (1810).
W.A.	*Annotations to Watson's 'Apology'* (1798).

References to passages quoted in the text are given, in square brackets, by the abbreviation of the title followed by the page number of the one-volume Nonesuch edition, edited by Geoffrey Keynes (1927).

I

LIFE AND WORKS

CHAPTER I

Childhood and Youth

O why was I born with a different face?
Why was I not born like the rest of my race?
When I look, each one starts! when I speak, I offend;
Then I'm silent & passive & lose every Friend. [*L.* 1081]

WILLIAM BLAKE was born in his father's house at 28 Broad Street, Golden Square, London, on the 28th of November 1757. He entered the English scene at a point when the great tide of eighteenth-century formalism and elegance was receding, leaving the shore littered with debris. The originators had disappeared; the imitators were busy taking their places. Instead of Locke, Hume, and Gibbon, the age was to have as its mentors Priestley, Hartley and Paine; Pope, Johnson and Gray were to be replaced by Erasmus Darwin, Hayley and the 'learned and awful Mrs Carter, a female Great Cham of literature, and protectress of "Religion and Morality"'. There were as yet no mutterings of the storm which at the century's end was to convulse Europe.

Of Blake's family antecedents little is known. His father, James Blake, was a substantial hosier. Though a Nonconformist, with Swedenborgian leanings, he had William baptised at 'Grinling Gibbons's ornate font in Wren's noble Palladian church of St James's'. The boy was the second of four sons; there was also a daughter, named Catherine after her mother, who outlived the rest of the family. Alexander Gilchrist in his *Life of William Blake* (1863)[1] suggests that William was 'different' from the start, mooned about the London streets, and went off for long solitary walks into the fields and lanes around the city.[2] Certainly it was not long before his

---

[1] From which the above quotations, and any others not specified in this First Part, are taken. Gilchrist's *Life*, the earliest full account of Blake, remains the most readable. I have used the Everyman reprint (1942), which contains valuable additional matter contributed by the editor, Ruthven Todd.

[2] Mrs George, in her *London Life in the Eighteenth Century*, brings evidence to show that by 1767 the surroundings of London had been rendered very unattractive. Jonas Hanway, the philanthropist, wrote: 'We have taken pains to render its environs

faculty of 'vision' made its appearance. He was only eight or ten when he saw a tree filled with angels, and when he told his father about it was barely saved by his mother's intervention from a thrashing for telling a lie. Later he saw other angels walking about among the haymakers in a summer field. The most awesome experience of all came when God Himself pressed His face to the window and peered in at him.

At so early an age the eternal world was opened to him, and the visionary experience clothed in its immediate aftermath with definite forms.

He was a strange being to come out of that respectable middle-class environment. From the beginning he had the gift of direct uninhibited speech about his experiences:

One day a traveller was telling bright wonders of some foreign city. "Do you call that splendid?" broke in young Blake; "I should call a city splendid in which the houses were of gold,[1] the pavement of silver,

---

displeasing both to sight and to smell. The chain of brick-kilns that surrounds us, like the scars of the small-pox, makes us lament the ravages of beauty and the diminution of infant aliment.' These brick-kilns, to which Blake refers so often in the imagery of his symbolic books, were among the Industrial Revolution's earliest efforts towards deforming England's green and pleasant land.

[1] This is the earliest reference we have to *Gold*, one of the predominant symbols of Blake's thought. Commentators have noted how constantly Blake incorporates into the mythological structure of the longer poems the streets and districts of London—'mournful ever-weeping Paddington', Lambeth, Primrose Hill and South Molton Street—but have not remarked that Golden Square itself, though never mentioned by name, is a far more pervasive idea. It would not be too much to say, indeed, that Blake's whole cosmography is based on the suggestions evoked by the collocation of these two words. The idea of a square—the quaternary—meets us everywhere, from the four seasons which open the *Poetical Sketches* to the Four Zoas and the fourfold city of Golgonooza. Just as the symbolism of *grey cold* is set against that of *golden heat* to point the contrast of energy and sterility in his writings, so too the *square* is set against the *circle* as a pattern of ordered freedom. Heaven is not for Blake as for Milton 'undetermined square or round', but very definitely 'the spiritual fourfold London'—Golden Square raised to the nth degree, as it were. 'Gold' and 'square'—the mathematical and the alchemical magic are here synthetised: the intellectual operation of the 'pure' mathematician links with the 'practical' technique of the alchemist in transmuting 'base' metals into gold. The *circle,* on the other hand, is the constant symbol of restriction, the astronomical heaven of Newton; and Blake's task, as it was the task of the ancient hermetists, is precisely that of squaring the circle, of building the New Jerusalem within and in opposition to the figure described by Urizen's compasses.

the gates ornamented with precious stones." At which outburst, hearers were already disposed to shake the head and pronounce the speaker crazed....

Thus the legend of 'mad Blake' had an early start.

There can have been little sympathy between James Blake and this queer child who saw angels and divine faces, and the very word 'father' was to appear in his writings with constant overtones of tyranny and oppression. Yet James Blake must have been a man of some comprehension and more than ordinary common sense, for he had the wit to see that his son would get nothing out of the current education of the day. He let him off school and at the age of ten William was allowed to follow his bent for art at 'Mr Pars' drawing-school in the Strand', where the boy learned to sketch by copying 'plaster casts after the antique'. Four years later he was apprenticed to Basire the engraver. He stayed with Basire seven years, and during this time made the drawings of tombs and sepulchral figures in Westminster Abbey which, we are told, laid the foundations of his life-long love for Gothic. 'Gothic is living form.' And while he was in the Abbey his visionary faculty was at work. On at least one occasion he saw a vision of Christ and the twelve apostles walking down the shadowy aisles.

It was during his apprenticeship to Basire that Blake learned to admire 'firm and correct outline'; indeed, the old engraver's drawing was altogether too firm, and even stiff, for the popular taste; and in later years Blake was to find this old-fashioned style a decided disadvantage when it came to competing with more 'modern' engravers such as Stothard and Bartolozzi. Another thing he learned at this time was the importance of colour—and he learned it, oddly enough, in the Abbey, where he discovered traces of the original colouring on the stone monuments and realised that the grey masses we admire nowadays are merely shadows of the full Gothic magnificence. But he never failed to subordinate colour to line. What angered him most when, in 1778, he became a student at the Royal Academy, was his teachers' failure to appreciate the greatness of line in Raphael and Michelangelo. They did their best to distract his attention to Rubens and the colourists. He was not a docile pupil:

I was once looking over the Prints from Rafael & Michael Angelo in the Library of the Royal Academy. Moser[1] came to me & said: "You should not Study these old Hard, Stiff & Dry, Unfinish'd Works of Art—Stay a little & I will shew you what you should Study." He then went & took down Le Brun's & Rubens's Galleries. How I did secretly Rage! I also spoke my Mind...

[*a line cut away by the binder*]

I said to Moser, "These things that you call Finish'd are not Even Begun; how can they then be Finish'd? The Man who does not know The Beginning never can know the End of Art."

There was a great deal besides to displease Blake at the Academy. He did not like drawing from the living model; he felt that this distorted his visionary insight—not because the model was alive, but because in keeping a set attitude it was erring against the energy of life. He detested the President, the great Reynolds himself, who severely criticised his early work; and all his life he opposed the idea of art as a social ornament for which Sir Joshua stood.

During this period Blake did a number of engravings, by far the best of which is that called *Glad Day*[2] (1780), showing a nude youth standing, or almost springing from the earth, surrounded by the radiance of dawn: under which at a later date he wrote the significant words, 'Albion arose from where he labour'd at the Mill with slaves: Giving himself for the Nations he danc'd the dance of Eternal Death'. It was by engraving that he had to earn his living—now, and all through his life. He often grudged the time and energy which he might have given to greater, more creative things, but he rarely turned out less than his best. He was a conscientious workman as well as a genius. He got to know Stothard and Flaxman: the one best known as an engraver, the other as a sculptor, and both destined to more fame and fortune than ever came Blake's way, though Flaxman at this period was earning a meagre living by designing pottery for the famous Josiah Wedgwood. It is interesting to note that Blake too, though at a later date—around 1815–16, when he was deep in the fires of inspiration which were forging *Jerusalem*—kept himself

[1] Moser, a Swiss by birth, was the first Keeper of the newly formed Royal Academy. The anecdote occurs in Blake's annotations to Reynolds' *Discourses* (Nonesuch edition, p. 975).

[2] See Plate I.

GLAD DAY

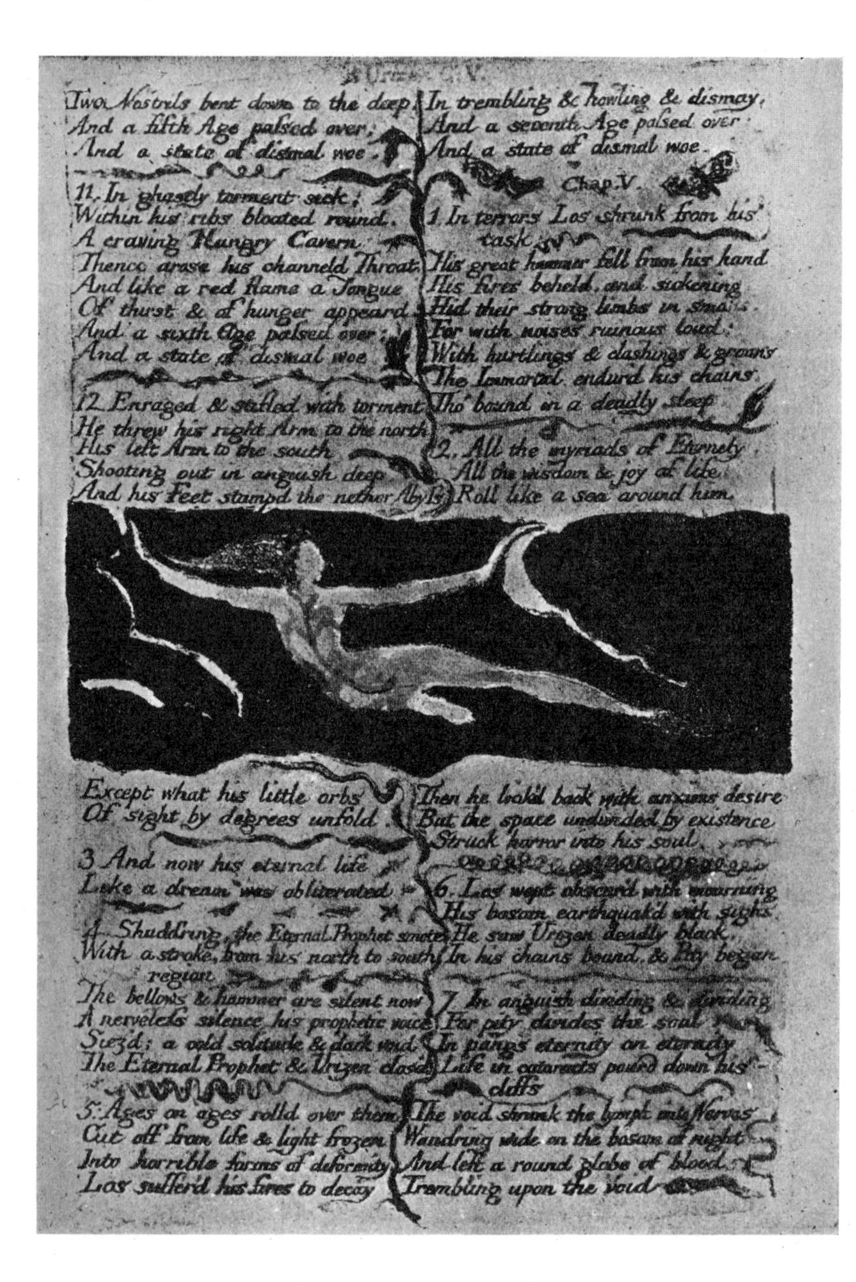

Two Nostrils bent down to the deep.
And a fifth Age passed over;
And a state of dismal woe.

11. In ghastly torment sick;
Within his ribs bloated round,
A craving Hungry Cavern;
Thence arose his channeld Throat,
And like a red flame a Tongue
Of thirst & of hunger appeard.
And a sixth Age passed over:
And a state of dismal woe.

12. Enraged & stifled with torment
He threw his right Arm to the north
His left Arm to the south
Shooting out in anguish deep,
And his Feet stampd the nether Abyss

In trembling & howling & dismay.
And a seventh Age passed over:
And a state of dismal woe.

Chap. V.

1. In terrors Los shrunk from his task:
His great hammer fell from his hand:
His fires beheld, and sickening,
Hid their strong limbs in smoke.
For with noises ruinous loud;
With hurtlings & clashings & groans
The Immortal endur'd his chains,
Tho' bound in a deadly sleep.

2. All the myriads of Eternity:
All the wisdom & joy of life:
Roll like a sea around him,

Except what his little orbs
Of sight by degrees unfold.

3. And now his eternal life
Like a dream was obliterated

4. Shuddring, the Eternal Prophet smote
With a stroke, from his north to south region
The bellows & hammer are silent now
A nerveless silence, his prophetic voice
Siez'd; a cold solitude & dark void
The Eternal Prophet & Urizen closd

5. Ages on ages rolld over them
Cut off from life & light frozen
Into horrible forms of deformity
Los suffer'd his fires to decay

Then he look'd back with anxious desire
But the space undivided by existence
Struck horror into his soul.

6. Los wept obscur'd with mourning
His bosom earthquak'd with sighs
He saw Urizen deadly black,
In his chains bound, & Pity began,

7. In anguish dividing & dividing
For pity divides the soul
In pangs eternity on eternity
Life in cataracts pourd down his cliffs
The void shrunk the lymph into Nerves
Wand'ring wide on the bosom of night
And left a round globe of blood
Trembling upon the Void

'THE SEVENTH AGE'
(from *The Book of Urizen*)

alive by producing designs for household crockery for the furnaces of Wedgwood's Etruria. Flaxman became one of Blake's best friends, second only in his affections to Fuseli, the eccentric Swiss painter and translator. Then there was Romney, who admired the drawings which Blake exhibited in the 1780 Academy and said they would stand with the historical paintings of Michelangelo.

1780: the date is significant for another landmark in Blake's life. It was in early June of this year that Lord George Gordon's anti-popery riots broke out and swept the city. In one vivid episode Blake was, involuntarily, a participant. Strolling along the street which led to Newgate, he was caught up in the mob which rolled down to the gates of the great prison and stormed it, releasing its three hundred inmates. It would be impossible to exaggerate the impression which this episode of violence and liberation made on Blake's mind. The themes of imprisonment and release are constant in his poetry; and the vividness of their presentation may owe much to this early incident.

Blake fell in love with 'a lively little girl' called Polly Woods, who had no objection to going out with him, but encouraged another admirer and laughed when Blake talked of marriage. Blake was hurt and jealous. Garrulous as lovers generally are about their woes and ecstasies, Blake was telling his story in the house of a friend; a pretty dark-eyed girl who sat listening in a corner was moved by compassion and said impulsively that 'she pitied him from her heart'. Impulsiveness was always the way to Blake's esteem; surprised and touched, he told her that he loved her for it, and married her a year later, 18 August 1782. Probably no man has regretted his marriage more, though his biographers tend to gloss this over and make out that the match was little short of idyllic. The facts, however, speak for themselves. William Blake, a great lover of children, was tied for forty-four years to a childless marriage. A man who was a 'mental prince' had to live hour in hour out with a woman who could not sign her name when she married him and never came to show signs of developing intelligence. A fervent believer in free love found himself under the effective domination of narrow-minded jealousy. The story is writ large in the lyrics and the symbolic books. Of course Catherine Boucher was a good wife, a very good wife, as far as her limitations went. She had great gifts of love and devotion. And Blake learned to be content. But it was not the happiness which he, above all men, should have found in marriage.

It appears that his son's union with a market-gardener's daughter was not acceptable to James Blake, and William had to find a new home. He took his young bride—she was twenty—to lodgings at 23 Green Street, Leicester Fields. It was about this time that Blake became acquainted with Flaxman's friend 'the accomplished Mrs Mathew', one of the outstanding blue-stockings of the day, who collected round her such lions as Mrs Montague, 'who gave the annual May Day dinner to the chimney sweepers', Mrs Elizabeth Carter, Mrs Barbauld, Mrs Hannah More, 'as yet young and kittenish, though not without claws', and the sagacious Dr Joseph Priestley. The conversation in this late eighteenth-century salon at 27 Rathbone Place was determinedly intellectual and improving. Blake was drawn in, he read his poems and even sang them to tunes of his own invention; but we can imagine how bored he must often have been. The atmosphere of moral uplift and literary repartee became stifling to his free spirit; and he did not like to know that his young wife was being snubbed and laughed at. His revolt is supposed to have been expressed in the farcical satire *An Island in the Moon*, but I shall shortly give reasons for supposing that this refers to quite a different gathering or gatherings. At all events, he did revolt, and Rathbone Place knew him no more.

Before he shook this improving dust off his feet, however, an event of the first importance for English poetry had taken place. The Mathews, who seem to have been decent souls enough, were impressed by the lyrics which Blake had recited at their *conversazioni*, and persuaded him to have them printed—undertaking to defray half the cost. Thus, in 1783, the *Poetical Sketches by W. B.* appeared, introduced by a modest—too modest—preface from the pen of the Rev. Henry Mathew:

> The following Sketches were the production of untutored youth, commenced in his twelfth, and occasionally resumed by the author till his twentieth year...Conscious of the irregularities and defects to be found in almost every page, his friends have still believed that they possessed a poetic originality, which merited some respite from oblivion....

The volume opens with a quartet on the seasons—four lyrics which blend a certain statuesque quality with a curious energy. It is surely not adventitious that this insistence on the quaternary comes so early in Blake's writing. And is it purely fanciful to detect in these vivid personifications the broad outlines of Los, Urizen, Tharmas and Luvah—the Four Zoas who are to dominate the symbolic works? Summer is surely Los:[1]

> O Thou, who passest thro' our vallies in
> Thy strength, curb thy fierce steeds, allay the heat
> That flames from their large nostrils! thou, O Summer,
> Oft pitched'st here thy golden tent, and oft
> Beneath our oaks hast slept, while we beheld
> With joy thy ruddy limbs and flourishing hair.

The last phrase anticipates all Blake was later to write of the glory of exuberant vitality. And in the last stanza of the poem summer, like Los in the later works, is associated with music, dance and poetry:

> Our bards are fam'd who strike the silver wire:
> Our youth are bolder than the southern swains:
> Our maidens fairer in the sprightly dance:
> We lack not songs, nor instruments of joy,
> Nor echoes sweet, nor waters clear as heaven,
> Nor laurel wreaths against the sultry heat. [*P.S.* 4]

—in which lines also (as elsewhere in these *Poetical Sketches*) Blake's almost aggressive Englishness becomes vocal.

If summer is Los by anticipation, winter is as obviously the icy and ominous figure of Urizen:

> Lo! now the direful monster, whose skin clings
> To his strong bones, strides o'er the groaning rocks:
> He withers all in silence, and his hand
> Unclothes the earth, and freezes up frail life. [*P.S.* 5]

And here, in this juxtaposition of heat and cold, of 'golden tent' and 'dark habitation', we have the clue to Blake's basic imagery throughout the length and breadth of his work. Already *evil* is equated with

---

[1] The name is simply 'Sol' reversed.

cold, *good* with *heat*. Blake has nothing complimentary to say of winter. He does not enlarge, as so many of our native poets have felt constrained to do, on the bracing effects of the winter climate of these islands. No: cold, snow, ice, frost, sleet, fog, and bitter winds are to him simply evil; and when he comes to paint the definitive picture of his evil spirit, Urizen, he is careful to surround him with all these wintry attributes. The sun and its rays, on the other hand, are the very principle of life, and the word 'golden' the most precious in his vocabulary. The 'Age of Gold' in *A Little Girl Lost* (*Songs of Experience*) is 'free from winter's cold', and that is the first thing to be said about it.

The new magic which Blake brought into the English lyric is heard in his first lines—the opening of *To Spring*:

> O thou with dewy locks, who lookest down
> Thro' the clear windows of the morning, turn
> Thine angel eyes upon our western isle,
> Which in full choir hails thy approach, O Spring!

This combination of energy with massive drawing remains, throughout his work, one of Blake's cardinal qualities. These figures are no mere Augustan personifications. Already Blake is developing his peculiar humanisation of non-human things: a humanisation which is so far from humanism. The process is precisely the opposite to that whereby Wordsworth assimilates his old leech-gatherer to a rock or a cloud. Note how penetrated it all is with light:

> all our longing eyes are turned
> Up to thy bright pavillions...

and the sense of smell, too, is acute:

> let our winds
> Kiss thy perfumed garments; let us taste
> Thy morn and evening breath... [*P.S.* 3]

in a directness of sensuous experience which was something new in English eighteenth-century verse. Every detail is intensely visualised. Even the diction has largely escaped from the neo-classical fetters, and the rhythm follows its own laws. We are already in the golden world of Blake's imagination, seeing 'not with but through the eye', in these lines of *To Autumn*:

> "The narrow bud opens her beauties to
> The sun, and love runs in her thrilling veins;
> Blossoms hang round the brows of morning, and
> Flourish down the bright cheek of modest eve." [*P.S.* 4]

Autumn, as a personification, we may perhaps identify as an early sketch of Tharmas, the body, singing his 'lusty song of fruits and flowers', while spring, the emotional season, fits in well with the later conception of Luvah, the passions.

The famous lines *To the Evening Star* strike an even more original note than the Four Seasons. The star draws 'the blue curtains of the sky', scatters 'silver dew on every flower'; and there is perfection in the phrasing of

> Let thy west wind sleep on
> The lake; speak silence with thy glimmering eyes,
> And wash the dusk with silver. [*P.S.* 5–6]

Words here have become the scarce-veiled expression of a spiritual perception extraordinarily acute. The resemblance is to nothing in the national literature, but rather to the hymns of the *Rig-Veda*; the hymn *To Night* in its English translation at least strongly recalls the rhythm and atmosphere of Blake's poem. But the Vedas, according to Dr Joseph Priestley's *Comparison of the Institutions of Moses with those of the Hindoos and other ancient Nations* (1799), had not yet been translated into any European language.

The longer poems, which show the influence of Ossian, Chatterton, Shakespeare, Spenser and other Elizabethans, and the Nordic cult of the time, are less important; though even in these many hints of Blake's later themes may be found. Urizen we meet again in the figure of Gwin, King of Norway; and once Albion appears, though in feminine guise, in the Ossianic fragment *The Prologue to King John*. We note too the image of the lost traveller in *The Couch of Death*:

> "I seem to walk through a deep valley, far from the light of day, alone and comfortless!...I walk in regions of Death, where no tree is; without a lantern to direct my steps, without a staff to support me...." [*P.S.* 42]

This theme is to be taken up again and amplified in the *Songs of Innocence and Experience*.

A War Song to Englishmen is perhaps the most curious, and the least successful, of these pieces. We see that Blake had not yet reached that position of complete pacifism and hatred of war which was to be so marked later. But the patriotism of the poem is an uneasy one. Blake is not sure of himself. In the unfinished dramatic piece *King Edward the Third*, on the other hand, he paints a golden picture of an England at peace, with a firmness of touch significantly in contrast with the fumblings of the *War Song*:

> Then shall England's verdure shoot, her fields shall smile,
> Her ships shall sing across the foaming sea,
> Her mariners shall use the flute and viol,
> And rattling guns, and black and dreary war,
> Shall be no more. [*P.S.* 37]

The sense of unsureness, however, which appears in several of the poems may have been the reason why Blake himself appears to have cared so little for the *Poetical Sketches*. He let them sink into oblivion. They contain a number of perfect poems, they abound in shining phrases which pierce the imagination, but their general effect is of unreality. Blake had yet to attain that precision, that barebone inevitability of phrase, which marks his greatest work.

This first literary production was not followed up for six long years—years of struggle and disappointment. More and more he found from experience how little his peculiar style of engraving pleased the popular taste. The suave and conventional designs of Stothard were preferred to his. He saw himself reduced—now and throughout his life—to the task-work of engraving the designs of artists, including Stothard, whom he knew to be infinitely below him in inventive power. Sometimes his resentment broke out in the form of epigrams written in the notebook which he never intended for publication:

> S[tothard] in Childhood on the Nursery floor
> Was extreme Old & most extremely poor.
> He is grown old & rich & what he will:
> He is extreme old & extreme poor still. [*Ep.* 847]

For in spite of all the frowns of fortune Blake never for a moment doubted his own powers, and he knew where those powers lay—in the ability to see into the life of things, an ability which the child possesses but which designers like Stothard have never known.

In 1784 two designs of Blake's were hung in the Royal Academy: *War unchained by an Angel—Fire, Pestilence and Famine following*; and *A Breach in a City—The Morning after a Battle*. Blake's mind is still moving, we note, on the theme which had inspired some of the grimmest lines in the *Poetical Sketches*, and was to be to the fore in all his work—the horror and inhumanity of war. At the following year's Academy he exhibited rather more conventional water-colours: an illustration of Gray's *The Bard*, and three subjects taken from the Biblical story of Joseph and his brethren.

Blake's father died in 1784, and William returned to Broad Street—No. 27, next door to his mother and his elder brother James who had succeeded to the business. There, in partnership with an old fellow-apprentice of the Basire days, James Parker, he set up a print shop. Blake's brother Robert lived with them, and it was a fruitful and loving partnership between the two brothers; though not so much to the taste of Catherine, as it appears. For Robert was clearly a man of quick intelligence, and sympathised with William's mystical ideas—and the poor wife must often have felt herself left out of the picture. We even have an isolated instance of injustice on William's part:

> One day a dispute arose between Robert and Mrs Blake. She, in the heat of discussion, used words to him his brother (though a husband too) thought unwarrantable. A silent witness thus far, he could now bear it no longer, but with characteristic impetuosity—when stirred—rose and said to her: "Kneel down and beg Robert's pardon directly, or you never see my face again!" A heavy threat, uttered in tones which, from Blake, unmistakably showed it was *meant*. She, poor thing! 'thought it very hard', as she would afterwards tell, to beg her brother-in-law's pardon when she was not in fault! But being a duteous, devoted wife, though by nature nowise tame or dull of spirit, she *did* kneel down and meekly murmur: "*Robert, I beg your pardon, I am in the wrong*." "Young woman, you lie!" abruptly retorted he; "*I* am in the wrong!"

It was a great blow to William, then, when Robert died at the beginning of 1787. He had watched over his brother all through his sickness, and nursed him without rest during the final fortnight. As Robert died, William saw his spirit rising and disappearing 'through the matter-of-fact ceiling, clapping its hands for joy'—a touch which may remind us of the details of William's own death forty years later. Blake never lost the sense of his favourite brother's presence, and often talked with him 'in vision'.

It was at this time that he began experimenting with his 'new way of printing' in monochrome from copper-plate, a process in which he accomplished miracles of lovely design. He always insisted that the secret had been given him by Robert from the unseen world. His first two essays in the new process took the form of prose 'tracts': *There is no Natural Religion* and *All Religions are One*, engraved *c.* 1788. The first contains a series of anti-rationalist aphorisms, protesting against the Lockean doctrine that Man's desires are limited by his senses, and ending with the profoundly Blakean (and, one might add, Christian) dictum,

> He who sees the Infinite in all things, sees God. He who sees the Ratio only, sees himself only.
> Therefore God becomes as we are, that we may be as he is. [*Did.* 148]

The rest of Blake's work was to give the elaboration of this gnomic utterance. The second tract is headed *The Voice of one crying in the Wilderness*. It is a defence of the Poetic Genius as the source of all true knowledge: as, indeed, the true Man, from whose division all things are derived. These are essays in the theory of vision, provoked no doubt by the shock of his brother's death and the need to protest that the dead are not beyond our companionship. But before long Blake was to produce the proof of vision itself in the unmistakable flowering of his poetic gifts: the *Songs of Innocence*.

In 1787 the partnership with Parker was broken off, and the Blakes left Broad Street for 28 Poland Street. Print-selling was abandoned, and Blake had to rely once more on his graver for a living. Yet he found time, *c.* 1788, to read carefully, and annotate, Lavater's *Aphorisms on Man* (translated by Fuseli with a frontispiece, which Blake engraved for him), and Swedenborg's *Wisdom of Angels concerning Divine Love and Divine Wisdom*. Blake had much in common with both these men: his heart was drawn to Lavater's simple human piety, and his mind to the boldly unorthodox cosmology of Swedenborg. But for Blake they did not go far enough.

Lavater's moral standpoint is too timid, too negative, too conventional. He accepts the old divisions into vices and virtues, commending these and condemning those. Like all moralists he stigmatises as vices those manifestations of energy which Blake had been taught 'from Hell' to regard as 'staminal virtues', and confounds these with the real vices which originate in weakness. 'Active Evil', says Blake, 'is better than Passive Good':

> As I understand Vice it is a Negative. It does not signify what the laws of Kings & Priests have call'd Vice; we who are philosophers ought not to call the Staminal Virtues of Humanity by the same name that we call the omissions of intellect springing from poverty.
>
> Every man's leading propensity ought to be call'd his leading Virtue & his good Angel. But the Philosophy of Causes & Consequences misled Lavater as it has all his Cotemporaries. Each thing is its own cause & its own effect....But the origin of this mistake in Lavater & his cotemporaries is, They suppose that Woman's Love is Sin; in consequence all the Loves & Graces with them are Sins. [*L.A.* 932]

The conclusion is significant: Blake makes clear his belief that sex is the source of energy and the staminal virtues, and traces the falsity and puerility of orthodox thought on every vital subject to this initial falsification: the belief that sexual love is sin. In Blake's view the full mental and physical union of human beings was the first and necessary step to the reintegration of being which he called re-entry into the eternal world. This note on Lavater is Blake's first full and explicit statement of this cardinal doctrine.

Thou shalt serve God with the good impulse and also with the evil impulse. The old Jewish saying might well have been written by Blake himself: certainly he would have approved of it as a guide to morals. Good and evil are the eternal contraries which are never destroyed: not even in Eden. What is destructible is not the contraries but the negative—*vice.* Idleness is a negative, the sin of Sodom; deceit too, that obscure feminine quality which usurps the place of true love. And in the Lavater *marginalia* Blake mentions others:

> Murder is Hindering Another. Theft is Hindering Another. Backbiting, Undermining, Circumventing, & whatever is Negative is Vice.
>
> [*L.A.* 932]

But there are wonderful things in Lavater and in Blake's comments. Here are a few of them:

To abstain from laughing, and exciting laughter, merely not to offend, or to risk giving offence, or not to debase the inward dignity of character —is a power unknown to many a vigorous mind (L.). *I hate scarce smiles: I love laughing* (B.). [*L.A.* 904]

Hell is the being shut up in the possession of corporeal desires which shortly weary the man, for ALL LIFE IS HOLY (B.) [*L.A.* 913]

Keep him at least three paces distant who hates bread, music, and the laugh of a child (L.). *The best in the book!* (B.) [*L.A.* 913]

Whatever is visible is the vessel or veil of the invisible past, present, future—as man penetrates to this more, or perceives it less, he raises or depresses his dignity of being (L.). *A vision of the Eternal Now* (B.). [*L.A.* 917]

He, who has frequent moments of complete existence, is a hero, though not laurelled; is crowned, and without crowns, a king; he only who has enjoyed immortal moments can reproduce them (L.). *O that men would seek immortal moments! O that men would converse with God!* (B.). [*L.A.* 922]

Forwardness nips affection in the bud (L.). *The more is the pity* (B.). [*L.A.* 927]

The comments on Swedenborg's *Divine Love and Divine Wisdom* are on the whole sympathetic. There was much in Swedenborg's teachings which chimed with Blake's own beliefs. Had not Swedenborg declared the year 1757—the year of Blake's birth—to have inaugurated a new dispensation with the Last Judgement? Blake's parents, his friend Flaxman, and Blake and Catherine themselves for a while, were members of Swedenborg's New Jerusalem Church. The coincidences between Swedenborg's teaching and Blake's are too numerous to mention: though we must not suppose that it was always from Swedenborg that Blake borrowed these bricks for his own building. Blake often went back beyond Swedenborg to Boehme. There he found such doctrines as the Universal Man, the system of correspondences, the bright and the dark sun, the New Jerusalem. But these ideas as reflected in Swedenborg's astonishingly literal and matter-of-fact mind bear little organic relation to the same Behmenist ideas as absorbed into Blake's philosophy. The system of correspondences itself, which is the keystone of Swedenborg's edifice—the belief that everything in heaven and earth has its prototype within the body of Man—is turned upside down in Blake's world-scheme. For him, as we know, the material world is a fiction: there can therefore be no true 'correspondence' between the spiritual body and the gross universe. The whole idea is an allegory, and will vanish into smoke, with the material universe itself, once a man has come to a 'last judgement', i.e. realised his true nature as God.

Blake's first comment on the *Divine Love and Divine Wisdom* is in opposition to Swedenborg's doctrine of the will. It is an important announcement, and a milestone to mark for us Blake's progress in wisdom:

> There can be no Good Will. Will is always Evil; it is pernicious to others or suffering. If God is anything he is Understanding. [*S.D.L.* 933]

The conception of will as evil is central in Blake; and this conception breaks down the whole framework of conventional morality, and character, and social thinking, on which our lives to-day (in spite of Freud and the other psychologists) are constructed.

This Understanding or Heaven, Blake continues, 'is acquir'd by means of Suffering & Distress & Experience'. He opposes Swedenborg's teaching that Understanding can be acquired by the Sciences:

> Study Sciences till you are blind, Study intellectuals till you are cold, Yet science cannot teach intellect. Much less can intellect teach Affection. How foolish then is it to assert that Man is born in only one degree, when that one degree is reception of the 3 degrees, two of which he must destroy or close up or they will descend; if he closes up the two superior, then he is not truly in the 3d, but descends out of it into meer Nature or Hell. Is it not also evident that one degree will not open the other, & that science will not open intellect, but that they are discrete & not continuous so as to explain each other except by correspondence, which has nothing to do with demonstration; for you cannot demonstrate one degree by the other; for how can science be brought to demonstrate intellect without making them continuous & not discrete? [*S.D.L.* 938]

Understanding is an activity—*the* activity—of the whole man. But Blake welcomes the statement that there is no other idea of God than that of a Man: and comments:

> Man can have no idea of any thing greater than Man, as a cup cannot contain more than its capaciousness. But God is a man, not because he is so perceiv'd by man, but because he is the creator of man. [*S.D.L.* 934]

We note that at this early stage in his thinking Blake has not perfected his characteristic doctrine of expansion and contraction, by which (as we shall see later) he safeguards at the same time the unity and the variety of Eternity. In these notes on Swedenborg he has to adopt the theory of numerous infinities in order to preserve the variety in unity. Swedenborg confounds essence with identity; Blake comments:

Essence is not Identity, but from Essence proceeds Identity & from one Essence may proceed many Identities, as from one Affection may proceed many thoughts. Surely this is an oversight.

That there is but one Omnipotent, Uncreate & God I agree, but that there is but one Infinite I do not; for if all but God is not Infinite, they shall come to an end, which God forbid.

If the Essence was the same as the Identity, there could be but one Identity, which is false. Heaven would upon this plan be but a Clock; but one & the same Essence is therefore Essence & not Identity.

[*S.D.L.* 935–6]

In the later annotations to Swedenborg's *Wisdom of Angels concerning Divine Providence* Blake is more severe. His thought is now moving far beyond any system of correspondences; and he is detecting in Swedenborg an element of predestinarianism:

Predestination after this Life is more Abominable than Calvin's, & Swedenborg is Such a Spiritual Predestinarian....Cursed Folly!

[*S.D.P.* 947]

Some time before 1789 Blake wrote the satire-fantasy which he called *An Island in the Moon*, and which exists only in an unfinished state. He never engraved it. This is generally supposed to be a lampoon on the literary circle at Mrs Mathew's tea-parties, but the reference to the moon in the title gives us the clue. Somehow or other Blake had got to know about the famous Lunar Society of Birmingham, a vigorous scientific club, the members of which met once a month at one another's houses, in rotation, and at the time of the full moon so as to be able to see their ways home afterwards. It is of course unlikely that Blake should ever have attended one of the meetings. These were held in or near Birmingham, since most of the members lived in that part of England. They were a distinguished if motley crowd. Among them we may note Dr Erasmus Darwin, James Watt, Dr Joseph Priestley, Josiah

Wedgwood the potter, Matthew Boulton, and the mathematician Dr William Small.[1] Blake, we know, was on terms of intimacy with Priestley, and his friend Flaxman worked for Wedgwood and for Matthew Boulton the manufacturer. Boulton, in partnership with Watt whose inventions he financed, was responsible for a good deal of the machinery which was being installed all over England in Blake's day, and his name was widely known. He was co-founder with Darwin of the Lunar Society. What is particularly interesting, when we remember the way Blake picked up topographical names and wove them into the fabric of his prophecies, is that Boulton, in 1784, built the famous Albion Mill on the south side of the Thames near Blackfriar's Bridge. This, a flour mill to serve the metropolis, was looked upon as one of the mechanical wonders of the age. It was just beginning to prove a commercial success when it was burned down on March 3rd, 1791, barely six years after its completion, and before the third intended engine had been installed.[2] 'Albion' and 'Mill'—the two words become henceforward prime symbols in Blake's work of the enslavement of the human mind through machinery (the engines of Watt and Boulton) and rationalist philosophy (Darwin and the Lunar Society). The connection is still more precisely seen when we read[2] of the rotative engine which operated in the Albion Mill, with its 'sun and planets gear', and remember Urizen, 'prince of the starry wheels', and the great Mill in which he set the Sons of Albion to toil unceasingly.[3]

In 1789, again, we find Blake's friend, the bookseller Joseph Johnson, publishing the Second Part of Erasmus Darwin's *The Botanic Garden*. This was called *The Loves of the Plants*. The First Part, *The Economy of Vegetation*, was held back until 1791; but it was finished, and there is no doubt Blake saw a copy, before 1789. Blake contributed five plates to *The Economy of Vegetation*, engraved from Fuseli's designs: four of them are drawings of Wedgwood's Portland Vase, and the fifth is an impressive emblem of *The Fertilization of Egypt*. *The Botanic Garden* as a whole, and more especially *The Economy of Vegetation*, is a work which Blake must have detested from his heart. It is rationalistic, scientific, deistical in its attitude,

---

[1] Dr Small died in 1775.

[2] H. W. Dickinson, *Matthew Boulton* (Cambridge, 1937).

[3] Cf. also the inscription (added about 1800) to *Glad Day*, quoted above, p. 6.

mock-heroic and grotesquely artificial in its diction. There is evidence that Blake read it carefully, and that he had it often in mind in later years when he was writing his great symbolic poems—as a polar opposite.

A good deal of *The Economy of Vegetation* is given up to celebrating the triumphs of steam and machinery. There is a long account of the Albion Mill, for example, in the Additional Notes. And the cantos are interspersed with lengthy prose 'interludes' in which Darwin gives full expression to his materialism and more than Lockean aesthetics. Blake must have ground his teeth in fury to think that he was forced by dire necessity to engrave illustrations for such a work! No wonder his anger vented itself in satire (a *genre* which ten or more years earlier he had stigmatised as a 'foul contagion'); he rejoiced to pour his scorn on the Lunar Society and the whole rational experimental movement for which it stood.[1]

Blake's first meeting with Priestley was probably at one of Mrs Mathew's tea-parties. Later, both men attended the gatherings at Joseph Johnson's bookshop which I describe in a later chapter. Here, no doubt, the activities of the Lunar Society, and the writings of Erasmus Darwin and Miss Seward, were discussed at length—both writers being among Johnson's authors. 'Thrown early among the authors who resorted to Johnson, the bookseller', Palmer tells us, 'he [Blake] rebuked the profanity of Paine, and was no disciple of Priestley'. There is also the possibility that Blake attended the meetings of another group, somewhat similar to the Lunar Society, and including some of its members, which were held at Slaughter's Coffee House in London. Of this group Richard Lovell Edgeworth (himself a 'Lunatic') writes:

> We practised every means in our power, except personal insult, to try the temper and understanding of each candidate for admission. Every prejudice, which his profession or situation in life might have led him to cherish, was attacked, exposed to argument and ridiculed. The argument was always ingenious, and the ridicule sometimes coarse.[2]

---

[1] Yet even from *The Botanic Garden* Blake could learn something. There is a footnote on p. 24 of the 1791 edition of Part II, describing the horrors of the Bastille, which probably inspired Blake's picture of the 'dens' in *The French Revolution* [*F.R.* 175–6].

[2] Hesketh Pearson, *Doctor Darwin*.

This might as easily be a description of the conversation in *An Island in the Moon*. Godwin too turned up at Johnson's dinners; he belonged, moreover, to 'a private debating society that met once a week to discuss such subjects as Fame, Tribunes, Marriage, Incest, and A God'.[1]

There was, then, this wealth of discussion groups in the society to which Blake belonged in the last decades of the eighteenth century. And there are two main facts about the burlesque itself which point to a target other than Mrs Mathew's salon. The subjects discussed are mainly scientific and philosophical, not literary or philanthropical. And these topics arose in the course of meetings which were held at the various speakers' houses *in turn*. These facts fit in perfectly with an ascription to the Lunar Society.

Blake's commentators have been content to pass over *An Island in the Moon* with a shudder. It has never received the attention it deserves as our only surviving example of Blake's skill in dialogue and as an important social document. Yet the piece is an outstanding success on many counts. It has wit, vivacity, and great naturalness of dialogue. From it we gain an insight into many of the interests of the early Blake: we learn what was the *negative* impulse behind the *Songs of Innocence*, three of which appear in their first shape in this satire. And we are presented with sharply distinguished pen-pictures of several of Blake's important contemporaries.

The influence of *Gulliver's Travels* is apparent in the opening paragraph:

> In the Moon is a certain Island near by a mighty continent, which small island seems to have some affinity to England, &, what is more extraordinary, the people are so much alike, & their language so much the same, that you would think you was among your friends. In this Island dwells three Philosophers—Suction the Epicurean, Quid the Cynic, & Sipsop the Pythagorean. I call them by the names of those sects, tho' the sects are not ever mention'd there, as being quite out of date; however, the things still remain, and the vanities are the same. [*I.M.* 865]

Here, surely, we have the Swiftean ironic poise, the calm detached amusement, the fluid colloquial manner, taken off to the life. We shall find other evidence in the *Island* of Blake's powers of mimicry.

[1] Ford K. Brown, *William Godwin*.

The three philosophers are shown sitting together, 'thinking of nothing'. A number of other characters appear, including one Mrs Gimblet whose likeness is caught in a single Dickensian phrase:

The corners of her mouth seem'd—I don't know how, but very odd, as if she hoped you had not an ill opinion of her,—to be sure, we are all poor creatures!

We are introduced to Etruscan Column the Antiquarian, who can be no other than Josiah Wedgwood, the founder of the Etruria pottery works;[1] and to Inflammable Gass the Wind-finder, alias Dr Joseph Priestley.[2] The Pythagorean playing with the cat is probably Erasmus Darwin himself, whose predilection for a favourite Snow the Persian is dwelt on in Anna Seward's biography. All three are shown together in a passage where Blake's psychological insight creates vivid satire:

This was the situation of this improving company when, in a great hurry, Inflammable Gass the Wind-finder enter'd. They seem'd to rise & salute each other. Etruscan Column & Inflammable Gass fix'd their eyes on each other; their tongues went in question & answer, but their thoughts were otherwise employ'd. "I don't like his eyes", said Etruscan Column. "He's a foolish puppy", said Inflammable Gass, smiling on him. The 3 Philosophers—the Cynic smiling, the Epicurean seeming studying the flame of the candle, & the Pythagorean playing with the cat—listen'd with open mouths to the edifying discourses. [*I.M.* 866]

The edifying discourses range over many topics. Everyone speaks at cross-purposes, no one pauses to understand his neighbour, there is complete disagreement on every subject. The first theme of discussion is Voltaire; and the exchanges become so heated that the participants are on the verge of blows when Obtuse Angle enters and calms everyone down. Obtuse Angle may perhaps be identified with Richard Lovell Edgeworth, who was an amateur of mathematics.

---

[1] In *The Economy of Vegetation* Erasmus Darwin gives a detailed description of Wedgwood's Portland Vase (of which Blake did some designs) and lays stress on a broken classical *column* represented on the vase.

[2] The name inflammable gas comes directly from *The Economy of Vegetation*, where it is used in a note on Priestley's chemical experiments.

A whole crowd of new characters then come in, including Steelyard the lawgiver, who may be a portrait of Godwin—a figure drawn from quite another milieu than the Lunar Society:

> When Steelyard, the lawgiver, coming in stalking—with an act of parliament in his hand, said that it was a shameful thing that acts of parliament should be in a free state, it had so engrossed his mind that he did not salute the company.
>
> Mrs Gimblet drew her mouth downwards. [*I.M.* 868]

At a second meeting, this time 'in Obtuse Angle's study', the conversation turns on surgery. Here Blake's indignation at the treatment of the poor in hospitals again reminds us of Dickens. This, he seems to say, is the cost in human agony of the craze for experiment which began with Sir Francis Bacon:

> "Ah!" said Sipsop, "I only wish Jack Tearguts had had the cutting of Plutarch. He understands Anatomy better than any of the Ancients. He'll plunge his knife up to the hilt in a single drive, and thrust his fist in, and all in the space of a Quarter of an hour. He does not mind their crying, tho' they cry ever so. He'll swear at them & keep them down with his fist, & tell them that he'll scrape their bones if they don't lay still & be quiet. What the devil should the people in the hospital that have it done for nothing make such a piece of work for?" [*I.M.* 873]

The Cynic then sings a 'song of surgery' that is so very cynical that even Sipsop is disgusted:

> "Ah," said Sipsop, "you think we are rascals—& we think you are rascals. I do as I chuse. What is it to any body what I do? I am always unhappy too. When I think of Surgery—I don't know. I do it because I like it. My father does what he likes & so do I. I think, somehow, I'll leave it off. There was a woman having her cancer cut, & she shriek'd so that I was quite sick." [*I.M.* 874]

Fantasy as the *Island* is, we see it is deadly serious fantasy. Blake's social conscience is awake as always; the horrors of surgery without anaesthetics were present to him as were the horrors of the little chimney-sweeps and the factory-workers. But the woman having her cancer cut does not appear in the *Songs of Experience*. Her agony would have burst and shattered even that capacious framework. It was one function of *An Island in the Moon* to teach Blake what to leave out of his art.

The next meeting is at Steelyard's house. There is a good deal of social chit-chat, and Godwin's humourless gravity is cleverly sketched:

With great solemnity he address'd the company in these words:

"They call women the weakest vessel, but I think they are the strongest. A girl has always more tongue than a boy. I have seen a little brat no higher than a nettle, & she had as much tongue as a city clark; but a boy would be such a fool, not have any thing to say, and if anybody ask'd him a question he would put his head into a hole & hide it. I am sure I take but little pleasure. You have as much pleasure as I have. There I stand & bear every fool's insult. If I had only myself to care for, I'd wring off their noses."

To this Scopprell answer'd, "I think the Ladies' discourses, Mr. Steelyard, are some of them more improving than any book. That is the way I have got some of my knowledge."

"Then," said Miss Gittipin, "Mr Scopprell, do you know the song of Phebe and Jellicoe?"

"No, Miss," said Scopprell.

Then she repeated these verses, while Steelyard walk'd about the room:

Phebe, dressed like beautie's Queen,
Jellicoe in faint pea green,
Sitting all beneath a grot
Where the little lambkins trot;

Maidens dancing, loves a-sporting,
All the country folks a-courting,
Susan, Johnny, Bet, & Joe
Lightly tripping on a row.

Happy people, who can be
In happiness compar'd with ye?
The Pilgrim with his crook & hat
Sees your happiness compleat."

"A charming song, indeed, Miss," said Scopprell. Here they receiv'd a summons for a merry making at the Philosopher's house. [*I.M.* 877–8]

Miss Gittipin's song is a brilliant caricature of the milk-and-water school of pastoral verse so popular at the time. All the recognised ingredients are here: the shepherd and shepherdess, the grot, the lambs, a country dance, and the pilgrim pausing on his lonely way to give a benevolent blessing. But by the most delicate touches of absurdity Blake makes the whole thing ridiculous: 'faint pea green', 'the little lambkins trot', and the very homely names of the country nymphs and swains.

This deliciously absurd mimicry of the prevalent poetic fashions is continued in the next chapter. Amid more scurrilous verse directed against Dr Johnson, and in a convivial atmosphere of rum-and-water, Miss Gittipin, who 'sings like a harpsichord', delights the company with a rendering of 'This frog he would a-wooing ride'. "Hang your serious songs!" Sipsop breaks in, and gives them a piece of sheer nonsense: "Fa ra so bo ro"; to which Quid, shouting "Hang Italian songs! Let's have English! English genius for ever! Here I go—" counters with a delightful parody of the sentimental ballad, beginning:

"Hail Matrimony, made of Love,
To thy wide gates how great a drove
On purpose to be yok'd do come!
Widows & maids & youths also,
That lightly trip on beauty's toe,
Or sit on beauty's bum." [*I.M.* 880]

In this chapter we see Blake thoroughly enjoying himself. An excellent drinking song ends the party.

The next chapter, which is short enough to be quoted in full as a first-rate example of Blake's sprightly dialogue, is concerned with the serious business of Dr Priestley's scientific experiments:

Thus these happy Islanders spent their time. But felicity does not last long, for being met at the house of Inflammable Gass the windfinder, the following affairs happen'd.

"Come, Flammable," said Gibble Gabble, "& let's enjoy ourselves. Bring the Puppets."

"Hay,—Hay," said he, "you—sho—why—ya, ya. How can you be so foolish? Ha! Ha! Ha! She calls the experiments puppets!"

Then he went up stairs & loaded the maid with glasses, & brass tubes, & magic pictures.

"Here, ladies & gentlemen," said he, "I'll shew you a louse, or a flea, or a butterfly, or a cockchafer, the blade bone of a tittleback. No, no. Here's a bottle of wind that I took up in the boghouse, and—O dear, O dear, the water's got into the sliders! Look here, Gibble Gabble! Lend me your handkerchief, Tilly Lally."

Tilly Lally took out his handkerchief, which smear'd the glass worse than ever. Then he screw'd it on. Then he took the sliders, & then he set up the glasses for the Ladies to view the pictures. Thus he was employ'd, & quite out of breath. While Tilly Lally & Scopprell were pumping at the air-pump, Smack went the glass.

"Hang!" said Tilly Lally.

Inflammable Gass turn'd short round & threw down the table & Glasses, & Pictures, & broke the bottles of wind, & let out the Pestilence. He saw the Pestilence fly out of the bottle, & cried out, while he ran out of the room:

"Come out! Come out! We are putrified! We are corrupted! Our lungs are destroy'd with the Flogiston. This will spread a plague all thro' the Island!"

He was downstairs the very first. On the back of him came all the others in a heap.

So they need not bidding go. [*I.M.* 882–3]

This magnificent piece of grotesquery provides the real climax to the *Island* as we have it in its unfinished state. Another chapter follows, but it transports us into a different world—the world of the *Songs of Innocence*—for it is here that we first catch the music of three of the most magical of Blake's songs. Mr Obtuse Angle is invited to sing (they are all together again at Steelyard the Lawgiver's house)—and the great music begins:

> Upon a holy thursday, their innocent faces clean,
> The children walking two & two in grey & blue & green,

—and when the song was finished 'they all sat silent for a quarter of an hour, & Mrs Nannicantipot said, "It puts me in Mind of my mother's song"...', and sings them the *Nurse's Song*.

The third Song of Innocence is contributed by Quid the Cynic. It is *The Little Boy Lost*. After this 'nobody could sing any longer' for a while; then they pluck up heart again and return to the mocking vein with imitations of popular ballads, sentimental songs, and Handelian recitatives. The narrative closes, after a gap where at least one leaf is missing, with an allusion to Blake's discovery of illuminated printing: with which we shall deal in the next chapter.

Why was *An Island in the Moon* written? Mainly, I think, to let off steam. Blake was in the habit throughout his life of relieving his feelings of anger and exasperation by scribbling epigrams in his note-book; they were intended for no eye but his own; and the *Island* is simply an extended epigram. But besides this, there was a more positive reason for writing. Blake clearly wished to straighten out his own ideas, to see just where he stood with reference to the controversies of his day, and he found it easiest to conduct this exploration of his own ideas through the concrete medium of fiction. We can regard the *Island* as so much *detritus* which Blake had to throw out of his mind before he could take the step forward into the lucid world of the *Songs of Innocence*. The *Island* is, in this sense, Blake's purgation. But it is also a means by which he made plain to himself and to us his realisation of the immensely divided character of his own time. In the three philosophers, Suction, Quid and Sipsop, and their adherents, we recognise the three aspects of contemporary thought that Blake was to spend his life in attacking: mere sensuality and *laissez-faire*,[1] lack of faith, and scientific determinism and materialism.

The silliness of the conversation in the *Island* and the constant bickering and misunderstanding remind us that the modern world, while deeply opposed to the spiritual life, is also deeply divided against itself. This is at once the occasion for grosser social misery and the possibility of a rebirth. What form that rebirth should take is naturally not adumbrated in the satire. We must look for the full expression of Blake's doctrine of reintegration in the *Songs of Innocence and Experience* which are now to follow.

A word may be opportune here on Blake's reading and his general intellectual background. The idea still current of Blake as an uncultivated naïf must be abandoned when we consider not only the intellectual level of the society to which he had access for the major part of his life but also the great variety of literature with which he was obviously acquainted. "I never look upon him as an unfortunate man of genius," said one who knew him. "He knew every great man of his day." Among his friends he was now beginning to count Paine, Priestley and Godwin. At Joseph Johnson's weekly meetings[2] he took part in discussions of politics, philosophy, religion and

---

[1] It would not be an irrelevance in Blake's eyes that Boulton and Wedgwood, two prominent members of the Lunar Society, were also considerable employers of labour in factory and pottery-works. Scientific experimentalism and exploitation of the poor go together.

[2] See Ch. III.

literature, and learned to hold his own in argument. 'Thrown early among the authors who resorted to Johnson, the bookseller', Samuel Palmer writes, 'he rebuked the profanity of Paine, and was no disciple of Priestley'; though we may conjecture that Mary Wollstonecraft's views were more to his taste. As for his reading, the *Poetical Sketches* bear witness to his study of Milton, Spenser and the Elizabethans generally, the Augustans, and Chatterton. Milton and Shakespeare were his constant companions. His comments on Chaucer in the *Descriptive Catalogue* show how deeply he could penetrate into the spirit of the Middle Ages. In occult and mystical writings his reading was extensive. And nothing is more characteristic of his seriousness than the attention he devoted to the philosophical literature of his own land. He tells us that 'when very Young' he read 'Burke's Treatise on the Sublime & Beautiful...Locke on Human Understanding & Bacon's Advancement of Learning'. Later he went carefully through Berkeley, as I shall show in the second part of this study, and formed his own opinion of that philosopher. There is evidence that he had also looked into Newton's *Principia*. His *marginalia* on Watson and Thornton show how to the end he kept abreast of the things that interested him in contemporary literature.

Frederick Tatham's testimony is conclusive. 'Some men muse and call it thinking, but Blake was a hard worker; his thought was only for action, as a man plans a house, or a general consults his map and arranges his forces for a battle. His mental acquirements were incredible; he had read almost everything in whatsoever language, which language he always taught himself. His conversation, therefore, was highly interesting, and never could one converse on any subject with him, but they would gain something quite as new as noble from his eccentric and elastic mind. It is a remarkable fact that among the volumes bequeathed by Mrs Blake to the author of this sketch, the most thumbed from use are his Bible and those books in other languages. He was very fond of Ovid, especially the *Fasti*. He read Dante when he was past sixty, although before he never knew a word of Italian.'[1]

---

[1] *The Letters of William Blake, together with his Life*, by F. Tatham. Edited by A. G. B. Russell.

CHAPTER II

Innocence and Experience

> Ah, Sun-flower! weary of time,
> Who countest the steps of the Sun,
> Seeking after that sweet golden clime
> Where the traveller's journey is done:
>
> Where the Youth pined away with desire,
> And the pale Virgin shrouded in snow
> Arise from their graves, and aspire
> Where my Sun-flower wishes to go. [*S.E.* 74]

BY the end of 1788 William Blake had finished writing the collection of lyrical poems he was to call *Songs of Innocence*. He wished to publish them, but he had small faith in the booksellers. Besides, he had conceived his ideas in the parallel forms of poetry and design. He must find a method of production which conserved the unity of his conceptions.

The problem was solved when, one night, Robert's spirit appeared to him and indicated the method of 'illuminated printing'.

'The subject of anxious daily thought passed—as anxious meditation does with us all', writes Gilchrist, '—into the domain of dreams and (in his case) of visions':

> In one of these a happy inspiration befell, not, of course, without supernatural agency. After intently thinking by day and dreaming by night, during long weeks and months, of his cherished object, the image of the vanished pupil and brother at last blended with it. In a vision of the night, the form of Robert stood before him, and revealed the wished-for secret, directing him to the technical mode by which could be produced a facsimile of song and design.
>
> On his rising in the morning, Mrs Blake went out with half a crown, all the money they had in the world, and of that laid out one shilling and tenpence on the simple materials necessary for setting in practice the new revelation. Upon that investment of one shilling and tenpence he started what was to prove a principal means of support through his future life—the series of poems and writings illustrated by coloured plates, often

highly finished afterwards by hand—which became the most efficient and durable means of revealing Blake's genius to the world.[1]

Thus the *Songs of Innocence* was printed, and each copy hand-coloured—a laborious process in which Catherine helped her husband. The work was completed in 1789; only twenty-one original copies are now known to exist. The price was five shillings.

The new volume is the record of Blake's return to the visionary ecstasy of childhood. He had lost it for a while. Six years had passed since his marriage to Catherine Boucher, six years in many ways of disappointment both within and without. And especially the disappointment, we may surmise, of being childless; and the disappointment of incompletely satisfied passion. The *Songs* mark, then, a return, not a continuance. It is a return to childhood. It is a child who, in the introductory song, tells Blake to 'sit him down and write'; it is of children and for children that he sings. The poems are radiant with that fresh unclouded vision which is of childhood and to which the mystic longs to attain. No other verse in English reaches this perfection; in the best, such as Wordsworth's lyrics, we have a sense of strain, of simplicity degenerating into *simplesse*. And Blake tells us that it is children who understand his visions best.

There is in all good mystical writing, when once we are attuned to it, an extraordinary flavour of immediacy. This immediacy expresses itself in two ways. First we receive the impression of first-hand experience. A treatise like *The Cloud of Unknowing* or the *Centuries of Meditations* affects us as a lyric does: it is a direct transcription of reality. And in so far as the experience is potentially available to all of us (unlike the lyrical experience of a great poet) it is all the more impressive, all the more immediate. '*There* we have been': and could be again, if we desired to fulfil the necessary conditions.

In the second place, we feel the certitude that we are coming into direct contact with the mind of the writer in a sphere of relationship which is oddly familiar. We find the writer: and we find ourselves in the writer.

We find the writer—for the simple reason that the mystic does not hide himself, wears no singing robes, no masks. The poet, the man of letters, all too often writes from an impure motive or with

[1] From Gilchrist's *Life*, Ch. IX.

impure technique. He has one eye on his subject, the other on himself and his readers. He is concerned with what sort of effect he is making. He is getting *himself* across, his private, personal experience, which he cannot help feeling is so remarkable, and, indeed, unique. So, to some extent, and largely unconsciously, he poses. A veil intervenes between himself and his reader. The mystic, on the other hand, writes at the end of a long process of 'self-naughting', of doing away with masks and veils and everything that obscures the real self. Personality—the structure of habit-patterns, passions, weaknesses, and vices to which we give that name—has already been destroyed. Moreover, in writing of his experience he has no motive in view but the good of his reader. Fame, wealth, 'self-expression', are ideas meaningless to him. This fierce sincerity is at once apparent in his writing. He is speaking, not from his own centre, but from God. His experience is both individual and universal: and that is why we find *ourselves* in what he says, in what he divulges of his own mind. For we *are* all one in that ultimate fundamental experience.

Not all mystics have had the natural literary gift adequate to the full expression of their meaning. But those who have that gift—Eckhart, Fénelon, Law, Blake—are among the most fascinating and human of all writers.

The key-note is, of course, simplicity. Simplicity of form, purity of diction, boldness and brevity of illustration: these are the qualities we note in the direct transcription of the vision. And these are the qualities, pre-eminently, that we find in *Songs of Innocence and Experience*. The same fundamental patterns are repeated over and over again: the soul losing itself, wandering in the wilderness, being found, and restored to a primitive happiness; or the interplay of contraries, lamb and tiger, youth and age, God and Man, night and day, black boy and white boy, freedom and slavery. Monotony is avoided by stanza variation and by the intense energy that informs each lyric. The diction, to a large degree monosyllabic, is crystal clear. The images are drawn from the simplest natural sights and sounds:

> The sun descending in the west,
> The evening star does shine;
> The birds are silent in their nest,
> And I must seek for mine.

The moon like a flower
In heaven's high bower,
With silent delight
Sits and smiles on the night. [S.I. 60]

The quality I have been attempting to describe is best summed up in Blake's own word 'Innocence'. The poet's style must be innocent of subterfuges and literary devices if he is to write about innocence. It must possess simplicity, and it must possess, above all, unity.

What Blake understood by 'innocence' is a complex thing. It includes vision: all the senses open to Eternity to a degree never to be attained in later life, save through 'the poetic genius'; love and forgiveness, implicit in the absence of the ideas of good and evil; impulse: the instinctive response to vision; energy: the child playing among the vital forms of the universe; and simplicity, the absence of semblances. The intensely humanising vision of the child is precisely Blake's vision. The child does not think to make distinctions between its own existence and that of a horse, a dandelion or an earwig, until grown-ups impress it with the idea of separateness. This is the vision we have in the exquisitely tender *A Dream*. Even the quivering antennae of the little emmet appear visible in the movement and atmosphere of

Troubled, 'wilder'd, and forlorn,
Dark, benighted, travel-worn,
Over many a tangled spray,
All heart-broke I heard her say:

"O, my children! do they cry?
Do they hear their father sigh?
Now they look abroad to see:
Now return and weep for me." [S.I. 52]

By an extraordinary sympathy Blake projects himself into the mind of the ant, not in the fabular manner of Aesop or Kipling which is essentially moral and *pretending*, but by reason of his conviction of the unity of life in all things.[1] It is for this reason that the providential

---

[1] The finest expression of this conviction is the *Auguries of Innocence* (see below, pp. 131–3).

appearance of 'the watchman of the night' strikes us as perfectly right and without a trace of sentimentality. We are living throughout the *Songs of Innocence* within the mind of the child, and to that mind this is the way things ought to happen; while to the seer's mind, on another though allied plane, this is the way things do happen, for nothing is lost in Eternity.

The theme of loss and finding again runs through the *Songs of Innocence*. Blake's thought plays constantly between the cosmic loss—the Fall, Man's exclusion from his home in Eternity—and the individual cases which he makes images of his great theme:

In futurity
I prophetic see
That the earth from sleep
(Grave the sentence deep)

Shall arise and seek
For her maker meek;
And the desart wild
Become a garden mild. [*S.I.* 52–3]

And it is through 'an improvement of sensual enjoyment' (Blake's later phrase in *The Marriage of Heaven and Hell*) that this is to come about. The golden lion who finds the sleeping Lyca (*The Little Girl Lost*) is a potent symbol of sexual experience. Innocence is surrounded by energetic powers:

Leopards, tygers, play
Round her as she lay,
While the lion old
Bow'd his mane of gold

And her bosom lick,
And upon her neck
From his eyes of flame
Ruby tears there came;

While the lioness
Loos'd her slender dress,
And naked they convey'd
To caves the sleeping maid. [*S.I.* 54]

Green, the colour of life and hope, is prominent in these lyrics. The children play 'under leaves so green', on the 'Ecchoing Green';

the released chimney-sweepers run laughing and leaping 'down a green plain'.

> The meadows laugh with lively green,
> And the grasshopper laughs in the merry scene, [*S.I.* 67]

and, in a last perfect expression of the thought which links children and the green things of the earth and the peace of the mystic,

> When the voices of children are heard on the green
> And laughing is heard on the hill,
> My heart is at rest within my breast
> And everything else is still. [*S.I.* 63]

Paradise Lost and Paradise Regained—and the regaining is through reconciliation. The lion of Love in *The Little Girl Found* is reconciled to the father and mother, sexual love to 'storgous appetite'; and in *Night* to the lamb (sexual inexperience) on which he has preyed. The little black boy is made one with his white brother. Here Blake just touches on the theme to which he is later to devote so much of his attention. The *Songs of Experience* will elaborate it. Though there is laughter and joy in the hearts of children, we are not allowed to forget the darkness and cruelty with which they are surrounded, the man-made shadow. But already the light is dawning. What Man has made of Man will be forgotten in the sunlight of the New Age. The *Songs of Innocence* end with a significant appeal to the young to forsake the errors of their elders. *The Voice of the Ancient Bard*, the immortal Los, is heard:

> Youth of delight, come hither,
> And see the opening morn,
> Image of truth new born.
> Doubt is fled, & clouds of reason,
> Dark disputes & artful teazing.
> Folly is an endless maze,
> Tangled roots perplex her ways.
> How many have fallen there!
> They stumble all night over bones of the dead,
> And feel they know not what but care,
> And wish to lead others, when they should be led.
> [*S.I.* 68]

Professor L. C. Martin, in his essay *Henry Vaughan and the Theme of Infancy*,[1] writes: 'We have to consider not a simple expression of the Platonic theory or myth, but a fusion of it with the widespread sentiment which attributes a special innocence and insight to children. The occurrence in literature of this fusion is relatively rare....' And much rarer, we may note, at the end of the eighteenth century than in the middle of the seventeenth. Between Vaughan and Traherne, who are both poets of this fusion, and Blake, a long rationalist process intervenes.[2] Yet his very antagonism to that process may have sent him with more vehemence

> to travell back
> And tread again that ancient track.

Blake, like Vaughan and Traherne, revelled in images of brightness, freshness and purity; finding no place for these in the grimy London of his day, he constructs a Golden Age, a pastoral paradise of innocence and love, which he fills with shepherds and shepherdesses, snow-white lambs, and little children playing. It is unlikely that he read Vaughan's poems, and Traherne he could not have known. But how delighted he would have been with Traherne's *The Salutation*, with its almost Blakean phrases:

> These little Limmes,
> These Eys and Hands which here I find,
> These rosie Cheeks wherwith my Life begins,
> Where have ye been? Behind
> What Curtain were ye from me hid so long!
> Where was? in what Abyss, my Speaking Tongue?

and its dwelling on the ideas of *gold* and *organisation*:

> New Burnisht Joys!
> Which yellow Gold and Pearl excell!
> Such Sacred Treasures are the Lims in Boys,
> In which a Soul doth Dwell;
> Their Organized Joynts, and Azure Veins
> More Wealth include, then all the World contains.

---

[1] *Seventeenth Century Studies presented to Sir Herbert Grierson* (Oxford, 1938).

[2] Professor Martin, in the essay quoted, does not acknowledge the fusion in Blake. To my mind it is implicit in all that Blake wrote, and especially in *Thel* and the *Songs*.

How agreeable, too, to Blake's thought is the famous passage from the *Centuries* which describes how the child's mind was corrupted and turned aside by adults from the pure joy of imagination to the futile pleasures of possessions and power:

> The corn was Orient and Immortal Wheat, which never should be reaped, nor was ever sown. I thought it had stood from everlasting to everlasting. The Dust and Stones of the Street were as precious as GOLD: the Gates were at first the End of the World. The Green Trees when I saw them first through one of the Gates Transported and Ravished me, their sweetness and unusual Beauty made my Heart to leap, and almost mad with ecstasie, they were such strange and Wonderful Things. The Men! O what Venerable and Reverend Creatures did the Aged seem! Immortal Cherubims! And young Men Glittering and Sparkling Angels, and Maids strange Seraphic Pieces of Life and Beauty! Boys and Girles Tumbling in the street, and playing, were moving Jewels. I knew not that they were Born or should Die; But all things abided Eternally as they were in their Proper Places. Eternity was Manifest in the Light of the Day, and something infinite Behind everything appeared: which talked with my Expectation and moved my Desire. The Citie seemed to stand in Eden, or to be Built in Heaven. The Streets were mine, the Temple was mine, the People were mine, their Clothes and Gold and Silver were mine, as much as their Sparkling Eyes, Fair Skins and ruddy faces. The Skies were mine, and so were the Sun and Moon and Stars, and all the World was mine; and I the only Spectator and Enjoyer of it. I knew no Churlish Proprieties, nor Bounds, nor Divisions: but all Proprieties and Divisions were mine: all Treasures and the Possessors of them. So that with much adoe I was corrupted, and made to learn the Dirty Devices of this World. Which now I unlearn, and become, as it were, a little Child again that I may enter into the Kingdom of God.

To accept, to trust, to believe, to love: these are the prerogatives of innocence. To suffer, to doubt, to sin, to hate: these are the activities of experience. With much ado the child is corrupted and made to learn the dirty devices of the world. Innocence and experience are, in Blake's phrase, the 'Two Contrary States of the Human Soul'. And 'Without Contraries is no progression'. The spiritual warfare is the struggle between these states: and wisdom is their recognition and harmonisation on a higher level. No one can remain in the state of innocence, nor should he wish to do so; but it can be re-entered through the understanding of experience. The wanderer returns, bringing his sheaves with him. Thus Blake's *Songs of Innocence* are followed, in 1794, by the *Songs of Experience*.

It is worth while breaking the strict chronological sequence of our narrative to consider the *Songs of Experience* now, in conjunction with the *Songs of Innocence*. That Blake wished them to be so considered is certain, as he himself collected them and bound them together in one book.

The atmosphere of the new volume presents a striking contrast to that of the old. The warm pastoral note has disappeared: we find ourselves more in the town than the country. And the intensity of Blake's indignation (for these are, above all, poems of indignation) is reflected in the tighter rhythms and sharper imagery, the brilliant use of denunciatory repetition.

The prophetic note which had ended the *Songs of Innocence* sounds again, and more forcibly, in the *Introduction* to this second volume:

> Hear the voice of the Bard!
> Who Present, Past, & Future, sees;
> Whose ears have heard
> The Holy Word
> That walk'd among the ancient trees,
>
> Calling the lapsed Soul,
> And weeping in the evening dew;
> That might controll
> The starry pole,
> And fallen, fallen light renew!
>
> "O Earth, O Earth, return!
> Arise from out the dewy grass;
> Night is worn,
> And the morn
> Rises from the slumberous mass.
>
> Turn away no more;
> Why wilt thou turn away?
> The starry floor,
> The wat'ry shore,
> Is giv'n thee till the break of day." [S.E. 69]

Already we have passed out of the simple personal innocence of the *Songs of Innocence* into the very central chamber of Blake's mature thought. The word of God calls the fallen universe to return to its home in Eternity. The soul of Man must no longer be content with the material glory: the starry floor of heaven, and the great sea, are merely the 'mundane shell' separating the soul from chaos. These things are given only 'until the break of day'. When full understanding comes, when the vision is complete, they must be transcended and consumed in 'the burning fire of thought'.

But the time of redemption is not yet. *Earth's Answer* is a pitiful cry of incapacity, of imprisoned energy longing yet unwilling to be free. 'Starry Jealousy', later known as Urizen, the ancient Reason who brought about the primal Fall, still controls the motions of impulse and the strength of love. A mature philosophy of the relations of man and woman and the meaning of sex is contained in this short poem, later to be elaborated through the whole of Blake's vast undertaking.

Free Love bound with jealousy, the partial theme of *Earth's Answer*, is also the theme of *The Clod and the Pebble*, *The Angel*, *My Pretty Rose Tree*, *The Garden of Love*, and *A Little Girl Lost*. For Blake, love between man and woman was not an exclusive passion rooted in the principle of property, but a form of energy in unity expanding into many forms. How different he found the conception of love in actual fact, as he looked around him at his friends, or even in his own home, where he had been prevented from taking a 'handmaid' by his wife's tears! The one aspect of love is pure and bright:

> "Love seeketh not Itself to please,
> Nor for itself hath any care,
> But for another gives its ease,
> And builds a Heaven in Hell's despair."

but the other aspect is dark as death:

> "Love seeketh only Self to please,
> To bind another to Its delight,
> Joys in another's loss of ease,
> And builds a Hell in Heaven's despite." [*S.E.* 70]

Like Shelley, Blake would not be one of 'that great sect' who bind themselves to a single partner, and so through life

> With one fast friend, perhaps a jealous foe
> The longest and the dreariest journey go.

He believed in a community of love, in the ability to enjoy many modes of sensual pleasure, and through a wide range of physical unions to attain a new apprehension of Eternity. Modern disciples of Blake have seized delightedly on this side of his thought as a licence for promiscuity. Blake would regard them with the same abhorrence that D. H. Lawrence felt for Casanova. But I leave this subject for later development.

Blake's social conscience is seen clearly at work in the *Songs of Experience*. The evils of poverty, the exploitation of the poor and particularly the children of the poor, the incomprehension of the adult for the child, of the man for the insect, of man for man: all these aspects of a fallen society are pressed home in a series of consummate lyrics. The burning intensity of Blake's vision was something new in English poetry. Without expostulating, without screaming, he conveys the sense of indignation and judgement. And how vivid are his phrases! The little chimney-sweeper, set to work while still an infant for its pious father and mother, is seen as

> a little black thing among the snow. [*S.E.* 71]

Blake hears the charity children singing hymns in St Paul's on Holy Thursday, and his heart is filled with pity:

> Is that trembling cry a song?
> Can it be a song of joy?
> And so many children poor?
> It is a land of poverty! [*S.E.* 71]

Here, as so often in the twin volumes, the dark *Holy Thursday* of *Songs of Experience* forms a contrast to the bright lyric of the same name in *Songs of Innocence*.

The apathy of the Church, its support of vested interests, its crushing of natural joy, are also poignantly illustrated. 'Thou shalt not' is written over the chapel which the religious have built in the midst of the Garden of Love, and the pleasant walks are filled with tombstones instead of flowers,

> And Priests in black gowns were walking their rounds,
> And binding with briars my joys & desires. [*S.E.* 75]

The little vagabond tells his mother that he prefers the ale-house to the church because there he is happy and warm, whereas in church he is cold and miserable. Religion itself, the religion of mysteries and ceremonies, is pilloried in *The Human Abstract*. Blake shows that all those virtues which are deemed specifically Christian by the pious spring from poverty, mental and material, from cruelty and the wish to dominate others—all those things, in short, which are the bitter enemies of the spiritual life:

> Pity would be no more
> If we did not make somebody Poor;
> And Mercy no more could be
> If all were as happy as we. [*S.E.* 76]

Jealousy, fear and unbelief enter into all the relations of life. The new-born child even is not free, as Blake shows in *Infant Sorrow*. The Nurse, in *Nurse's Song*, is envious of the simple joy of the children playing, and spoils it. The young girl jealously and fearfully shuts herself up from the 'fiery joy' of love. The insulted friend nurses his anger, practises deceit, and is glad to see the other die from his hatred. The child who enunciates the profound truth

> "Nor is it possible to Thought
> A greater than itself to know" [*S.E.* 78]

is burnt to death by the priests. All passions, feelings, thoughts, actions, are enclosed in the Mundane Shell, bound down to matter and to the corruption which matter is heir to, and can only be freed by a resurrection into the new life. The new life will come by annihilation of the selfhood, through love and understanding; and future generations of men will look back with incredulity on this present age:

> Children of the future Age
> Reading this indignant page,
> Know that in a former time
> Love! sweet Love! was thought a crime. [*S.E.* 79]

On the practical level, the contrast between the *Songs of Innocence* and the *Songs of Experience* represents simply Blake's perception of good and evil in the world: a moral judgement such as any observer might have made. But within the framework of his own life and work the second volume marks another step along the mystic way: the step taken when the first ecstatic joy of illumination is over and the narrow path of purgation lies before the seeker. We must not push this phraseology of orthodox mysticism too far, however: there is little trace in Blake of the Western 'dark night of the soul', nor should we expect it in a spirit so alien to asceticism.

Tiriel, the first of the symbolic books, was written just after the *Songs of Innocence*. It is an elaborate figurative expression of Blake's belief that the Fall consisted in replacing imagination by law. It is also, among other things, an allegory of happy, 'lawless' family life (Har, Heva, Mnetha), and unhappy, disciplined family life (Tiriel and his children). Here for the first time Blake used the loping heptameter which is to be the staple metre for his longer poems. As all the basic ideas of *Tiriel* are stated more clearly in the later prophecies, we need not linger over this rather immature work.

A much more attractive poem than *Tiriel*, and a much deeper one, is *The Book of Thel*, also etched in 1789. There is a spring-like atmosphere about *Thel*, 'the freshness of the early world', an intense realisation of the individuality of common things. The theme is the pre-existence of the soul and its unwillingness to enter the living grave of earthly existence. Thel is a spirit-maiden, the youngest of 'the daughters of the Seraphim' who 'lead round their sunny flocks' in the vales of Paradise. She is melancholy, for she feels within herself the intimation of a terrible duty and a change: the passage from purely spiritual existence to the life of the body, which appears to Thel nothing less than extinction,—'who shall find my place?'—for she is quite unable to see to the other side of the 'grave'. She laments, and her lament is answered by the spiritual form of the Lily of the Valley, who tells her that even the humble plant has its place in the whole and is visited by God—'then why should Thel complain?'. Thel is still unconvinced, and the Lily calls upon the

Cloud to explain why he does not protest when the hour of his dissolution is upon him.

"O maid, I tell thee, when I pass away
It is to tenfold life, to love, to peace and raptures holy:
Unseen descending, weigh my light wings upon balmy flowers,
And court the fair-eyed dew to take me to her shining tent:"
[*B.Th.* 170]

Thel now points out that such optimism is all very well for the Cloud, which has a function in life, and therefore may rightly be spared extinction:

"But I feed not the little flowers; I hear the warbling birds,
But I feed not the warbling birds; they fly and seek their food:
But Thel delights in these no more, because I fade away;
And all shall say, 'Without a use this shining woman liv'd,
Or did she only live to be at death the food of worms?'"
[*B.Th.* 170–1]

The Cloud takes her up on her last word:

"Then if thou art the food of worms, O virgin of the skies,
How great thy use, how great thy blessing! Every thing that lives
Lives not alone nor for itself." [*B.Th.* 171]

It is an early statement of a doctrine which was to form an important aspect of Blake's thought: 'everything that lives is holy'.

The Cloud in his turn calls upon the Worm to appear in its naked helplessness. Blake's 'double vision' sees it not only as a worm, but 'like an infant wrapped in the Lilly's leaf': a favourite image, as anyone may verify by looking through Blake's designs. The Worm cannot speak, but the Clod of Clay speaks for it—clay, the humblest and darkest of created things, yet in its loving serviceableness the foundation of all:

"But, he, that loves the lowly, pours his oil upon my head,
And kisses me, and binds his nuptial bands around my breast,
And says: 'Thou mother of my children, I have loved thee
And I have given thee a crown that none can take away.'
But how this is, sweet maid, I know not, and I cannot know;
I ponder, and I cannot ponder; yet I live and love." [*B.Th.* 172]

In which last lines Blake admirably expresses the instinctive life of the unconscious.

Convinced at last, Thel, the virgin soul, lies down in the grave-plot of clay, and prepares to take upon herself mortality. But she discovers only too soon the horror of her new condition: she finds that her senses, which had expanded in joy in the morning air of Eternity, are now restricted to the five material ones. Even the sense of touch, the medium of love, is cramped in flesh:

> "Why a tender curb upon the youthful burning boy?
> Why a little curtain of flesh on the bed of our desire?"
>
> [*B.Th.* 173]

Unable to bear the mortal imprisonment, Thel flees back into the world of Eternity.

The outburst of the French Revolution and its progress exercised a tremendous influence on Blake. He was by nature a rebel, though his revolutionary principles went deeper than any mere idea of social or political change. Yet he joined the 'Friends of Liberty' in England, and associated with such radicals as Tom Paine and such philosophers as Godwin. Godwin's principles of human perfectibility through the improving of outward conditions could never satisfy a mind which would be content with nothing short of a rebirth of the whole man in each individual; Blake did not fall into the snare which was to shackle so many of the best energies of Wordsworth and Shelley. Nevertheless he too, like Wordsworth and Coleridge, greeted in the French Revolution

> France standing on the top of golden hours
> And human nature seeming born again.

His first reaction to the great cataclysm is expressed in the poem *The French Revolution*—the only verse of his, besides *Poetical Sketches*, which found its way into print during his lifetime. The publisher was Joseph Johnson, of St Paul's Churchyard, who forms one link between Blake and the famous Lunar Society.

Of *The French Revolution, a Poem in Seven Books*, only the first book survives. It may be that Blake himself destroyed the MS. of the remaining six when the September massacres convinced him that his prophecy of a golden age was not going to be realised in the immediate future. It may be that, disgusted by the course of events, he never wrote more than the one book. What remains is a curiosity among Blake's longer poems, a foretaste of the great symbolical works yet containing a mixture of history, drama and allegory such as he did not attempt again.

'The dead brood over Europe', the poem begins; and the action is heavy with the sense of dead things crushing the springs of life.

> The ancient dawn calls us
> To awake from slumbers of five thousand years. [*F.R.* 174]

In the Bastille every form of torture and injustice is concentrated; at Versailles the King and his counsellors are preparing the instruments of oppression. But 'the Commons convene in the Hall of the Nation', and prisoners everywhere feel the impulse of freedom. Even among the nobles themselves there is realisation of the spirit of change which is abroad. The various speakers rise one by one to give their opinions of what is best to be done to restore peace to France. The King himself presages disaster. Then 'the ancientest Peer', the Duke of Burgundy, rises to urge war against the Commons in defence of the ancient prerogatives, the civilisation of the rich and noble:

> "Shall this marble built heaven become a clay cottage, this earth an oak stool, and these mowers
> From the Atlantic mountains mow down all this great starry harvest of six thousand years?" [*F.R.* 178]

The Atlantic mountains, we must note, are always with Blake the realms of Eternity, and the starry heavens the symbol of perverted reason and law: thus the revolutionary movement is heralded as the expression in time of that rebirth into Eternity for which 'all creation groaneth and travaileth in pain together until now'.

The Archbishop of Paris, a typical Blakean priestly villain, foresees the downfall of both nobility and clergy, and urges the imprisonment of the seditious deputies; otherwise

> "The priest [shall] rot in his surplice by the lawless lover, the holy beside the accursed,
> The King, frowning in purple, beside the grey plowman, and their worms embrace together." [*F.R.* 181]

But the Duke of Orleans, expressing Blake's own convictions, arises 'generous as mountains' and replies that if nobility is true nobleness it cannot be overthrown, nor can it be founded on the misery of the lower estate:

"Is the body diseas'd when the members are healthful? can the man be bound in sorrow
Whose ev'ry function is fill'd with its fiery desire? can the soul whose brain and heart
Cast their rivers in equal tides thro' the great Paradise, languish because the feet,
Hand, head, bosom, and parts of love follow their high breathing joy?"
[*F.R.* 183]

Through the mouth of Orleans Blake utters his belief that the individual cannot be subjected to laws, for each man is unique,

"...fire delights in its form.
But go, merciless man! enter into the infinite labyrinth of another's brain
Ere thou measure the circle that he shall run. Go, thou cold recluse, into the fires
Of another's high flaming rich bosom, and return unconsum'd, and write laws.
If thou canst not do this, doubt thy theories; learn to consider all men as thy equals,
Thy brethren, and not as thy foot or thy hand..." [*F.R.* 183–4]

The Abbé Sieyès is now admitted to Versailles as the people's messenger, and tells the Council of France's sufferings. Burgundy answers him with defiance and the threat of armed force, and Sieyès returns to the Assembly. Here Mirabeau calls on Lafayette as the nation's general to order the army to remove ten miles from Paris. The order is obeyed, and the King and his nobles are left defenceless.

So ends the first and only surviving book of *The French Revolution*, a poem not wholly successful as it stands but containing some brilliant phrases and a foretaste of Blake's apocalyptic manner. It adds nothing to what we already know of his thought, unless it be the momentary identification of the French Revolution with the beginning of the New Age of which he was the prophet. Yet there is a strong power of dramatisation in the situations and in the characters which are clearly if slightly marked. It is our last contact with the earth and with pure history in the poems of William Blake. Henceforth we are to travel as best we can through those extraordinary worlds of the imagination which have so much that is strange and yet, as I have already suggested, so much that is familiar, for they are the regions of the human mind.

CHAPTER III

The Fires of Orc

All Penal Laws court Transgression & therefore are cruelty & Murder. The laws of the Jews were (both ceremonial & real) the basest & most oppressive of human codes, & being like all other codes given under pretence of divine command were what Christ pronounced them, The Abomination that maketh desolate, i.e. State Religion, which is the source of all Cruelty. [*W.A.* 963]

It was in the years 1791 to 1794 that Blake's mind was most powerfully exercised with the thoughts of revolution which had received expression in his last poem. He had found his way into a revolutionary clique. At Joseph Johnson's house over the bookshop in St Paul's Churchyard there met week by week some of the most advanced thinkers of the day: Dr Joseph Priestley, William Godwin, Tom Paine, Mary Wollstonecraft, Dr Price—and Blake himself. These 'Liberty Boys' hailed the French Revolution with joy, but only Blake, we are told, went so far as to wear the *bonnet rouge* in broad daylight in the streets of London. He abandoned this perilous gesture only when the September massacres had disillusioned him of his high hopes of the millenium. In 1791 Paine published the First Part of his *Rights of Man*, running the risk of imprisonment and even death. The Second Part appeared in 1792. Pitt's government issued a proclamation against seditious publications. Danger was coming closer to the Liberty Boys, and with rapid strides:

In September a French deputation announced to Paine that the department of Calais had elected him member of the National Convention. Already as an acknowledged cosmopolitan and friend of man, he had been declared a citizen of France by the deceased Assembly. One day in this same month, Paine was giving at Johnson's an idea of the inflammatory eloquence he had poured forth at a public meeting of the previous night. Blake, who was present, silently inferred from the tenor of his report that those in power, now eager to lay hold of noxious persons, would certainly not let slip such an opportunity. On Paine's rising to leave, Blake laid his hand on the orator's shoulder, saying: "You must not go home, or you are a dead man!" and hurried him off on his way to France, whither he was now in any case bound, to take his seat as French legislator. By the time Paine was at Dover, the officers were in his house... and some twenty minutes after the custom house officials at Dover had turned over his slender baggage with, as he thought, extra malice, and he had set sail for Calais, an order was received from the Home Office to detain him.[1]

What a contrast to the genteel teaparties at Mrs Mathew's these ardent political meetings must have seemed to Blake! He joined fully in the discussions, combating Paine's and Priestley's and Godwin's religious views while concurring in their social and political aspirations. There was not only the intrinsic interest of the subjects discussed—there was also, as Paine's peril had emphasised, the spice of adventure. It was really dangerous to discuss radical ideas at this time in England, and still more dangerous to publish them. It is surmised that Blake's *The French Revolution* never got beyond the proof-sheet stage because he, or Johnson, was afraid to publish it. We know that Johnson, in spite of his friendship and sympathy with Paine, dared not undertake the publication of the First Part of the *Rights of Man* in 1791; we also know that he was prosecuted a few years later; and that he was imprisoned in 1798 for selling a copy of Gilbert Wakefield's *Reply to the Bishop of Llandaff's Address*—the same Bishop of Llandaff who excited Blake's ironic comments on his *Apology for the Bible*.[2]

The year 1792 is a blank as far as Blake's writing is concerned though he no doubt continued to earn a meagre livelihood by engraving. Sir Joshua Reynolds, his old enemy, died in February; it was sixteen years later that Blake wrote his comments on the *Discourses*. Blake's mother also died in this year. In 1793 he moved to 13 Hercules Buildings, Lambeth; and the following seven years were to be the most productive and prosperous of his career. For a time Catherine even kept a servant, but she soon found that she preferred to do all the housework herself. And she continued to help her husband in the printing and colouring of his books. In a *Prospectus*, etched in 1793, Blake announces the completion of

[1] Gilchrist, *Life of Blake*, Ch. XI. 'Spite of unworldliness and visionary faculty', Gilchrist comments, 'Blake never wanted for prudence and sagacity in ordinary matters.'

[2] See below, Ch. XIX. Johnson was the publisher of Mary Wollstonecraft's *Rights of Women* (1792) and Godwin's *Political Justice* (1793).

'works (he is not afraid to say) of equal magnitude and consequence with the productions of any age or country'. He speaks of the new method of printing which he has invented 'in a style more ornamental, uniform, and grand, than any before discovered'. This was no empty boast, as the rapid production of many masterpieces of coloured printing, and the illustrations to such works as Young's *Night Thoughts*, amply demonstrated. Blake was beginning to be spoken about in the artistic world, and a few people realised the genius of his designs, though many considered him a madman. He made a good friend in Thomas Butts the Muster-Master General, who gave him encouragement and bought his work (sometimes one drawing a week) for nearly thirty years, turning his house in Fitzroy Square into a veritable Blake gallery. It is to Butts, Gilchrist tells us, that we owe the story of Mr and Mrs Blake being discovered by him one day in the summerhouse of their garden freed from 'those troublesome disguises' which have draped the human form since the Fall. "Come in!" cried Blake, "it's only Adam and Eve, you know!" There is nothing intrinsically improbable or important about this story, but it has roused much comment among the more prudish of Blake's admirers. Butts is said later to have denied the story.

In this year 1793 Blake got through a great deal of work both in designing and writing; we are not surprised to come across this memorandum, dated June: 'I say I shan't live five years, And if I live one it will be a Wonder'; for the vehemence of his thought must often have seemed likely to prove too strong for his body. When the fit of inspiration was on him, we are told, he would rise from his bed in the night and see visions and write down what he saw; and Catherine would get up too and sit quietly beside him, stirring neither hand nor foot but staying his beating mind with her silent presence. His output for this year includes *The Marriage of Heaven and Hell*; *A Song of Liberty*; *Visions of the Daughters of Albion*; *America*; *The Gates of Paradise*; and various minor lyrics. In these poems the burning fire of thought shines bright and clear. Blake is working out the metaphysical foundations of the system he is to elaborate in the longer prophetic books.

The Gates of Paradise was added to in 1818, when almost all the text was supplied to accompany the plates. These designs were originally inscribed *For Children*: the title was changed to *For the*

Sexes when the text was added. It will be better to consider designs and text together later on.

The Marriage of Heaven and Hell is a collection of prose passages preceded by a verse 'Argument'. It is the completest expression of Blake's philosophy up to date, and in a sense he was never to go beyond this clear and succinct exposition of 'the everlasting gospel'. I shall be referring again and again to its teaching in the second part of this book, so there is no need here to give more than a synopsis. As the title suggests, Blake is dealing with the problem of evil, and indeed with the mystery of life itself, so obviously beyond good and evil and yet evoking in man a moral response.

The first prose passage announces the beginning of 'a new heaven', as proclaimed by Swedenborg, 'the Angel sitting at the tomb'. The resurrection of Man into unity is to begin. 'Now is the dominion of Edom, & the return of Adam into Paradise.' And this return is to be accomplished by accepting the tension of the contraries in Man.

> Without Contraries is no progression. Attraction and Repulsion, Reason and Energy, Love and Hate, are necessary to Human existence.
>
> From these contraries spring what the religious call Good & Evil. Good is the passive that obeys Reason. Evil is the active springing from Energy.
>
> Good is Heaven. Evil is Hell. [*M.H.H.* 191]

Blake is carrying on, as we can see, from his comments on Lavater. In doing so in this vein, he is enunciating a new psychology, an account of Man radically different from the formulations of post-Renaissance tradition. He is preaching the acceptance of the human *totality*; he is denying the right of repressive codes to dwarf and amputate any expression of life.

The second passage gives us 'The Voice of the Devil'—i.e. of pure energetic wisdom. How does the moral code come to exist? this voice asks in effect. By imagining a body separate from the soul, and insisting that the bodily energies must be repressed in favour of the soul. As a consequence of this false teaching, it is supposed 'that God will torment Man in Eternity for following his Energies'.

What restrains desire, we are told in the following section, is *Reason*—a purely passive thing, but exerting like all passive things a strong *vis inertiae*. Here Blake gives an analysis of the theme of

Paradise Lost from the point of view of his own theory of reason and desire. The Messiah in *Paradise Lost* is reason, and Satan is the principle of energy. Milton has told the story upside down; and that is why in 1804 Blake had to set to work to retell the drama. For Milton has been led astray by his Puritanism, the error of the moral code, and must be redeemed.

This ends the first or purely didactic part of *The Marriage of Heaven and Hell.* There follows a series of Proverbs of Hell, preceded by a 'Memorable Fancy' in which Blake describes how he collected these proverbs while walking about among the fires of hell—the burning ideas of his own imagination. These proverbs are too numerous to comment upon in full. They are full of wisdom, and successive readings bring out further depths of meaning. Many of them are concerned with the dangers of repression, the importance of giving full scope to one's energies and desires:

> The road of excess leads to the palace of wisdom.
> He who desires but acts not, breeds pestilence.
> Sooner murder an infant in its cradle than nurse unacted desires.
> [*M.H.H.* 192–5]

Others speak of the double vision:

> A fool sees not the same tree that a wise man sees.
> When thou seest an Eagle, thou seest a portion of Genius; lift up thy head!
> The roaring of lions, the howling of wolves, the raging of the stormy sea, and the destructive sword, are portions of eternity, too great for the eye of man.[1] [*M.H.H.* 193–4]

Or we have the fourfold vision, the direct experience of eternity:

> One thought fills immensity.
> The soul of sweet delight can never be defil'd.
> To create a little flower is the labour of ages.
> [*M.H.H.* 193–4]

And with these a multitude of precepts deriving from them, extolling the life of the imagination and the virtue of forgiveness. All are directed to the great end of Blake's 'prophecy': the re-integration of the human image.

---

[1] But not too great for the *mind* of Man, seeing not *with* but *through* the eye.

The sequence of prose passages is now resumed. Didactic utterances are alternated with 'memorable fancies': all teach the same lesson that Man's purpose on earth is to raise himself and others 'into a perception of the infinite'. Blake returns to the prophetic announcement with which he began, that the New Age is at hand:

> For the cherub with his flaming sword is hereby commanded to leave his guard at tree of life; and when he does, the whole creation will be consumed and appear infinite and holy, whereas it now appears finite & corrupt.
>
> This will come to pass by an improvement of sensual enjoyment.
>
> [*M.H.H.* 197]

In other words, it is by understanding the senses as what they really are, 'the chief inlets of soul in this age', and enjoying their data to the full, using them as windows into Eternity and not as mere channels of information about matter or instruments of pleasure, that we shall 'melt apparent surfaces away and display the infinite which was hid'. Blake takes his own technique of etching as the type and symbol of this new technique of understanding.

> If the doors of perception were cleansed every thing would appear to man as it is, infinite.
>
> For man has closed himself up, till he sees all things thro' narrow chinks of his cavern. [*M.H.H.* 197]

And we are to cleanse the doors of perception, the senses, not by denying them and cramping them, but by indulging them to the uttermost: by letting the full river of life sweep through them.

In the *Song of Liberty* with which the *Marriage* ends, Blake's vision rises to ecstasy in a free-verse canticle which looks forward to the mythology of the prophetic books. He calls upon the nations to break their bonds and participate in the liberation which comes with the New Age. We have the first mention by name of Urthona, the noblest of the Four Zoas, while Urizen, Tharmas, Vala and the revolutionary Orc are referred to in unmistakable terms. The book ends with the Chorus:

> Let the Priests of the Raven of dawn no longer, in deadly black, with hoarse note curse the sons of joy. Nor his accepted brethren—whom, tyrant, he calls free—lay the bound or build the roof. Nor pale religious letchery call that virginity that wishes but acts not! [*M.H.H.* 204]

In *The Marriage of Heaven and Hell* Blake has triumphantly completed the statement of a new psychology which he began in the tractates *There is no Natural Religion* and *All Religions are one.* The basic contraries of human nature are here firmly stated and related to the cosmic drama which is to form the subject of the long symbolic books. Blake's vision pierces through the political and social anomalies of his age to the disintegration of the personality which over-development of reason has brought about. Here is no crude doctrine of perfectibility such as we find in Godwin's prose or Shelley's verse. The analysis is deeper and more original—anticipating, indeed, the basic discoveries of Freud.

It is plain that in *The Marriage of Heaven and Hell* Blake is occupied above all with the sexual problem: the dilemma of sex as a source of delight and energy being restrained by the moral code. In the *Visions of the Daughters of Albion* he gives a symbolic and narrative form to the conclusions he has come to in the prose work. Henceforth, indeed, symbolic narrative is to replace straightforward philosophical statement as the medium for his ideas. For through symbolic narrative he was able to combine in a single pattern all the planes on which his insight was functioning: philosophical, social, political, psychological, aesthetic, historical. The *Visions* are an allegory of the workings of instinct under the bond of law, with a musical structure in which questionings about the instincts of animals is a recurrent theme. Oothoon, 'the soft soul of America', is the name given to Thel since she has now entered the body (which in Blake's symbolic cosmology is represented by the West). She represents instinct innocent and undefiled; and when she sees the Marigold (like the Sunflower of *Songs of Experience* an image of sensual pleasure) she wishes to pluck it—but is afraid, for the narrow prison of the body has already brought its doubts and fears:

> "Art thou a flower? art thou a nymph? I see thee now a flower,
> Now a nymph! I dare not pluck thee from thy dewy bed!"
>
> The Golden nymph replied: "Pluck thou my flower, Oothoon
> the mild!
> Another flower shall spring, because the soul of sweet delight
> Can never pass away." She ceas'd, & clos'd her golden shrine.

> Then Oothoon pluck'd the flower, saying: "I pluck thee from thy bed,
> Sweet flower, and put thee here to glow between my breasts,
> And thus I turn my face to where my whole soul seeks."
>
> [*V.D.A.* 205–6]

It is for Theotormon she seeks, the principle of free, active desire; but all too soon she finds herself in the snares of Bromion, conventional morality, who violates her. Theotormon falls into agonies of jealousy, and refuses to see that Oothoon cannot be defiled by an enforced prostitution. Oothoon tells him that purity is not a physical thing: it consists in vision, in understanding. The five senses are not all, she insists; all living creatures have different instincts and different joys, so none should condemn another. Still Theotormon refuses to be convinced, and Oothoon accuses Urizen (now first mentioned by name) of the authorship of all their woe in striving to conform everything to his own image:

> "O Urizen! Creator of men! mistaken Demon of heaven!
> Thy joys are tears, thy labour vain to form men to thine image.
> How can one joy absorb another? are not different joys
> Holy, eternal, infinite? and each joy is a Love." [*V.D.A.* 210]

Then follows a magnificent exposition of the folly of attempting a uniformity of manners and actions and thoughts which is the very antithesis of true unity. For unity consists in the free play of contraries. 'One Law for the Lion & Ox is Oppression.' And now Blake, through the mouth of Oothoon, goes on to speak in burning words of the misery of sexual servitude, of marriage in which there is no love. Religion and the moral code have their part to play in the tragedy:

> "With what sense does the parson claim the labour of the farmer?
> What are his nets & gins & traps; & how does he surround him
> With cold floods of abstraction, and with forests of solitude,
> To build him castles and high spires, where kings & priests may dwell;
> Till she who burns with youth, and knows no fixed lot, is bound
> In spells of law to one she loaths? and must she drag the chain
> Of life in weary lust? must chilling, murderous thoughts obscure
> The clear heaven of her eternal spring; to bear the wintry rage
> Of a harsh terror, driv'n to madness, bound to hold a rod
> Over her shrinking shoulders all the day, & all the night

To turn the wheel of false desire, and longings that wake her womb
To the abhorred birth of cherubs in the human form,
That live a pestilence & die a meteor, & are no more?" [*V.D.A.* 211]

After acclaiming infancy as the period of unrestrained sexuality, Oothoon ends her outburst with a panegyric of free love which holds no measure of jealousy. 'Every thing that lives is holy', she reiterates. But her arguments are unavailing—

. . . Theotormon sits
Upon the margin'd ocean conversing with shadows dire. [*V.D.A.* 215]

In *America*, to which he gives the name *A Prophecy*, Blake returns from the theme of sexual liberty to that of political and social emancipation which he has already treated in *The French Revolution*; but now the historical order is completely penetrated by and subservient to the eternal order. The symbolic action of the poem is puzzling to those who read Blake chronologically, for the vision of Orc in chains with which it begins is only comprehensible when we are acquainted with the events described in *The Book of Urizen* (1794). The *Preludium* tells how 'red Orc' (the principle of Revolution) breaks his chains and unites with 'the shadowy Daughter of Urthona' (Nature), who is dumb until this moment. Only when the natural order is penetrated by revolt does it come really to life. The centuries have waited for this event.

"I know thee, I have found thee, & I will not let thee go:
Thou art the image of God who dwells in darkness of Africa,
And thou art fall'n to give me life in regions of dark death." [*A.* 217]

Then follows the prophecy, a relation of events of which the *Preludium* has given the spiritual significance. The action may be divided into ten sections. In the first five lines, we are shown the discontent in America, and the threatenings of England. Then follows Washington's accusation of English tyranny. Next, a vision of Orc is seen 'o'er the Atlantic sea'. Orc sings a song of revolt and liberation. Albion's angel accuses Orc of being Antichrist. Orc replies by defiance, and insists that holiness is of the spirit:

The Terror answer'd: "I am Orc, wreath'd round the accursed tree:
The times are ended; shadows pass, the morning 'gins to break;
The fiery joy, that Urizen perverted to ten commands,

What night he led the starry host thro' the wide wilderness,
That stony law I stamp to dust; and scatter religion abroad
To the four winds as a torn book, & none shall gather the leaves;"
[*A.* 220]

Aroused by this challenge, Albion's angel sounds the trumpet to war: but in vain; the colonies support Washington. The thirteen original states revolt, animated by the example of 'Boston's Angel'. The War of Independence ensues, and the English are defeated. Finally, the *inner* significance of the revolt is driven home by Blake: it is a defeat for Urizen, and therefore not only a political triumph for Orc but a psychological one as well:

The doors of marriage are open, and the Priests in rustling scales
Rush into reptile coverts, hiding from the fires of Orc,
That play around the golden roofs in wreaths of fierce desire,
Leaving the females naked and glowing with the lusts of youth.
[*A.* 226]

This sexual preoccupation, which Blake could not keep out of so political-seeming a poem as this on the American revolt, reaches its height in the third poem of the trilogy, *Europe*, which was etched in 1794 but had better be considered now, disregarding strict chronological order. *Europe* is also a 'prophecy': it consists of an introductory section found in only two copies, a 'Preludium', and a narrative which breaks away from history altogether and is content to be purely symbolic. The introduction gives us Blake's most brilliant description of his doctrine of the senses:

"Five windows light the cavern'd Man: thro' one he breathes the air;
Thro' one hears music of the spheres; thro' one the eternal vine
Flourishes, that he may recieve the grapes; thro' one can look
And see small portions of the eternal world that ever groweth;
Thro' one himself pass out what time he please; but he will not,
For stolen joys are sweet & bread eaten in secret pleasant." [*Eu.* 232]

It is a reiteration of the doctrine of the *Marriage*: the five senses are the chief inlets of soul in this age; cleanse them by vigorous enjoyment, and Man steps into Eternity. But Man will not: he prefers the perverted joys of secrecy, especially in sex. He gets a thrill from thinking that he is being naughty. He shrinks back from liberty.

The *Preludium* gives the lament of Nature—nature, the vegetable universe formed, as we shall see later, when Urizen committed his initial crime—on being compelled to bring forth so many strange forms, in such vast suffering. Only the prophetic vision of a birth which will compass the infinite, the birth of Christ (identified with Orc), is able to console her. The *Prophecy* itself begins with a passage imitative in matter and manner of Milton's *Ode on the Morning of Christ's Nativity*. But soon we find Blake returning to the contemplation of that sexual dilemma which obviously absorbed his attention at this period. Los, the prophetic genius, is attempting to restore Urizen to his true place in the South (to restore, that is, reason to its right sphere, the intellect). He calls on his son Orc, the spirit of revolution, to help him. But unfortunately Los is not at one with his Emanation Enitharmon, who represents inspiration; and she, in her female weakness, sets up wrong ideals of morality. She wishes woman to have dominion over man, and she knows she can bring this about by making woman's love a mysterious and suspected thing. She sends her children out into the world to preach this doctrine:

> "Go! tell the Human race that Woman's love is Sin;
> That an Eternal life awaits the worms of sixty winters
> In an allegorical abode where existence hath never come.
> Forbid all Joy, & from her childhood shall the little female
> Spread nets in every secret path." [*Eu.* 235]

The first error is the persuasion that sexual love is sinful; men are led to believe this by the promise of religion that if they suppress their desires they will go to heaven after their death. But there is no such heaven: Eternity is entered on this side of the grave, if at all; and the poor fools are simply deluded. This is the holy alliance of the women and the priests. Joy is stigmatised as criminal, and modesty and coquetry are taught to 'little females' from their infancy. Such is Blake's analysis of the situation.

Enitharmon then sleeps eighteen hundred years, 'a female dream'. It is Blake's way of accusing the centuries which followed the birth of Christ, up to his own day, of rejecting vision and art. Christ's salvation has been brought to nought by cunning, and the Catholic Church has declined into priestcraft and ceremony. In a magnificent phantasmagoric image Blake expresses the spiritual confusion of European history:

> Shadows of men in fleeting bands upon the winds,

a line in which the inner eye sees these figures like leaves blown across the dark horizon of the centuries. It is Urizen who is now the arbiter of Man's destiny, and the Ten Commandments are the law which he must follow. He raises the Druid temple at 'golden Verulam', and the serpent religion spreads over the whole earth:

> Thought chang'd the infinite to a serpent, that which pitieth
> To a devouring flame; and man fled from its face and hid
> In forests of night: then all the eternal forests were divided
> Into earths rolling in circles of space, that like an ocean rush'd
> And overwhelmed all except this finite wall of flesh.
> Then was the serpent temple form'd, image of infinite
> Shut up in finite revolutions, and man became an Angel,
> Heaven a mighty circle turning, God a tyrant crown'd. [*Eu.* 237]

Enitharmon in her sleep is delighted to see this reign of repression, with 'Thou shalt not' written over the doors and 'Fear' over the chimneys. Orc, however, the spirit of revolt, is active: the moment comes when he essays to blow the trumpet of the Last Judgement. But the time is not yet; the trumpet is seized by 'a mighty Spirit from the land of Albion, nam'd Newton'—he blows the trumpet and, instead of the dead rising,

> myriads of Angelic hosts
> Fell thro' the wintry skies seeking their graves,
> Rattling their hollow bones in howling and lamentation. [*Eu.* 240]

Thus a still grimmer form of materialism is loosed upon the world! Enitharmon awakes at last, but she has not repented of her error; she continues to instruct her daughters in the arts of deceit, until Orc is aroused and appears in the red flames of the French Revolution. Enitharmon is dismayed, and Los the spirit of prophecy calls all his sons to the spiritual warfare with error—a warfare which will be recounted at length in the later symbolic books.

CHAPTER IV

The Myth

I must Create a System or be enslav'd by another Man's. [*J.* 564]

FLAXMAN returned to England and to Blake's circle in 1794: his seven years in Italy had been devoted to studying the antique; he returned 'with well-stored portfolios, with more than ever classicised taste, and having made at Rome for discerning patrons those designs from Homer, Aeschylus, and Dante which were afterwards to spread his fame through Europe'. He was made R.A. immediately. Blake continued to engrave from his designs and remained his friend (with some periods of estrangement, to which the epigrams bear eloquent witness) up to Flaxman's death a year before his own. Flaxman appears to have been genuinely fond of Blake, and to have had some kind of puzzled inkling of his greatness. In a letter of 1800 Blake thanks God for Flaxman's friendship. Among his heavenly friends he lists Milton, Ezra, Isaiah and Shakespeare; among his friends on earth he counts Fuseli, Hayley and Flaxman—and Flaxman's principal virtue seems to be that he 'knows to forgive Nervous Fear'.

In 1794 Blake engraved, besides his *Songs of Experience*, finished this year, *The Book of Urizen*, which gives us the first of his narratives of the Fall. There are several of these Fall narratives interspersed among the episodes of the symbolic books which we are now about to study, and it may be convenient to summarise their variations, together with the preceding myth of the Golden Age.

The language in which we discuss ideas which are independent of space and time is, unfortunately, the same everyday language which has been woven on the looms of space and time. There is no special metaphysical speech. The more we attempt to describe, to elucidate, the more we falsify. For the mystic the problem is even more acute, since now the reason itself, with its categories, is impotent. Metaphysics has managed, through the ages, to establish a skeleton structure of thoughts, if not a universal vocabulary. But the mystic is compelled to

> fix his thought upon
> That quarter where all thought is done:
> Who can distinguish darkness from the soul?

Who indeed? and on the whole the greatest mystics have preferred to accept darkness itself as their vehicle of suggestion. The *via negativa* is superior to the *via affirmativa*. Dionysius speaks of the Divine Dark, and East and West join in saying of the supreme reality: *Not that.*

When we come to consider the origins of Blake's mythological scheme, we are faced with a grave difficulty. We can hardly think of 'origin' without appending the idea 'in time'. We are impelled to ask: *When* did this happen? and by this question we mean: At what point in a frame of reference based on the revolutions of the earth round the sun? Blake did not choose the *via negativa* to express his vision. His mind was too dynamic, too Western if you like, for that approach. He used a mythology, and by doing so he tied himself down to temporal and spatial symbols. But we cannot rest in the symbols; we must constantly see beyond them to the reality. And the reality exists in Eternity, not in time. The reality *is* Eternity.

Man as he is now is 'that great and true *Amphibium*', living 'in divided and distinguished worlds'. His home is Eternity, but his existence is caught up in the meshes of time and space. This antithesis tortures him until he realises his true being, and sets foot on the road that leads back to Eternity. To point out this road is the task of poets and prophets. They sing of a Golden Age when this division did not exist. They tell of a Fall into division, and foretell a Resurrection into Unity.

Of Eternity we can only say that *it is*; and Blake would add—in the mind of every man, the imagination. But leaving aside that corollary for later study, let us fix our thoughts upon Eternity as independent of duration, not as something formed of an infinite catena of intervals of time—and thus understand that we cannot rightly speak of the Golden Age as being *before* time and space, except for the purposes of myth. We cannot say, 'There was a time when Eternity alone existed, and the universe was not'. For in the word 'time' we have again slipped into the temporal idea.

Thus words fail us; but with this caution in our minds, let us still say: 'In the beginning was Eternity, and time and space were not.' Let this remain a purely verbal statement, for it is what flows from it, in the doctrine of the Fall, that is important. The idea of Eternity will only become real to us when, later on in this book, I suggest what it means in the business of actual living. What can be said at this point about Blake's conception of the Golden Age is only useful as laying the foundation of the myth in which the doctrine is given flesh and blood and bones.

Before time and space were, Eternity was: and Eternity was the mode of existence of the Universal Man. Outside him, nothing. No earth, no planets; 'Earth was not: nor globes of attraction'; only the spiritual body of Man. And in this spiritual body, 'four faces', which Blake calls the four Zoas: Urthona, or Los, who is the imagination and dwells in the symbolic North; Urizen, or reason, who dwells in the South; Luvah, the passions, in the East; and Tharmas, the body, in the West. These powers live in harmony with one another and with their 'emanations', which do not become separate (and thus describable) until the Fall. Each, moreover, has his station in an organ of sense: Urthona in the ears, Urizen in the eyes, Luvah in the nostrils, and Tharmas in the tongue.

The senses of the Universal Man were not limited in scope like ours. Our senses are weak and fallible. They give us some knowledge of a material world around us, filled with a number of separate objects, some of them living, others dead. In many ways they deceive us. And as we grow older, they decay with the material body of which they are a part.

In Eternity this was not so. The senses of the Universal Man were infinite in scope, granting him an intensity of perception, and a variety of perceptions, quite unknown to us. Now these senses had one great power: they were 'all-flexible'. They could be expanded or contracted at will. When expanded, Man saw himself as Unity. When contracted, he saw himself as Diversity.

Here we have the key to the whole range of Blake's vision. It is the solution to the hoary philosophical problem of the One and the Many; it is the solution to the metaphysical trinity of God, Man, and Nature. It is an idealism more radical than Berkeley's and at the same time more consistent. It has room for a Fall (which Berkeley's system does not really admit) with all its corollaries of sin and pain. It leaves room for the individual, and for his various passions and aspirations.

Contracting his senses, Man sees himself as one man among his fellow-men. He sees, under their spiritual forms, animals, rivers, rocks and cities, and 'all the furniture of Heaven and Earth'. Not as we see them now, dead or only half-alive:

> A Rock, a Cloud, a Mountain,
> [Are] now not Vocal as in Climes of happy Eternity
> Where the lamb replies to the infant voice, & the lion to the man of years
> Giving them sweet instructions; where the Cloud, the River & the Field
> Talk with the husbandman & shepherd. [*F.Z.* 357]

In the Golden Age all things, being part of Humanity, were alive and vocal. There was a constant interchange between Man and that part of his being which, when he pleased, he saw as exterior to himself:

> the Bodies in which all Animals & Vegetations, the Earth & Heaven
> Were contain'd in the All Glorious Imagination. [*J.* 642]

The essence of Eternity is freedom. Where there is unity there can be no bondage and no lordship. All things, the four Zoas and the Eternal Ones who are the thoughts of Humanity, work for the Universal Man, because they are aspects of him. His nature is of infinite richness, in which every quality, whether 'good' or 'evil', lives in a contrapuntal relation with its neighbours. No sooner does sin appear as a form of energy than it provokes forgiveness. No sooner does error show itself than it is challenged and through the tension of combat changed into its direct opposite. Every energy exists and is recognised; and 'Energy is Eternal Delight'.

It is no static bliss that Blake envisages in his Golden Age. There is spiritual hunting and spiritual war in the clash of contraries; the great primal vices and virtues of humanity in constant tension bring forth ever new forms. The idea of a moral code is utterly alien to unfallen Man:

> "O Times remote!
> When Love & Joy were adoration,
> And none impure were deem'd:
> Not Eyeless Covet,

Nor Thin-lip'd Envy,
Nor Bristled Wrath,
Nor Curled Wantonness;

But Covet was poured full,
Envy fed with fat of lambs,
Wrath with lion's gore,
Wantonness lull'd to sleep
With the virgin's lute
Or sated with her love;

Till Covet broke his locks & bars
And slept with open doors;
Envy sung at the rich man's feast;
Wrath was follow'd up and down
By a little ewe lamb,
And Wantonness on his own true love
Begot a giant race." [*B.L.* 267]

Here we see the operation of the dialectical process, the transmutation of 'base' passions into pure gold, the road of excess leading to the palace of wisdom. 'Virtues' are produced from 'vices' by letting the vices have their head! In Eternity, 'exuberance is beauty' whatever the form it takes. What is *not* beauty is all that proceeds from restriction, egotism and withdrawal from the human family. We note that Blake includes in the present list even envy, which later (in the annotations to Lavater's *Aphorisms*) takes its place among the vices springing from weakness. But this is only because envy in Eternity is an expression of desire uncurbed by reason which can be immediately satisfied and so brought to 'sing at the rich man's feast'. It is an evil being put off continually.

The Universal Man, seen as a unity, has the form of Christ, who is also called the Divine Vision. He is Man's consciousness of his unity; and if we bear this in mind, we shall understand why Blake wrote at the heading of his *Jerusalem* the words Μόνος ὁ Ἰησοῦς and why the single devotion to Jesus runs through all his thought. It is Christ alone who can save the Fallen Man—Albion, who is Man unconscious of his unity—and die for him by taking upon Himself generation *in complete consciousness of what He is doing.*

Another great symbol in the eternal world is Jerusalem, the Pleroma or aggregate of the minute particulars. She is the Bride of Christ and the Emanation of the Universal Humanity. In yet another aspect, she is the light given out by every particular form in Eternity:

> & the form is the Divine Vision
> And the Light is his Garment.

In every individual man she is the spirit of liberty, in which men can meet and communicate. But if she separates from Man (as happens in the world of generation) she is seen as Vala—Nature, the sexual delusion who is the cause of jealousy and strife.

> "When in Eternity Man converses with Man, they enter
> Into each other's Bosom (which are Universes of delight)
> In mutual interchange, and first their Emanations meet
> Surrounded by their Children; if they embrace & comingle,
> The Human Four-fold Forms mingle also in thunders of Intellect;
> But if the Emanations mingle not, with storms & agitations
> Of earthquakes & consuming fires they roll apart in fear;
> For Man cannot unite with Man but by their Emanations
> Which stand both Male and Female at the Gates of each Humanity."
>
> [*J.* 729]

In Eternity, then, there is no sex; man is a unity, possessing a double emanation which we can think of, in our terms, as male and female. But in time,

> The Feminine separates from the Masculine & both from Man,
> Ceasing to be His Emanations, Life to Themselves assuming:
>
> [*J.* 733]

Thus sex, which in this world can be the supreme way back to unity and thus to Eternity, is also the supreme obstacle. 'The sexual garments sweet Grow a devouring Windingsheet.' Woman is jealous: she wants the whole of a man's life for herself; nothing is left for God. She creates a religion of sexual mystery; she gets power through the moral law. Not so in the Golden Age. There, male and female emanations live in harmony within every man, and within the four Zoas. Enitharmon is the feminine emanation of Los, Enion of Tharmas, Vala of Luvah, and Ahania of Urizen. None claims separate existence.

All this sounds very tedious and allegorical, and I put down these correspondences here simply as a mechanical guide to what might otherwise give unnecessary difficulty. No breath of the life of Blake's thought comes from them until they are seen animated in the lines of *The Four Zoas* and *Urizen*; until, for example, we hear Ahania singing of the joys of her eternal existence:

> "Where is my golden palace?
> Where my ivory bed?
> Where the joy of my morning hour?
> Where the sons of eternity singing
>
> To awaken bright Urizen, my king,
> To arise to the mountain sport,
> To the bliss of eternal valleys;..." [*B.A.* 265]

Such are the main outlines of the Golden Age as it presented itself to Blake. This is the basis of the myth—or, as Blake would call it, vision as opposed to fable or allegory.[1] And the essence of myth is that it is that which is believed. Blake perfectly believed in this state of man which precedes the Fall. 'I look back', he writes to Flaxman (21 September 1800), 'into the regions of Reminiscence & behold our ancient days before this Earth appear'd in its vegetated mortality to my mortal vegetated eyes'. He lived in constant communion with Los and with Urizen and with the beings that appear to our clouded vision as rocks and trees and streams. He saw them in their true lineaments, in the world of his imagination. He saw their bliss in the Golden Age; and he saw, too, how they had fallen from bliss to disunion and misery.

What is the meaning of this gigantic framework? Is it a perverse piece of obscurantism?[2] If we think so we shall be denying to Blake

[1] 'Fable or Allegory are a totally distinct & inferior kind of Poetry. Vision or Imagination is a Representation of what Eternally Exists, Really & Unchangeably' [*V.L.J.* 828–9].

[2] As Dr Tillyard would seem to suggest in his *Poetry: Direct and Oblique*. 'How effective the repeated symbol could be we may realise if we imagine Blake's making the best use of his early successes. Having established certain admirable symbols in *Songs of Innocence and Experience*, like the lamb, the tiger, the rose, the watery shore, he throws away the enormous advantages of being able to use them again and painfully labours to create afresh a symbolism that lacks all the initial advantages of his previous creations. The normal mind leaps to greet Blake's tiger, it is persuaded to accept with strong approval his rose, and it can see some sense in the notion of making the watery shore signify the margin between material and eternal. With Los and Enitharmon it has to start at scratch, and it is hopelessly discouraged at the perverse steeplechase it is expected to run. Had Blake repeated his early symbols,

even the vestiges of that reputation for balanced judgement and insight which he will probably have won in our minds, assuming that we started with the *Poetical Sketches* and the *Songs of Innocence and Experience*. Is it not wiser to believe that he was *forced* into inventing and elaborating this symbolism by the fact that he had something to communicate which he could communicate in no other way, something novel, something incommensurate with anything that had gone before?

The Fall came with the disruption of this primeval unity. It is not an event which takes place in time and space.

> "The Sin was begun in Eternity and will not rest to Eternity
> Till two Eternitys meet together." [*M.* 485]

And it began with the Four Zoas, whom we have just pictured living in the freedom of diversity within the unity of the Eternal Man. Peace and joy, light and understanding, were universal through the interplay of contraries. But one of the Four Living Creatures, the rational principle to which Blake gives the name of Urizen, was not content: he wished to usurp all power and conform all things to his own image. As a result he brought about division in Eternity, was cast out by his indignant peers, and organised the material world as his private kingdom where reason should reign supreme. Thus the external universe as we now see it, with its starry heavens, its seas, rocks, beasts and flowers, and all mankind, is the creation of Urizen. Urizen is Blake's version of the Jehovah of the Old Testament, the creator of this world, the Father of Jealousy: a mistaken demon not to be worshipped:

> Thinking as I do that the Creator of this World is a very Cruel Being, & being a Worshipper of Christ, I cannot help saying: "the Son, O how unlike the Father!" First God Almighty comes with a Thump on the Head. Then Jesus Christ comes with a balm to heal it. [*V.L.J.* 844]

Blake is not always consistent in his presentation of the action of the Fall, as we shall see in our analyses of the prophetic books. In the

he would have extracted from them a colossal force.' But we can only conclude that Blake refrained from repeating his early symbols (or repeated them in more limited contexts) simply because they were no longer adequate to what he had to express.

Book of Urizen and its sequels he shows the abstract reason revolting against unity and shrinking back into itself and being materialised. That is quite clear: reason divorced from understanding hates the creative diversity of Eternity and wishes to rule, subjecting every other manifestation of life to its own standard. Hence comes the split in personality and the secession of the individual ego from the race-consciousness. When this happens the soul is clouded with materialism and the spiritual eye darkened, so that only a material universe, composed of strictly discrete forms, is seen. Thus, in this initial version, the guilt is ascribed to the reasoning faculty.

But in the later myth of *The Four Zoas* there is an important variant. The first account is now felt to be too simple to do justice to the inner facts, to satisfy Blake's growing experience. Reason is still the demiurge, the immediate builder of the material universe: but is he the prime *cause* of the Fall? Blake now goes back behind reason to the passions. He had disagreed with Milton that passion was the dominant motive of the Fall: now he comes to agree with him, but gives his own peculiar twist to the argument. The Eternal Man who is 'in the beginning' lives ideally in enjoyment of every aspect of his being. Of these aspects four are prominent: the imagination (Los), the reason (Urizen), the passions (Luvah), and the instincts or body (Tharmas). So long as these aspects are held in fluid interplay, all is well. But Man (Albion) is led astray by his passions, and begins to worship them. He permits himself to be dominated by Luvah, and only recovers in time to appeal to Urizen for help. But already the balance of consciousness has been disturbed—the excess in the direction of passion has to be remedied by an excess in the direction of reason. Urizen seizes all power into his hands, banishes Luvah, and initiates the egotistic universe of matter. Tharmas is precipitated in a material form as the ocean, and Los, separating from his emanation Enitharmon (inspiration), is engaged in an eternal struggle from now on to redeem man from the effects of his folly. This involves warfare with Urizen. Man falls into the world of generation, and the phenomenal universe is detached from his body.

In a still later form of the myth, in *Jerusalem*, Blake has passed to another position. He is no longer content with his picture of separate human elements revolting against a totality: he now presents Albion himself as the guilty one, murdering Luvah, consciously seceding from Eternity, and losing himself in the 'valleys dark' of self-hood.

The basis of Blake's myth is no more personal than its philosophy: we find its guiding features in the Bible, the Hindu scriptures, in the Cabbala, in Jakob Boehme, and in the Gnostic writings of Marcion and Valentinus. Blake was well acquainted with this literature. But the vesture of the myth is original—its personages, cosmology and episodes—and came directly from what Blake saw in vision. He did not concoct a mythology by association: he wrote down his own direct experiences of the world of the imagination.

It is impossible to claim that Blake's myth is lucid and attractive as a whole. To most minds it is too violent and apocalyptic. It gives too much of the anguish and stress of the imagination, and not enough of its calm and felicity. No doubt this fact is due in part to deep personal causes in Blake's own mind. He felt frustrated in many directions, and he was agonisingly conscious of the spiritual blindness and gross materialism of his age. These feelings did not help to preserve his aesthetic balance.

Moreover, he tried to cram too much into his myth. His subject-matter has too wide a scope for clarity. Everything Blake knew and felt—the details of his own life, his quarrels and grievances, his attitude to contemporary society, his views on politics and social questions—was woven, not always skilfully, into the vast web. The result is the very opposite of that clarity and precision, that 'bounding line' in art, that Blake praised so much. His poetry is not disciplined enough.

The identities of the *dramatis personae*, even, are not fixed. Imagine the confusion in the reader of *Othello* if the hero of that play suddenly became identified with Iago! Yet that, or something like it, is what happens again and again in the symbolic books. Blake's practice seems in conflict with his teaching. 'Nothing in Eternity changes into another thing', he writes. Yet Albion is amalgamated with Urizen, Orc with Luvah, Milton with Los, and Heaven with Hell.

It is of course perfectly possible for the hard-working student of the symbolic books to prove to his own satisfaction that the framework is a unity, that there is a very good reason for these transformations, and that a profound psychological meaning is at the bottom of it all. We believe that all this is true. Through all one's grapplings with Blake's system there does grow in one a profound respect for his intelligence and his inner consistency. But for the moment we are considering the *aesthetic* impact of the symbolic books on the reader—on the careful and persistent reader. The effect is one of confusion and obscurity. We cannot enjoy *Jerusalem* as we enjoy *Paradise Lost* or *The Prelude.*

This is understandable when we remember that Blake was primarily interested not in poetry but in truth. He is speaking as a prophet. He shared with Paine the belief that poetry and prophecy are one and the same thing, but he was never immediately concerned with the *presentation* of his message. It was the message itself that was vitally important. The words, he firmly believed, were dictated to him by a higher source—and the images and episodes were a direct transcription from incidents in Eternity, revealed through Vision. This attitude did not exclude subsequent verbal revision.

Now this prophetic attitude, this trusting to truth to create its own form, worked supremely well, as we have seen, in the brief lyrics of the *Songs of Innocence and Experience.* There, a single idea or flash of emotion, acutely realised, could be trusted to fuse every element into a perfect whole. But the material of a long poem must be marshalled. There must be a beginning, a middle, and an end; and there must be a proper balance and connection of parts within the whole. Blake never wholly achieved this.

The result of his failure is twofold. In the first place, we have the general effect of confusion and complexity, of difficulty; yet this effect does not necessarily put us off reading Blake. It may spur us on. The first impression of unintelligibility withers away on persistent reading, and as the basic idea-framework becomes apparent we are stimulated to thought. Blake's obscurity puts us on our mettle, because we begin to suspect that it is an obscurity which originates in real depth of thought and not in mere incapacity for lucid expression.

The danger now is that our reading of Blake may degenerate into a kind of cross-word puzzle solving. A good deal of the writing of Blake's commentators is of this description. We suspect in reading them that they are very much concerned with making the details of the external framework fit and that in the process the essence of

Blake's teaching has evaporated. We lose what little light we had already.

The second result of Blake's unique concern with truth is the occurrence in the symbolic works of long tracts of verse of quite extraordinary intensity and beauty. It is as though the turbid matrix from time to time crystallises out—and we get something which would have been impossible apart from the matrix. To my mind these passages surpass anything else I know in poetry. Here Blake gets down to the bare bones of truth and at once the bones put on flesh and blood and rise up in resurrection and sing.

The Blakean myth covers the whole course of human history. It is also an allegory of eternal events proceeding in the human imagination. The second sense is 'truer' than the first, as will be apparent if we agree that time itself is an illusion and that consequently all events in time are purely figurative.

To the supreme reality Blake gives many names: Eternity, Eden the land of life, Paradise. He identifies this reality with the human imagination. All men are united in this realm, but refuse to see their unity. They *want* to be separate, they cling to the selfhood. And from this foolish clinging all their miseries arise. For the selfhood is the great source of illusion.

Blake symbolises this egotism through the myth of a Fall. In the individual this Fall comes after the period of childhood, the age of innocence. In early childhood there is no sense of separateness, for the separating faculty, the reason, has not yet developed.[1] When it does so, the ego shrinks into itself, and considers the rest of mankind as separate and inimical. It begins to build round itself a wall of private lusts and fears and hatreds. With these it identifies itself, and Eternity (the consciousness of unity in joy and freedom) is lost:

> And now his eternal life
> Like a dream was obliterated. [*B.U.* 251]

Now the ego desires more and more to protect itself against all other egos and to feed on them. It formulates laws of morality and justice, or uses those already in existence to exploit other personalities. But

---

[1] Cf. above, Ch. II.

the further it shrinks from the consciousness of Eternity the more miserable it becomes, for Man's home is in Eternity and he is never happy until he is there again. Man is sick; and a healing process is therefore necessary.

The healing process is possible for the material world because in spite of everything it is not wholly under the domination of Urizen. Los, the spirit of prophecy or the Poetic Genius, takes pity on the world of generation as soon as it is created, and enters it along with Urizen (with whom in Eternity he was united). The course of history now takes the shape of a struggle between these two great opponents, imagination for ever attempting to define error so that, when it is understood, it may be cast out: preparing a way for man to return to Eternity.

Man as he now is, of course, is merely a minute division of the Eternal Man. He is wrapped in error, bound by reason, shackled by law; his once numerous senses are reduced to five, and only through one of them can he escape directly to the Eternal World. This sense, the energy we call sex, is cramped, restricted, defiled, perverted in every possible way by subjection to the laws of the jealous Urizen, who does not wish to see Man find himself again. But a champion enters the lists: Christ, the Universal Humanity who redeems not only Man but Urizen also through love, assuming 'the dark Satanic body in the Virgin's womb'.

Such, in meagre outline (and we shall have to amplify and modify, as well as explain, here and there), is the scheme of all the symbolic books. The scheme may be regarded, I have suggested, as a historical one, in six parts: (i) the Fall; (ii) the Druidical Age; (iii) the Patriarchal Age; (iv) classical times; (v) the Christian era; (vi) the New Age. But this is simply an externalisation of the psychological drama. The gigantic figures of Blake's mythology are not alien to us, not beings that we are to wonder at from a distance. We are meant to recognise them as the denizens of our own brains—archetypes, as Jung would call them, belonging to that 'collective unconscious' in which all men share.

> [For] in the Brain of Man we live & in his circling Nerves,...
> Where Urizen & all his Hosts hang their immortal lamps.
>
> [*F.Z.* 290]

The *Preludium* to *The Book of Urizen* is very short:

> Of the primeval Priest's assum'd power,
> When Eternals spurn'd back his religion
> And gave him a place in the north
> Obscure, shadowy, void, solitary.
>
> Eternals! I hear your call gladly.
> Dictate swift winged words & fear not
> To unfold your dark visions of torment. [*B.U.* 243]

Such is the theme, such the invocation. Two points call for comment: Blake's implicit identification of the disruptive reason with the 'assum'd power' of priesthood; and his conviction that he writes his verses under the direct inspiration of 'Eternals'. This conviction we shall find reiterated throughout the prophecies. The word *dictation* is significant. The vigorous trimeter, the new form in which Blake writes his 'dark visions', certainly gives the impression of inspired energy.

The Book is divided into chapters. The first shows Urizen forming a void in Eternity, a 'soul-shudd'ring vacuum'—which we may perhaps identify with the Newtonian void which is the sensorium of God.[1] Urizen engages in endless calculations, and in a long struggle with Chaos. From his encircling clouds the 'rolling of wheels' can be heard: a mechanical universe. And over it all there broods a deathly cold. The Fall has taken place.

In the second chapter Urizen draws up a moral code. He sounds a trumpet (as, we remember, Newton had done in *Europe*) and gathers the 'myriads of Eternity' round his hidden dwelling-place to hear his decree:

> "From the depths of dark solitude, From
> The eternal abode in my holiness,
> Hidden, set apart, in my stern counsels,
> Reserv'd for the days of futurity,
> I have sought for a joy without pain,
> For a solid without fluctuation...." [*B.U.* 244]

He has formed books of metals, and in them written the secrets of his

[1] See below, Ch. XVIII.

solitary 'wisdom'; among them, the 'seven deadly sins of the soul'. He has invented moral laws to combat these sins: laws

"...of peace, of love, of unity,
Of pity, compassion, forgiveness;
Let each chuse one habitation,
His ancient infinite mansion,
One command, one joy, one desire,
One curse, one weight, one measure,
One King, one God, one Law." [*B.U.* 245]

The delightful diversity of Eden has thus been reduced to a sterile uniformity, and impulse codified into law. Attempting to improve on Eternity, Urizen has created 'a universe of death'. The other Eternals are confounded at this horror, and in the third chapter Los is commissioned to separate off the world of Urizen from Eternity. It is appropriate that this task should be entrusted to Los, for in Eden he and Urizen were intimately connected, as reason should always be with inspiration and vision. Now Urizen sleeps a 'stony sleep' after all his labours. In chapter four Los chains Urizen, who begins to materialise: first the skeleton, then the heart and veins, then sight, hearing, smell and taste. Error is taking on a concrete form so that, eventually, it may be cast off: one of Blake's constant doctrines. In the fifth chapter we find Urizen already chained; in his new material form he has quite forgotten Eternity. And now there comes a change in Los too. It is an axiom of Blake's that 'we become what we behold'; and Los, watching over Urizen, is smitten with pity, an emotion unknown in Eternity. 'Pity divides the soul', and thus

...the Eternal Prophet was divided
Before the death image of Urizen. [*B.U.* 252]

Los's emanation, Enitharmon who is inspiration, separates from him as the first female. Sexuality has begun. The Eternals, horrified at this innovation (for in Eternity there is no division into sexes, Man being androgynous) curtain off Los and Enitharmon from the sight of Eden.

In the next chapter Los embraces the female, who shows typically feminine wiles in refusing his advances and fleeing 'in perverse and cruel delight'. Los follows, and 'begets his likeness on his own divided image'. In the course of time Orc is born, the Human Shadow. Enitharmon suckles the child; and soon Los begins to feel the pangs of jealousy: a new intrusion in the universe, the dire fruit of sexuality. Urizen gains his first victory over Los when the father binds his son to the Rock of the Decalogue with the chain of jealousy. Urizen hears the howlings of Orc and awakens:

> And Urizen, craving with hunger,
> Stung with the odours of Nature,
> Explor'd his dens around.
>
> He form'd a line & a plummet
> To divide the Abyss beneath;
> He form'd a dividing rule;
>
> He formed scales to weigh,
> He formed massy weights;
> He formed a brazen quadrant;
> He formed golden compasses,
> And began to explore the Abyss;
> And he planted a garden of fruits. [*B.U.* 255]

Chapter eight describes Urizen's voyage of exploration through chaos. His sons and daughters cannot keep his laws, and he weeps in hypocritic pity. As he wanders, a cold shadow follows him like a spider's web: this is the Net of Religion, 'twisted like to the human brain'.

This net is powerful enough to restrain the impulses of Urizen's children, and very soon they find themselves shrinking to 'reptile forms of seven feet stature'; their senses are reduced and limited; and men as we now know them come into being:

> No more could they rise at will
> In the infinite void, but bound down
> To earth by their narrowing perceptions
> They lived a period of years;
> Then left a noisom body
> To the jaws of devouring darkness. [*B.U.* 258]

Some of Urizen's sons, however, escape the Net of Religion: of these Fuzon is the leader, and together with his brethren he leaves the pendulous earth.

The narrative is continued in *The Book of Ahania* (1795). Fuzon, who represents passion, is indignant with his father's laws of repression. He throws his wrath at Urizen in the shape of a great burning globe, which pierces his loins. Now Urizen divides, as Los had done before him; and his parted soul is Ahania, whom he calls Sin. (Blake's debt to Milton is particularly obvious here.) Fuzon thinks he has killed his father; but Urizen is one of the Eternals, and cannot die; he prepares a poisoned rock, and shoots it at Fuzon from a bow which he makes from the ribs of the serpent of materialistic science. This rock is the Table of the Law. Fuzon appears to be slain, and Urizen nails his body to the Tree of Mystery. The arrows of pestilence fly around the corpse—pestilence which must always result when passion is crucified on religion.

The book ends with the lament of Ahania 'weeping upon the void':

> "Why didst thou despise Ahania
> To cast me from thy bright presence
> Into the World of Loneness?" [*B.A.* 264]

She recalls the days when Urizen occupied his rightful place in Eden, when he delighted in her love:

> "When he gave my happy soul
> To the sons of eternal joy,
> When he took the daughters of life
> Into my chambers of love...." [*B.A.* 265]

But now, she concludes, there is nothing but division, fear, and jealousy.

It is not easy to grasp exactly what Blake meant by his figure of Ahania, the emanation of Urizen. Like all the other emanations, she 'lives from the life of the male', and exists to give joy and repose to Urizen after his labours of Eternity—labours which are here expressed as sowing:

> "Then thou with thy lap full of seed,
> With thy hand full of generous fire
> Walked forth from the clouds of morning,
> On the virgins of springing joy,
> On the human soul to cast
> The seed of eternal science.

> The sweat poured down thy temples;
> To Ahania return'd in evening,
> The moisture awoke to birth
> My mother-joys, sleeping in bliss." [*B.A.* 265–6]

Ahania, we surmise, is the principle of repose and of *desire*. Urizen repudiates desire, counts it sin, and feels himself weakened by giving way to it. In *The Four Zoas* we shall find this repudiation more clearly stated. For the moment it is enough to note that Urizen has now gone through a three-fold separation: from the life of Eternity, from his particular brotherhood with Los and Enitharmon (imagination and inspiration), and from desire.

The Book of Los (1795) takes us back to the events of the Fall, but now Los, and not Urizen, holds the chief place in the drama. We have a preface by Eno, the Earth-mother,

> Sitting beneath the eternal Oak, [*B.L.* 267]

and lamenting the passing of the golden age of Eternity when there were no restrictions on desire. We are again told the tale of Urizen's creation of the material universe, with Los compelled to stand by and watch until he can refrain no longer: he breaks through 'the vast solid' and falls until at last, like Urizen, he organises himself in material form. He creates light, and begins to bind Urizen. He forms the sun, and fastens Urizen to it; but the cold spirit of reason is too strong for the sun of poetry and puts it out.

In *The Song of Los*, which also belongs to 1795, Blake tells how the 'philosophy of the five senses' (the same pilloried in *The Marriage of Heaven and Hell*) arose in Africa, and social iniquity in Asia. The *Song* is clearly anterior in its action to the two earlier books *Europe* and *America*. Blake's hatred of abstractions which invariably solidify into laws restraining the passions is evident in the first part of this poem; and as usual it is the Greeks (with the Egyptians) that he blames for disseminating the errors of logic:

> To Trismegistus, Palamabron gave an abstract Law:
> To Pythagoras, Socrates & Plato. [*S.L.* 273]

In modern times, Newton and Locke carry on the vast delusion; and the Asiatic kings use a tyranny over the body as well as the mind to enslave their subjects:

"To turn man from his path,
To restrain the child from the womb,
To cut off the bread from the city,
That the remnant may learn to obey,

That the pride of the heart may fail,
That the lust of the eyes may be quench'd,
That the delicate ear in its infancy
May be dull'd, and the nostrils clos'd up,
To teach mortal worms the path
That leads from the gates of the Grave." [*S.L.* 275]

The poem ends with a forecast of the victory of Orc, who comes, in the words of a letter written this same year to George Cumberland, 'to prove to the abstract philosophers that Enjoyment & not Abstinence is the food of intellect'.

These early prophetic books, and much of *The Four Zoas* too, are concerned with giving an account of the Creation as it presented itself to Blake's imagination. It should be remembered that Blake's is not the only essay in reinterpretation of the Biblical narrative. Following the account in *Paradise Lost*, which seems to have given the fillip to English poets and poetasters, we have such works as Sir Richard Blackmore's *Creation* (1712), Henry Brooke's *Universal Beauty* (1735), and Erasmus Darwin's *The Temple of Nature* (1803). The trend in all these was deistic or scientific, or both. It is partly in reaction to this trend that Blake writes his 'prophecies'. Another influence is that of Hindu philosophy, in which the late eighteenth century was taking considerable interest. Besides the translations of Sir William Jones and Wilkins from the Sanskrit, there were such popular treatises as Dr Priestley's *A Comparison of the Institutions of Moses with those of the Hindoos and other ancient Nations* (1799), in which many topics of interest to Blake are discussed.

The production of *Urizen*, *Ahania*, and *Los*, arduous as it was, did nothing towards providing the Blakes with bread and butter. Blake's engraving of other men's designs, and his own original works, had to go on. In 1793 he produced two prints, one on the subject of Ezekiel xxiv. 16, and the other illustrating the Book of Job—an anticipation of the famous later series, the *Illustrations to the Book of Job.* In 1795 he helped to illustrate Captain J. G. Stedman's *Narrative of a Five Years' Expedition, against the Revolted Negroes of Surinam.* Negroes and revolt, we notice, are much in evidence in his writings around this date. In the same year he produced a splendid series of colour-prints, including *Nebuchadnezzar, Newton, The Elohim creating Adam,* and *The Lazar-House.* During 1795–6 we find Blake busy illustrating a new English edition of Bürger's *Lenore.* And it was in 1796 that he began his most ambitious piece of illustrating—the designs for a *de luxe* edition of Young's *Night Thoughts.* Unfortunately the edition failed to catch the public taste and never got beyond the first part, which appeared in 1797 and contained 43 plates by Blake. Blake had already completed the whole set of drawings for the *Night Thoughts*—537 designs in all, according to Frederic Shields.[1] In 1799 he exhibited a picture, *The Last Supper*, in the Academy.

Meanwhile he had started work on *The Four Zoas.*

---

[1] Gilchrist, *op. cit.* pp. 116–17.

CHAPTER V

'*The Four Zoas*'

> The Song of the Aged Mother which shook the heavens with wrath,
> Hearing the march of long resounding, strong heroic Verse
> Marshall'd in order for the day of Intellectual Battle.
> The heavens quake, the earth was moved & shudder'd, & the mountains
> With all their woods, the streams & valleys wail'd in dismal fear.
> [*F.Z.* 277–8]

ALL the fundamental questions which he had raised in the minor prophetic books Blake now proceeds to explore in detail. The chart of his explorations he calls *The Four Zoas*. This is his longest work with the exception of *Jerusalem*: and by far his most baffling. The original title of the poem, which is dated 1797 but was written and revised from 1795 to 1804, was 'Vala / or / The Death and Judgement / of the Ancient Man / A Dream of Nine Nights'; which Blake later altered to 'The Four Zoas / The Torments of Love & Jealousy in / The Death and Judgement / of Albion the Ancient Man'.

In his *Descriptive Catalogue* of 1809 Blake refers to this poem, though not by name, while explaining his painting *The Ancient Britons*. He describes himself as an inhabitant of Eden:

> ...and if every thing goes on as it has begun, the world of vegetation and generation may expect to be opened again to Heaven, through Eden, as it was in the beginning.
>
> The Strong Man represents the human sublime. The Beautiful Man represents the human pathetic, which was in the wars of Eden divided into male and female. The Ugly Man represents the human reason. They were originally one man, who was fourfold; he was self-divided, and his real humanity slain on the stems of generation, and the form of the fourth was like the Son of God. How he became divided is a subject of great sublimity and pathos. The Artist has written it under inspiration, and will, if God please, publish it; it is voluminous, and contains the ancient history of Britain, and the world of Satan and of Adam. [*D.C.* 796–7]

This long poem as we now have it (Blake left it in manuscript, and in a confused state with many variant passages) is, as the above description suggests, an account of the divisions and conflicts of the four components of the Ancient Man. There are sections of direct narrative, not always consecutive, interspersed with retrospective accounts of the Fall, not always agreeing with one another. In fact we cannot consider *The Four Zoas* to be a whole. It is a workshop, from which Blake took material from time to time as he needed it and wove it into the fabric of *Milton* and *Jerusalem*. But in its freshness and spontaneity it is in many ways superior to the two later poems.

I do not propose to go through *The Four Zoas* in full detail. That has been done often enough. What follows is a very brief analysis of the narrative, so far as it can be pieced together, with comments on its significance.

Night the First is a kind of Prologue. The Fall has taken place, and there is universal distress. War is imminent among the fallen Zoas, who are thus described:

> Four Mighty Ones are in every Man; a Perfect Unity
> Cannot Exist but from the Universal Brotherhood of Eden,
> The Universal Man, To Whom be Glory Evermore. Amen.
> What are the Natures of those Living Creatures the Heav'nly
>   Father only
> Knoweth. No Individual knoweth, nor can know in all Eternity.
>
> Los was the fourth immortal starry one, & in the Earth
> Of a bright Universe, Empery attended day & night,
> Days & nights of revolving joy. Urthona was his name
> In Eden; in the Auricular Nerves of Human Life,
> Which is the Earth of Eden, he his Emanations propagated,
> Fairies of Albion, afterwards Gods of the Heathen.
>   Daughter of Beulah, Sing
> His fall into Division & his Resurrection to Unity:
> His fall into the Generation of decay & death, & his
> Regeneration by the Resurrection from the dead. [*F.Z.* 278]

We can now identify the Strong Man, the Ugly Man, and the Beautiful Man of Blake's description. The Beautiful Man who represents the 'human pathetic' must be Luvah, the passions; for Los we know to be 'the fourth' who is 'like the Son of God', and Urizen we know to be 'the human reason', while Tharmas is clearly the Strong Man. He represents the body, with its energy and instincts. In spite of his strength he is 'the mildest son of heaven'.[1]

It is with his division, and not with Luvah's, that the action opens. His separated emanation is Enion, the Earth-mother (the Eno of *The Book of Los*). It is she who brings into being the illusion, Nature, who is also called Vala: material forms only are presented when spiritual energy is withdrawn. And in the moral sphere, as Enion clearly sees,

> "All Love is lost: Terror succeeds, & Hatred instead of Love,
> And stern demands of Right & Duty instead of Liberty."
>
> [*F.Z.* 279]

The cosmos is now the domain of 'vegetable' existence, devoid of spiritual meaning. Tharmas accepts this doom, and sets in motion his Circle of Destiny: the sequence of time and the extension of space which must replace the timelessness and ubiquity of Eden until the moment of regeneration comes:

> Tharmas groan'd among his Clouds
> Weeping; then bending from his Clouds, he stoop'd his innocent head,
> And stretching out his holy hand in the vast deep sublime,
> Turn'd round the circle of Destiny with tears & bitter sighs
> And said: "Return, O wanderer, when the day of Clouds is o'er."
>
> [*F.Z.* 280]

And saying this, he 'sinks down into the sea', entering the world of generation which is woven by Enion. His first station is in the 'female dream' called Beulah, which in Blake's symbolic cosmogony is a realm of shadows separating Eternity from the Chaos formed by Urizen.

Now that the world of generation is a fact, and Eternity has been disrupted, time and space begin. In this early version of the myth, Nature is formed by the union of Enion and the spectre of Tharmas: and from Nature time and space are born—Los and Enitharmon. But Los is also the spirit of prophecy, and Enitharmon is inspiration; and Los foretells the coming of Christ in the fullness of time. Los

---

[1] Cf. Letter 48, to Hayley (28 September 1804): 'I had the pleasure of a call from Mrs Chetwynd and her brother, a giant in body, mild and polite in soul, as I have, in general, found great bodies to be.' [*L.* 1106].

'keeps the divine vision in time of trouble', but Enitharmon's inspiration is obscured in the world of matter, and she turns to the wiles of the female, rousing Los's 'alternate Love & Hate' by her 'Scorn & Jealousy'. In *Night the First* the account of Los and Enitharmon's doings is most confused, being interspersed with narratives of the Fall and references to the Council of God which meets 'in Great Eternity' to form plans for the redemption of the fallen universe. There is no doubt that many elements of the myth have been carelessly thrown together here.

Enitharmon in her jealousy and opposition to Los repudiates the prophetic vision and calls on Urizen to descend and take possession of fallen man:

> Descend, O Urizen, descend with horse & chariot!
> Threaten not me, O visionary; thine the punishment.
> The Human Nature shall no more remain, nor Human acts
> Form the rebellious Spirits of Heaven, but War & Princedom,
> & Victory & Blood." [*F.Z.* 290]

At this, Urizen does descend, proclaiming himself to be 'God from Eternity to Eternity', and offering Los partnership. If Los will consent to tyrannise over Luvah (the Emotions and Passions), Urizen will give him authority over all the hosts of heaven.[1]

This temptation of Los (who from time to time in the prophecies is specifically identified with Christ) at once recalls the Gospel story. Los refuses indignantly, and Urizen again asserts the claim of reason to be sole lord of the world:

> "Obey my voice, young Demon; I am God from Eternity to Eternity.
> Art thou a visionary of Jesus, the soft delusion of Eternity?
> Lo I am God, the terrible destroyer, & not the Saviour.
> Why should the Divine Vision compell the sons of Eden
> To forego each his own delight, to war against his spectre?
> The Spectre is the Man. The rest is only delusion & fancy."
> [*F.Z.* 291]

In these words Urizen lays bare the motive which has led him to rebel against the unity of Eden. The Divine Vision will not allow

[1] This is the ideal state of partnership between reason and imagination against the affections envisaged by Bacon in the *Advancement of Learning* (see below, Ch. XIII).

Man to identify himself with his spectre (i.e. his naked reasoning power), but insists that every element in the human totality must be respected. Moreover, every Eternal must 'forego each his own delight' (in Urizen's perverted phrase)—must, that is, renounce his selfhood and recognise that he is part of a whole. The initial crime of Urizen was to withdraw from the whole into solitude.

Here the narrative is abruptly broken off, and we have some fleeting pictures of the reconciliation of Los and Enitharmon, and of Luvah and Vala his emanation standing separated 'in the bloody sky'. Then comes the marriage feast of Los and Enitharmon, with a bridal song celebrating war and bloodshed. Meanwhile, 'far in Night repell'd', Enion laments for the cruelty of Nature:

> "Why does the Raven cry aloud and no eye pities her?
> Why fall the Sparrow & the Robin in the foodless winter?
> Faint, shivering, they sit on leafless bush or frozen stone
> Wearied with seeking food across the snowy waste, the little
> Heart cold, and the little tongue consum'd that once in thoughtless joy
> Gave songs of gratitude to waving cornfields round their nest."
>
> [*F.Z.* 296–7]

The image of 'nature red in tooth and claw' is certainly not hidden from Blake, as it so often seems to be from Wordsworth. It must be confessed that it is these vivid passages of direct observation and feeling that we look for and enjoy most in *The Four Zoas*, amid all the confusion of the symbolic machinery.

With another abrupt transition, we are shown the Eternal Man arriving at 'the Palm Tree & the Oak of Weeping which stand upon the Edge of Beulah'; he sinks down from the Saviour's arms and is gently laid on 'the Rock of Ages'. Man is now, we gather, definitely fallen into the world of generation where he must remain until the Circle of Destiny is complete.

At this point there comes a striking interpolation in the shape of a Fall narrative. Messengers from Beulah arrive to tell the Council of God (which seen as One Man is Jesus the Christ) of the plight of the fallen Man; and their narrative takes us back to the origin of the Fall. Here we are shown a different and more complicated state of affairs than the simple revolt of reason given in *The Book of Urizen*. We learn that, while Albion was sleeping in his tent, Urizen and

Luvah conferred. Urizen tells Luvah to go into the South, while he himself will establish his kingdom in the North, and make war on all the sons and daughters of Eternity until he is acknowledged sole king. Luvah refuses, not for honourable reasons but because he too has the idea of smiting Albion and making himself supreme. And he does actually begin a personal war against the Universal Man.

It is now that Urthona (Los) divides, in horror at what he sees and hears; and he falls into the world of Tharmas. Urizen and his hosts retreat into the North,

> leaving the rage of Luvah
> To pour its fury on himself & on the Eternal Man. [*F.Z.* 301]

When the messengers from Beulah have finished their report, the Council elect Seven Watchers to guard the fallen Man; 'the Seventh is named Jesus'.

Night the Second continues this interpolated narrative of the Fall. Smitten by Luvah, Albion calls upon Urizen to help him, and gives up his sceptre before falling into the sleep of death. Now Urizen is master of the ruined universe. He begins the building of the Mundane Shell, the world of material existence, and casts Luvah into 'the Furnaces of affliction'. The passions, in other words, are henceforth declared unlawful. Vala, Luvah's emanation, delights to feed the furnaces. Urizen, 'the great work master', continues to build his universe as a defence against Chaos, the world of Ulro which surrounds him on all sides. This is not the vital order of Eternity, but the order of law which is death; yet it is permitted by the Council of Heaven to prevent Man from falling into non-entity. In the midst of it all Urizen's palace is built. Here Ahania is seen reposing 'on a White Couch', or hovering over his head. (We are still dealing with the interpolated Fall narrative: Ahania has not yet been cast out.) She is now a jealous emanation, for the love and faith of Eternity have vanished; and she has to be kept alive with 'lives of Victims sacrificed upon an altar of brass'. Desire, in non-symbolic terms, can now be appeased only with the torment of its object.

In lines of splendid verse Blake describes the construction of the Mundane Shell:

> But infinitely beautiful the wondrous work arose
> In sorrow and care, a Golden World whose porches round the heavens
> And pillar'd halls & rooms reciev'd the eternal wandering stars.

> A wondrous golden Building, many a window, many a door
> And many a division let in & out the vast unknown.
> Circled in infinite orb immoveable, within its walls & cielings
> The heavens were clos'd, and spirits mourn'd their bondage night & day,
> And the Divine Vision appear'd in Luvah's robes of blood.
>
> [*F.Z.* 312]

We see, then, that Blake is perfectly ready to admit the wonder and glory of the stellar universe—and who better than he has described that glory both in its astronomical aspects and in 'the minute particulars' of bird and flower and insect! But for all that it is a *dead* universe, when viewed as material; it is too poor to produce one seed. All its life comes from the life of Eternity. And that is why the Divine Vision, Jesus, must appear in Luvah's robes of blood—the blood of sacrifice. Luvah, who is love, has been cast into the furnaces and sealed; and therefore the Divine Vision himself must take on Luvah's functions that the universe may not forget the power of love.

Now the stars are created to form the outer barrier of the Mundane Shell:

> Thus were the stars of heaven created like a golden chain
> To bind the Body of Man to heaven from falling into the Abyss.
> Each took his station & his course began with sorrow & care.
>
> [*F.Z.* 313]

Note how Blake dwells on the sorrow and care with which the stellar universe functions, in direct contrast to such popular views as those expressed by Addison in his famous hymn. Blake often refers to the stars, never with that approbation which made Arnold invite humanity to emulate their courses, but with a due appreciation of their beauty. It is the *voids between the stars* which excite his indignation: these are the Satanic wheels of the mill which grinds Albion to powder; and he associates them expressly with the name of Newton.

From this account of the Fall we return to the story of the jealous combats of Los and Enitharmon. These Eternals have not yet lost the powers which were theirs in Eden:

> For Los & Enitharmon walk'd forth on the dewy Earth
> Contracting or expanding their all flexible senses

At will to murmur in the flowers small as the honey bee,
At will to stretch across the heavens & step from star to star,
Or standing on the Earth erect, or on the stormy waves
Driving the storms before them, or delighting in sunny beams,
While round their heads the Elemental Gods kept harmony. [*F.Z.* 314]

This power of expanding or contracting the senses is possessed by all in Eternity. It is Blake's solution, derived perhaps from Boehme, of the dilemma of the one and the many. We know that Man in Eternity is One; but that One is a Family, not a Solitude. Man when he wishes can think of himself as One; or when he wishes he can think of himself as many, and see multitude: all the denizens of Eternity as separate individuals dwelling in the varied landscape of Eden. The first mode he experiences by *expanding* his senses, the second by *contracting* them. We can do the same thing on earth by retreating to a distance, when we see a hill as a uniform shape of green, or by coming near again, when all the blades of grass and the insects and birds become visible. But we cannot 'in this age' see the whole human family as one: this faculty was lost at the Fall, and can only be recovered when the last judgement comes to pass in each man.

The self-torments of Los and Enitharmon are vividly described, and Enitharmon sings a song about the pleasures of 'fierce jealousy'. It is the woman's triumph. But Enion, still wandering far out in the void, is heard bemoaning the 'new order' of pain and hypocrisy which has come upon the universe:

"I am made to sow the thistle for wheat, the nettle for a nourishing dainty.
I have planted a false oath in the earth; it has brought forth a poison tree.
I have chosen the serpent for a councellor, & the dog
For a schoolmaster to my children.
I have blotted out from light & living the dove & nightingale,
And I have caused the earth worm to beg from door to door....
What is the price of Experience? do men buy it for a song?
Or wisdom for a dance in the street? No, it is bought with the price
Of all that a man hath, his house, his wife, his children.
Wisdom is sold in the desolate market where none come to buy,
And in the wither'd field where the farmer plows for bread in vain."
[*F.Z.* 318]

It is such passages as these which encourage the reader of Blake to continue his efforts to understand the longer poems. For they have such an accent of sincerity, such a burning energy, that it is plain that a powerful original experience underlies the bare monosyllabic expression. No other poet speaks like Blake, directly from the source of consciousness. In all other poets, even the greatest, we are conscious of the presence of *art*: the writer is aware he is producing poetry, he is assuming an attitude. With Blake we are conscious only that he is proclaiming truth; his findings turn out to be poetry, but they are spoken *as truth*.

The third Night recounts the ejection of Ahania; a retelling of *The Book of Ahania*. The scene is laid in the Palace of Urizen. Ahania, moved by Enion's lament, begs her lord not to 'look upon futurity'—to remain content with the Eternal Now. But Urizen persists in looking into the future: he foretells the birth of Orc, and cries,

> "Alas for me! what will become of me at that dread time?"
>
> [*F.Z.* 321]

Ahania beseeches Urizen to return to his obedience to the Eternal One. "Leave all futurity to him." And here, in Ahania's speech, we are given yet another version of the Fall:

> "Why didst thou listen to the voice of Luvah that dread morn
> To give the immortal steeds of light to his deceitful hands?"
>
> [*F.Z.* 321]

Reason has yielded his dominion to the passions. Man worships a 'watery image of himself', gives himself over to sentiment and weakness. He allows his feminine emanation to gain power over him. And this is the cause of Luvah's smiting of Albion. At this point, as in the earlier account, Albion calls on Urizen to redress the balance, and the supreme authority which for a moment he had resigned to Luvah is now assumed permanently by Urizen. Luvah and Vala divide; and, Ahania ends,

> "All is Confusion. All is tumult, & we alone are escaped."
>
> [*F.Z.* 324]

Urizen is furious at this objective account of the Fall. He asserts his sole Godhead, and seizing Ahania by the hair casts her out into Non-Entity. In so doing he himself falls down into the sea of Tharmas, who is materialised by the shock,

Crying: "Fury in my limbs! destruction in my bones & marrow!
My skull riven into filaments, my eyes into sea jellies
Floating upon the tide wander bubbling & bubbling,
Uttering my lamentations & begetting little monsters
Who sit mocking upon the little pebbles of the tide
In all my rivers & on dried shells that the fish
Have quite forsaken." [F.Z. 327]

Hearing the voice of her beloved Tharmas, Enion again breaks out into one of the lamentations that punctuate *The Four Zoas* like the choruses of a Greek tragedy. She begs Tharmas not to drive her quite away into the void:

"Make me not like the things forgotten as they had not been.
Make me not the thing that loveth thee a tear wiped away." [F.Z. 328]

The fourth Night is largely concerned with Tharmas, as the previous Night had been with Urizen. Tharmas is the 'parent power', the most innocent of the Zoas, as representing the body in Man; and he cannot help feeling love and pity for Enion. But all hope is fled. He curses Urizen and Luvah for bringing about this confusion, and commands Los to rebuild the universe. Los refuses to obey him, as he had refused Urizen before; but for a different reason. He has gone over to the enemy. He acclaims Urizen as king. He accepts the new order; but asserts that now Urizen is fallen into the deep it devolves upon him, Los, to rule over all things. However, Tharmas soon shows Los that he is not all-powerful by rending Enitharmon from his side; and Los becomes the Spectre of Urthona. Now it is Tharmas' turn to proclaim himself God:

"Now all comes into the power of Tharmas. Urizen is fall'n
And Luvah hidden in the Elemental forms of Life & Death.
Urthona is My Son. O Los, thou art Urthona, & Tharmas
Is God. The Eternal Man is seal'd, never to be deliver'd.
I roll my floods over his body, my billows & waves pass over him,
The sea encompasses him & monsters of the deep are his companions.
Dreamer of furious oceans, cold sleeper of weeds & shells,
Thy Eternal form shall never renew, my uncertain prevails against thee."[1]
[F.Z. 334–5]

---

[1] The idea seems to have come from Berkeley's *Siris*, paragraph 313: 'It was the Platonic doctrine, that human souls or minds descended from above, and were sowed

Tharmas restores Enitharmon to Los, but Los is compelled to carry out his bidding and build a stony universe around the fallen Urizen. Here the narrative repeats the story told in *The Book of Urizen* and *The Book of Los*.

This fourth Night ends with a petition from the Daughters of Beulah to the Divine Vision, the Saviour. The Divine Vision, we remember, is composed of all those Eternals who have not fallen with Albion: seen as One Man they are the Saviour, Jesus Christ. The Daughters of Beulah are the emanations of Eternity. They beseech the Saviour to help them, for they are terrified by the events of the Fall. And Jesus responds by fixing in Albion the two limits: the limit of opacity, beyond which blindness to truth and feebleness of vision may not go; and the limit of contraction, beyond which division may not go:

> The Saviour mild & gentle bent over the corse of Death,
> Saying, "If ye will Believe, your brother shall rise again."
> And first he found the Limit of Opacity, & nam'd it Satan,
> In Albion's bosom, for in every human bosom these limits stand.
> And next he found the Limit of Contraction, & nam'd it Adam,
> While yet those beings were not born nor knew of good or Evil.
>
> [*F.Z.* 340]

The divine hand now touches the starry wheels, and 'limit was put to Eternal Death'. But Los becomes transformed into a material shape, and in *Night the Fifth* both Los and Enitharmon are seen within the bounds of space and time, no longer with expansive senses as before, but

> Shrunk into fixed space, stood trembling on a Rocky cliff,
> Yet mighty bulk & majesty & beauty remain'd, but unexpansive.
>
> [*F.Z.* 341]

Now the fiery Orc is born, as in *The Book of Urizen*, and chained by his jealous father to the Rock of the Decalogue. But his spirit is not

---

in generation; that they were stunned, stupified, and intoxicated by this descent and immersion into animal nature; and that the soul, in this ὀνείρωξις or slumber, forgets her original notions, which are smothered and oppressed by many false tenets and prejudices of sense. Insomuch that Proclus compares the soul, in her descent invested with growing prejudices, to Glaucus diving to the bottom of the sea, and there contracting divers coats of seaweed, coral, and shells, which stick close to him, and conceal his true shape.'

subdued, and in a brilliant pictorial passage we are told of revolution's transforming power:

> His limbs bound down mock at his chains, for over them a flame
> Of circling fire unceasing plays; to feed them with life & bring
> The virtues of the Eternal worlds, ten thousand thousand spirits
> Of life lament around the Demon, going forth & returning.
> At his enormous call they flee into the heavens of heavens
> And back return with wine & food, or dive into the deeps
> To bring the thrilling joys of sense to quell his ceaseless rage.
> His eyes, the lights of his large soul, contract or else expand:
> Contracted they behold the secrets of the infinite mountains,
> The veins of gold & silver & the hidden things of Vala,
> Whatever grows from its pure bud or breathes a fragrant soul:
> Expanded they behold the terrors of the Sun & Moon,
> The Elemental Planets & the orbs of eccentric fire. [*F.Z.* 346]

Then Los is sorry for what he has done, and tries to free Orc; but in vain, for the chains of jealousy have taken root in the very structure of the world. Urizen, who has been awakened from his stony sleep by the howlings of Orc, ends the fifth Night with a song of repentance for his sin, and of momentary hope in the spirit of revolution:

> "I will arise, Explore these dens, & find that deep pulsation
> That shakes my cavern with strong shudders; perhaps this is the night
> Of Prophecy, & Luvah hath burst his way from Enitharmon.
> When Thought is clos'd in Caves Then love shall shew its root in Deepest Hell." [*F.Z.* 351]

In the sixth Night Urizen explores his dens—a section closely recalling Satan's journey through Chaos in *Paradise Lost.* He meets his three daughters, but they repudiate him; and he turns south into the world of Tharmas. Tharmas confronts the tyrant; and Urizen journeys towards 'the dark world of Urthona', meeting all the monsters of the deep,

> the forms of tygers & of Lions, dishumaniz'd men.
> Many in serpents & in worms, stretched out enormous length
> Over the sullen mould & slimy tracks, obstruct his way. [*F.Z.* 356–7]

In the East, the region of Luvah, he falls into the void (for Luvah, we remember, has been shut up and sealed); but

> The ever pitying one who seeth all things, saw his fall,
> And in the dark vacuity created a bosom of clay. [*F.Z.* 358]

In time he is able to continue his journey. He carries with him his books of moral precepts and his iron pen,

> Still to be written & interleav'd with brass & iron & gold,
> Time after time, for such a journey none but iron pens
> Can write And adamantine leaves recieve, nor can the man who goes
> The journey obstinate refuse to write time after time. [*F.Z.* 359]

Urizen wearies of this chaos, and plans another ordered world, forming vast instruments to measure out space and build his kingdom. And everywhere he goes he drags behind him the Web of Religion. Next he travels North into the world of Urthona or Los, who thrusts him back into the 'dire web'. But he finds Orc, the bound spirit of revolt, and in *Night the Seventh* tries to curb his power. Orc at first defies Urizen: "Curse thy hoary brows!" Then Urizen calls up his daughters to knead the Bread of Sorrow; and he reads moral precepts from his book of brass. Orc finds himself overcome against his will by Urizen's hypocrisy, and changes into a serpent which climbs coiling up the Tree of Mystery. Revolt has been overcome by reason. Meanwhile Los and Enitharmon converse in the shadow of the dismal tree. Los is miserable that he can no longer enjoy Enitharmon's love: Enitharmon rejoices because she has the power to make Los miserable. The two parts of prophecy, poetry and inspiration, are at variance, and in consequence the Spectre of Urthona appears. Enitharmon addresses the Spectre and gives yet another account of the Fall.

She describes Albion in Eternity walking among the Flowers of Beulah—the emanations, or softly feminine aspects of the Eternal Man. He falls in love with his emanation, Vala, and 'faints' in sweet bliss. He gives way to his purely emotional side, and as a result Urizen appears to right the balance: but this time Urizen is represented as the child of Albion and Vala:

> There he revel'd in delight among the Flowers.
> Vala was pregnant & brought forth Urizen, Prince of Light,
> First born of Generation. [*F.Z.* 375]

Albion forgets Eternity, dallying too long in the inferior delights of the feminine world; and Urizen confers with Luvah, with the results already described by the messengers from Beulah in *Night the First.*

The Spectre of Urthona, in reply, puts the same Fall narrative in another way, somewhat resembling Ahania's account in *Night the Third.* One dread morn, he says,

> "The manhood was divided, for the gentle passions, making way
> Thro' the infinite labyrinths of the heart & thro' the nostrils issuing
> In odorous stupefaction, stood before the Eyes of Man
> A female bright. I stood beside my anvil dark, a mass
> Of iron glow'd bright prepar'd for spade & plowshares: sudden down
> I sunk with cries of blood issuing downward in the veins
> Which now my rivers were become, rolling in tubelike forms
> Shut up within themselves descending down...."[1] [*F.Z.* 376–7]

Again we are given the impression that the original cause of the Fall was a weakness in Man by which he gave way to 'the gentle passions' and allowed himself to be absorbed by sentiment; then, finding himself powerless to resist, resigned his authority into the hands of reason. In so doing he upset the whole economy of the Eternal World.

The only means of return to Eden, the Spectre of Urthona now announces, is by self-annihilation: and first Los, and his Spectre, and Enitharmon, must reunite. Los accepts this truth, but Enitharmon with feminine deceit flees to the Tree of Mystery. Los builds Golgonooza, the City of Art (in its widest sense); and in so doing is astonished to find that he has become at peace with Urizen his enemy. Art is the reconciliation of poetry, inspiration and reason: or, as Blake concisely expresses it in another place, 'Art is the forgiveness of sins'. We shall have more to say about this doctrine in discussing Blake's thought as a whole.

There is a second version of *Night the Seventh*, differing in many particulars from the one we have just considered. In this, Urizen proceeds to organise the human world of trade and commerce, and to initiate the exploitation of the poor and defenceless. He builds also the Temple of Religion,

---

[1] Cf. Berkeley's *Siris*, paragraph 32: 'A body, therefore, either animal or vegetable, may be considered as an organised system of tubes and vessels, containing several sorts of fluids.'

> allegoric of the Generations
> Of secret lust, when hid in chambers dark the nightly harlot
> Plays in Disguise in whisper'd hymn & mumbling prayer. The priests
> He ordain'd & Priestesses, cloth'd in disguises beastial,
> Inspiring secrecy; & lamps they bore: intoxicating fumes
> Roll round the Temple.... [*F.Z.* 387]

In such a passage all Blake's hatred for institutional religion and ceremony is revealed. He invariably associates sexual 'deceit' or secrecy with religion. The mystery in which woman hides her charms and the mystery of the priests is one and the same.

There is great strife in the eternal world between the four Zoas. Urizen is triumphant, and the Age of Reason produces a materialist civilisation despising the simple arts of life and exchanging them for machines. Here Blake is clearly thinking of the Industrial Revolution of which he was a witness.

Among all the conflicts and perversions of the eternal powers, Tharmas, the body, has preserved his innocence (according to this closing passage of *Night the Seventh*, which however agrees ill with some descriptions that have gone before). Blake thus expresses his belief in the essential rightness of the body, though it is bound in material forms. Vala, who is Nature or Material Beauty, is reproved by Tharmas for delighting in the wars of Urizen, and she repents, turning again to the glories of the eternal world of which she is the mirror.

The eighth Night opens with the Council of God again meeting as one Man, Jesus,

> Upon the Limit of Contraction to create the Fallen Man. [*F.Z.* 398]

This limit is now fixed, and Man begins to wake on the Couch of Death—he sneezes seven times, and a tear of blood drops from each eye. Los and Enitharmon become conscious of the Divine Vision, and unite in works of mercy. But Urizen makes preparations for war:

> Horrible hooks & nets he form'd, twisting the cords of iron
> And brass, & molten metals cast in hollow globes, & bor'd
> Tubes in petrific steel, & ramm'd combustibles, & wheels
> And chains & pullies fabricated all round the Heavens of Los. [*F.Z.* 402]

In defence, Los builds the walls of Golgonooza. Within them, Enitharmon works at her looms, weaving bodies for the spectres—

the naked desires and aspirations of humanity—until these appear as 'a vast family, wondrous in beauty & love', which is also the 'Universal Female' Jerusalem. And Jerusalem, as we already know, is the totality of Man's vision of the infinite: the true emanation of Albion, of which Vala is only the 'vegetated shadow'.

The Sons of Eden round the Lamb of God sing the beginning of Redemption:

> "We now behold the Ends of Beulah, & we now behold
> Where death Eternal is put off Eternally.
> Assume the dark Satanic body in the Virgin's womb,
> O Lamb Divine! it cannot thee annoy. O pitying one,
> Thy pity is from the foundation of the World, & thy Redemption
> Begun Already in Eternity. Come then, O Lamb of God,
> Come, Lord Jesus, come quickly." [*F.Z.* 408]

Meanwhile the war raging around the gates of Golgonooza takes a human form, 'seen in the aggregate', and this form is hermaphroditic. At last it gives birth to the being called Satan,

> A male without a female counterpart, a howling fiend
> Forlorn of Eden & repugnant to the forms of life. [*F.Z.* 408]

The Lamb of God descends in pity, and is judged by the Synagogue of Satan, in which Vala sits triumphant 'in the cruelties of holiness'. He is condemned to death, and crucified on the Tree of Mystery. We then have a remarkable conflation of Blake's myth with the Gospel story. Los takes the Body down from the Cross, with Jerusalem weeping over it, and lays it in the sepulchre which he had hewn in the Rock of Eternity for himself. He confesses that he too has pierced the Son of God; and because Christ by His death has defined error, Los is now able to reveal truth in words of prophecy. He announces the doctrine of States, later to be revealed more fully in *Milton*.

Urizen begins to 'stonify'—that is, his error is now made apparent through Christ's passion—and he assumes a dragon form. Though this seems the nadir of his degradation, it is really the beginning of his restoration to unity; for error once defined can be put off:

> now he finds in vain
> That not of his own power he bore the human form erect,
> Nor of his own will gave his Laws in times of Everlasting. [*F.Z.* 416]

The other Zoas, too, fall into the stony stupor of error, and again Ahania's voice is heard lamenting in the void. But Enion, the Generative instinct, replies with a song of hope:

> "The Lamb of God has rent the Veil of Mystery, soon to return
> In Clouds & Fires around the rock & the Mysterious tree.
> And as the seed waits Eagerly watching for its flower & fruit,
> Anxious its little soul looks out into the clear expanse
> To see if hungry winds are abroad with their invisible array,
> So Man looks out in tree & herb & fish & bird & beast
> Collecting up the scatter'd portions of his immortal body
> Into the Elemental forms of every thing that grows....
> And in the cries of birth & in the groans of death his voice
> Is heard throughout the Universe: wherever a grass grows
> Or a leaf buds, The Eternal Man is seen, is heard, is felt,
> And all his sorrows, till he reassumes his ancient bliss."
>
> [*F.Z.* 420–1]

This passage, with its instinctive sympathy for every form of life, and its impassioned conviction of the unity of being, is among the best things in Blake. His verse glows with hope, and his intelligence, as always, is perfectly at home with conceptions from which the ordinary mind would shrink in alarm at the unusual and the gigantic. We may apply to his confident insight into the life of flowers and stars the lines he applies to his two immortals:

> At will to murmur in the flowers small as the honey bee,
> At will to stretch across the heavens & step from star to star.
>
> [*F.Z.* 314]

But the triumph of vision is not yet. Though Christ's coming makes a radical change in the cosmic order by rendering error manifest, its final effect (the resurrection into unity) is postponed eighteen hundred years by the rise of Natural Religion or Deism. It seems as though Mystery has been destroyed, but she revives in another form.

Night the Ninth has the sub-title *The Last Judgment.* Los is terrified at the death of Jesus and fails to see that only the material body remains in the sepulchre, while His spirit stands beside them. Los therefore tears down the heavens; the 'fires of Eternity', intellectual fires, stream into the material world and the Last Trump is sounded. Kings are hurled from their thrones, tyrants are smitten by those they have oppressed, and

> From the clotted gore & from the hollow den
> Start forth the trembling millions into flames of mental fire,
> Bathing their limbs in the bright visions of Eternity. [*F.Z.* 425]

All Nature feels the shock; the Tree of Mystery goes up in fire and everything is purified from error by the march of 'living flames winged with intellect & Reason'.

From this vision of purgation and judgement we are abruptly transported to 'a Horrible rock far in the South', on which the Eternal Man is lying. It is not clear whether we are to take what follows as a continuation of the narrative we have just been considering, or whether it is an alternative form of the judgement theme. The Eternal Man awakes, and bemoans his hapless state:

> "When shall the Man of future times become as in days of old?
> O weary life! why sit I here & give up all my powers
> To indolence, to the night of death...?" [*F.Z.* 427]

He calls Urizen to return to his ancient allegiance:

> "Come forth from slumbers of thy cold abstraction! Come forth,
> Arise to Eternal births! Shake off thy cold repose,
> Schoolmaster of souls, great opposer of change, arise!" [*F.Z.* 428]

Urizen at first does not answer, and Albion calls again, threatening to seize Urizen's sceptre and cast him out into the indefinite:

> "Thy self-destroying, beast form'd Science shall be thy eternal lot.
> My anger against thee is greater than against this Luvah,
> For war is energy Enslav'd, but thy religion,
> The first author of this war & the distracting of honest minds
> Into confused perturbation & strife & horrour & pride,
> Is a deciet so detestable that I will cast thee out
> If thou repentest not, & leave thee as a rotten branch to be burn'd
> With Mystery the Harlot & with Satan for Ever & Ever.
> Error can never be redeemed in all Eternity,
> But Sin, Even Rahab, is redeem'd in blood & fury & jealousy—
> That line of blood that stretch'd across the windows of the morning—
> Redeem'd from Error's power. Wake, thou dragon of the deeps!"
> [*F.Z.* 429]

Then Urizen weeps, anxious to reassume his human form. He wishes he had never looked into futurity, never built

> . . . arches high, & cities, turrets & towers & domes
> Whose smoke destroy'd the pleasant gardens, & whose running kennels
> Chok'd the bright rivers; burd'ning with my Ships the angry deep;
> Thro' Chaos seeking for delight, & in spaces remote
> Seeking the Eternal which is always present to the wise;
> Seeking for pleasure which unsought falls round the infant's path
> And on the fleeces of mild flocks who neither care nor labour."
> [*F.Z.* 430]

He renounces futurity, shakes the snows from off his shoulders, and rises in radiant youth.

Now 'the bursting Universe explodes', and the Last Judgement begins. The oppressed judge their tormentors and punish them,

> And every one of the dead appears as he had liv'd before,
> And all the marks remain of the slave's scourge & tyrant's Crown,
> And of the Priest's o'ergorged Abdomen, & of the merchant's thin
> Sinewy deception, & of the warrior's outbraving & thoughtlessness
> In lineaments too extended & in bones too strait & long. [*F.Z.* 433]

The Four Zoas reassume their functions, and reverse the work of Urizen, restoring the plough and other 'rural works' (Blake always gives a pastoral character to his Eden), and destroying the instruments of war. Urizen drives the 'Plow of ages' over all his universe, and begins to sow the seed of a new humanity. Then, with his wearied sons, he rests, awaiting the harvest,

> And bright Ahania took her seat by Urizen in songs & joy.
> [*F.Z.* 437]

Urizen addresses Luvah and Vala, commanding them to be henceforth 'servants to the infinite & Eternal of the Human form'. In a significant passage exactly recalling the Introduction to *Songs of Experience*, Nature is called upon to arise 'from the dews of death'.

> She rises among flowers & looks toward the Eastern clearness,
> She walks yea runs, her feet are wing'd, on the tops of the bending grass,
> Her garments rejoice in the vocal wind & her hair glistens with dew.
> [*F.Z.* 439]

The idyll that follows, relating the reconciliation of Luvah and Vala, resembles *The Book of Thel* in its pellucid pastoral atmosphere, and forms a most effective contrast to the terrific imagery of the rest of the poem. The brotherhood of Eden is emphasised when we find Vala bringing Tharmas and Enion together again; the two become little children and so find their happiness. But Blake makes it clear that this is only a shadow 'in Vala's world' of the glories of Eternity.

The human harvest ripens, and Urizen, shouting "Times are Ended!", gathers in the sheaves, spreading a feast in the 'bright South' for the Eternal Man. Individual human forms are dissolved, together with those of 'beasts & worms & creeping things'. Albion invites all the Eternals to the feast; they look around them, appalled by the separateness of the generative world, and announce the truth that

> "Not for ourselves, but for the Eternal Family we live.
> Man liveth not by Self alone, but in his brother's face
> Each shall behold the Eternal Father & love & joy abound."
> [*F.Z.* 450]

When morning dawns, Urizen rises to thresh the grain:

> And all Nations were threshed out, & the stars thresh'd from
> their husks. [*F.Z.* 451]

Tharmas takes the winnowing fan, and separates the grain from the chaff. The Eternal Man tells Luvah that the grapes are ripe, and Luvah passes them through the winepress; 'the great winepress of the wrath of God' of Revelation xiv, which is war.

There follows a description of the treading of the grapes by the sons of Luvah—a description which though brilliant is added to and improved in *Milton*, where it is called the winepress of Los. Finally Urthona grinds the new corn, and bakes the Bread of Ages. The poem ends in the dawn of Eternity:

> The Sun has left his blackness & has found a fresher morning,
> And the mild moon rejoices in the clear & cloudless night,
> And Man walks forth from midst of the fires: the evil is all consum'd.
> His eyes behold the Angelic spheres arising night & day;
> The stars consum'd like a lamp blown out, & in their stead, behold
> The Expanding Eyes of Man behold the depths of wondrous worlds!
> One Earth, one sea beneath; nor Erring Globes wander, but Stars
> Of fire rise up nightly from the Ocean; & one Sun

> Each morning, like a New born Man, issues with songs & joy
> Calling the Plowman to his Labour & the Shepherd to his rest.
> He walks upon the Eternal Mountains, raising his heavenly voice,
> Conversing with the Animal forms of wisdom night & day,
> That, risen from the Sea of fire, renew'd walk o'er the Earth.
>
> [*F.Z.* 459]

'Renew'd' is the important word; for, as Blake tells us again and again, nothing is lost; every form of life is preserved in Eternity, but under its spiritual lineaments. This is the significance of the mill and the winepress: the material vesture, the husk of the corn and the skin of the grape, must be cast away before reality can appear as it is, infinite. Therefore those who love the beauty of this world have nothing to fear, for every detail is eternal, and will be enjoyed to the full by the infinite faculties of the new-born man.

The foregoing synopsis of this long and complicated poem has left many things unmentioned and more unexplained. The reason for this is obvious: *The Four Zoas* is not a unity, and only confusion and darkening of counsel could result from trying to make it out to be so. It does however tell a story, and that story, in its essentials, I have tried to trace.

What is it that Blake is trying to do? Several things. He is relating an original vision of the nature of things: a metaphysics. He is making a criticism of the existing social and religious order: an indictment. He is attempting a description of mental states exceedingly subtle and intricate: a psychology. And all this within the framework of the poem, illustrated of course by his own designs. The task is an immense one.

Now to-day, if a writer were to engage on any of these tasks, he would be able to proceed along certain well-defined roads. Let us take the metaphysical problem. Here Blake was confronted by the difficulty that no existing metaphysical system was of use to him in his attempt to describe his peculiar perception of reality. The philosophy of the age, as we have seen, was materialistic. It was obsessed by the enormous prestige of science, and particularly by the achievement of Newton in astronomy and physics. Even the traditional Christian metaphysics was dominated by the idea of law and tended more and more to become simple 'Natural Religion'.

Then, secondly, in the sphere of social thinking, the reaction to the French Revolution was acute in England. Repressive legislation was in full swing. And the Radicals, such as Tom Paine and Godwin, were themselves of a materialistic, Lockean, ameliorationist bent entirely alien to Blake's visionary enthusiasm. Lastly, where psychology is concerned, we must remember that Blake was treading quite new paths without a guide. He is a pioneer in this field, for it is practically certain that he knew nothing of Leibniz's speculations on the subconscious mind. The current ideas were those of Locke: a 'fortuitous concourse of memories' is the way Blake expresses in *Jerusalem* the Lockean association of ideas. And Locke's theories had been carried to their conclusions by Hartley and Erasmus Darwin—conclusions naturally distasteful to Blake.

We see, then, that Blake had really to create his own system 'or be enslav'd by another Man's'. And we must remember that his mind was not that of a psychologist, a metaphysician or a sociologist; he was a poet, an artist, and a mystic. He saw reality in terms of figures, forms, and colours, or in apprehensions too subtle to be expressed even in his own winged words. Looking into the depths of his imagination, he perceived conflicts of mental forces which previous writers had not even referred to. He was convinced that his consciousness was not a continuum of perceptions and sense-data; he discerned within himself strange depths and heights of the spirit. He saw, exultingly, that 'we are greater than we know'. And his object was to trace with absolute fidelity the inner life as he saw it. He was assured that his own mind was no different, essentially, from other men's; and he thought therefore that what he traced in his own consciousness was valid for all humanity.

The violence and complexity of his presentation may be explained, partly, by his desire to convey the sensation of energy in these wars of the intellect—energy, which he held to be the source of all truth. To him, the mental warfare was far more terrible than any war of swords and spears. Partly, we may regard this violence as his exasperated reaction against the complacent materialism of the age. His irritation with the pointless notion-bandying of London clubs is reflected in *An Island in the Moon*; his disgust with the general torpor of late eighteenth-century England finds a vehement outlet in the howlings and bludgeonings of *The Four Zoas*. But there is another and deeper reason for the complicated machinery of this strange poem.

It has sometimes been suggested that the essence of Blake's thought lies in his aphorisms, his gnomic sayings in *The Marriage of Heaven and Hell*, *The Everlasting Gospel*, the lyrics and so on. In this he resembles every great original teacher. But such logoi are susceptible of endless misinterpretation, especially when, as in Blake's case, they are 'contraries', instinct with paradox. This misinterpretation, or over-emphasis of one side of the teaching, usually takes place through the development of a 'doctrine' in an organised ecclesiastical framework.

Blake escapes this fate by something little short of a miracle. He forestalls the systematisers by erecting his own system, majestic and complete, yet quite obviously *inapplicable in a mechanical way as it stands*. It must be reinterpreted again and again before it can have any meaning for the individual searcher after truth; and each new discoverer will be so dissatisfied with the way his predecessors have interpreted it that he will be driven to make his own exegesis. There can be no dogma. Christ's teaching it was possible for the moralists to codify and petrify because it contained terms already familiar to His Jewish hearers, which they were able to apply in their old traditional sense as soon as the first impulse of the Gospel had passed away. The parables live on, it is true, to be a stumbling-block to many an earnest moralist and Judaiser. But Blake was determined that the fluid balance of his thought should be maintained, and he preferred to be obscure and elusive rather than suffer the fate of final and permanent misinterpretation. His doctrine is open to every man according to his needs and his intellectual power. *Each man's wisdom is peculiar to his own individuality.* There can be no codification of Blake's thought, no short cut to understanding:

> That which can be made Explicit to the Idiot is not worth my care. The wisest of the Ancients consider'd what is not too Explicit as the fittest for Instruction, because it rouzes the faculties to act. [*L.* 1039]

We know that Blake addressed his teaching, not to his own perverse and foolish generation, but to 'the young men of the new age'. What is still more remarkable is that he should have appreciated the fate to which his writings were likely to be subjected, and nipped the mischief in the bud. Whether this plan was wholly instinctive, or to some degree conscious, we cannot know; nor, in any case, is the point of much importance. It is certain that Blake would have said that his visions are valid, for that is how he *saw*; just as certainly he would have admitted that his expression of them is in groups of symbols organised by the mind.

Perhaps the best way to study Blake, in order to get at the heart of his mystery, is to isolate the gnomic sayings in the prophetic books and elsewhere, to connect them with *The Proverbs of Hell*, and to ponder them in their inter-relations. Where difficulties of interpretation arise, where the mutual operation of contraries is not immediately apparent, the reader should refer to the framework of the prophetic books and there consider the partial expression in its relation to the whole. For the mythological framework determines the tone, the attitude, and the sequence in which the sentences should be read. It gives them their setting in the world of Eternity (which is 'ever-growing', not static); it avoids the danger of literal and partial interpretation. Many of the sayings of *The Proverbs of Hell* cannot be understood apart from the longer poems. We need the ninth Night of *The Four Zoas*, for instance, to grasp in all its completeness the proverb *Drive your cart and your plow over the bones of the dead.* And *All wholesome food is caught without a net or a trap* is more than a pious piece of vegetarian propaganda.

CHAPTER VI

Felpham

We have had but little time for viewing the Country, but what we have seen is Most Beautiful, & the People are Genuine Saxons, handsomer than the people about London. [*L.* 1053]

BLAKE'S letters form a most valuable commentary on his life and work. The first in date that survives (6 December 1795) is addressed to George Cumberland, the artist, one of Blake's oldest friends; it contains a characteristic gird at Locke, and the opinion I have already quoted: 'Peace & Plenty & Domestic Happiness is the Source of Sublime Art, & [you will] prove to the Abstract Philosophers that Enjoyment & not Abstinence is the food of Intellect.' Blake was never weary of opposing the romantic notion, favoured by the rich and comfortable, that genius works best on a crust of bread in a garret.

Though he quarrelled with many of his friends, usually over the question of his visions, Blake could be remarkably generous in his encouragement of those he loved. He valued Flaxman, for instance, far above his worth. And in his letters—especially the earlier ones—we find him every now and then striving to accommodate his thought and expression to his correspondents. It is not that he was hypocritical or servile. He simply did what most of us do in letter-writing: he sought to please. As he grew older, and became indifferent to criticism, or felt surer of sympathy from a few tried friends, his letters reflect his mind more closely.

It was Cumberland who, in 1799, put Blake in touch with the Reverend Dr John Trusler, author of *Hogarth Moralised* and *The Way to be Rich and Respectable*. Dr Trusler engaged Blake as an illustrator, but the connection proved an unsatisfactory one. Dr Trusler wanted clear, straightforward, prosaic illustration to suit his didactic text; Blake's imagination, as usual, flew away with him and he produced symbolic designs quite beyond the Doctor's comprehension. There is a letter dated 16 August 1799, in which Blake gives some valuable statements of his ideas on inspiration. He begins by acknowledging his singularity: 'my Style of Designing is a Species by itself, & in this which I send you [I] have been compell'd by my Genius or Angel to follow where he led....' He has tried hard to follow the Doctor's instructions, but in vain. As for his designs,

> tho' I call them Mine, I know that they are not Mine, being of the same opinion with Milton when he says That the Muse visits his slumbers & awakes & governs his song when Morn purples the East, & being also in the predicament of that prophet who says: "I cannot go beyond the command of the Lord, to speak good or bad." [*L.* 1038]

These references to Milton and the prophet are significant; they show in how exalted a light Blake viewed his art, and his determination never to sink below his best for the sake of gain: a resolution he maintained to the end of his life.

Blake's views on art are amplified in a second letter (23 August 1799), in which he gets angry and in effect calls Dr Trusler a fool:

> I had hoped your plan comprehended All Species of this Art [Moral Painting], & Expecially that you would not regret that Species which gives Existence to Every other, namely, Visions of Eternity. You say that I want somebody to Elucidate my Ideas. But you ought to know that What is Grand is necessarily obscure to Weak men. That which can be made Explicit to the Idiot is not worth my care. The wisest of the Ancients consider'd what is not too Explicit as the fittest Instruction, because it rouzes the faculties to act. [*L.* 1038–9]

That is plain enough, if not too plain. The note of uncompromising honesty which sounds in Blake's letters marked his conversation too, and we cannot wonder that he soon found the 'Way to be Rich and Respectable' closed to him.

He goes on to make one of the longest and most pertinent of his prose announcements. It must be quoted in full:

> I have therefore proved your Reasonings Ill proportion'd, which you can never prove my figures to be; they are those of Michael Angelo, Rafael & the Antique, & of the best living Models. I percieve that your Eye is perverted by Caricature Prints, which ought not to abound so much as they do. Fun I love, but too much Fun is of all things the most loathsom. Mirth is better than Fun, & Happiness is better than Mirth.

I feel that a Man may be happy in This World. And I know that This World Is a World of Imagination & Vision. I see Every thing I paint In This World, but Every body does not see alike. To the Eyes of a Miser a Guinea is far more beautiful than the Sun, & a bag worn with the use of Money has more beautiful proportions than a Vine filled with Grapes. The tree which moves some to tears of joy is in the Eyes of others only a Green thing which stands in the way. Some see Nature all Ridicule & Deformity, & by these I shall not regulate my proportions; & some scarce see Nature at all. But to the Eyes of the Man of Imagination, Nature is Imagination itself. As a man is, so he sees. As the Eye is formed, such are its Powers. You certainly Mistake, when you say that the Visions of Fancy are not to be found in This World. To Me This World is all One continued Vision of Fancy or Imagination, & I feel Flatter'd when I am told so. [*L.* 1039–40]

'As a man is, so he sees.' This axiom that knowledge can only be a function of the knower, that being must come before knowing, that neither the reason nor the observation alone can deal with the data presented by reality, is central for Blake's thought. It is interesting to come across it so early and so cogently expressed.

Blake goes on to say that he has found many who can elucidate his visions, and especially children (to whom we may suppose the Doctor's book to be primarily addressed). The whole letter is a stirring apology, but naturally it failed of its object. We are not surprised to find that Dr Trusler scribbles on the back of Blake's letter the single comment: 'Blake, dim'd with Superstition.'

But the defence is continued in a letter to Cumberland (26 August 1799) in which Blake expresses his thanks for the introduction to Dr Trusler. 'I cannot paint Dirty rags & old shoes where I ought to place Naked Beauty or simple ornament.' The Doctor has affirmed his desire to live only in this world; which, in Blake's eyes, is sufficient to show 'the difference between the doctrines of Dr Trusler & those of Christ'.

The lengthy pronouncement on imagination and vision which Blake makes in his letter to Trusler is worth some attention. We note that he is here able to praise Nature, which in the prophetic books he so mercilessly chastises, because he is now speaking of Nature as seen through but not with the eye: *natura naturans* rather than *natura naturata.* Of course this defence, with its reliance on a more than Berkeleyan idealism, is the last thing to appeal to Dr Trusler. And is there a wicked reference, one wonders, to the Doctor's *The Way to be Rich and Respectable* in the comment on the miser and his bag worn with the use of money? It links up, at any rate, with that other comparison between the sun and a guinea, written eleven years later in his description of the *Vision of the Last Judgment*:

> "What," it will be Question'd, "When the Sun rises, do you not see a round disk of fire somewhat like a Guinea?" O no, no, I see an Innumerable company of the Heavenly host crying, "Holy, Holy, Holy is the Lord God Almighty." I question not my Corporeal or Vegetative Eye any more than I would Question a Window concerning a Sight. I look thro' it & not with it. [*V.L.J.* 844]

But by 1810 he had come to see that he could not speak well of Nature without being misunderstood: his hearers insisted on supposing that he referred to the physical creation. Therefore the passage just quoted is immediately preceded by this corrective:

> Error is Created. Truth is Eternal. Error, or Creation, will be Burned up, & then, & not till Then, Truth or Eternity will appear. It is Burnt up the Moment Men cease to behold it. I assert for My Self that I do not behold the outward Creation & that to me it is hindrance & not Action; it is as the dirt upon my feet, No part of Me. [*V.L.J.* 844]

This burning up of error, and the resurrection of the eternal world, Blake has described in the last book of *The Four Zoas*.

In 1800 Blake was introduced by Flaxman to William Hayley, a popular poetaster, memoir-writer and art dilettante. In the same year his canvas *The Loaves and Fishes* was exhibited at the Academy. The picture seems symbolical and prophetic: for four years Hayley was to provide Blake's loaves and fishes, to feed him with hope and to damp the fires of his genius alternately. At first, the prospects were rosy enough. Hayley was well-off; there seemed no reason why he should not become Blake's permanent patron. He poured out a constant stream of epic and didactic verse, metrical dramas, memoirs, and other works, all calling for illustration to eke out the thin veins of meaning. Flaxman had been Hayley's friend for some twenty years, and had taught his illegitimate son, Thomas Alphonso, the arts of drawing and sculpture. An engraving of Thomas Alphonso's head, after a medallion by Flaxman, was the first piece of work Blake did for Hayley. It was to be published in the Bard's *Essay on Sculpture* (1800); but Hayley was not satisfied with the likeness, and certain alterations had to be made. Blake writes from Hercules Buildings on 1 April 1800:

> With all possible Expedition I send you a proof of my attempt to Express your & our Much Beloved's Countenance. Mr Flaxman has seen it & approved of my now sending it to you for your remarks. Your Sorrows and your dear son's May Jesus and his Angels assuage & if it is consistent with his divine providence restore him to us & to his labours of Art & Science in this world. So prays a fellow sufferer & Your humble servant, Willm. Blake. [*L.* 1042–3]

The sorrow referred to was Thomas Alphonso's illness; unfortunately divine providence had other plans, and the 'young sculptor' died, leaving 'our poor bard', in Gilchrist's acid comment, 'to solace himself in his own way, by inditing sonnets to his child's memory, "on his pillow", at four o'clock in the morning; a daily sonnet or two soon swelling into manuscript volumes'.

A letter of sympathy came from Blake on May 6, offering the consolations of his own faith in immortality:

> I know that our deceased friends are more really with us than when they were apparent to our mortal part. Thirteen years ago I lost a brother, and with his spirit I converse daily and hourly in the spirit, and see him in my remembrance, in the regions of my imagination. I hear his advice, and even now write from his dictate. Forgive me for expressing to you my enthusiasm, which I wish all to partake of, since it is to me a source of immortal joy, even in this world. By it I am the companion of angels. May you continue to be so more and more; and to be more and more persuaded that every mortal loss is an immortal gain. The ruins of Time build mansions in Eternity. [*L.* 1043]

On July 2 we find Blake writing to George Cumberland in a tone of great enthusiasm about Cumberland's plan for a National Gallery of painting and sculpture. Blake himself is just beginning 'to Emerge from a deep pit of Melancholy, Melancholy without any real reason for it, a Disease which God keep you from & all good men'. He is still employed 'in making Designs & little Pictures with now & then an Engraving & find[s] that in future to live will not be so difficult as it has been'. He is astonished at the elegance of modern London, the number of booksellers and printshops.

We may well think that there was good reason for Blake's 'melancholy' at this time, when we consider not only his failure to gain public recognition, but also the vast amount of work, both in design and poetry, which he had produced during the past ten years. The symbolic books could only have been gestated through intense spiritual and mental activity: a reaction was inevitable, and the surprising thing is that it was not more serious. Blake had reached a turning-point in his life. His metaphysical system and his symbolic framework were now complete: the later works would amplify and illustrate his central position, but not substantially modify it. He was tired, and when the opportunity came for a change of scene, he was ready to take it.

The opportunity came through Hayley. The 'bard of Sussex', as he delighted to call himself, was a close friend of William Cowper; and shortly after Cowper's death on 25 April 1800, he undertook to write a memoir of the poet, which he asked Blake to illustrate. Hayley's home was at Felpham in Sussex, and he suggested to Blake that he might move to the same neighbourhood while he was working on the plates. Blake welcomed the plan—partly because it gave him an escape from the pressure of Johnson's and Fuseli's disapproval of his uncommercial 'enthusiasm', as we see from the letter of 10 January 1802, to Thomas Butts.[1] Catherine was equally in favour. We find her writing to Mrs Flaxman in a letter of September 14:

> My husband has been obliged to finish several things necessary to be finished before our migration; the Swallows call us, fleeting past our window at this moment. O how we delight in talking of the pleasure we shall have in preparing you a summer bower at Felpham, & we not only talk, but behold! the Angels of our journey have inspired a song to you. . . .[2] [*L.* 1047]

and she includes a lyric by William, who, in a letter two days earlier to Flaxman, has enthusiastically declared: 'It is to you I owe all my present Happiness', for now, he goes on in verse, 'now

---

[1] Quoted below, p. 113.
[2] Signed 'Catherine Blake', but the whole letter is in her husband's hand.

Flaxman hath given me Hayley his friend to be mine'. It is indeed a time of rejoicing. Already Felpham is ceasing to be just a sea-side village in Sussex: it is ready to be absorbed into the framework of Blake's visionary world. In a letter of September 16 to Hayley he writes:

> Eartham [Hayley's previous residence] will be my first temple & altar....My Wife is like a flame of many colours of precious jewels whenever she hears it named....My fingers emit sparks of fire with Expectation of my future labour.... [*L.* 1048]

On the 18th, after a long and tiring but happy journey, Blake and his wife and sister arrived at Felpham almost on the stroke of midnight, and moved into a six-roomed cottage which Blake had rented from the landlord of the Fox Inn for £20 a year. At first all was perfection and delight. On the 21st Blake writes to Flaxman:

> Dear Sculptor of Eternity,
>
> We are safe arrived at our Cottage, which is more beautiful than I thought it, & more convenient. It is a perfect Model for Cottages &, I think, for Palaces of Magnificence, only Enlarging, not altering its proportions, & adding ornaments & not principals. Nothing can be more Grand than its Simplicity & Usefulness. [*L.* 1048]

After these original views on architecture, he goes on to say that he has begun to work: Felpham is more spiritual than London:

> Heaven opens here on all sides her golden Gates; her windows are not obstructed by vapours; voices of Celestial inhabitants are more distinctly heard, & their forms more distinctly seen; & my Cottage is also a Shadow of their houses. [*L.* 1049]

A description of his journey from London by post-chaise follows; after which he soars to yet more fervent heights:

> And Now Begins a New life, because another covering of Earth is shaken off. I am more famed in Heaven for my works than I could well concieve. In my Brain are studies & Chambers filled with books & pictures of old, which I wrote & painted in ages of Eternity before my mortal life; & those works are the delight & Study of Archangels. Why, then, should I be anxious about the riches or fame of mortality? [*L* 1049]

—in which his belief in the pre-existence of the soul is clearly asserted, and also his faith in the merit of his writings and designs.

In a letter two days later to Thomas Butts, he tells the same story, but with some additions:

> Mr Hayley reciev'd me with his usual brotherly affection. My Wife & Sister are both very well, & courting Neptune for an Embrace, whose terrors this morning made them afraid, but whose mildness is often Equal to his terrors. The villagers of Felpham are not meer Rustics; they are polite & modest. Meat is cheaper than in London, but the sweet air & the voices of winds, trees & birds, & the odours of the happy ground, makes it a dwelling for immortals. Work will go on here with God speed. —A roller & two harrows lie before my window. I met a plow on my first going out at my gate the first morning after my arrival, & the Plowboy said to the Plowman, "Father, The Gate is Open." [*L.* 1050]

What doubt could there be after that! Blake felt that through the lips of the ploughboy the eternal powers had spoken.[1] He is confident that a period of useful and inspired work lies before him at Felpham. Butts replies in a friendly but more guarded strain: he does not know whether Blake will be a better artist or a better poet from his change of environment, but he is sure he will be a better man. Or it will not be Hayley's fault! He hopes that Blake's peculiar opinions, 'which have been equally prejudicial to your Interest & Happiness, will now disperse as a day-break Vapour', and Blake will become an orthodox Churchman. So little sympathy and understanding did Blake receive, even from his closest friends, where his inner life was concerned. To this letter Blake replied with somewhat Jesuitical mildness, promising in future to be 'the determined advocate of Religion & Humility, the two bands of Society'. But a poem which he enclosed shows how far he was from changing his mode of vision, and how different his idea of religion was from that of the Archbishop of Canterbury. It is a poem in which we recapture for a brief moment the tone of the *Songs of Innocence*, as though all the bitterness and anguish of experience, so strongly felt in the symbolic books, had been washed away in the sea and sunbeams of Felpham.[2]

---

[1] Remembering, perhaps, Jakob Boehme's account of his illumination: 'In this my earnest and Christian Seeking and Desire...the Gate was opened to me, that in one Quarter of an Hour I saw and knew more than if I had been many years together at an University....' *Aurora* (vol. 1, p. 15, of English translation, 1764).

[2] See below, pp. 407–10, for a discussion of this important poem.

Then, too, Blake got on so well with William Hayley! The insipid bard of *The Triumphs of Temper* had clearly mastered his own lessons, or else had taught them to Blake. Blake even admired Hayley's verses and rated them (in this letter to Butts) above his own. He was soon hard at work on a frieze of heads of the poets (including Milton, Homer, Camoens, Ercilla, Ariosto and Spenser) for the Bard's library. He was so happy in his cottage that he was almost afraid. He worked diligently at his engravings for the *Life of Cowper* and found an unsuspected pleasure in that poet's letters: 'perhaps, or rather Certainly, the very best letters that ever were published', a verdict in which posterity has generally concurred.[1] And in a letter to Flaxman of October 1801 he expresses his faith that the millennium itself is dawning on earth, now that peace with Napoleon has been concluded: 'The Kingdoms of this World are now become the Kingdoms of God & His Christ, & we shall reign with him for ever & ever. The Reign of Literature & the Arts commences. Blessed are those who are found studious of Literature & Humane & polite accomplishments. Such have their lamps burning & such shall shine as the stars'—sentences in which the influence of Hayley and that of the Authorised Version are equally evident.

Among the engravings Blake did for Hayley at this time may be mentioned: designs for a ballad, *Little Tom the Sailor*, and for a series of ballads 'On Anecdotes relating to Animals', and six engravings for the twelfth edition of the famous *Triumphs of Temper*. Moreover Hayley was getting commissions for Blake to paint miniatures of the local gentlefolk. Blake evidently detested the work, but Hayley's kindness on behalf of his protégé cannot be denied. His letters are full of 'our good Blake', 'our excellent Blake', 'our kind Blake', 'the warmhearted, indefatigable Blake'—who, it seems, not only produced the illustrations for the *Life of Cowper* but acted as Hayley's secretary and amanuensis. The intimacy between the two men grew apace: by the end of 1801 we hear (from Hayley, in a letter to Cowper's cousin, the Rev. John Johnson) that they are reading Cowper's translation of the *Iliad* together and

[1] Note that Blake writes 'published'—not 'written': just one small instance of the sagacity and discrimination which he maintained in the midst of his 'enthusiasm' and which bespeak a balanced as well as a sensitive mind.

comparing it with the Greek as they proceed. How much of Blake's later castigation of Homer and the Greeks owes its virulence, we wonder, to memories of these half-hours with the best authors?[1] Some relic of the trend of Hayley's critical opinions is preserved in two lines of *Blake's Apology for his Catalogue*:

> Thus Hayley on his Toilette seeing the sope,
> Cries, "Homer is very much improved by Pope". [*Ep.* 856]

Soon, indeed, the depressing effect of constant companionship with Hayley becomes apparent. Writing to Thomas Butts on 11 September 1801, Blake strikes this ominous note:

> Time flies faster (as seems to me) here than in London. I labour incessantly & accomplish not one half of what I intend, because my Abstract folly hurries me often away while I am at work, carrying me over Mountains & Valleys, which are not Real, in a Land of Abstraction where Spectres of the Dead wander. This I endeavour to prevent & with my whole might chain my feet to the world of Duty & Reality; but in vain! the faster I bind, the better is the Ballast, for I, so far from being bound down, take the world with me in my flights, & often it seems lighter than a ball of wool rolled by the wind. Bacon & Newton would prescribe ways of making the world heavier to me,[2] & Pitt would prescribe distress for a medicinal potion; but as none on Earth can give me Mental Distress, & I know that all Distress inflicted by Heaven is a Mercy, a Fig for all Corporeal! Such Distress is My mock & scorn. Alas! wretched, happy, ineffectual labourer of time's moments that I am! who shall deliver me from this Spirit of Abstraction & Improvidence?
> [*L.* 1056–7]

Abstract folly! here indeed is a change from Blake's gay self-confidence, the sureness of his mission which glowed in the letters to Dr Trusler. It is a passage in which an acute division appears for the

---

[1] As, no doubt, his most scurrilous diatribe against Klopstock took its rise from this episode recorded in Hayley's diary: 'Read the death of Klopstock in the newspaper of the day, and looked into his Messiah, both the original and the translation. Read Klopstock into English to Blake; and translated the opening of his third canto, where he speaks of his own death' (26 and 29 March 1803). Cf. Blake's 'When Klopstock England defied' (Nonesuch edition, p. 103).

[2] This is evidently a reminiscence of Bacon, *Novum Organum*: 'The understanding must not therefore be supplied with wings, but rather hung with weights, to keep it from leaping and flying.'

first time (and I think the last) in Blake's mind. 'Temptation will not come in this kind again.' There is the deep, permanent conviction of happiness, the assurance that in his innermost being he is invulnerable; and there is the new, agonising idea, obviously implanted by Hayley, a man he loves and admires, that his visions are a mere waste of time and opportunity, that he should be busy painting miniatures of Lord Egremont, of Petworth and Miss Harriet Poole; and—even more agonising—that the lands and persons he sees in his imagination are nothing more than 'abstractions'. This, to one with Blake's hatred of abstraction, is a terrifying thought. No wonder that the later epigrams on Hayley are so bitter.[1] For Hayley had done Blake the greatest of wrongs. He had made him, for a moment, doubt himself. 'Corporeal friends are spiritual enemies.'

To these discontents more material ones were added with the discovery that the beautiful cottage was not so healthy as it had at first appeared. Both Blake and Catherine, we learn from a letter of January 1802 to Butts, have been very ill. The cottage is damp: Catherine has been constantly afflicted by rheumatism and ague. And now, too, Blake is finding out Hayley's faults:

> I find on all hands great objections to my doing anything but the meer drudgery of business, & intimations that if I do not confine myself to this, I shall not live; this has always pursu'd me. You will understand by this the source of all my uneasiness. This from Johnson & Fuseli brought me down here, & this from Mr. H. will bring me back again; for that I cannot live without doing my duty to lay up treasures in heaven is Certain & Determined, & to this I have long made up my mind.

There follows a magnificent exposition of Blake's belief in his mission as prophet of the eternal world:

> I am not ashamed, afraid, or averse to tell you what Ought to be Told: That I am under the direction of Messengers from Heaven, Daily & Nightly; but the nature of such things is not, as some suppose, without trouble or care. Temptations are on the right hand & left; behind, the

---

[1] E.g. that quoted below, p. 129, footnote; and the following:

To H[*ayley*]

Thy Friendship oft has made my heart to ake:
Do be my Enemy for Friendship's sake. [*Ep.* 850]

The first book of *Milton* is full of resentment on this same account.

sea of time & space roars & follows swiftly; he who keeps not right onward is lost, & if our footsteps slide in clay, how can we do otherwise than fear & tremble? but I should not have troubled You with this account of my spiritual state, unless it had been necessary in explaining the actual cause of my uneasiness, into which you are so kind as to Enquire; for I never obtrude such things on others unless question'd, & then I never disguise the truth.—But if we fear to do the dictates of our Angels, & tremble at the Tasks set before us; if we refuse to do Spiritual Acts because of Natural Fears or Natural Desires! Who can describe the dismal torments of such a state!—I too well remember the Threats I heard!—"If you, who are organised by Divine Providence for spiritual communion, Refuse, & bury your Talent in the Earth, even tho' you should want Natural Bread, Sorrow & Desperation pursues you thro' life, & after death shame & confusion of face to eternity. Every one in Eternity will leave you, aghast at the Man who was crown'd with glory & honour by his brethren, & betray'd their cause to their enemies. You will be call'd the base Judas who betray'd his Friend!"—Such words would make any stout man tremble, & how then could I be at ease? But I am no longer in That State, & now go on again with my Task, Fearless, and tho' my path is difficult, I have no fear of stumbling while I keep it. [*L.* 1061–2]

All Blake's splendid courage and contempt for the main chance come out in this letter; as well as his absolute faith in his visions. Through holding to this faith and courage throughout his life he condemned himself to poverty and loneliness, but at the same time procured the leisure to write out and engrave his vision of truth.

There is a gap of almost a year before the next letter to Butts. A strangeness has grown up between the friends; Butts is dissatisfied with the designs which Blake has been executing for him, and Blake has been 'very Unhappy' about other matters and so has not written. But now all is well:

Tho' I have been very unhappy, I am so no longer. I am again Emerged into the light of day; I still & shall to Eternity Embrace Christianity and Adore him who is the Express image of God; but I have travel'd thro' Perils & Darkness not unlike a Champion. I have Conquer'd, and shall Go on Conquering. Nothing can withstand the fury of my Course among the Stars of God & in the Abysses of the Accuser. My Enthusiasm is still what it was, only Enlarged and confirm'd. [*L.* 1065]

Ill news, perhaps, for the prosaic Butts who had hoped that the sea air and sensible company of Felpham would sweep the fanatic cobwebs from Blake's poor deluded brain! And the bad impression would be strengthened by the second letter that Blake wrote on the same day, finding that he 'had not said half what [he] intended to say', and enclosing a copy of verses 'composed above a twelvemonth ago'. These verses are the celebrated poem on the thistle, in which Blake expounds his doctrine of double vision. I consider these verses in a later chapter.

Such moments of spiritual enlightenment, however, are few. The continual strain of coping with Hayley's advice, threats and jealousy was too much for Blake, and in a letter to his brother James (30 January 1803) he expresses his determination to return to London. Hayley is jealous just as Stothard was; he is frightened by Blake as a poet and holds diametrically opposite views of painting. Blake has been very ill at Felpham and he is now convinced that 'the air tho' warm is unhealthy'. But he has done a lot of work, has made some money and looks forward with great hopes to the future. He is full of plans for publishing. Catherine has been busy too, and Blake now quite fancies himself as a man of affairs. 'In short I have got everything so under my thumb that it is more profitable that things should be as they are than any other way, tho' not so agreeable, because we wish naturally for friendship in preference to interest.' Poor Blake! It is pathetic to witness the children of light attempting to ape the children of this world.

Writing to Thomas Butts on April 25 he reiterates his determination to get back to London—for precisely the same reason that had induced him to go to Felpham:

> That I can alone carry on my visionary studies in London unannoy'd, & that I may converse with my friends in Eternity, See Visions, Dream Dreams & prophecy & speak Parables unobserv'd & at liberty from the Doubts of other Mortals; perhaps Doubts proceeding from Kindness, but Doubts are always pernicious, Especially when we Doubt our Friends. Christ is very decided on this Point: "He who is Not With Me is Against Me." There is no Medium or Middle state; & if a Man is the Enemy of my Spiritual Life while he pretends to be the Friend of my Corporeal, he is a Real Enemy—but the Man may be the friend of my Spiritual Life while he seems the Enemy of my Corporeal, but Not Vice Versa. [*L.* 1073]

The same letter gives news of Blake's literary work during his three years at Felpham: the composition of a long epic poem, taken down from immediate dictation (from the spirit world), 'twelve or sometimes twenty or thirty lines at a time, without Premeditation & even against my Will'. This poem is no doubt *The Four Zoas*, although we may assume *Milton* also to have been begun during this period. Blake believes that the writing of this epic was the grand reason for his being sent to Felpham.

Mr Hayley, we learn from Blake's next letter to Butts (July 6), is quite agreeable to Blake's return and 'there is all the appearance in the world of our being fully employ'd in Engraving for his projected Works, Particularly Cowper's Milton. . . .These works will be ornamented with Engravings from Designs from Romney, Flaxman & Yr. hble Servt., & to be Engrav'd also by the last mention'd.' Alas for such hopes! no engravings by Blake were included in the published work. The same letter of July 6 gives a further account of Blake's new poem as

> a Sublime Allegory, which is now perfectly completed into a Grand Poem. I may praise it, since I dare not pretend to be any other than the Secretary; the Authors are in Eternity. I consider it as the Grandest Poem that this World Contains. Allegory addressed to the Intellectual powers, while it is altogether hidden from the Corporeal Understanding, is My Definition of the Most Sublime Poetry; it is also somewhat in the same manner defin'd by Plato. This Poem shall, by Divine Assistance, be progressively Printed & Ornamented with Prints & given to the Public. [*L.* 1076]

This, of course, did not come to pass: *The Four Zoas* remained in manuscript; but much of its matter was used in *Milton* and *Jerusalem*.

Hayley has seen part of the poem '& has looked with sufficient contempt to enhance my opinion of it'. And he likes Blake's designs as little as his verses, so that Blake has been 'forced to insist on his leaving me in both to my own Self Will; for I am determin'd to be no longer Pester'd with his Genteel Ignorance & Polite Disapprobation. I know myself both Poet & Painter, & it is not his affected Contempt that can move me to any thing but a more assiduous pursuit of both Arts.'

One of the few 'events' in Blake's life, if we may use that word to mean stirring outward occurrences, was reported in his next letter to Butts from Felpham, dated 16 August 1803.

I am at Present in a Bustle to defend myself against a very unwarrantable warrant from a Justice of Peace in Chichester, which was taken out against me by a Private in Captn. Leathes's troop of 1st or Royal Dragoons, for an assault & seditious words. The wretched Man has terribly Perjur'd himself, as has his Comrade; for, as to Sedition, not one Word relating to the King or Government was spoken by either him or me. His Enmity arises from my having turned him out of my Garden, into which he was invited as an assistant by a Gardener at work therein, without my knowledge that he was so invited. I desired him, as politely as was possible, to go out of the Garden; he made me an impertinent answer. I insisted on his leaving the Garden; he refused. I still persisted in desiring his departure; he then threaten'd to knock out my Eyes, with many abominable imprecations & with some contempt for my Person; it affronted my foolish Pride. I therefore took him by the Elbows & pushed him before me till I had got him out; there I intended to have left him, but he, turning about, put himself into a Posture of Defiance, threatening & swearing at me. I, perhaps foolishly & perhaps not, stepped out at the Gate, &, putting aside his blows, took him again by the Elbows, &, keeping his back to me, pushed him forwards down the road about fifty yards—he all the while endeavouring to turn round & strike me, & raging & cursing, which drew out several neighbours; at length, when I had got him to where he was Quarter'd, which was very quickly done, we were met at the Gate by the Master of the house, The Fox Inn (who is the proprietor of my Cottage), & his wife & Daughter & the Man's Comrade & several other people. My Landlord compell'd the Soldiers to go in doors, after many abusive threats against me & my wife from the two Soldiers; but not one word of threat on account of Sedition was utter'd at that time. This method of Revenge was Plann'd between them after they had got together into the stable. This is the whole outline.

[*L.* 1078–9]

One does not know which aspects to remark more in this vividly reported episode—Blake's cool courage and resourcefulness, his physical strength, or the calm recital of the whole affair. He goes on to give a full account of the sequel. The dragoon, John Scholfield, and his comrade, Private Cock, have laid a charge of sedition and assault against him, and he has appeared before the Bench of Justices at Chichester and been forced to find bail. He is to be tried at the

Quarter Sessions, to be held after Michaelmas. The accusation is that he uttered seditious words and 'Damn the King', which he hotly denies. The letter ends with a short and plaintive poem, of which the first verse is adapted from his earlier *Mary*:[1]

> O why was I born with a different face?
> Why was I not born like the rest of my race?
> When I look, each one starts! when I speak, I offend;
> Then I'm silent & passive & lose every Friend. [*L.* 1081]

Blake certainly was not silent and passive when it came to his defence against the charge laid by Scholfield. He drew up a most vigorous and effective *Memorandum* for the use of his counsel. He stood his trial for High Treason (an offence punishable by death) on 11 January 1804. Catherine used to tell long after how his vehement cries of "False!" at each successive perjury of Scholfield's electrified the court. Hayley stood by him, and he was acquitted amid the applause of those present. The incident left a profound impression on Blake's mind, and the two soldiers appear as the demons Skofeld and Cox in the majestic framework of the later symbolic books.

Blake was lucky to escape. One of the magistrates, it is known, was against him; and if he had been identified as the London Blake, the notorious Radical, the friend of Godwin and Paine who had worn the red cap of liberty in the London streets it would have gone hard with him. Fortunately the trial was held in Chichester. It is quite possible, too, that Scholfield and his friend were not lying all the time; that the words "Damn the King!" and other seditious expressions did in fact pass Blake's lips in his excitement—though he may have forgotten the fact later.

Hayley, though Blake's spiritual enemy, acted like a true corporeal friend during this contretemps; and Blake was duly grateful.[2] The Bard had met with an accident a few days before the trial opened. 'It was of a kind, however', writes Gilchrist, who can never resist the temptation to make Hayley look absurd, 'to which he was pretty well accustomed. A persevering and fearless rider, he was in the eccentric habit of using an umbrella on horseback, to shade his eyes;

[1] See *Miscellaneous Poems*, p. 115.

[2] At first; later it appears that he came to believe in the monstrous idea that Hayley had engineered the whole episode to ruin him. See below, pp. 128–9.

the abrupt unfurling of which was commonly followed, naturally enough, by the rider's being forthwith pitched on his head. He had, on this occasion, lighted on a flint with more than usual violence; owing his life, indeed, to the opportune shield of a strong new hat.' This accident, with its consequences of a bump and a bandage, did not keep Hayley away from his friend's side at the trial; for which fortitude we may render him due honour.

Blake had now been living in London, at 17 South Molton Street (which was to be his home for nearly seventeen years) since September 1803, returning to Sussex only to stand his trial in January 1804. Business was coming in, we learn from a letter of December 13. Johnson the bookseller has told him that there is no want of work. He hopes 'yet to make a figure in the great dance of life' (27 January 1804).[1]

Suddenly, in a letter to Hayley of October 23, we have one of those announcements which mark milestones in Blake's spiritual career:

> For now! O Glory! and O Delight! I have entirely reduced that spectrous fiend to his station, whose annoyance has been the ruin of my labours for the last passed twenty years of my life. He is the enemy of conjugal love and is the Jupiter of the Greeks, an iron-hearted tyrant, the ruiner of ancient Greece. I speak with perfect confidence and certainty of the fact which has passed upon me. Nebuchadnezzar had seven times passed over him; I have had twenty; thank God I was not altogether a beast as he was; but I was a slave bound in a mill among beasts and devils; these beasts and these devils are now, together with myself, become children of light and liberty, and my feet and my wife's feet are free from fetters. [*L.* 1108]

He ascribes this liberation to the three years' rest from perturbation which he has enjoyed at Felpham; but we must remember he is addressing Hayley. The immediate cause of his enlightenment, the catalytic agent, as it were, is a visit to the Truchsessian Picture

[1] And Flaxman writes to Hayley, as late as 14 November 1805: '...you will be glad to hear that Blake has his hands full of work for a considerable time to come, and if he will only condescend to give that attention to his wordly concerns which everyone does that prefers living to starving, he is now in a way to do well....' (From F. Tatham, *The Letters of William Blake*, pp. 186–7.)

Gallery, an exhibition of alleged old masters recently opened in New Road, opposite Portland Place. Among the painters represented were many of Blake's favourites, including Michelangelo, Dürer, Holbein, and da Vinci. It was on the day following his visit, he tells us, that

> I was again enlightened with the light I enjoyed in my youth, and which has for exactly twenty years been closed from me as by a door and by window-shutters. . . . Dear Sir, excuse my enthusiasm or rather madness, for I am really drunk with intellectual vision whenever I take a pencil or graver into my hand, even as I used to be in my youth, and as I have not been for twenty dark, but very profitable, years. [*L.* 1108–9]

What are we to make of this amazing statement that the light has been closed from Blake for exactly twenty years? The period includes all Blake's writing with the exception of the *Poetical Sketches* and a few fragments of Ossianic prose, and almost all the designs. In what sense has this long period been devoid of light? It cannot be the light of Eternity, for we already have abundant evidence in Blake's own words that he is always conscious of writing from the immediate dictation of heavenly powers.

The problem is a difficult one, and a commentator can but hazard a guess. Perhaps the reference to the spectrous fiend who is 'the enemy of conjugal love' may give us the clue. Twenty years would carry us back to 1784, two years after Blake's marriage to Catherine Boucher. It is at this time, I surmise, that Blake became conscious of two things; first, that it was unlikely that his wife would bear him a child, and, secondly, that she would not have him form a liaison with another woman. Now, for the first time, Blake felt the full strength of the bonds of marriage, and of the malice of that spectrous fiend jealousy—whom he afterwards identified thoroughly with Urizen or Jupiter, the god of the Greeks.

In what respect can the power of jealousy be said to have hampered his work during these twenty years? The answer is found in the poems themselves. The theme of jealousy runs through the *Songs of Experience*, through the lyrics of the Rossetti manuscript, through the minor prophetic books, and is even incorporated into the title as well as the texture of *The Four Zoas*. Blake has suddenly realised, in this flash of vision, how different his work might have been if this obsession had not run through it and corrupted it. How clear and strong its outlines, how full of joy and laughter its content, if jealousy had not distorted his view! And he realises this now because for one moment, in the presence of great art, he has stepped out of his selfhood. His personal anguish disappears and once again, as in the days of his youth, he finds innocence. At that moment the world is recreated.

And this, perhaps, is the reason Blake did not engrave *The Four Zoas*, did not revise it, even, but went on to his great epics of reconciliation. *Milton* and *Jerusalem* are utterly different in spirit from the earlier prophecy. They are calmer and brighter: the hurt and the jealousy have gone out of them. It is probable, to carry our surmise one step further, that this change of tone corresponds to a real change in Blake's personal life: a change which means a settling down to closer companionship with Catherine, a sharing of his great mind with her more limited but loving mind, a renouncing of his hopes of a passionate and fruitful union with another woman.

But this, let it be emphasised again, is the merest surmise. We cannot know precisely what Blake meant in his confession to William Hayley. All we can say for sure is that there is a change in his work after this date; and this change is towards a serener vision, a less tormented symbolism. It is as though Blake were saying: What I told you in *The Four Zoas* was true, the light was really from the world of Eternity, but it was shining through a mind thrown out of true by passion. There was too much William Blake in it, and not enough of Eternity. And one thing we shall notice, in tracing the growth of Blake's conception of Christ in a later chapter, is that the figure of Jesus becomes much more vivid and definite in his work after this date.

CHAPTER VII

Years of Struggle

> The Angel that presided o'er my birth
> Said, "Little creature, form'd of Joy & Mirth,
> Go love without the help of any Thing on Earth." [*M.P.* 124]

THE fair prospects on which Blake had nourished his hopes on leaving Felpham were to remain prospects only. It was his belief that 'every man ought to be a judge of pictures, and every man is so, who has not been connoisseured out of his senses'; but he soon found that his taste and that of the public differed widely. He was now living at 17 South Molton Street, working hard, with Catherine's help, at engraving which brought in very little money. *Milton* and *Jerusalem* were going forward: but there was no living to be made out of *them*! All hopes of a patron had disappeared; Blake was still working for Hayley, but Hayley was now a falling star in the firmament of letters. He is engaged in January 1805 in designing and engraving five prints for Hayley's *Ballads founded on Anecdotes relating to Animals*: on which *Ballads* his remarks are painfully obsequious: 'Truly proud I am', he writes, 'to be in possession of this beautiful little estate....I shall consider myself a robber to retain any more than you at any time please to grant'. But it is not long before we find him writing in his notebook such epigrams as:

> My title as a Genius thus is prov'd:
> Not Prais'd by Hayley nor by Flaxman lov'd. [*Ep.* 851]

The *Ballads*, that 'beautiful little estate', was a complete failure: the reading public was beginning to wake up to the flimsiness of the Hermit's pretensions and crying out for richer and spicier fare. Scott was more in the fashion than these dying moans of the eighteenth century. And Blake's engravings appeared simply ridiculous to the reviewers. The flimsy reed on which he had so long and so unwillingly leant was broken at last, the smoking flax quenched. Hayley never regained his popularity.

TWO DESIGNS FOR HAYLEY'S *BALLADS*

PLATE IV

46

Or if we wish a fourth, it is a friend——
But friends how mortal! dangerous the desire.
Take Phœbus to yourselves, ye basking bards!
Inebriate at fair fortune's fountain-head;
And reeling through the wilderness of joy;
* Where sense runs savage broke from reason's chain,
And sings false peace, till smother'd by the pall.
My fortune is unlike; unlike my song;
Unlike the DEITY my song invokes.
I to day's soft-eyed sister pay my court,
Endymion's rival! and her aid implore;
Now first implored in succour to the muse.
Thou who didst lately borrow Cynthia's form,
And modestly forego thine own! O thou
Who didst thyself, at midnight hours, inspire!
Say, why not Cynthia patroness of song?
As thou her crescent, she thy character
Assumes; still more a goddess by the change.
Are there demurring wits, who dare dispute
This revolution in the world inspired?
Ye train pierian! to the lunar sphere,
In silent hour address your ardent call
For aid immortal—less her brother's right.
She, with the spheres harmonious, nightly leads
The mazy dance, and hears their matchless strain;
A strain for gods, denied to mortal ear.
Transmit it heard, thou silver queen of heaven!
What title or what name endears thee most?
Cynthia! Cyllene! Phœbe!—or dost hear
With higher gust fair P——d of the skies?

A PAGE FROM YOUNG'S *NIGHT THOUGHTS*

So it went hard with Blake. In his commonplace book for Tuesday, 20 January 1807, we find the simple and terrible entry: 'Between Two & Seven in the Evening—Despair.' He breaks off his *Milton* after only two books have been written. When, in 1809, Hayley's *Life of Romney* was published, the majority of the engravings were by one Caroline Watson who had supplanted Blake in the Bard's esteem. And now he fell into the hands of an exploiter more unscrupulous and more cunning than Hayley: the ex-engraver and print-seller Cromek. When Cromek discovered him in 1805, Blake's affairs were at their lowest ebb; according to the Yorkshireman's jeering letter of May 1807, he was in fact reduced to living on half-a-guinea a week. The wily Cromek was quick to see the commercial value of some of Blake's work, and bought his illustrations to Blair's *The Grave* for twenty guineas. There were twelve of these, and it was expressly stipulated that Blake should engrave them for the forthcoming edition of the poem. He did actually engrave one or two; but when the book finally appeared the engravings were by Schiavonetti, a pupil of Bartolozzi. Blake was furious at this piece of sharp practice and vented his rage in devastating entries in the notebook:

> Cr[omek] loves artists as he loves his Meat.
> He loves the Art, but 'tis the Art to Cheat,

and

> A Petty Sneaking Knave I knew—
> O Mr. Cr[omek], how do ye do? [*Ep.* 848]

Even while Schiavonetti was working on Blake's designs, Cromek would drop in from time to time at Blake's rooms and look around for anything else he could steal. Blake had been making a pencil drawing of his *Canterbury Pilgrims*; Cromek's vulture eye lit on this, and he suggested to Blake that he might let him have it to give to Schiavonetti to engrave. Blake turned down the idea indignantly; but Cromek was not to be outdone. He went to the artist Stothard and suggested a picture portraying the Canterbury Pilgrims. Whether or not he told Stothard that Blake was already working on the subject, or how much of Blake's original idea he passed on to him, is uncertain. The general lay-out of the two finished pictures is certainly very much the same. However this may be, Blake was furious when he learned of the new knavery that had been practised on him, and his anger overflowed into the *Descriptive Catalogue* which he wrote and had printed for his Exhibition of paintings in 1809.

> Such are the characters [he writes of the figures in his *Canterbury Pilgrims*] that compose this Picture, which was painted in self-defence against the insolent and envious imputation of unfitness for finished and scientific art; and this imputation, most artfully and industriously endeavoured to be propagated among the public by ignorant hirelings. The painter courts comparison with his competitors, who, having received fourteen hundred guineas and more, from the profits of his designs in that well-known work, Designs for Blair's Grave, have left him to shift for himself, while others, more obedient to an employer's opinions and directions, are employed, at a great expence, to produce works, in succession to his, by which they acquired public patronage. This has hitherto been his lot—to get patronage for others and then to be left and neglected, and his work, which gained that patronage, cried down as eccentricity and madness; as unfinished and neglected by the artist's violent temper; he is sure the works now exhibited will give the lie to such aspersions. [*D.C.* 789–90]

It is painful to hear such a man defending himself, to catch the note of childlike bewilderment and pain; it is more painful to consider the distress that had driven the greatest designer of his age, as Palmer rightly called him, to such shifts. The exhibition which opened in May 1809 in his brother's shop in Broad Street, Golden Square—his childhood home—was Blake's last attempt to capture the attention of the public. 'In my beginning is my end.' The exhibition was a dismal failure. The admittance fee was *2s. 6d.* with a descriptive catalogue included: a prose key to the exhibits which is itself a most interesting piece of Blakean propaganda for his favourite ideals in art. It opens with an uncompromising attack on the colourists:

> The eye that can prefer the Colouring of Titian and Rubens to that of Michael Angelo and Rafael, ought to be modest and to doubt its own powers. [*D.C.* 778]

From this it is an easy step to the personal question:

> Mr. B. appeals to the Public, from the judgment of those narrow blinking eyes, that have too long governed art in a dark corner. [*D.C.* 778]

Then follows a spirited account of each of the sixteen pictures, including the *Canterbury Pilgrims*. Much of Blake's comment must inevitably have seemed sheer lunacy to the critics of the time. In what other light than madness could such remarks as the following have appeared to these sobersides?

> The two pictures of Nelson and Pitt are compositions of a mythological cast, similar to those Apotheoses of Persian, Hindoo, and Egyptian Antiquity, which are still preserved on rude monuments, being copies from some stupendous originals now lost or perhaps buried till some happier age. The Artist having been taken in vision into the ancient republics, monarchies, and patriarchates of Asia has seen those wonderful originals, called in the Sacred Scriptures the Cherubim, which were sculptured and painted on walls of Temples, Towers, Cities, Palaces, and erected in the highly cultivated states of Egypt, Moab, Edom, Aram, among the Rivers of Paradise, being originals from which the Greeks and Hetrurians copied Hercules Farnese, Venus of Medicis, Apollo Belvidere, and all the grand works of ancient art. [*D.C.* 780]

Then follows, of course, an attack on the Greeks, Blake's favourite bugbear.

Blake's critical excursus on the characters of Chaucer's *Prologue* is justly famous. Charles Lamb praised it at the time it appeared—'a most spirited criticism on Chaucer, but mystical and full of Vision'. Mystical it certainly is: Blake cannot comment even on the earthy medieval Chaucer without bringing in his doctrine of the Four Zoas:

> Chaucer's characters are a description of the eternal Principles that exist in all ages....Visions of these eternal principles or characters of human life appear to poets, in all ages; the Grecian gods were the ancient Cherubim of Phoenicia; but the Greeks, and since them the Moderns, have neglected to subdue the gods of Priam. These gods are visions of the eternal attributes, or divine names, which, when erected into gods, become destructive to humanity. They ought to be the servants, and not the masters of man, or of society. They ought to be made to sacrifice to Man, and not man compelled to sacrifice to them; for when separated from man or humanity, who is Jesus the Saviour, the vine of eternity, they are thieves and rebels, they are destroyers. [*D.C.* 787, 788]

The long and vigorous analysis of Chaucer's characters is too well-known to need comment or exposition. It is yet another expression of Blake's 'indomitable Englishry'. The most interesting fact to note, perhaps, is that Blake's mystical interpretation of the pilgrims, whatever we may think of it, does not in the least diminish the acuteness of his criticism as a purely literary *tour de force*. No better criticism on Chaucer has ever been written.

The picture of *The Ancient Britons*, too, calls forth some of Blake's most characteristic pronouncements on history, mythology, the resurrection into unity, the non-progressiveness of art, and nudism. He has learned from Jacob Bryant and other historians that the Ancient Britons were

> naked civilized men, learned, studious, abstruse in thought and contemplation; naked, simple, plain in their acts and manners; wiser than after-ages. [*D.C.* 796]

He has also discovered that all nations originally had one language and one religion, which was the religion of Jesus, the everlasting gospel of forgiveness and art. It is the survival of this religion, in however mutilated a form, which makes for greatness in art; and this is why we cannot say that one age or individual is greater than another, if both are inspired. There are no degrees in inspiration. Blake was one of the first to perceive the falsity of the idea that art can improve through widening knowledge or slicker technique.[1]

Finally he gives us, in his notes on *Ruth—A Drawing*, his golden rule in art. This is the rule that Blake comes back to again and again; he applies it to his visions, and indeed makes it a touchstone to distinguish real vision from mere fancy and day-dreaming. If the vision is of figures and objects which are perfectly distinct in every detail, more so than in 'real life', it may be accepted as authentic. If, on the other hand, the impression is blurred and generalised, we must reject it:

> The great and golden rule of art, as well as of life, is this: That the more distinct, sharp, and wirey the bounding line, the more perfect the work of art, and the less keen and sharp, the greater is the evidence of weak imitation, plagiarism, and bungling. [*D.C.* 805–6]

In May 1809 Blake issued a prospectus of his proposed engraving of the Canterbury Pilgrims 'fresco', to be ready, size three feet one inch by one foot, in September 1810. He invites subscriptions:

---

[1] See below, Ch. XXIII, for a fuller discussion of Blake's views on art.

'FOUR GUINEAS, Two to be paid at the time of Subscribing, the other Two, on delivery of the Print.'

Valuable as Blake's *Descriptive Catalogue* is to us to-day as an aid to understanding his views on art and vision, it cannot be doubted that it did a lot to damage what little reputation he had in his own day. Crabb Robinson was unsympathetic, and the *Examiner*, Robert Hunt's paper, downright abusive. It is with somewhat wry amusement, remembering the protection afforded by the law of libel to the versifiers of our own day, that we read the following strictures on one of the greatest of writers and painters:

> If besides the stupid and mad-brained political project of their rulers, the sane part of the people of England required fresh proof of the alarming increase of the effects of insanity, they will be too well convinced from its having lately spread into the hitherto sober regions of art....Such is the case with the productions and admirers of William Blake, an unfortunate lunatic, whose personal inoffensiveness secures him from confinement, and, consequently, of whom no public notice would have been taken, if he was not forced on the notice and animadversion of the *Examiner* in having been held up to the public admiration by many esteemed amateurs and professors as a genius in some respect original and legitimate....Thus encouraged, the poor man fancies himself a great master, and has painted a few wretched pictures, some of which are unintelligible allegory, others an attempt at sober character by caricature representation, and the whole 'blotted and blurred' and very badly drawn. These he calls an Exhibition, of which he has published a Catalogue, or rather a farrago of nonsense, unintelligibleness and egregious vanity, the wild effusions of a distempered brain....

It may be imagined that Blake was deeply indignant and hurt at this vicious attack. He defended himself in the *Public Address* of 1810 (which however remained in manuscript), and was not deterred from the idea of another exhibition. He worked hard at his great 'fresco' of the Last Judgement. And in the *Public Address*, amid all the grumblings at Stothard, Romney, Flaxman, Bartolozzi, Woolett, Hayley, and others, we find precious notes on Blake's principles of art and life. He insists on the truth that idea and expression are not two things but one, and cites

> a Poem signed with the name of Nat Lee, which perhaps he never wrote & perhaps he wrote in a paroxysm of insanity, In which it is said that

Milton's Poem is a rough Unfinish'd Piece & Dryden has finish'd it. Now let Dryden's Fall & Milton's Paradise be read, & I will assert that every Body of Understanding must cry out Shame on such Niggling & Poco-Pen as Dryden has degraded Milton with. [*P.A.* 820]

The superiority of Milton was always apparent to Blake, and of course to many other critics of discrimination; but Dryden's was still a name to conjure with. Blake saw Milton's greatness as clearly as he saw that of Chaucer, and he discerned its foundation in brilliance of imagination and corresponding strength of invention and poetic technique. Dryden was able to try his improver's hand on Milton's rough original because Dryden's age really believed that it had taken a step forward in every branch of literature. But once scrutinised by the criticism of Blake, Coleridge, and Hazlitt such a view became untenable.

It is in his manuscript notes on the great picture, *A Vision of the Last Judgment*, also written in 1810, that Blake gives the clearest expression (outside the prophetic books, of course) to his theories of vision and imagination. These important notes are left for discussion to a later chapter, together with his marginalia (*c.* 1808) on Sir Joshua Reynolds' *Discourses*.

In 1808 Blake exhibited for the last time at the Royal Academy: *Christ in the Sepulchre guarded by Angels* and *Jacob's Dream*.

Epigrams from Blake's notebook showing his resentment at the treatment he had received from Hayley, Stothard and Cromek have already been quoted. There are others which give more lengthy expression to his sense of grievance; and one in particular, written in the heroic couplet, shows that this still rankled after Cromek's death in March 1812. It is worth quoting in full for the light which it throws, too, on Blake's relations with Hayley during the Felpham period.

The passage, as it stands in the notebook, begins in the middle of what was evidently a narrative of some extent. The person speaking appears to be Stothard himself, engaged in delivering a funeral oration on his friend Cromek. The first four lines refer, probably, to Cromek's expedition to Dumfries in search of unpublished poems by Robert Burns.[1] The next four lines concern Cromek's engagement

---

[1] See Gilchrist's *Life of William Blake*, Ch. XXVI, for details.

of Stothard as engraver. Here the name Stothard is disguised under the sarcastic appelation of Stewhard:

> And his legs carried it like a long fork,
> Reach'd all the way from Chichester to York,
> From York all across Scotland to the Sea;
> This was a Man of Men, as seems to me.
> Not only in his Mouth his own Soul lay,
> But my Soul also would he bear away.
> Like as a Pedlar bears his weary Pack,
> So Stewhard's Soul he buckl'd to his Back. [*Ep.* 845]

He is anxious to patronise and exploit Blake too:

> But once, alas! committing a Mistake,
> He bore the wretched Soul of William Blake
> That he might turn it into Eggs of Gold;
> But neither Back nor mouth those Eggs could hold.
> His under jaw drop'd as those Eggs he laid,
> And Stewhard's Eggs are addled & decay'd.

Next comes a reference to the attack on Blake in Robert Hunt's *Examiner*, already noticed. Here Blake is given the name of Death, which sticks to him throughout the remaining lines of the poem:

> The Examiner, whose very name is Hunt,
> Call'd Death a Madman, trembling for the affront,
> Like trembling Hare sits on his weakly paper
> On which he us'd to dance & sport & caper.

In the next six lines Cromek (Yorkshire Jack Hemp) and one 'Daw' who is perhaps Stothard under yet another name are associated with Hayley (Felpham Billy). The passage is important not only in suggesting that Blake and Hayley went out riding together, but also for the reference to 'Billy's Lawyer & Dragoon'. Does this really mean that Blake believed Hayley to have been responsible for the Scholfield episode? It is not the only passage in Blake's notebook which makes this grave—and, it would seem, crazy—accusation.[1]

---

[1] 'When H[ayley] finds out what you cannot do,
That is the very thing he'll set you to.
If you break not your Neck, 'tis not his fault,
But pecks of poison are not pecks of salt.
And when he could not act upon my wife
Hired a Villain to bereave my Life.' [*Ep.* 849]

Yorkshire Jack Hemp & gentle, blushing Daw
Clap'd Death into the corner of their jaw,
And Felpham Billy rode out every morn
Horseback with Death over the fields of corn,
Who with iron hand cuff'd in the afternoon
The Ears of Billy's Lawyer and Dragoon. [*Ep.* 845–6]

The rest of the poem refers to Blake's resistance to exploitation by Cromek and Stothard. Cromek is now given the name of Screwmuch:

And Cur, my Lawyer, & Dady, Jack Hemp's Parson,
Both went to Law with Death to keep our Ears on.
For how to starve Death we had laid a plot
Against his Price—but Death was in the Pot.[1]
He made them pay his Price, alack a day!
He knew both Law & Gospel better than they.
O' that I ne'er had seen that William Blake,
Or could from death Assassinetti wake!
We thought—Alas, that such a thought should be!—
That Blake would Etch for him & draw for me.
For 'twas a kind of Bargain Screwmuch made
That Blake's designs should be by us display'd,
Because he makes designs so very cheap.
Then Screwmuch at Blake's soul took a long leap.
'Twas not a Mouse—'twas Death in a disguise,
And I, alas! live to weep out mine Eyes.
And Death sits laughing on their Monuments,
On which he's written, "Reciev'd the Contents."
But I have writ—so sorrowful my thought is—
His Epitaph, for my tears are aqua fortis:
"Come Artists, knock your heads against this stone
For Sorrow that our friend Bob Screwmuch's gone."
And now, the Muses upon me smile & Laugh,
I'll also write my own dear Epitaph,
And I'll be buried near a Dike
That my friends may weep as much as they like:
"Here lies Stewhard the Friend of All, &c."

Blake's resentment against Cromek was justified enough, but one hardly knows how to take his accusations against Hayley. The

---

[1] The reference is to II Kings iv. 40.

charitable supposition would be that he wrote the lines not seriously but in a fit of passion.

During his Felpham sojourn Blake had been working on a number of poems which are best discussed together. They include the long *Mental Traveller*, *Milton*, and several short lyrics. *The Mental Traveller* is an extremely cryptic poem in quatrains: as to its meaning, one reader's guess seems as good as another's. It is based on Blake's favourite dichotomies of male and female, age and youth, freedom and bondage, and is cyclic in its action. The well-known *Auguries of Innocence* is simpler. It is composed of a number of gnomic couplets which embody much of Blake's wisdom in striking and memorable form. These couplets have been arranged by Blake's editors. If we seek for a guiding thread to the *Auguries*, we may find it in Mr E. M. Forster's counsel, 'Only connect!' Blake shows us that the Universe, spiritual and material, is a subtle web of interrelations: no action can be called trifling, for it has the most far-reaching consequences. A strong but lyric indignation runs through the verses: indignation against injustice and cruelty and stupidity, expressed in phrases unrivalled for condensed power.

In the famous opening quatrain Blake gives the formula for the good life: the point of view from which nature and man are to be considered in the ensuing verses:

> To see a World in a Grain of Sand
> And a Heaven in a Wild Flower,
> Hold Infinity in the palm of your hand
> And Eternity in an hour. [*M.P.* 118]

Then comes a series of couplets chastising the stupidity which ill-treats animals and fails to see them as part of the great human totality:

> A Robin Red breast in a Cage
> Puts all Heaven in a Rage.
> A dove house fill'd with doves & Pigeons
> Shudders Hell thro' all its regions.
> A dog starv'd at his Master's Gate
> Predicts the ruin of the State.
> A Horse misus'd upon the Road
> Calls to Heaven for Human blood.

Each outcry of the hunted Hare
A fibre from the Brain does tear.
A Skylark wounded in the wing,
A Cherubim does cease to sing.... [*M.P.* 118]

Verses on unbelief follow, linked up with his lines on animals and birds:

The Bat that flits at close of Eve
Has left the Brain that won't Believe.... [*M.P.* 118]

and he curses those that mock the faith of a little child:

He who mocks the Infant's Faith
Shall be mock'd in Age & Death.
He who shall teach the Child to Doubt
The rotting Grave shall ne'er get out. [*M.P.* 120]

Cruelty to children, especially in the form of 'education' or discipline, always arouses his indignation:

The Babe that weeps the Rod beneath
Writes Revenge in realms of death. [*M.P.* 120]

Next comes the turn of the prostitute and the gambler:

The Whore & Gambler, by the State
Licenc'd, build that Nation's Fate.
The Harlot's cry from Street to Street
Shall weave Old England's winding Sheet.
The Winner's Shout, the Loser's Curse,
Dance before dead England's Hearse. [*M.P.* 121]

And finally we have a concise expression of Blake's faith in vision:

We are led to Believe a Lie
When we see [with] not Thro' the Eye
Which was Born in a Night to perish in a Night
When the Soul Slept in Beams of Light.
God appears & God is Light
To those poor Souls who dwell in Night,
But does a Human Form Display
To those who Dwell in Realms of day. [*M.P.* 121]

These couplets are not sentimentality, but vision in the highest degree. The human form which is revealed by Jesus is more real than the impersonal image of light; and it includes the meanest creature that breathes. The *Auguries of Innocence* are a brilliant statement of the unity of all life. 'Every thing that lives is holy', and we cannot wrong the humblest of living things without injuring the whole of which we too are a part.

CHAPTER VIII

'Milton'

I saw Milton in Imagination And he told me to beware of being misled by his Paradise Lost. In particular he wished me to shew the falsehood of his doctrine that the pleasures of *sex* arose from the fall. The fall could not produce any pleasure. [Blake, reported by H. Crabb Robinson, *Diary*, 17 Dec. 1825]

WHAT precisely did Milton mean to Blake? We know from numerous scattered references that he was one of the earliest and most consistent influences on Blake's thought—

Milton lov'd me in childhood & shew'd me his face. [*L.* 1046]

—and we know that as early as *Poetical Sketches* Blake had chosen a Miltonic theme for treatment in *Samson*; while in *The Marriage of Heaven and Hell* he had criticised the basis of Milton's doctrine of reason and passion.

We shall return to the *Marriage* in a moment. *Milton* is not an easy poem to understand. It is the product of an intense struggle in Blake's own mind, a struggle complicated by his relations with Hayley at Felpham, but concerned chiefly with the question that always haunted him: how had it come about that England, once the seat of inspiration and vision, was now the dispenser of rationalism to Europe—the land of Bacon, Newton and Locke? It is with this problem that Blake is going to grapple anew in *Milton.* And he is going to use Milton himself, the poet of vision writing in the century of experiment, to exteriorise this problem.

As always, the situation has its several aspects: historical, religious, psychological. In the case of Milton the historical aspect—and more especially the biographical details—takes on an unwonted importance for Blake. In many respects he could identify himself with the seventeenth-century poet. He, too, felt his work to be 'doctrinal to a nation'; he, too, felt directly inspired; he too, was an apostle of liberty in an age of restrictions. And—to come down to the more personal question—he had known something of Milton's disappointment in an early marriage, and something of Milton's revolt.

We cannot, then, understand fully what Milton meant to Blake until we have first made a brief enquiry into what Milton meant to his own age, and where he stands in the tradition of English thought which flows down to Blake. We cannot understand the basic *motif* of Blake's *Milton* until we have scrutinised the motives which led Milton to write *Paradise Lost* and the attitudes which that poem contains to some of Blake's own major interests—reason and passion, the senses, nature, and the eternal world.

To begin with, let us consider the 'climate of opinion' into which *Paradise Lost* was born.

Poetry, in the mid-seventeenth century, finds itself in an awkward position. "The new philosophy calls all in doubt", John Donne pathetically remarks in 1611; by 1667, the date of the publication of *Paradise Lost*, there was not so much doubt as a horrid certainty. Materialism was winning all along the line. The reign of the saints had ended; Charles II, the Hobbesian monarch, was on the throne. And poetry, which had been sneered at in *The Advancement of Learning* and bludgeoned in *Leviathan*, had not yet learned to accommodate herself to the new world-picture, had not accepted the rôle, which she played so gracefully in the next century, of delighting with agreeable fictions and charming with variety of numbers. The poets, and especially John Milton, still believed in the seriousness of their art, still believed that they could instruct, enlighten, and 'justify the ways of God to men'.

Milton's task was, in effect, the reassertion of certain values which he clearly saw were in danger of being lost in the world of his day. Against the current materialist attitude, of which Hobbes is the prime exponent, he asserts the Christian cosmogony with its insistence on the primacy of spirit and the existence of the soul. He confronts Hobbes' dark picture of man in a state of nature with the idyll of our first parents in Eden. God, who is fading away into a mathematical diagram, is brought back with startling vividness as the Hebrew Creator and governor. And a serious if unsuccessful attempt is made to support free-will against Hobbesian determinism. In this task Milton was equipped with learning and perseverance, with a superb imagination and a still more superb magniloquence. He had behind him, too, the authority of the Scriptures, as yet unimpaired in the popular mind.

I am not suggesting, of course, that Milton's sole object in writing *Paradise Lost* and *Paradise Regained* was to combat seventeenth-century rationalism. He had as well the ambition to become the Homer of his country; to write an English epic which should stand side by side with those of Greece and Rome and be found not inferior to Italian models. Moreover, Milton was himself deeply tinged with the rationalism of his age, as Blake well perceived; and the interest for us in the present study is the conflict between the rational and the prophetic elements in Milton, which Blake equated with the struggle between Jehovah and Satan. Milton did not work out this conflict while on earth, and the theme of Blake's symbolic book *Milton* is the account of his second visit to earth to find 'self-annihilation'. But, all the same, Milton stands with the Cambridge Platonists in protest against the growing materialism of contemporary thought.

The Genesis myth presents us with an extraordinary tangle of symbolism, chaotic enough in Milton's mind and still more confused when reflected through Milton's mind into Blake's. We know that for Blake the original Fall took place in Eternity, and consisted in the usurpation of reason over the passions, the body and the imagination. In the Bible story, and in Milton, it is Satan who engineers the Fall by persuading Eve to eat of the fruit of the Tree of the Knowledge of Good and Evil. Satan, therefore, from Blake's original standpoint, is Urizen. But from Milton's point of view (deeply rooted in the facts of his private life) the Fall consists in the usurpation of 'upstart passions' over reason. Satan thus represents passion or impulse in revolt against reason. The confusion that this produces is shown in the well-known passage from *The Marriage of Heaven and Hell*:

> Those who restrain desire, do so because theirs is weak enough to be restrained; and the restrainer or reason usurps its place & governs the unwilling.
>
> And being restrain'd, it by degrees becomes passive, till it is only the shadow of desire.
>
> The history of this is written in Paradise Lost, & the Governor or Reason is call'd Messiah.
>
> And the original Archangel, or possessor of the command of the heavenly host, is call'd the Devil or Satan, and his children are call'd Sin & Death.

But in the Book of Job, Milton's Messiah is call'd Satan.

For this history has been adopted by both parties.

It indeed appear'd to Reason as if Desire was cast out; but the Devil's account is, that the Messiah fell, & formed a heaven of what he stole from the Abyss.

This is shewn in the Gospel, where he prays to the Father to send the comforter, or Desire, that Reason may have Ideas to build on; the Jehovah of the Bible being no other than he who dwells in flaming fire.

Know that after Christ's death, he became Jehovah.

But in Milton, the Father is Destiny, the Son a Ratio of the five senses, & the Holy-ghost Vacuum!

Note: The reason Milton wrote in fetters when he wrote of Angels & God, and at liberty when of Devils & Hell, is because he was a true Poet and of the Devil's party without knowing it. [*M.H.H.* 191–2]

That Milton was of the devil's party means, in Blake's terminology, that he was, like all true poets, on the side of exuberance, energy and excess. And here Blake lays a critical finger on precisely the contradiction we so often feel in Milton's poetry: a contradiction which may be expressed as the conflict between the Puritan and the man of the Renaissance, or between the imaginative artist with all his love of beauty and the ascetic for whom chastity is the prime virtue. The pathos of all Milton's verse is the result of this tension—pathos which gives an almost unbearable beauty to lines like

> Return Alpheus, the dread voice is past
> Which shrunk thy streams, return Sicilian muse

in which we feel the tenderness of one telling a child that he can come out of his hiding-place, for the bogy-man has gone by. The dichotomy is most apparent in *Comus*, where all Milton's passion for sensuous beauty is in conflict with his convictions that chastity and abstinence are essential for the good life. So great is the sensuous intensity, and so consummate the rhetoric in which this intensity is conveyed in *Comus*, that the reader finds himself altogether on the enchanter's side and against the two brothers. Milton writes in fetters when he supports chastity, at liberty when he celebrates excess.

From his notes on the illustrations to *L'Allegro* and *Il Penseroso*, it is clear that Blake felt the same energy and exuberance in the first of these poems, while in the second he felt Milton's prophetic power.

Under a print illustrating Mirth and her companions, from *L'Allegro*, Blake writes,

> Solomon says, "Vanity of Vanities, all is Vanity", & What can be Foolisher than this? [*M.Pr.* 896]

About the fourth design he writes,

> Mountains, Clouds, Rivers, Trees appear Humanized on the Sunshine Holiday. [*M.Pr.* 894]

and the last design shows how

> The youthful Poet, sleeping on a bank by the Haunted Stream by Sun Set, sees in his dream the more bright Sun of Imagination under the auspices of Shakespeare & Johnson, in which is Hymen at a Marriage & the Antique Pageantry attending it. [*M.Pr.* 895]

In most of these early verses there were things to make Blake believe that Milton was a fellow-spirit. The progress of thought in the *Ode on the Morning of Christ's Nativity* is very much in line with Blake's. He imitates the theme, the mood and the metre of the Hymn in the beginning of *Europe.*

Milton was agreeable to Blake on a number of counts. In the first place, he too was a prophet, a man who felt himself dedicated and marked out to teach divine truth by direct inspiration.[1] In the famous passage from the *Reason of Church Government* Milton states his charter with a contempt for Blake's bugbear Memory which must have delighted the heart of that champion of Imagination: a charter derived

> not by the invocation of Dame Memory and her Siren daughters, but by devout prayer to that eternall Spirit who can enrich with all utterance and knowledge, and sends out his Seraphim with the hallow'd fire of his Altar to touch and purify the lips of whom he pleases.[2]

And he was, like Blake, a prophet of England. The patriotism of the two men is very much alike; not a jingoism, but a mystic conviction

[1] 'Milton, in his old age, sitting in his "mossy cell", contemplating the constellations, surrounded by the spirits of the herbs and flowers, bursts forth into a rapturous prophetic strain.' [*M.P.* 896].

[2] Blake quotes this passage in the margin of his copy of Reynolds' *Discourses.*

that God has and always has had a work for England to do. We might trace much of Blake's belief in the early greatness of Britain, and his opinions on the Druids of Albion, to casual remarks in Milton's prose.[1]

Blake's sense of kinship with Milton, however, goes deeper than this. He recognised two qualities in Milton which were also predominant in himself. The first was energy, manifesting itself as exuberance and sensuality. The second was rebellion.

I have already referred to the love of sensual beauty in *Comus*. It is evident too in the descriptions of Eden in *Paradise Lost*, and in its frankest guise in the picture of conjugal bliss between Adam and Eve.[2] Such passages were of the highest interest and importance to Blake. In face of a social convention and a religious code which forbade the frank acceptance of the body and its delights, Blake could feel himself supported by this great name, the greatest poetic name since Shakespeare. Blake was not deceived by the narrow and life-denying cult of chastity which obtruded itself from time to time in Milton's writings. He knew that such aberrations were the product of the other Milton—not the inspired poet and prophet, but the Milton controlled by Urizen, the Milton who wrote in chains. This chained Milton had been growing within the free Milton who at twenty-two had assured the amorous nightingale that

> Whether the Muse, or Love call thee his mate,
> Both them I serve, and of their train am I.

But Blake could see him clearly, and in *Milton* he repays his debt by disengaging him completely from his fetters.

As for Milton the rebel, he was plain enough for the dullest eye to see. A rebel in politics, in religion and in morals. In politics, he opposed the Hobbesian idea of despotic monarchy; and when he found out how despotic a presbytery could be, he opposed that too.

---

[1] E.g. in the *Doctrine and Discipline of Divorce*, where Milton says that if the Parliament accepts his proposals, 'it would not be the first, or second time, since our ancient Druides, by whom this Iland was the Cathedral of Philosophy to France, left off their pagan rites, that England hath had this honour vouchsaft from Heav'n, to give out reformation to the World.' See, too, *Areopagitica* (Nonesuch Milton, p. 716).

[2] Cf. also the 'thousand raptures between those two lovely ones farre on the hither side of carnall enjoyment' of *Tetrachordon*.

In religion, he was the sworn foe of priestcraft, superstition and ceremony. In morals he attempted a revolution in sexual matters by promulgating ideas both of divorce and of polygamy: in which latter doctrine Blake was wholeheartedly with him. Milton is, indeed, the greatest apostle of liberty, besides Blake, in our literature; and in questions where he has a personal stake in sensual or spiritual liberty he can defend it with all the suasiveness of the humanist:

> He who wisely would restrain the reasonable Soul of man within due bounds, must first know himself perfectly, how far the territory and dominion extends of just and honest liberty. As little must he offer to bind that which God hath loos'n'd, as to loos'n that which he hath bound. The ignorance and mistake of this high point, hath heapt up one huge half of all the misery that hath bin since *Adam*. In the Gospel we shall read a supercilious crew of masters, whose holinesse, or rather whose evil eye, grieving that God should be so facil to man, was to set straiter limits to obedience, then God had set; to inslave the dignity of man, to put a garrison upon his neck of empty and overdignifi'd precepts: And we shall read our Saviour never more greev'd and troubl'd, then to meet with such a peevish madnesse among men against their owne freedome. How can we expect him to be lesse offended with us, when much of the same folly shall be found yet remaining where it lest ought, to the perishing of thousands. The greatest burden in the world is superstition; not only of Ceremonies in the Church, but of imaginary and scarcrow sins at home.[1]

I have quoted the passage at such length to show quite clearly the extraordinary identity of Milton's attitude here with Blake's. No wonder Blake tells us that 'Milton lov'd me in childhood & shew'd me his face'. He was, in fact, the one great poet in English history combining prophetic imagination, sensuality and revolt to whom Blake could appeal as a precedent and feel supported by.

Why, in this case, should Blake have described Milton once to Crabb Robinson 'as being at one time a sort of classical Atheist', and why should he feel the need to write a symbolic work in which Milton could be delivered from mortal error? For a reason which is writ large in the pages of *Paradise Lost*, a poem which influenced Blake more than any writing outside the Bible itself. *Paradise Lost* is the record of Milton's submission to error.

---

[1] *The Doctrine and Discipline of Divorce.* Cf. Ch. xv below, pp. 297–8.

In religion, to begin with, Milton's rebelliousness took the form of an extreme and militant Protestantism. His prose pamphlets are full of virulent abuse of popes, priests and prelates. Now Protestantism consists essentially in following the inner light instead of the light of authority and tradition. It is true that Protestantism bows to the authority of the Bible; but the Bible is to be interpreted by each believer according to his own inner light. ('Both read the Bible day and night, But thou read'st black where I read white.')

Milton's religion cannot be listed in any of the accepted Protestant categories. He was an eclectic, picking a heresy here and a heresy there, adding one or two of his own, and fusing them in the fierce crucible of his mind. But the fusion could not be quite complete; we do not wonder that there are asperities and contradictions. Milton is defending religion in a rationalist age, and his own mind is as 'amphibious' as that of any other seventeenth-century thinker. Constantly, in reading *Paradise Lost*, we are shifting from one plane of understanding to another.

The first great difficulty lies in the Biblical basis of the poem—the Genesis narrative. Whatever construction Milton puts on this story—literal, allegorical, or moral—it has elements which fit in badly with his rooted convictions. One of these convictions is that there is no such thing as true liberty which is untested. Virtue consists in standing the trial of temptation and moral hardship. We remember the noble passage from *Areopagitica*:

I cannot praise a fugitive and cloister'd vertue, unexercis'd and unbreath'd, that never sallies out and sees her adversary, but slinks out of the race, where that immortall garland is to be run for, not without dust and heat. Assuredly we bring not innocence into the world, we bring impurity much rather: that which purifies us is triall, and triall is by what is contrary. That vertue therefore which is but a youngling in the contemplation of evill, and knows not the utmost that vice promises to her followers, and rejects it, is but a blank vertue, not a pure; her whitenesse is but an excrementall whitenesse.[1]

[1] This is nearly, but not quite, Blake's doctrine; and we may think of the *Songs of Innocence and Experience* as his correction of this passage of the *Areopagitica*. We do bring innocence into the world, but it is not the wise innocence of experience mastered. It is the latter which is won by 'what is contrary'.

But *Areopagitica* was published in 1644, *Paradise Lost* in 1667. The one is written in the full glow of anticipation of the reign of the saints. The other is the work of a lonely, blind, disappointed yet indomitable old man.

The liberty and virtue which Adam and Eve possess in Eden are of the fugitive and cloistered kind. And Milton in spite of all his efforts to make his version of the Fall seem a tragedy, cannot help giving the impression that the 'Paradise within thee, happier far' which Michael promises is well bought by the loss of innocence. For this, of course, is what *Paradise Lost*, on one plane, means. In Eden our first parents are children—docile and quite uninteresting children. In such a state no drama, no struggle and no development is possible. They must emerge from the state of innocence into the state of experience. They must know Good and Evil. They must pass through, and in the end combine, 'the two contrary states'. *Paradise Lost* must show the inevitability of this process.

This—and now I speak from Blake's standpoint—is what *Paradise Lost* should have been. But it was not. Milton fell under the domination of his spectre, reason: and this captivity vitiated his whole poem.

We may note, in the first place, that Milton alters the mystical significance of the story by taking all intrinsic importance from the Tree of the Knowledge of Good and Evil. It is not a special tree, he says: that it is so, that it will confer supernatural powers on man, is merely the Serpent's suggestion to entrap Eve. The Tree is a test of obedience and nothing more. Any tree would have done; Jehovah happened to choose this one. The crux of the matter lies not in man's aspiring to a forbidden knowledge, but in his disobedience to an arbitrary command, enforced by a threat.

Here we have Blake's Urizen-Jehovah tyrant plainly declaring himself. Against such a tyrant the first duty is defiance and rebellion. Lucifer, in *Paradise Lost*, does rebel. But does Milton take his side? No: he ranges himself with the forces of oppression and sins against his own understanding. Throughout *Paradise Lost* he supports tyranny, law, cruelty, chastity and 'unorganised innocence'.

What, then, has happened to Milton's Protestant rebelliousness—to his following of the inner light against all authority? We can only think that the inner light has become darkened. And to see how this has come about we must examine afresh the motives which led Milton to write *Paradise Lost*.

The first motive, as already mentioned, is the desire to produce the great English epic poem. The second is to give expression to philosophic and religious ideas. The third is to set forth certain highly personal ideas about society, his own miserable state, and especially his low opinion of woman. And on this last consideration, as Blake saw with unerring insight, the tone of all the rest depends.

There is no need to go over the sad story of Milton's marital misfortunes. Whatever comfort he may have found in his second and third wives, there is no doubt that his first matrimonial failure affected him deeply. He had wanted a wife; he got one, and she turned out to be no mate for him. His spirit rebels against the chains with which he has bound himself; he agitates for a change in the laws of England, first for divorce, and then for polygamy. He gets neither; and, unable to throw off his chains, he looks into his own mind, he ponders the causes of his great disappointment, and he sees in his giving liberty to his sensual desires the cause of his misfortune. The cult of chastity which he has always practised will not allow him the satisfaction of promiscuous pleasure. Therefore Milton turns on pleasure itself, upon the sensual principle in his own make-up, and by a monstrous inversion constitutes it the author of his fall. Woman, woman with her devilish charms is the root of all evil.

Milton, thus, hands over the reins to reason. In *Paradise Lost* it is reason, 'the restrainer', who governs or should govern the Universe; so long as reason is followed all things subsist in a perfect order. Lucifer is the first to revolt; a very different revolt from that of Urizen against the infinite diversity in unity of the Eternal Man. For here, in Milton's version, Satan is the imaginative, romantic spirit, defying authority and rigid law—is, in fact, the fiery Orc. But Milton has subdued the long conflict in himself between reason and passion by giving the sovereignty to reason, his spectre, just as Albion does in *The Four Zoas*. That he has not subdued the conflict as completely as he thinks was pointed out by Blake in *The Marriage of Heaven and Hell*. Milton's Satan is not only rebellious: he is also, at least in the earlier books, generous and magnanimous, a lover of music and art. The building of Pandemonium, with its 'dulcet symphonies' and 'golden architrave', is a foreshadowing of Golgonooza; and what evil can there be in spirits that

> move
> In perfect *Phalanx* to the *Dorian* mood
> Of Flutes and soft Recorders?

The picture, on the other hand, which Milton gives of the Almighty, a crafty, smiling but insecure despot, surrounded by His golden lamps,[1] has all the characteristics of Blake's Urizen:

> Mean while th' Eternal eye, whose sight discernes
> Abstrusest thoughts, from forth his holy Mount
> And from within the golden Lamps that burne
> Nightly before him, saw without thir light
> Rebellion rising, saw in whom, how spred
> Among the sons of Morn, what multitudes
> Were banded to oppose his high Decree;
> And smiling to his onely Son thus said.

The Son, we note from the ensuing speech, is merely the reflection of the Father's glory and the instrument of His creative and punitory power. Milton will not admit the Second Person of the Trinity to equality with the First; and the Holy Ghost, as Blake perceived, is a 'Vacuum'. In *Paradise Lost* Milton has forsaken his old Platonism; combating rationalism, he 'becomes what he beholds', caught in the toils of Nature; not only are the angels rarefied forms of matter, but God Himself, out of whose substance the universe is made (and not out of nothing, as orthodoxy says[2]), must be of a material substance.

Let us turn, finally, to Milton's account of the Fall, the critical point of the epic. This is the theme of the Ninth Book, but already in Book VIII Adam, in discourse with Raphael, prepares our minds for the event. The beginning of the Eighth Book contains an anti-astronomical tirade from Raphael, in answer to Adam's request for an explanation of the how and why of the starry heavens. Raphael replies that Man is not here on earth to occupy his mind with such useless questions. It does not matter whether the earth moves round the sun or the sun round the earth; these facts

[1] Cf. 'In the Brain of Man we live & in his circling Nerves. . . Where Urizen & all his Hosts hang their immortal lamps.' [*F.Z.* 290]

[2] In this point too Blake follows Milton.

From Man or Angel the great Architect
Did wisely to conceal, and not divulge
His secrets to be scann'd by them who ought
Rather admire; or if they list to try
Conjecture, he his Fabric of the Heav'ns
Hath left to thir disputes, *perhaps to move*
His laughter at thir quaint Opinions wide[1]
Hereafter, when they come to model Heav'n
And calculate the Starrs, how they will weild
The mightie frame, how build, unbuild, contrive
To save appeerances, how gird the Sphear
With Centric and Eccentric scribl'd o're,
Cycle and Epicycle, Orb in Orb.[2]

The earth, Raphael continues, may be smaller than the sun, but it is not therefore less important. On the contrary, the earth is nobler, for it contains Man, the highest of all God's works; and it is for Man, and not for the material globe, that these heavenly bodies describe their complicated motions and exert their precious influences.[3]

It is now Adam's turn to speak. He gives Raphael an account of the creation of Eve, and speaks glowingly of her charms. Moved to thank God for this crowning blessing, he is yet not quite at ease. He knows he is a being whose supreme attribute is *reason*, and he wonders how it is that he can be moved so powerfully and so irrationally. The beauty of trees and flowers and the song of birds delight him too, but not like this—

but here
Farr otherwise, transported I behold,
Transported touch; here passion first I felt,
Commotion strange, in all enjoyments else
Superiour and unmov'd, here onely weake
Against the charm of Beauties powerful glance.

[1] My italics. A simple sense of humour is one of the more engaging characteristics of Milton's Deity.

[2] It is interesting to remember that in the years 1665–6, when *Paradise Lost* was being completed, a young scholar of Trinity was beginning a series of mathematical and astronomical studies which were to revolutionise the world picture. 'At such time', he tells us, 'I found the method of Infinite Series; and in summer 1665, being forced from Cambridge by the plague, I computed the area of the hyperbola at Boothby, in Lincolnshire....' And a year later (Dryden's 'Annus Mirabilis') he discovered the law of gravitation.

[3] All this, of course, would delight Blake. See below, Ch. XII.

Uxorious but bewildered, Adam wonders if Nature has failed in him, or perhaps 'more than enough' was taken from his side to fashion Eve; but Raphael replies 'with contracted brow' that Adam is not to accuse Nature. He must show his wisdom: he plainly perceives Eve to be inferior; let him then exercise due authority. The sense of touch is not such a 'dear delight' as Adam makes it out to be, for it is common to beasts as well as to men. True love has its seat in the reason and points the way to the love of God. Here we see Milton returning for a moment to his Platonism.

The stages of the Fall itself amply bear out Adam's view of the inferiority of woman. Eve's nature is predominantly sensual; ordinary hunger plays its part in inducing her to eat the fruit, and when she does so she 'ingorges greedily without restraint'. Her motives too in persuading Adam to share her crime are base: after all she may have to die for her sin, and in that case Adam had better die too:

> but what if God have seen,
> And Death ensue? then I shall be no more,
> And *Adam* wedded to another *Eve*,
> Shall live with her enjoying, I extinct;
> A death to think.

Milton here puts Eve in a very bad light. Adam's fall is nobler: he cannot bear to think of living without Eve, even if God does give him another consort. So he eats also:

> he scrupl'd not to eat
> Against his better knowledge, not deceav'd,
> But fondly overcome with Femal charm.

Adam, then, sins against his own reason; and once having done so, he becomes a prey to his passions. The first result of the Fall is lust; they weary themselves with 'amorous play' on a 'shady bank'; they sleep, and when they awake all is changed; they reproach each other, they quarrel,

> For Understanding rul'd not, and the Will
> Heard not her lore, both in subjection now
> To sensual Appetite, who from beneathe
> Usurping over sovran Reason claimd
> Superior sway.

Thus, for Milton, the Fall is the usurpation of the passions over reason, the precise contrary of Blake's view;[1] and woman is the instrument of destruction. And the result of the Fall is loss of liberty, as Michael tells the guilty pair before he ejects them from Paradise:

> yet know withall,
> Since thy original lapse, true Libertie
> Is lost, which alwayes with right Reason dwells
> Twinn'd, and from her hath no dividual being.

Such, in brief outline, are the aspects of Milton's mind and genius which would strike Blake most. He recognised in Milton the greatest of poets, and I have pointed out why he should; but he also saw in Milton the arch-promulgator of pernicious errors. Blake's symbolic works may be regarded as a rewriting of Milton's epics with an inversion, or subtle elaboration, of the rôles of passion and reason, and with a deeper meaning given to Christ and the Holy Ghost. Milton's Fall takes place in time, but for Blake

> The Sin was begun in Eternity and will not rest to Eternity
> Till two Eternitys meet together,

as he tells us in *Milton.*

Milton, a Poem in 2 Books (though more were probably intended) bears the motto from *Paradise Lost* 'To Justify the Ways of God to Men'. It was composed in part at Felpham and finished in London in 1808. There are only four copies, etched and coloured by Blake, in existence. The Preface, a first part in prose and a second in verse, carries on the themes of the *Descriptive Catalogue* and the *Vision of the Last Judgment.* In the prose part Blake condemns 'the Stolen and Perverted Writings of Homer & Ovid, of Plato & Cicero', and contrasts them with the inspired strains of the Bible. It is noticeable that *Milton* contains far more direct Biblical allusion than we find in *The Four Zoas.* The Bible is the only Sublime. 'Shakespeare & Milton were both curb'd by the general malady & infection from the silly Greek & Latin slaves of the Sword.' And this infection of rationalism continues. Blake calls upon the 'Young Men of the New Age' to revolt and oppose the false doctrines which are taught in

[1] At any rate, in the earlier and clearer form of the myth.

'the Camp, the Court & the University'; he implores the artists and sculptors to be true to their own imaginations, 'those Worlds of Eternity in which we shall live for ever in JESUS OUR LORD'. Then follows the famous poem, 'And did those feet in ancient time Walk upon England's mountains green?'—a supreme expression of Blake's determination to go on thinking and writing for his country's good. "Would to God that all the Lord's people were Prophets", Moses' cry from the Book of Numbers, are the concluding words of the Preface.

'...now no longer divided nor at war with myself...', Blake had written to Hayley in 1804, at the time he was making a final revision of *Milton.* This inner unity becomes apparent in the poem. It is more controlled; it has structure; it is free from the 'torments of jealousy' which gave rise to such wild and violent imagery in the earlier epic. The imagery of *Milton*, indeed, is drawn to a surprising degree from the world of nature; observed, it is true, not with but through the eye, yet observed in its minutest particulars. It might almost be called the epic of Nature, seen *sub specie æternitatis.* For it was Nature that Milton rejected, when he rejected his sixfold emanation, his three wives and three daughters, and the redemption of Nature is a corollary of Milton's self-annihilation. Hence the sheer joy in the life of flowers, birds and insects which runs through the poem. We see that Blake had used his three years in the country to good purpose, that his eyes and ears have been alert to every natural sight and sound.

Structurally, the poem consists of a redemption narrative interspersed with long passages of mystical teaching. The narrative is about Milton, who while on earth (as we have seen) had held wrong views of sex and nature, and was unkind to his womenfolk, but has repented of his error during the hundred years he has spent in heaven, and is anxious to atone for it. He is separated from his sixfold emanation, who wanders in the abyss in torment. Now at last he casts off his spectrous reason, the power which has dominated him hitherto—and descends again into the world of vegetation to redeem his emanation.

We note at the very beginning that this is to be a milder book than either *The Four Zoas* or *Jerusalem.* Blake invokes as his Muses the 'Daughters of Beulah', the softly feminine principle which in

Eden serves as a repose for the warriors wearied with their intellectual combats, and which in earthly existence is marriage itself. But in *Jerusalem* it will be the Saviour, the Divine Vision, who is invoked, and who dictates the very words of the song. There is a profound difference of emphasis. The action of *Milton*, important as it is, is secondary to the supreme theme of man's resurrection into unity.

'Come into my hand', so Blake calls to the Daughters of Beulah, the emanations of Eternity,

> By your mild power descending down the Nerves of my right arm
> From out the portals of my Brain, where by your ministry
> The Eternal Great Humanity Divine planted his Paradise
> And in it caus'd the Spectres of the Dead to take sweet forms
> In likeness of himself.... [*M.* 465]

'By your ministry....' Blake, now no longer divided, can look on sexual generation as a good, a *beatum peccatum*, as indeed it is in comparison with the nothingness man might have suffered after the Fall. It is Milton's error not to have recognised this. 'O blessed Generation, image of Regeneration', Blake cries later. In his poetry he has accepted Nature, though in his prose he may still think it necessary to be explicit against the material creation.

Then we have the theme stated:

> Say first! what mov'd Milton, who walk'd about in Eternity
> One hundred years, pond'ring the intricate mazes of Providence,
> Unhappy tho' in heav'n—he obey'd, he murmur'd not, he was silent
> Viewing his Sixfold Emanation scatter'd thro' the deep
> In torment—To go into the deep her to redeem & himself perish?
> That cause at length mov'd Milton to this unexampled deed,
> A Bard's prophetic Song! [*M.* 466]

The Bard, who may in fact be identified with Blake, sings the familiar story of the Fall, the Incarnation of Urizen and the Division of Los, as we have read it in *The Book of Urizen* and *The Four Zoas*:

> ...when Albion was slain upon his Mountains
> And in his Tent, thro' envy of the Living Form, even of the Divine Vision,
> And of the sports of Wisdom in the Human Imagination,
> Which is the Divine Body of the Lord Jesus, blessed for ever. [*M.* 466]

There follows the equally familiar story of the building of Golgonooza and the birth of Satan. The song continues with the account of a quarrel between Satan and Palamabron, in which Blake introduces in symbolic dress the history of his contests with Hayley during the Felpham period. Hayley's sneaking dislike is suggested:

> "If you account it Wisdom when you are angry to be silent and
> Not to shew it, I do not account that Wisdom, but Folly...."
>
> Mean while wept Satan before Los accusing Palamabron
> Himself exculpating with mildest speech,... [M. 468, 475]

We are shown the three Classes of Men: the Elect, who are obdurate in their selfhoods; the Redeemed, who turn to the Divine Vision; and the Reprobate, who never cease to believe. Hayley, here seen as Satan, belongs to the first class; Blake, as Palamabron, to the second. By the arts of mildness and cunning Satan persuades Los to give him Palamabron's horses of inspiration—in concrete terms, Hayley persuades Blake to prostitute his genius to worthless activity, such as painting miniatures for the Sussex gentry. The result is catastrophic, and a large part of the First Book is taken up with the consequences of this personal quarrel, interpreted in symbolic terms. Satan invents the seven deadly sins, and falls into Ulro. He calls himself God, and erects his mills for the enslavement of humanity.

The further details of the Bard's song are either too personal, or too repetitive of the action of *The Four Zoas*, to need setting forth here. When the song has ended,

> there was great murmuring in the Heavens of Albion
> Concerning Generation & the Vegetative power & concerning
> The Lamb the Saviour. [M. 487–8]

Then Milton rises in the midst of the assembly, and avows his resolution to return to earth:

> He took off the robe of the promise & ungirded himself from the oath of God.
> And Milton said: "I go to Eternal Death! The Nations still
> Follow after the detestable Gods of Priam, in pomp
> Of warlike selfhood contradicting and blaspheming.
> When will the Resurrection come to deliver the sleeping body
> From corruptibility? O when, Lord Jesus, wilt thou come?
> Tarry no longer, for my soul lies at the gates of death.
> I will arise and look forth for the morning of the grave:

I will go down to the sepulcher to see if morning breaks:
I will go down to self annihilation and eternal death,
Lest the Last Judgment come & find me unannihilate
And I be siez'd & giv'n into the hands of my Selfhood." [*M.* 488]

He accuses himself of sin in having deserted his emanation: in his selfhood he is precisely that Satan described by the Bard. Then he plunges into the Abyss.

On the verge of Beulah he enters his Shadow, and goes onward into the world of generation. First he sees Albion outstretched on the Rock of Ages, with the Sea of Time and Space rolling over him. Then, says Blake,

Then first I saw him in the Zenith as a falling star
Descending perpendicular, swift as the swallow or swift:
And on my left foot falling on the tarsus, enter'd there:
But from my left foot a black cloud redounding spread over Europe.
[*M.* 491]

The left foot is a symbol of the material world. Milton proceeds on his way through the recesses of the Mundane Shell towards Los and Enitharmon. The Shadowy Female (Vala) laments, and Urizen emerges 'from his Rocky Form & from his Snows' to bar Milton's passage. They fight, and Urizen tries to freeze Milton's brain with the icy waters of reason,

But Milton took of the red clay of Succoth, moulding it with care
Between his palms and filling up the furrows of many years,
Beginning at the feet of Urizen, and on the bones
Creating new flesh on the Demon cold.... [*M.* 495–6]

Against his will, reason is being endued with the warm flesh and blood of humanity. This 'moulding' is the eternal task of the poet, the maker. Moreover, in descending to redeem his sexual portion, Milton also redeems his spectre, and creates the whole man which he had never been before.

Now Rahab and Tirzah—moral virtue and Natural Religion—enter the lists against Milton: they mock at Jerusalem and the Lamb of God; but Milton pays no attention. He goes on with his work on Urizen. And Albion begins to turn on his couch,

Feeling the electric flame of Milton's awful precipitate descent. [*M.* 498]

Los, remembering an ancient prophecy that Milton would descend, goes in search of him.

When Milton enters Blake's left foot, Blake is enabled to 'see into the life of things', to have a new vision of the universe. He now becomes one man with Los,

> And all this Vegetable World appear'd on my left Foot
> As a bright sandal form'd immortal of precious stones & gold.
> I stooped down & bound it on to walk forward thro' Eternity.
>
> [*M.* 500]

Los reveals to Blake the glorious secret that not one moment of time is lost, 'nor one Event of Space unpermanent'. He greets the coming of Milton as the sign that six thousand years are passed away and the end is approaching. A vision of the great winepress follows, as we have seen it in the earlier epic, though with certain elaborations. And Los orders the human corn to be bound in the three classes described by the Bard. The First Book ends with an exposition of Blake's view on the nature of time and space.[1]

Book the Second opens in Beulah, 'a place where Contrarieties are equally True'. Beulah is a feminine world, as we have already seen, built around Great Eternity by the mercy of God: a world where the Emanations, who cannot bear the too terrible joy and sports of intellect, find refuge, and where Man also may repose awhile from his mental activities. Here dwells Ololon, who appears to be identified with Milton's sixfold emanation, though in an earlier text we have seen it stated that Milton's emanation is wandering solitary through the void. She prepares to descend, as Milton had done, into generation; and 'all the Living Creatures of the Four Elements' wail. These living creatures are the Zoas, who have partaken of mortality, and preach a materialistic doctrine which in the succeeding paragraph of the epic is opposed by a spiritual doctrine of creation. This opposition of the two views of Nature is a principal theme of *Milton*. Missing out the interpolated sheet 35, we come to the charge of the Divine Voice to Vala or Nature, stressing the truth that natural beauty was first formed to be a refreshment to the spirit of fallen Man, but has hardened into a system opaque to the Divine Vision.

---

[1] See below, Ch. XII.

Ololon now descends from Beulah,

> A long journey & dark thro' Chaos in the track of Milton's course, [*M.* 531]

and enters the Mundane Shell, surrounded by the four ruined universes of Urizen, Los, Tharmas and Luvah. She contrasts the state of physical war in the generative world with the spiritual combats of Eternity, and bewails the frozen bulk of Nature:

> "How are the Wars of Man, which in Great Eternity
> Appear around in the External Spheres of Visionary Life,
> Here render'd Deadly within the Life & Interior Vision?
> How are the Beasts & Birds & Fishes & Plants & Minerals
> Here fix'd into a frozen bulk subject to decay & death?
> Those Visions of Human Life & Shadows of Wisdom & Knowledge
>
> Are here frozen to unexpansive deadly destroying terrors,
> And War & Hunting, the Two Fountains of the River of Life,
> Are become Fountains of bitter Death & of corroding Hell. . . ."
> [*M.* 533–4]

Having entered the Polypus, or Ulro, Ololon appears as 'a Virgin of twelve years' before Blake in his cottage garden at Felpham, whither he has been taken by Los from Lambeth in order to write this account of eternal happenings. Ololon tells Blake that she has come to seek Milton. Milton's Spectre, i.e. his false rational power which he has now cast off but which is still active, hears this and appears, too, before Blake. In the form of this Spectre he sees all the false gods and churches of the world.

Now, however, because Milton has separated himself from his Spectre, the process of self-annihilation can begin. Milton addresses his Spectre thus:

> "Satan! my Spectre! I know my power thee to annihilate
> And be a greater in thy place & be thy Tabernacle,
> A covering for thee to do thy will, till one greater comes
> And smites me as I smote thee & becomes my covering.
> Such are the Laws of thy false Heav'ns; but Laws of Eternity
> Are not such; know thou, I come to Self Annihilation." [*M.* 541]

Blake, we see, is continuing with his purpose of rewriting *Paradise Lost*, of rectifying Milton's error. Just as in Book I he has shown that Satan fell, not from pride and ambition as Milton had said, but from hypocrisy, moral judgement and officious kindness, so now he is demonstrating that the laws of Eternity do not demand Satan's punishment and relegation to the pit, but watch over him and protect him until the time comes for him to be delivered. Milton continues:

> "Such are the Laws of Eternity, that each shall mutually
> Annihilate himself for others' good, as I for thee.
> Thy purpose & the purpose of thy Priests & of thy Churches
> Is to impress on men the fear of death, to teach
> Trembling & fear, terror, constriction, abject selfishness.
> Mine is to teach Men to despise death & to go on
> In fearless majesty annihilating Self, laughing to scorn
> Thy Laws & terrors, shaking down thy Synagogues as webs.
> I come to discover before Heav'n & Hell the Self righteousness
> In all its Hypocritic turpitude, opening to every eye
> These wonders of Satan's holiness, shewing to the Earth
> The Idol Virtues of the Natural Heart, & Satan's Seat
> Explore in all its Selfish Natural Virtue, & put off
> In self annihilation all that is not of God alone,
> To put off Self & all I have, ever & ever. Amen." [*M.* 541–2]

Satan defies Milton, asserting that he is God alone, opposed to Mercy and Jesus the Divine Delusion. But at this point the Trumpets of the Last Judgement sound, calling Albion to awake; he does so, and attempts to walk, but is not strong enough and has to sink down again upon his couch. For *Milton* is not the record of the universal Last Judgement, but only of a particular one, that of Milton and through Milton of Blake himself.

Next we have the meeting of Milton and Ololon. Ololon cannot yet completely understand Milton's self-annihilation: she is afraid that in its course the 'little ones, the Children of Jerusalem' (i.e. the minute particulars of human life) will be destroyed also. But Milton rebukes her and gives a clear exposition of doctrine:

> turning toward Ololon in terrible majesty Milton
> Replied: "Obey thou the Words of the Inspired Man.
> All that can be annihilated must be annihilated
> That the Children of Jerusalem may be saved from slavery.
> There is a Negation, & there is a Contrary:
> The Negation must be destroy'd to redeem the Contraries.

> The Negation is the Spectre, the Reasoning Power in Man:
> This is a false Body, an Incrustation over my Immortal
> Spirit, a Selfhood which must be put off & annihilated alway."
>
> [*M.* 545–6]

This statement is important and we must look more closely at its meaning. Ololon, we remember, is the emanation: that is, in each individual she is the feminine portion, representing the softer emotions and sentiments and particularly the instinct of self-preservation. She is that part of a man which fears that he will, in seeking for God alone, throw away all his human happiness and be left 'naked to laughter'. It is this shrinking fear which holds back many a man from the unitive life. But Milton teaches her that this fear is without foundation: only that which is annihilable can be annihilated, and what is annihilable is no part of reality. It is the outer covering or mask, the false shell which each man builds up around himself with the passing of years—the shell which hides his true nature even from himself, but to which, nevertheless, he clings with trembling fear. It is only when this shell has been sloughed off, this mask discarded, that the true joy can spring, the joy of being what one really is. Only then can the Children of Jerusalem, the minute particulars of Man's real identity, be redeemed from slavery. Ololon is confounding the negation with the contrary. The negation is the Spectre, the cold uncreative reason; the contraries are the ultimate paradoxes of a man's being, which ensure the springs of his energy. The selfhood, Blake is never tired of insisting, is a nothingness: yet it is to this nothingness that we sacrifice, perpetually, our happiness.

The poem ends with a vision of the Saviour coming, 'round his limbs The Clouds of Ololon folded as a Garment dipped in blood'; the Four Zoas sound their trumpets, and at this Blake's soul leaves its union with Milton and

> return'd into its mortal state
> To Resurrection & Judgment in the Vegetable Body,
> And my sweet Shadow of Delight stood trembling by my side.
>
> [*M.* 548]

All things are now ready for 'the Great Harvest & Vintage of the Nations'.

The years which followed the engraving of *Milton* are called 'years of deepening neglect' in Gilchrist's *Life*. This is not overstating the case or darkening the picture. Through his quarrel with Cromek and Stothard, and his girds at contemporary engravers in the *Descriptive Catalogue*, Blake had gone far to put himself out of the market. Joseph Johnson the publisher, who had always helped Blake as much as he could, died in 1809; and Hayley drops out of his life around this time too. George Cumberland continued faithful, and in 1818 introduced Blake to John Linnell, who, says Gilchrist, 'was to become the kindest friend and stay of the neglected man's declining years, and afterwards to be famous as one of our great landscape painters'.

The *Descriptive Catalogue* of 1809 was, as I have already suggested, Blake's last challenge to the world. When it became obvious that the society of his own day would regard him only as mountebank or madman, he accepted neglect and poverty. The minor lyrics of this time are eloquent of his mood:

> The Angel that presided o'er my birth
> Said, "Little creature, form'd of Joy & Mirth,
> Go love without the help of any Thing on Earth".
>
> [*M.P.* 124]

And again

> Since all the Riches of this World
> May be gifts from the Devil & Earthly Kings,
> I should suspect that I worship'd the Devil
> If I thank'd my God for Worldly things. [*M.P.* 126]

His declining years, until he met Linnell and his group, were lonely. Southey visited him and had no doubt he was insane. He had been shown something of *Jerusalem*, which he considered 'a perfectly mad poem'. In 1812 Blake exhibited his *Canterbury Pilgrims*, *Pitt* and *Nelson* at the Associated Artists in Water Colour Exhibition, but by 1817 he had so far disappeared from public view that William Paulet Carey writes: 'I never had the good fortune to see him; and so entire is the uncertainty, in which he is involved, that after many enquiries, I meet with some in doubt whether he is still in existence....' Meanwhile Blake managed to keep himself and Catherine alive, though little more, by engraving. He never lost confidence in his own abilities. 'I still go on', he writes in a lyric of this period,

> I still go on
> Till the Heavens & Earth are gone,
> Still admir'd by Noble minds,
> Follow'd by Envy on the winds,
> Re-engrav'd Time after Time,
> Ever in their youthful prime,
> My designs unchang'd remain.
> Time may rage but rage in vain.
> For above Time's troubled Fountains
> On the Great Atlantic Mountains,
> In my Golden House on high,
> There they Shine Eternally. [*M.P.* 127]

And quite undaunted he continued working at *Jerusalem.*

CHAPTER IX

'*Jerusalem*'

The Imaginative Image returns by the seed of
Contemplative Thought. [*V.L.J.* 829]

MOST of Blake's commentators assert their preference for *Milton* over *Jerusalem*. This is natural enough. *Milton* is simpler, crisper, and contains a large proportion of easily quotable verse dealing with Nature. *Jerusalem, The Emanation of the Giant Albion*, takes up once more, and for the last time, the theme of *The Four Zoas*; and develops it to a further degree of complexity. But there is this difference. *The Four Zoas* was not only complex: it was also confused. It was not a unity. *Jerusalem*, through all its windings, is a unity and we feel it as such. Blake rightly calls it in his prefatory *To the Public* 'this more consolidated and extended work'. 'Consolidation' is its great merit over the earlier poem.

The reason for this is not far to seek. The unity of the book lies in the unity of the hero. In *The Four Zoas* Blake's hesitations are obvious in the changes he made in the title. First he called the poem *Vala*; but the 'shadowy female' is far too indistinct to be a heroine. Then the Four Zoas were selected, and as an afterthought Albion was put into the sub-title; but the Zoas are only the servants of Man, and Man himself has fallen into the sleep of death. In *Milton*, on the other hand, a real person is chosen to be the hero of the poem, and by his union with Blake and with Los energy is given to the narrative. Now, in *Jerusalem*, he has found the greatest hero of all: not Jerusalem herself, who must continue to act the Andromeda part, but Jesus, the immortal Perseus of the narrative. In a later chapter I trace the growth of the figure of Jesus in Blake's mind. Here, it is sufficient to point out that *Jerusalem* is saturated with Christian doctrine, that the references to the New Testament are many and significant, and that regeneration has become identified with union with Christ. Jesus is at once the hero, the inspirer and fashioner, and the goal of the narrative. Albion has been quite cast out of his rôle as protagonist and has become identified in many respects with Urizen. His is the sin, his the responsibility for the revolt of the Zoas. We may regard *Jerusalem* as an extended commentary on the Pauline saying, 'As in Adam [Albion] all died, even so in Christ shall all be made alive'.

The Preface contains an immediate reference to oneness with Christ. After hoping 'that this more consolidated & extended Work will be as kindly recieved' as his former poems, Blake goes on:

> I also hope the Reader will be with me, wholly One in Jesus our Lord, who is the God of Fire and Lord of Love to whom the Ancients look'd and saw his day afar off, with trembling & amazement. [*J*. 550]

Blake's purpose now is to attempt a reinterpretation of Christian doctrine within the framework of his individual myth. But Christian doctrine means to Blake one thing above all others, and that is 'Forgiveness of Sins'. He continues, therefore:

> The Spirit of Jesus is continual forgiveness of Sin: he who waits to be righteous before he enters into the Saviour's kingdom, the Divine Body, will never enter there. I am perhaps the most sinful of men. I pretend not to holiness: yet I pretend to love, to see, to converse with daily as man with man, & the more to have an interest in the Friend of Sinners.

And here, obviously, we come to the idea of *self-forgiveness*. A man has to 'forgive himself the lot' before he can enter the Kingdom of Heaven. His misery, or hell, is caused by his remorse and self-laceration: the 'hope that is unwilling to be fed'. Hence Albion himself becomes the murderer; hence his fall is shown as a deliberate turning away down the valleys dark; hence too his regeneration is an escape from illusion into reality—'All was a Vision, all a Dream'. *Jerusalem* drops the theme of jealousy and pride to take up the psychologically much more subtle theme of self-tormenting.

In *Jerusalem*, again, Los is consistently in the right, and not shifting from good to bad as in *The Four Zoas*. Being identified with Christ ('the God of Fire') he is shown giving himself for Albion: he could live in Eternity if he wished, but he renounces this felicity and through love remains in the world of generation. Yet, even while in the world of generation, he does not fall into error.

After the uncompromising motto, Μόνος ὁ Ἰησοῦς, the poem starts in Miltonic fashion with a statement of the theme:

> Of the Sleep of Ulro! and of the passage through
> Eternal Death! and of the awaking to Eternal Life.
>
> This theme calls me in sleep night after night, & ev'ry morn
> Awakes me at sun-rise; then I see the Saviour over me
> Spreading his beams of love & dictating the words of this mild song.
> [*J.* 551–2]

Now Jesus Himself is the inspirer of the poem, and actually dictates the words which Blake writes. And a little later Blake states in no uncertain terms the splendid purpose of his writing:

> I rest not from my great task!
> To open the Eternal Worlds, to open the immortal Eyes
> Of Man inwards into the Worlds of Thought, into Eternity
> Ever expanding in the Bosom of God, the Human Imagination.
> O Saviour pour upon me thy Spirit of meekness & love!
> Annihilate the Selfhood in me: be thou all my life! [*J.* 554]

The Divine Voice calls on Albion to awake and 'expand'. 'But the perturbed Man away turns down the valleys dark.' The myth is being picked up from *Night the Seventh* (*a*) of *The Four Zoas*, in which the Shadow of Enitharmon gives the version of the Fall which shows Albion as wandering in the land of Beulah, making love to Vala and begetting Urizen. He forgets Eternity, and Urizen takes over the sceptre. Now we have the continuation of that myth. We are still in the framework of the Fall.

Albion rejects the Saviour as a delusion; he asserts that Man can live only by demonstration, and not by faith. His sin is selfishness, the refusal to share in the contrapuntal delights of Eternity, and from this refusal laws of moral virtue take their rise. There follows a picture of the divided universe: 'Cambridge & Oxford & London', obvious symbols of the intellect, are 'driven among the starry Wheels'—deluded, that is, with the philosophy of Newton and Locke. There is war over the whole earth, and the danger is that the sleeping Humanity may be destroyed thereby. The Starry Wheels drag Jerusalem (the minute particulars) eastwards into Non-Entity, and the cares of the Daughters of Beulah for Albion are in vain because of abstract philosophy.

Los, who is now permanently divided from Enitharmon, has a long argument with his Spectre. The Spectre tries to persuade him to look to his own welfare and not trouble any more about Albion. But Los is steadfast: he reproaches the Spectre and prophesies Albion's regeneration. Finally he compels his Spectre (the naked reason) to help him at his work in the furnaces, in the building of Golgonooza. This is described in great detail, together with the 'land of death eternal' or Ulro, and the Vegetative Universe:

> The Vegetative Universe opens like a flower from the Earth's center
> In which is Eternity. It expands in Stars to the Mundane Shell
> And there it meets Eternity again, both within and without,
> And the abstract Voids between the Stars are the Satanic Wheels.
>
> [*J.* 571]

From Golgonooza Los looks out and beholds all the chaos of the stricken universe. His city of art, which is also a citadel of forgiveness where the rhythm of Eternity may be made real and preserved in this world, is the vantage-point from which he can observe and act. He sees all the different forms of error ('the Cave, the Rock, the Tree, the Lake of Udan Adan'), and the symbols of spiritual forces ('the Cherub at the Tree of Life, also the Serpent Orc, the first-born, coil'd in the south, the Dragon Urizen, Tharmas the Vegetated Tongue').

It is significant that Orc, the force of violent revolution on which Blake relied so much in his earlier work, is now permanently *fallen* as the Serpent Orc; and that Urizen is exhibited in the form of permanent error as the Dragon.

Then comes a personal interpolation from Blake:

> I see the Four-fold Man, The Humanity in deadly sleep
> And its fallen Emanation, The Spectre & its cruel Shadow.
> I see the Past, Present & Future existing all at once
> Before me. O Divine Spirit, sustain me on thy wings,
> That I may awake Albion from his long & cold repose. [*J.* 574]

This long and cold repose is the work of Bacon, Newton and Locke, we are told once more, and it is against these that Los is working in his furnaces. But the Sons of Albion (the rationalists) meet to condemn Jerusalem (spiritual freedom) and proclaim their allegiance to Vala, the goddess Nature.

Now we pass back to a glimpse of Albion (Blake's technique often reminds us of that of the screen):

> Outstretch'd his Giant beauty on the ground in pain & tears:
> His Children exil'd from his breast pass to and fro before him,
> His birds are silent on his hills, flocks die beneath his branches,
> His tents are fall'n; his trumpets and the sweet sound of his harp
> Are silent on his clouded hills that belch forth storms & fire. [*J.* 583]

Jerusalem and Vala (who are reconciled in this part of the poem, and only separated in the foolish thoughts of the rationalists) discuss sin and love and forgiveness. Albion is obsessed by the idea of sin and wishes for annihilation. He rejects Jerusalem as sin, and invites Vala to kill him and drain his blood 'to the last drop', for he believes he has slain Luvah and therefore deserves punishment. But Jerusalem points out how contrary all this is to the law of Eternity:

> "Why should Punishment Weave the Veil with Iron Wheels of War
> When Forgiveness might it Weave with Wings of Cherubim?"
>
> [*J.* 591]

Albion is moved by Jerusalem's words, and he tries to escape the consequences of his error; but he is still too weak, and he sinks down 'between the Palm Tree & the Oak of weeping', as in *The Four Zoas*.

The theme of forgiveness is urged once more in the lamentation of the Daughters of Beulah with which the first chapter ends.

> "Why did you take Vengeance, O ye Sons of the mighty Albion,
> Planting these Oaken Groves, Erecting these Dragon Temples?
> Injury the Lord heals, but Vengeance cannot be healed.
> As the Sons of Albion have done to Luvah, so they have in him
> Done to the Divine Lord & Saviour, who suffers with those that suffer;
> For not one sparrow can suffer & the whole Universe not suffer also
> In all its Regions, & its Father & Saviour not pity and weep.
> But Vengeance is the destroyer of Grace & Repentance in the bosom
> Of the Injurer, in which the Divine Lamb is cruelly slain.
> Descend, O Lamb of God, & take away the imputation of Sin
> By the Creation of States & the deliverance of Individuals Evermore.
> Amen." [*J.* 596]

The Preface to Chapter Two is dedicated *To the Jews*. It claims that 'Britain is the Primitive Seat of the Patriarchal Religion', and that all the nations of the earth are united 'in One Religion, The

Religion of Jesus, the most Ancient, the Eternal & the Everlasting Gospel'. Abraham and Noah were Druids, whose parent was Albion; '& in his Chaotic State of Sleep, Satan & Adam & the whole World was Created by the Elohim'. Then follows a poem in quatrains on the same subject, in which recollections of Blake's childhood rambles in the country around London combine with his new-found delight in Jesus:

> The Jew's-harp-house & the Green Man,
> The Ponds where Boys to bathe delight,
> The fields of Cows by Willan's farm,
> Shine in Jerusalem's pleasant sight.
>
> She walks upon our meadows green,
> The Lamb of God walks by her side,
> And every English Child is seen
> Children of Jesus & his Bride. [*J.* 598]

In a final prose passage, Blake begs the Jews to take up the Cross and follow Jesus.

In this second chapter of *Jerusalem* Albion is plainly identified with Urizen. He is 'the punisher & judge', he condenses all the loves and ornaments of Eternity into solids, and insists that 'Man be separate from Man'. He is surrounded by snows and ice, and the Tree of Moral Virtue shoots up under his foot.

Why has Blake made this change in his myth? Why has Urizen been deposed from his station as arch-villain of the cosmic drama, and Albion placed there in his stead? I believe the answer to this question lies precisely in that statement which Blake made in a letter to Hayley, that he had subdued 'the spectrous fiend' and was now 'at unity with himself'. He feels now that he has given far too much importance to *jealousy* and *reason* (both of which he identifies with Urizen, 'the Zeus of the Greeks'), and not enough to the *sense of sin* which is so deep within Man that we have to regard it as an integral part of his innermost nature. This sense of sin, and this refusal to be redeemed, is something so vital that Blake could not represent it by the symbolism of the four Zoas: he had to represent it by Man himself. Here is another meaning of the phrase 'more consolidated' which Blake applies to this poem in his Preface.

Albion in his error is not left without a witness of truth. The Divine Vision appears 'like a silent Sun', and within it a Human

Form is seen. The Voice of the Lamb proclaims that there is a principle of evil within Albion, called here 'the Reactor', i.e. that which *acts back* in envy against joy, and that this principle can only be seen and cast out when it has formed itself into a system. The voice ends with the promise:

> "I come that I may find a way for my banished ones to return.
> Fear not, O little Flock, I come. Albion shall rise again." [*J.* 602]

At this point two figures make their way 'from Albion's darkening locks': they are Los and Enitharmon, who escape to tell the Saviour the story of Albion's fall. This is repeated verbatim from the Fall narrative supplied by Ahania in *Night the Third* of *The Four Zoas.*[1] Los prays the Saviour to come and save his little ones:

> "They mock at the Labourer's limbs: they mock at his starv'd Children:
> They buy his Daughters that they may have power to sell his Sons:
> They compell the Poor to live upon a crust of bread by soft mild arts:
> They reduce the Man to want, then give with pomp & ceremony:
> The praise of Jehovah is chaunted from lips of hunger & thirst."
> [*J.* 606–7]

In order to find out the cause of these perversions, Los takes 'his globe of fire' and searches the interior of Albion's bosom; he sees that all the Minute Particulars have been degraded, but cannot find the culprit, Satan. Moreover, he is aware, with Blake's new awareness of the absolute necessity of forgiveness, the absolute futility of judgement, that even if he found the guilty he could do nothing. To attempt to punish the guilty would mean the destruction of the innocent.

> "What shall I do? what could I do if I could find these Criminals?
> I could not dare to take vengeance, for all things are so constructed
> And builded by the Divine hand that the sinner shall always escape,
> And he who takes vengeance alone is the criminal of Providence.
> If I should dare to lay my finger on a grain of sand
> In way of vengeance, I punish the already punish'd. O whom
> Should I pity if I pity not the sinner who is gone astray?
> O Albion, if thou takest vengeance, if thou revengest thy wrongs,
> Thou art for ever lost! What can I do to hinder the Sons
> Of Albion from taking vengeance? or how shall I them perswade?"
> [*J.* 608–9]

---

[1] See above, p. 87.

Jerusalem and Vala, who were reconciled at the beginning of the poem, are now at odds, and quarrelling with all their might. Albion stands at his Eastern gate, 'ready to fall into Non-Entity'; and Los is terrified. Albion's Spectre appears, separate, and addresses Lockean doctrine to Albion:

> "I am your Rational Power, O Albion, & that Human Form
> You call Divine is but a Worm seventy inches long
> That creeps forth in a night & is dried in the morning sun,
> In fortuitous concourse of memorys accumulated & lost." [*J.* 611]

A conversation follows between Albion and Vala, in which that 'Shadowy Female' insists that she alone is beauty, thus denying the loveliness of the imagination which is Jerusalem. Los, standing at his anvil, hears these words, and is indignant at the arrogance of Woman who assumes all power to herself. Blake connects the female will, as always, with physical Nature and with rationalist philosophy.

At this point there comes an interposition of the Divine Hand, which fixes the limits of contraction and opacity in Albion's bosom. We are again shown the wrath of the Zoas, and Los is for a moment furious against Albion; but when he sees his plight, forgiveness returns, and in mercy he follows Albion into the void. Albion flees from love,

> but mild, the Saviour follow'd him,
> Displaying the Eternal Vision, the Divine Similitude,
> In loves and tears of brothers, sisters, sons, fathers and friends,
> Which if Man ceases to behold, he ceases to exist,
> Saying, "Albion! Our wars are wars of life, & wounds of love
> With intellectual spears, & long winged arrows of thought.
> Mutual in one another's love and wrath all renewing
> We live as One Man; for contracting our infinite senses
> We behold multitude, or expanding, we behold as one,
> As One Man all the Universal Family, and that One Man
> We call Jesus the Christ; and he in us, and we in him
> Live in perfect harmony in Eden, the land of life,
> Giving, recieving, and forgiving each other's trespasses.
> He is the Good shepherd, he is the Lord and master,
> He is the Shepherd of Albion, he is all in all,
> In Eden, in the garden of God, and in heavenly Jerusalem.
> If we have offended, forgive us; take not vengeance against us."
> [*J.* 620]

It is hardly necessary to emphasise the importance of this passage. Eternity is not a static condition of bliss, but a battle of thoughts and of love, in which sin may be committed, but is perpetually being forgiven. The senses there are infinite, and may be expanded to behold unity or contracted to behold diversity. The unity is Jesus. And the love of Jesus for Albion is so great that He is ready to ask forgiveness of him! This insistence on forgiveness is kept up in the pages which follow. We are shown that all things in Nature are human; that cities themselves are human, and that London and York and Canterbury are all ready to give themselves for Albion. Los, who 'was the friend of Albion who most lov'd him', and the other Zoas, are also willing to sacrifice themselves; and when it is found that the Fallen Man rejects their counsel and love, they try to bear him back on wings 'against his will thro' Los's Gate to Eden'. But this they cannot do, for

> the Will must not be bended but in the day of Divine Power. [*J.* 635]

Los therefore is charged by the other Eternals to watch over Albion; not as, in the earlier books, he watched over Urizen to bind and separate him, but to instruct him and bring him back home.

Finally the Saviour receives the Fallen Man and lays him on the Rock of Ages; and the Daughters of Beulah weep for Albion.

The Preface of the third chapter of *Jerusalem* is inscribed 'To the Deists'. The first part, in prose, attacks Natural Religion as the enemy of the human race. 'You, O Deists, profess yourselves the Enemies of Christianity, and you are so: you are also the Enemies of the Human Race & of Universal Nature. Man is born a Spectre or Satan & is altogether an Evil, & requires a New Selfhood continually, & must continually be changed into his direct Contrary.' Blake defends the enthusiasts, beginning with monks and coming down to Wesley and Whitefield, against the Deists' charge of hypocrisy. The monks condemned war and were therefore hateful to Gibbon and Voltaire. The closing verses ('I saw a Monk of Charlemaine') end with the celebrated lines:

> For a Tear is an Intellectual thing,
> And a Sigh is the Sword of an Angel King,
> And the bitter groan of a Martyr's woe
> Is an Arrow from the Almightie's Bow. [*J.* 649]

Chapter three takes up again the narrative of the building of Golgonooza. Los sings at his work, and the Daughters of Albion reply. Los's task is 'To Create a World of Generation from the World of Death'. Suddenly Urizen appears (he has hitherto been identified with Albion) and we find him also at work building his Temple of Nature. Much of what follows is repeated in other words from *The Four Zoas*. But a new element is introduced when the captive Jerusalem is comforted by a vision of Joseph and Mary: yet another instance of forgiveness. Mary is an adultress, but Joseph forgives and receives her. Mary gives the infant Jesus into the hands of Jerusalem. The Gospel history takes its course: Jesus is crucified and rises again, and His words comfort Jerusalem:

> "I am the Resurrection & the Life.
> I Die & pass the limits of possibility as it appears
> To individual perception. Luvah must be Created
> And Vala, for I cannot leave them in the gnawing Grave
> But will prepare a way for my banished-ones to return." [*J.* 669]

Vala, however, expresses her scorn for man: the male, she says, is himself a female, for he comes from woman. Her empire is associated with the Industrial Revolution, of which Blake gives us a description copied from the alternative version of *Night the Seventh* in *The Four Zoas*. Luvah, the passions, is sacrificed by the Spectre Sons of Albion on the Druid Stone of Salisbury. A long section follows connecting the Druids with the practitioners of science and natural religion. Finally all the Sons of Albion combine into a Polypus, and a religion of chastity arises, directed against Jerusalem.

The fourth and last chapter is addressed 'To the Christians', and headed by the well-known quatrain:

> I give you the end of a golden string,
> Only wind it into a ball,
> It will lead you in at Heaven's gate
> Built in Jerusalem's wall

—on which the comment of any interpreter of Blake may well be that it is not the end of a string he gives us, but a very tangled skein which has to be *un*wound 'with trouble and care' before its course can be followed!

There is a strong evangelical flavour about the beginning of the prose preface which opens this chapter. Blake is still thinking, we see, about Whitefield and Wesley:

> We are told to abstain from fleshly desires that we may lose no time from the Work of the Lord: Every moment lost is a moment that cannot be redeemed; every pleasure that intermingles with the duty of our station is a folly unredeemable, & is planted like the seed of a wild flower among our wheat: All the tortures of repentance are tortures of self-reproach on account of our leaving the Divine Harvest to the Enemy, the struggles of intanglement with incoherent roots. [*J.* 703]

But in the next sentence Blake's thought soars far beyond these prudential maxims, and he is back in his familiar world of the imagination:

> I know of no other Christianity and of no other Gospel than the liberty both of body & mind to exercise the Divine Arts of Imagination, Imagination, the real & eternal World of which this Vegetable Universe is but a faint shadow, & in which we shall live in our Eternal or Imaginative Bodies when these Vegetable Mortal Bodies are no more. [*J.* 703]

'I know of...no other Gospel....' It is plain that Blake's growing interest in Christianity, and the devotion to the person of Christ which we have noted in the later writings, is in no sense a modification of the beliefs he has held up to now. It is a reinforcement of them, a realisation that the truths he has spent his life in proclaiming are the very content of the Christian message. More and more, as the years pass, he is reading through the letter of the New Testament into its spirit: and that spirit is the Everlasting Gospel of forgiveness, imagination and creative activity. 'Is the Holy Ghost any other than an Intellectual Fountain?' he goes on to ask in this preface. The treasures which we are to lay up for ourselves in heaven are 'Mental Studies & Performances'. He appeals to the religious to discountenance anything which is in opposition to art and 'science'.

The poetic section of the Preface is written in one of Blake's rare passages of blank verse. It is once more directed against Natural Religion, and is full of the spirit of *The Everlasting Gospel.* Jesus is 'the bright Preacher of Life', inculcating the forgiveness of sins. Following this blank verse passage, three quatrains end the preface:

England! awake! awake! awake!
  Jerusalem thy Sister calls!
Why wilt thou sleep the sleep of death
  And close her from thy ancient walls?

Thy hills & valleys felt her feet
  Gently upon their bosoms move:
Thy gates beheld sweet Zion's ways:
  Then was a time of joy and love.

And now the time returns again:
  Our souls exult, & London's towers
Recieve the Lamb of God to dwell
  In England's green & pleasant bowers. [*J.* 705]

The narrative begins with a dramatic glimpse of Albion on his rock, attacked by the Spectres, which Los unceasingly drives away. Jerusalem is destitute, an outcast from Eternity. In a long lament she tells of the misery of creation. Vala replies, telling how Luvah had ordered her to murder Albion (yet another version of the Fall). She turns the Spindle of Materialism 'to weave Jerusalem a Body repugnant to the Lamb'.

On the summit of Skiddaw, the Daughters of Albion meet, and discuss their power over men. They refuse to give themselves to the gentle and contemplative, and reserve their favours for the warriors. Meanwhile Los, who is well aware of his eternal station as 'Urthona, keeper of the Gates of Heaven', is willing to vegetate in pangs of love if by so doing he can save Albion. He sings of the glory of Jerusalem; but Enitharmon, who suddenly appears at this point, repels him with female pride.

And now the terrible Covering Cherub is revealed, the supreme image of selfhood, 'the Antichrist accursed'. Within him a Double Female is enclosed, 'Religion hid in War, a Dragon red & hidden Harlot'. But this terrible vision, error made manifest, is the sign that the end is nigh. With prophetic fury Los proclaims his doctrine of forgiveness and worship:

"Go, tell them that the Worship of God is honouring his gifts
In other men & loving the greatest men best, each according
To his Genius which is the Holy Ghost in Man; there is no other
God than that God who is the intellectual fountain of Humanity.

> He who envies or calumniates, which is murder & cruelty,
> Murders the Holy-one. Go, tell them this, & overthrow their cup,
> Their bread, their altar-table, their incense & their oath,
> Their marriage & their baptism, their burial & consecration. [*J.* 736–7]

He sees the Briton, Saxon, Roman and Norman amalgamating 'into One Nation, the English', and taking refuge in Albion's loins. This is yet another sign of the end. Enitharmon is terrified that when Albion awakes she will vanish: like Milton's Eve she fears that then Los will 'Create another Female according to [his] Will'. Los answers that sexes must cease when Albion awakes and the life of Eternity is resumed.

Now Albion is ready to throw off his long trance; but England awakes first, fainting on Albion's bosom, and repents of her misdeeds. Her voice pierces Albion's ear, he rises, and walks 'into the Heavens'. Jesus appears

> standing by Albion as the Good Shepherd
> By the lost Sheep that he hath found, & Albion knew that it
> Was the Lord, the Universal Humanity; & Albion saw his Form
> A Man, & they conversed as Man with Man in Ages of Eternity.
> And the Divine Appearance was the likeness & similitude of Los.
> [*J.* 745]

Albion begs Jesus to tell him what he shall do: he knows that his selfhood, the Covering Cherub, is marching against the Lord from all corners of the earth. Jesus begs him not to be afraid: He must die for Albion, but He will rise again. Now the Covering Cherub tears them apart, but Albion loses his selfhood in contemplation of the Divine Mercy and the sublime loyalty of Los. He throws himself into the Furnaces of Affliction—and the moment he does so he is redeemed, for all is an illusion he himself has created by his lack of faith. The Four Zoas are immediately restored to their eternal stations, and shoot their bright arrows of love annihilating the 'Druid Spectre'. Eternity is restored. The moral law is destroyed, and the poem ends with the vision:

> All Human Forms identified, even Tree, Metal, Earth & Stone: all
> Human Forms identified, living, going forth & returning wearied
> Into the Planetary lives of Years, Months, Days & Hours; reposing,
> And then Awaking into his Bosom in the Life of Immortality.
>
> And I heard the Name of their Emanations: they are named Jerusalem.
> [*J.* 751]

So ends, in splendour, this long and difficult poem. Difficult, not because of sheer incoherence as *The Four Zoas* is, but by reason of the complexity of thought, the subtlety of the mental states described, and the interpolation of doctrinal passages which break the narrative. The foregoing analysis cannot pretend to have touched on more than a few of the threads of thought involved. Others of these will be woven into the discussion of Blake's philosophy in the second part of this study.

CHAPTER X

Last Years

> Re-engrav'd Time after Time,
> Ever in their youthful prime,
> My designs unchang'd remain.
> Time may rage but rage in vain.
> For above Time's troubled Fountains
> On the Great Atlantic Mountains,
> In my Golden House on high,
> There they Shine Eternally. [*M.P.* 127]

DETAILS of Blake's life between the years 1810 and 1817 are meagre indeed. Only one letter is extant, a short note to Josiah Wedgwood the younger about some engravings of Wedgwood ware that Blake was engaged on. Crabb Robinson did not meet Blake until 1825; but in his diary for 24 July 1811 he records a visit to Charles Lamb's, where he found a very large party, including Southey. Crabb Robinson reports:

> Southey had been with Blake & admired both his designs & his poetic talents at the same time that he held him for a decided madman. Blake, he says, spoke of his visions with the diffidence that is usual with such people & did not seem to expect that he shd. be believed. He shewed S[outhey] a perfectly mad poem called *Jerusalem*. Oxford Street is in Jerusalem.

No doubt it was Blake's sensing of his visitor's limitations that made him talk 'diffidently'. With more receptive minds he communed freely, but he held the sage's view of the uselessness of argument. 'When I tell any Truth', he observes in the *Public Address*, 'it is not for the sake of Convincing those who do not know it, but for the sake of defending those who do'.

The next entry comes in 1812. Crabb Robinson read some of Blake's poems to Wordsworth, who was pleased with them and considered that Blake had 'the elements of poetry a thousand times more than either Byron or Scott'. Three years elapse before the next reference. Flaxman had been speaking of Sharp the engraver, a follower of Joanna Southcott, who had tried to convert Blake:

As Fl[axman] judiciously observed, such men as B[lake] are not fond of playing the 2nd. fiddle. Hence B[lake] himself a seer of visions & a dreamer of dreams would not do homage to a rival claimant of the privilege of prophecy.

About the year 1818 Blake was writing *The Everlasting Gospel*, one of the most striking and pregnant of his poems. It was never finished, and there is no certainty about the order of the various passages as we find them scribbled down in Blake's notebook. But the poem has that gnomic quality which marks Blake's best verse, and we may set it side by side with the *Auguries* and the *Marriage* and the lyrics, as containing the quintessence of his thought. I discuss this poem at length in a later chapter.[1]

Probably in the same year Blake made additions to his *For Children: The Gates of Paradise*, which he had first engraved in 1793. It is a book of what the seventeenth century would have called 'emblems': symbolic pictures accompanied by a verse commentary. Blake changes the title to *For the Sexes: The Gates of Paradise*, and adds the commentary with a Prologue and Epilogue.

The Frontispiece shows a caterpillar on an oak leaf bending over a chrysalis on a lower leaf. The head of a child emerges from the chrysalis, and the 'Key' tells us:

> The Catterpiller on the Leaf
> Reminds thee of thy Mother's Grief. [*G.P.* 761]

The couplet is taken from the *Auguries of Innocence*. Beneath this emblem is another couplet:

> The Sun's Light when he unfolds it
> Depends on the Organ that beholds it. [*G.P.* 752]

In other words, we can see nothing unless we have vision: if we have vision, we can see 'the human face divine' in the caterpillar and the chrysalis.

The Prologue enforces the teaching of the forgiveness of sins:

> Mutual Forgiveness of each Vice,
> Such are the Gates of Paradise.

[1] See Ch. xx below.

Against the Accuser's chief desire,
Who walk'd among the Stones of Fire,
Jehovah's Finger Wrote the Law:
Then Wept! then rose in Zeal & Awe,
And the Dead Corpse from Sinai's heat
Buried beneath his Mercy Seat.
O Christians, Christians! tell me Why
You rear it on your Altars high. [*G.P.* 753]

When even Jehovah repented of inventing the Decalogue, why do so-called Christians make it a chief tenet of their faith?

The first emblem shows a woman pulling a child by the hair out of the ground; she is under a weeping-willow tree, and holds another child, which she has just 'gathered', in her left arm. The vegetable universe is human too, as well as the animal represented by the caterpillar; and in the corresponding 'key' Blake explains the significance of the emblem.

My Eternal Man set in Repose,
The Female from his darkness rose
And she found me beneath a Tree,
A Mandrake, & in her Veil hid me.
Serpent Reasonings us entice
Of Good & Evil, Virtue & Vice. [*G.P.* 761]

The Female is plainly Vala, or Nature, who arises as in the prophetic books from the sleeping Albion, finds the individual rooted under the Tree of Mystery, and hides him in her veil of material creation.

Four emblems follow of Man in the four elements. Water is the symbol of 'Doubt Self Jealous', earth of melancholy, air of shame and fear, while fire shows Urizen blind with shield and spear. The sixth emblem is of a winged child breaking from an egg in the midst of space; the commentary suggests that this is a type of Man breaking through the veil of death into new life. In the seventh, a boy is chasing a fairy and trying to catch her in his hat, while a second little figure lies dead on the ground. The commentary is not very helpful, but we may surmise that this is a warning against 'binding to oneself a joy': the fairies of love are not to be caught but to be kissed on the wing, as it were. The eighth emblem, a naked youth about to hurl a dart at an old man seated on a rock and holding a sword, carries the motto:

> My Son! my Son! thou treatest me
> But as I have instructed thee. [*G.P.* 762]

—in short, murder and ingratitude are the natural result of current religious instruction. The ninth, powerful in its simplicity, pictures a male figure beginning to climb up a long ladder to the moon, while two female figures stand by. The cry, 'I want! I want!', is written below. Even more striking is the tenth emblem: a dark and stormy sea, with a hand and arm stretched out, and a head sinking beneath the waves: 'Help! Help!'. The commentary is illuminating:

> In Time's Ocean falling drown'd. [*G.P.* 762]

Aged Ignorance appears in the next design, sitting beneath the Tree of Mystery. The sun is rising, but the old man has his back to it; and with an enormous pair of scissors he is clipping the wings of a child who is longing to fly into the light of freedom.

> Holy & cold, I clip'd the Wings
> Of all Sublunary Things,
> And in Depths of my Dungeons
> Closed the Father & the Sons, [*G.P.* 762]

—the second couplet referring to emblem twelve, which shows Ugolino and his sons and grandsons in the dungeon. 'Does thy God, O Priest, take such vengeance as this?' runs the caption beneath. The theme of the next emblem is immortality: the spiritual body is shown rising from the corpse of an old man, while his family gaze in astonishment. In emblem fourteen the traveller hastening home through gathering shadows is depicted; he arrives at death's door in emblem fifteen; and there finds, in the last design, the worm which weaves around his bones as the caterpillar had spun her cocoon around his infancy:

> Thou'rt my Mother from the Womb,
> Wife, Sister, Daughter, to the Tomb,
> Weaving to Dreams the Sexual strife
> And weeping over the Web of Life. [*G.P.* 762]

The Epilogue is addressed 'To the Accuser who is The God of This World', convicting Satan of stupidity in not distinguishing the eternal from the transitory, the state from the individual:

> Truly, My Satan, thou art but a Dunce,
> And dost not know the Garment from the Man.
> Every Harlot was a Virgin once,
> Nor can'st thou ever change Kate into Nan.
>
> Tho' thou art Worship'd by the Names Divine
> Of Jesus & Jehovah, thou art still
> The Son of Morn in weary Night's decline,
> The lost Traveller's Dream under the Hill. [*G.P.* 763]

It was in the same year 1818 that Blake met John Linnell, a young painter who became almost a son to him and introduced him to a group of young men who took up his ideas with enthusiasm—in so far as Blake's ideas were open to them. Among them was John Varley, an art teacher and founder of the Society of Painters in Water-Colours, 'a landscape designer of much delicacy and grace', as Gilchrist calls him. Varley was interested in 'the occult', and cultivated Blake for the sake of his visionary powers. He encouraged Blake to draw from spirit-models: Wat Tyler, the Man who built the Pyramids, Richard Cœur-de-Lion, William Wallace, Edward the First, and the famous 'Ghost of a Flea' were all set down on paper in Varley's presence. Varley gave even more importance to these manifestations than did Blake himself, and in spite of Blake's protests that Varley and Linnell could do exactly the same thing if they liked, he persisted in regarding Blake as a magician who could call up spirits at will.

Some small income must have been derived in this obscure period of Blake's life from the sale of his engraved books, which Linnell probably pushed as much as he could among his friends. We have also the evidence of a letter of 9 June 1818 to the botanist and antiquarian Dawson Turner, giving a list of these books, with prices which show a considerable rise from the days when the *Songs of Innocence* could be bought for five shillings. This work now costs three guineas, and *Milton*, the only major prophecy listed, is priced at ten guineas. It was through Linnell or Varley, again, that Blake obtained the commission to do the illustrations, or some of them, for

Dr Thornton's edition of Virgil's *Pastorals*. This was the third edition of 1821. For the first and last time in his career Blake attempted wood-engravings; the results are among the most striking products of his genius. By some magic he gives us the impression of pastoral landscapes in the golden age—not Virgil's golden age, perhaps, or Dr Thornton's, but rather that eternal world of his own imagination. Dr Thornton and his publishers considered these so odd that they were for sending them back, and were only restrained by hearing the favourable opinion of Linnell, Lawrence and other experts. Not quite overcoming his fears, the Doctor added a special note to the effect that 'they display less of art than genius, and are much admired by some eminent painters'. We are reminded of the Rev. Henry Mathew's Preface to the *Poetical Sketches*.

About 1819 we find Blake annotating Spurzheim's *Observations on the Deranged Manifestations of the Mind, or Insanity*. There are not many of these notes, but they are interesting. He is struck by the passage, 'Whatever occupies the mind too intensely or exclusively is hurtful to the brain, and induces a state favourable to insanity, in diminishing the influence of the will'. He does not comment on this statement, but his marking it shows that he was giving the idea some consideration. Another passage deals with religious insanity, and particularly the effects of Methodism. Blake notes:

> Cowper came to me and said: "O that I were insane always. I will never rest. Can you not make me truly insane? I will never rest till I am so. O that in the bosom of God I was hid. You retain health and yet are as mad as any of us all—over us all—mad as a refuge from unbelief—from Bacon, Newton and Locke." [*Marginalia*, 1020]

It is difficult to interpret this cryptic passage. It has been quoted as a proof that Blake recognised he was insane. But this is going too far. It is Cowper who makes the charge: Blake does not comment on it. Blake was not a Methodist, and there is no reason why he should apply Spurzheim's diagnosis to himself.

Blake engraved a *Laocoon Group c.* 1820, and surrounded it with gnomic sentences recalling the *Proverbs of Hell* in style. They are penetrated with a conviction of the all-importance of Christianity, and advance a characteristic fusion of Christianity with art. Morality and war are again attacked:

If Morality was Christianity, Socrates was the Saviour.
Art Degraded, Imagination Denied, War Governed the Nations.
Spiritual War: Israel deliver'd from Egypt, is Art deliver'd from Nature & Imitation.
A Poet, a Painter, a Musician, an Architect: the Man Or Woman who is not one of these is not a Christian.
You must leave Fathers & Mothers & Houses & Lands if they stand in the way of Art.
Prayer is the Study of Art.
Praise is the Practise of Art.
Fasting &c., all relate to Art.
The outward Ceremony is Antichrist. [*L.G.* 764]

Further sentences stress the identity between the Eternal Body of Man, the Divine Body, Jesus, and the imagination; attack the money motive which lies at the bottom of modern civilisation; reject Nature as being 'Satan's Wife, War & Misery'; declare that the Bible is the great code of art; and finally announce the purpose of living.

The Whole Business of Man Is The Arts, & All Things Common. No Secresy in Art. [*L.G.* 766]

There are also strictures on the classics: 'The Gods of Greece & Egypt were Mathematical Diagrams—See Plato's Works'; and these are amplified in the pamphlet *On Homer's Poetry & On Virgil*, engraved about the same time. 'The Classics!' he cries, 'it is the Classics, & not Goths nor Monks, that Desolate Europe with Wars'. Blake ascribed many of our errors to the false notions of warlike heroism inculcated by Homer and Virgil:

Sacred Truth has pronounced that Greece & Rome, as Babylon & Egypt, so far from being parents of Arts & Sciences as they pretend, were destroyers of all Art. Homer, Virgil & Ovid confirm this opinion & make us reverence The Word of God, the only light of antiquity that remains unperverted by War. Virgil in the Eneid, Book vi, line 848, says "Let others study Art: Rome has somewhat better to do, namely War & Dominion."

Rome & Greece swept Art into their maw & destroy'd it; a Warlike State can never produce Art. It will Rob & Plunder & accumulate into one place, & Translate & Copy & Buy & Sell & Criticise, but not Make. Grecian is Mathematic Form: Gothic is Living Form. Mathematic Form is Eternal in the Reasoning Memory: Living Form is Eternal Existence.

[*Homer & Virgil*, 768]

It is difficult to see how Blake arrived at this admiration for the Old Testament, which in his notes on Watson's *Apology* he calls 'an Example of the possibility of Human Beastliness in all its branches'. The Israelites are remarkable for the poverty of their artistic productions, outside the realm of literature; and the annals of the Old Testament are strewn with records of battles, massacres and treachery.

About 1820, too, Blake made some marginal notes in his copy of Bishop Berkeley's curious little treatise, *Siris*, which from a consideration of the virtues of tar-water rises to the heights of Neo-Platonic speculation. The relevance of these notes is assessed in Part II of this book.[1]

In 1821 Blake moved to his final lodging-place at 3 Fountain Court, Strand. Gilchrist describes the neighbourhood as 'an old-fashioned respectable court in 1821...its red-brick houses with over-hanging cornices dating from the end of the seventeenth and beginning of the eighteenth century'. Here was engraved in 1822 the short dramatic poem *The Ghost of Abel, A Revelation in the Visions of Jehovah seen by William Blake.* It is dedicated 'To LORD BYRON in the Wilderness: What doest thou here, Elijah? Can a Poet doubt the Visions of Jehovah? Nature has no Outline, but Imagination has. Nature has no Tune, but Imagination has. Nature has no Supernatural & dissolves: Imagination is Eternity.' It is clear that Blake has been reading *Cain* and *Manfred*: At first sight there would appear to be little in common between the great poseur and the apostle of self-annihilation; but Blake recognised in Byron the spirit of revolt, and that energy which is eternal delight. He would be entirely in sympathy with Byron's rejection of the false morality and corrupt politics of the age. But as the dedication shows, he considered Byron wrong in fleeing from human society into the wilderness, and rejecting vision. The scene of *The Ghost of Abel* is 'A rocky

---

[1] Ch. XVIII, pp. 336–345. See also pp. 289 and 337, footnote, for suggestion that Blake read *Siris* before *c.* 1788.

Country'. Adam and Eve are mourning over the body of Abel, while Jehovah stands above. Jehovah calls Adam, who refuses to listen, for he thinks God has deceived him in promising that the woman's seed shall bruise the serpent's head. Eve also declares her unbelief:

> Is this the Promise of Jehovah! O, it is all a vain delusion,
> This Death & this Life & this Jehovah! [*G.A.* 769]

The ghost of Abel appears, crying out for Cain's blood. Adam and Eve think that all is delusion, that they must die an eternal death. But suddenly in spiritual vision they see the Form Divine, and Abel living in Eternity. Eve asks whether it would not be better to believe vision 'with all our might & strength, tho' we are fallen & lost?' Abel cannot forgive: he still cries for vengeance, for the Accuser has entered into him as into his house,

> And He doth rule over Me; therefore My Soul in fumes of Blood
> Cries for Vengeance, Sacrifice on Sacrifice, Blood on Blood!
> [*G.A.* 771]

Jehovah replies that he has given a Lamb to be sacrificed for the transgressor, but Abel is not appeased, and sinks down into the ground, from which rises 'Satan, Armed in glittering scales, with a Crown & a Spear'. He demands human blood and not the blood of bulls or goats, and no atonement. Jehovah himself shall be sacrificed to him on Calvary. Jehovah replies that such is his will,

> that Thou Thyself go to Eternal Death
> In Self Annihilation, even till Satan, Self-subdu'd, Put off Satan
> Into the Bottomless Abyss, whose torment arises for ever & ever.
> [*G.A.* 771]

The drama ends with a chorus of angels singing the covenant of the forgiveness of sins.

It was in December 1825 that Henry Crabb Robinson met Blake for the first time, and now the entries in his diary begin in earnest. The meeting took place at one of the parties given by Mr Charles Aders, 'a wealthy merchant of an old German family; a liberal and art-loving man, whose doors were always open to literary men and artists', as Gilchrist describes him. Not only the most prominent painters of the time, but also writers of the calibre of Coleridge and Lamb attended the Aders' parties, and it is probable that Blake met Coleridge at one of them. Crabb Robinson describes this 10th December as 'a very remarkable & interesting evening', and it was clearly Blake's conversation that struck him, for he wrote down an extensive report of what the poet-artist had said. 'Shall I call him Artist or Genius—or Mystic or Madman? Probably he is all. He has a most interesting appearance. He is now old, pale with a Socratic countenance and an expression of great sweetness but bordering on weakness except when his features are animated by expression & then he has an air of inspiration about him. The conversation was on art & on poetry & on religion, but it was my object & I was successful in drawing him out & in so getting from him an avowal of his *peculiar* sentiments. I was aware before of the nature of his impressions or I shd. at times have been at a loss to understand him.' These diary entries of Henry Crabb Robinson's are by far the most extensive notes on Blake by a contemporary that we possess, and are of the greatest interest and value. Crabb Robinson has many of the qualities of a trained observer. But we should beware of accepting his reports of Blake's conversation as being on quite the same level of evidential value as Blake's own written works. Many commentators on Blake have made this mistake. Accurate reporter as Crabb Robinson may have been, we must remember that the value of his notes to us is simply that of hearsay evidence, and the evidence too of a man whose mind was not in the least in tune with Blake's mystical vision and therefore very apt unconsciously to distort what Blake said to him. With this caution we may go on to study his report of Blake's conversation, carefully testing every detail by what we already know of Blake's doctrine from his written works.

Blake talked of his visions, of having conversed with Socrates and Jesus Christ, and 'eagerly concurred' in Crabb Robinson's suggestion that the soul, to be immortal, must have pre-existed. 'We are all coexistent with God, Members of the Divine body. We are all partakers of the divine nature.' On being questioned concerning the divinity of Christ, 'He said—*He is the only God*—But then he added— "And so am I & so are you".' Crabb Robinson reports Blake as speaking of the errors of Jesus Christ: 'He was wrong in suffering himself to be crucified. He should not have attacked the govt. He had no business with such matters.' We should beware, however, of taking these casual jottings as evidence that Blake had entirely abandoned the beliefs of *Jerusalem* and *The Everlasting Gospel.* Crabb Robinson may have misunderstood the exact sense of Blake's remarks.

We feel more at home with his opinions on education. 'There is no use in education. I hold it wrong. It is the great sin. It is eating of the tree of the Knowledge of good & evil. That was the fault of Plato—he knew of nothing but of the Virtues and Vices And good & evil. There is nothing in all that. Everything is good in God's eyes.'

Blake seems to have talked long and vehemently at this meeting. There are dicta on art, on Swedenborg and Dante, which fit in with what we already know. Even more interesting are his opinions on Wordsworth:

> W[ordsworth] he thinks is no Xn. but a Platonist—he askd me—Does he believe in the Scriptures. On my answering in the affirmative he said he had been much pained by readg. the introduction to the Excursion. It brought on a fit of illness. The passage was produced & read
>
> *Jehovah,—with his thunder & the choir*
> *Of shouting angels, & the empyreal thrones—*
> *I* pass *them unalarmed.*
>
> This *pass them unalarmed* greatly offendd Blake. Does Mr Wordsw[orth] think his mind can *surpass* Jehovah? I tried to twist this passage into a sense correspondg with Blake's own theories but failed, And Wordsw[orth] was finally set down as a pagan. But still with great praise as the greatest poet of the age.

Wordsworth's nature-worship, his allegiance to 'the hallowed and pure motions of the sense', worried Blake, and in his annotations to the *Poems* of 1815 (written 1826) he comments: 'I see in Wordsw. the natural man rising up agst. the spiritual man continually, & then he is no poet but a heathen philosopher at Enmity agst. all true poetry or inspiration.' He repudiates Wordsworth's 'natural piety': 'There is no such thing as natural piety because the natural man is at enmity with God.' There we have Christianity speaking, and Blake is right in thinking Wordsworth is not a Christian. He has neither the Christian heights nor the Christian depths. Wordsworth was a born mystic who took the wrong turning: who allowed his eye to be seduced by the forms of things, who remained content with flashes of vision in his childhood and made no attempt to train his faculty, and was surprised and hurt to find it die away at last.

The paradox is that to the end Wordsworth remained a stranger, and a frightened stranger, in his phenomenal universe, because his love was based on the sense of ownership, and tainted with fear at the thought of being deprived. In the Lake District he had made a corner in the universe. He fixed his affections on rocks and stones and trees and wanted man to become as like them as possible—a desire precisely the contrary of Blake's. This is an effort at unification which closely resembles the primal error of Urizen: 'this sanctity of Nature given to man'.

The grave deterioration of Wordsworth's work from about 1805 onwards has not escaped notice, but the reasons given to explain it have sometimes been superficial. The failure of the French Revolution, the aftermath of the Annette Vallon episode, the break with Coleridge: these may have been contributory factors, but not principal ones. Wordsworth's mind was from the beginning the battleground of two opposed faculties: the power of intense visualisation with the bodily eye, and the gift of mystical vision. The record of his spiritual life is the story of an attempt to reconcile these 'discordant qualities', and of the gradual supersession of vision by visualisation. We note that it is when he is away from his dominating mountain scenery that he produces his best poems. Here Blake's comment is valuable: 'Natural objects always did & now do weaken, deaden & obliterate Imagination in me. W. must know that what he writes valuable is not to be found in Nature.' And of course Wordsworth, at the bottom of his heart, knew this. He admits as much as Blake could ever demand in the *Excursion*:

> Too, too contracted are these walls of flesh,
> This vital warmth too cold, these visual orbs,
> Though inconceivably endowed, too dim
> For any passion of the soul that leads
> To ecstasy; and all the crooked paths
> Of time and change disdaining, takes its course
> Along the line of limitless desires.

Wordsworth was awakened to the eternal world through sense-perceptions to a greater degree than Blake, but he failed to step beyond: something hard, unexpansive within him caused him to draw back, to cling to the palpable (as, in the notes to the *Immortality Ode*, he tells us he clung to the post) where Blake let himself go in an act of faith. He was afraid of losing his selfhood, of being carried away into 'strange seas of thought, alone'; so he clung to the familiar things and made them into a hard shell. Blake was right when he commented on the *Excursion* passage already quoted from Crabb Robinson:

> Solomon, when he Married Pharoah's daughter & became a Convert to the Heathen Mythology, Talked exactly in this way of Jehovah as a Very inferior object of Man's Contemplation; he also passed him by unalarm'd & was permitted. Jehovah dropped a tear & follow'd him by his Spirit into the Abstract Void; it is called the Divine Mercy. Satan dwells in it, but Mercy does not dwell in him; he knows not to Forgive.
>
> [*Marginalia*, 1026]

In this passage Blake clearly identifies Wordsworth with the Albion whom in *Jerusalem* he had shown rejecting the Divine Vision and pursuing his own way 'down the valleys dark'. The aim of this 'unexpansive' Wordsworth is to prove to his own satisfaction that there is no conflict between Nature and the spirit; to show

> How exquisitely the individual Mind
> (And the progressive powers perhaps no less
> Of the whole species) to the external World
> Is fitted:—& how exquisitely, too,
> Theme this but little heard of among Men,
> The external World is fitted to the Mind.

Blake took the trouble to copy out as well as annotate this passage from the *Excursion*: it struck him as a crucial expression of the doctrine that Man's evolution is towards a closer and closer identification of himself with Nature, and not, as Blake believed, that Man's evolution must be away from Nature and towards increasing spiritual consciousness, if he is not to perish. 'You shall not bring me down to believe such fitting & fitted', he notes dryly. For Blake the mind of Man and the physical universe are not 'fitted' but in a state of tension, for Nature is a petrified expression of the Eternal never passing beyond a fixed perfection, while Man's expression is incomplete and dynamic.

On 17 December 1825 Crabb Robinson called on Blake at Fountain Court. 'I found him in a small room which seems to be both a working room & a bed-room. Nothing could exceed the squalid air both of the apartment & his dress, but in spight of dirt, I might say filth, an air of natural gentility is diffused over him....'

Other observers, it should be noted, emphatically deny the charges of dirt and squalor. Blake's room, they affirm, was scrupulously clean though bare and unadorned. Crabb Robinson found Blake at work on his Dante designs: 'Of which I have nothing to say but that they evince a power of grouping & of throwing grace & interest over conceptions most monstrous & disgusting, which I shd. not have anticipated.' The talk turned once more on education: Blake approved only training in the fine arts and the use of the imagination. 'He denied that the natural world is anything. It is all nothing & Satan's empire is the empire of nothing.'

> Of the faculty of Vision he spoke as One he has had from early infancy. He thinks all men partake of it, but it is lost by not being cultivated. And he eagerly assented to a remark I made that All men have all faculties to a greater or less degree.—I am to renew my visits & to read Wordsworth to him of Whom he seems to entertain a high idea.

There was another visit on the 24th and Crabb Robinson read 'Wordsworth's incomparable Ode which he heartily enjoyed... the parts of Wordsworth's Ode which he most enjoyed were the most obscure & those I the least like & comprehend'. In his *Reminiscences* he expands this note as follows:

> On the 24th I called a second time on him, & on this occasion it was that I read to him *Wordsworth's Ode* on the supposed pre-existent state, & the subject of W.'s religious character was discussed when we met on the 18th of Feb. & the 12th of May. I will here bring together W. Blake's declaratns. concerning W. & set down his marginalia in the 8vo. edit. A.D. 1815. Vol. I. I had been in the habit when reading this marvellous Ode to friends, to omit one or two passages, especially that beginning
>
> But there's a tree, of many one
>
> lest I shd. be rendered ridiculous, being unable to explain precisely *what* I admired—not that I acknowledged this to be a fair test. But with Blake I cd. fear nothing of the kind, & it was this very Stanza wh. threw him almost into an hysterical rapture. His delight in W.'s poetry was intense. Nor did it seem less notwithstanding by the reproaches he continually cast on W. for his imputed worship of Nature, wh. in the mind of Blake constituted Atheism.

It is easy for us to see why the *Ode* should have affected Blake so strongly; and especially the stanza mentioned. It is the most visionary passage in the poem; it acknowledges the wide gap between imagination, the eternal world, and mere delight in Nature. Wordsworth has been describing the joy of the earth on this spring morning: the warmth of the sun, the flowers, the cry of lambs and the sound of streams. Then comes the realisation:

> I hear, I hear, with joy I hear!
> But there's a tree, of many, one,
> A single field which I have looked upon,
> Both of them speak of something that is gone:
> The pansy at my feet
> Doth the same tale repeat:
> Whither is fled the visionary gleam?
> Where is it now, the glory and the dream?

This, to Blake's mind, is the call of the lapsed soul realising that her kingdom is not of this world. 'The fool sees not the same tree that the wise man sees.' Here Wordsworth for once, in Blake's view, is the wise man: he sees the tree as symbol, not as vegetation. He looks beyond matter to the eternal form. Nature is not enough.

Three visits are recorded for 1826. The first, on January 6, receives but a short notice. Crabb Robinson had 'procured him two subscriptns for his Job from Geo Procter & Basil Montagu'. This, of course, refers to the famous series of illustrations to the Book of Job which Blake had now completed. Then follows a curious note: 'The oddest thing he said was that he had been commandd to do certain things that is to write abt Milton And that he was applauded for refusing.' As we know, Blake *had* written about Milton, in the symbolic book of that name, and had doubtless felt himself applauded for complying with the heavenly behest. It would seem that Crabb Robinson's understanding had slipped here. The second visit was on February 18. Again Blake talked of Wordsworth, then passed on to the Bible, 'and warmly declared that all he knew was in the Bible, but then he understands by the Bible the spiritual sense'. He said, according to our diarist, that he had composed six or seven epic poems as long as Homer, and twenty tragedies as long as *Macbeth*. On the third visit, June 13, there was talk of a community of women, which shocked Crabb Robinson into notes in German.

That Blake's health was failing in these days we know from the letters. The illness, said to be gallstones, dates back to 1824.

A letter to John Linnell tells us: 'A return of the old shivering fit came on this Morning as soon as I awaked & I am now in Bed, Better & as I think almost well...these attacks are too serious at the time to permit me to be out of Bed, but they go off by rest, which seems to be All that I want.' Another letter of 10 November 1825 relates that he is again in bed; and in 1826 he writes (February 1):

> I am again laid up by a cold in my stomach; the Hampstead Air, as it always did, so I fear it always will do this, Except it be the Morning air; & That, in my Cousin's time, I found I could bear with safety & perhaps benefit. I believe my Constitution to be a good one, but it has many peculiarities that no one but myself can know. When I was young, Hampstead, Highgate, Hornsea, Muswell Hill, & even Islington & all places North of London, always laid me up the day after, & sometimes two or three days, with precisely the same Complaint & the same torment of the Stomach, Easily removed, but excruciating while it lasts & enfeebling for some time after. [*L.* 1130]

In another letter of the same year he complains of 'this abominable Ague, or whatever it is'. He has to work in bed. By May things are worse.

> I have had another desperate shivering Fit; it came on yesterday afternoon after as good a morning as I ever experienced. It began by a gnawing Pain in the Stomach, & soon spread a deathly feel all over the limbs, which brings on the shivering fit, when I am forced to go to bed, where I contrive to get into a little perspiration, which takes it quite away. It was night when it left me, so I did not get up, but just as I was going to rise this morning, the shivering fit attacked me & the pain, with its accompanying deathly feel. I got again into a perspiration, & was well, but so much weaken'd that I am still in bed. This entirely prevents me from the pleasure of seeing you on Sunday at Hampstead, as I fear the attack again when I am away from home. [*L.* 1132]

Collins's Farm, North End, Hampstead, was at this time John Linnell's home. Here Blake spent many a happy Sunday when he was well enough to travel; Mrs Linnell welcomed him, and he was a great favourite with the children, who, 'whenever he was expected, were on the qui vive to catch the first glimpse of him from afar'. 'One of them', writes Gilchrist, 'who has now children of her own, but still cherishes the old reverence for "Mr Blake", remembers thus watching for him when a little girl of five or six; and how, as he walked over the brow of the hill and came within sight of the young ones, he would make a particular signal....She remembers how Blake would take her on his knee, and recite children's stories to them all: recollects his kind manner; his putting her in the way of drawing, training her from his own doings. One day he brought up to Hampstead an early sketch-book, full of most singular things, as it seemed to the children. But, in the midst of them, they came upon a finished Pre-Raphaelite-like drawing of a grasshopper, with which they were delighted.' And that Blake was an accomplished composer of children's verses may be judged from a surviving specimen:

Mr Blake's Nursery Rhyme

The sow came in with the saddle,
The little pig rocked the cradle,
The dish jumped o' top of the table
To see the brass pot swallow the ladle.
The old pot behind the door
Called the kettle a blackamoor.
'Odds bobbs' said the gridiron, 'can't you agree?
I'm the head constable, bring them to me.'

These were happy days for Blake. Hampstead was open country then, and he loved it all. Gilchrist gives us a pleasant glimpse of the old man enjoying the calm of evening. '[He] would often stand at the door, gazing, in tranquil reverie, across the garden toward the gorse-clad hill. He liked sitting in the arbour, at the bottom of the long garden, or walking up and down the same at dusk, while the cows, munching their evening meal, were audible from the farmyard on the other side the hedge. He was very fond of hearing Mrs Linnell sing Scottish songs, and would sit by the pianoforte, tears falling from his eyes, while he listened to the Border melody to which the song is set commencing:

O Nancy's hair is yellow as gowd,
And her een as the lift are blue.

To simple national melodies Blake was very impressionable, though not so to music of more complicated structure. He himself still sang, in a voice tremulous with age, sometimes old ballads, sometimes his own songs, to melodies of his own.'

At Hampstead indeed Blake, in the evening of his life, found again all the things he had loved: children, and flocks and herds and flowers, and music, and books, and above all the company of friends. 'William Blake', he writes himself down in William Upcott's autograph album, 16 January 1826, 'one who is very much delighted with being in good Company'. He was revered by John Linnell and the group of young artists and writers who met at his house: John Varley and his brother Cornelius, William Mulready, famous as painter and pugilist, H. J. Richter, and Frederick Tatham. They listened with respect to his doctrines, and were deeply influenced by his designs and paintings. 'It is a touching sight', Gilchrist remarks, 'to summon before one's mental eyes, this of the grey-haired visionary, opening his soul to these fresh-hearted youths. They all came to know one another, and would often meet and talk over their views on art; other views than were commonly current in that era of Lawrence, Martin Arthur Shee and the rest. Blake and his house used to be familiarly spoken of among them as "The House of the Interpreter". I can still trace something of the mystic poet's influence, surviving the lapse of more than thirty years, in all who ever knew and loved Blake; as of men who once in their lives had, as it were, entertained an angel *not* unawares.' This feeling of reverence is conveyed, too, in the letter from Samuel Palmer which Gilchrist transcribes in his *Life*: a document too long to be quoted here, and too full of important detail to be cut down.

It was under commission from Linnell that Blake began, in 1825, his illustrations to Dante. In order better to understand the text of the *Divina Commedia*, he set to work at the age of sixty-eight to learn Italian, and he is said to have succeeded in this, sufficiently for his purpose, in the course of a few weeks. He died before the series of illustrations was completed, but the hundred sketches, and the seven engraved plates, indicate that the glory of these engravings might even have surpassed his *Inventions* to the Book of Job.

A letter to Linnell of 2 July 1826 mentions these engravings. The opening paragraph is ominous:

My Dearest Friend, This sudden cold weather has cut up all my hopes by the roots. Every one who knows of our intended flight into your delightful Country concur in saying: "Do not Venture till summer appears again." I also feel Myself weaker than I was aware, being not able, as yet, to sit up longer than six hours at a time; & also feel the Cold too much to dare venture beyond my present precincts. My heartiest Thanks for your care in my accomodation, & the trouble you will yet have with me. But I get better & stronger every day, tho' weaker in muscle & bone than I supposed....

I intend to bring with me, besides our necessary change of apparel, Only My Book of Drawings from Dante & one Plate shut up in the Book. All will go very well in the Coach, which, at present, would be a rumble I fear I could not go thro'. So that I conclude another Week must pass before I dare Venture upon what I ardently desire—the seeing you with your happy Family once again, & that for a longer period than I had ever hoped in my healthfull hours. [*L.* 1133]

A letter three days later still contains hopes of improvement—'my Plan is diet only'—and begs Linnell not to worry about him. 'You have a Family, I have none; there is no comparison between our necessary avocations.' The same letter congratulates Linnell on 'the receit of another fine Boy'. But still the visit is postponed. On Sunday afternoon, July 16, he is complaining of 'a species of delirium and Pain too much for Thought'; this passes, but then (letter of July 29) 'Comes Another to hinder my Progress, call'd The Piles, which, when to the degree I have had them, are a most sore plague & on a Weak Body truly afflictive'. By August 4 he is feeling 'Well enough to come'.

A note in Crabb Robinson's *Reminiscences*, dated 13 June 1826, shows that the old heretic had not sunk into conventionalism, as Wordsworth was to do, in his declining years. 'He was as wild as ever...but he was led to-day to make assertions more palpably mischievous if capable of influencing other minds and immoral, supposing them to express the will of a responsible agent than anything he had said before.'

Flaxman died on the 7th of December, and Crabb Robinson records another visit:

It was, I believe on the 7th of December that I saw him last. I had just heard of the death of Flaxman, a man whom he professed to admire, & was curious how he wd. receive the intelligence. It was as I expected. He had been ill during the summer, & he said with a smile, 'I thought I shd. have gone first.' He then said, 'I cannot think of death as more than the going out of one room into another'. And Flaxman was no longer thought of. He relapsed into his ordinary train of thinking.

It is plain that Crabb Robinson was shocked by this insensibility, this want of the right expressions of grief and horror. His is the surprise of a man for whom a belief in immortality is something purely abstract: he is quite incapable of understanding the attitude of a man who holds it as a reality.

Crabb Robinson seems to have called on Blake for the last time on Friday, February 2 1827. He took along with him a young German painter named Götzenberger, who was highly impressed by the Dante engravings and said on his return to Germany, "I saw in England many men of talents, but only three men of Genius, Coleridge, Flaxman & Blake, & of these Blake was the greatest". It was about this time, too, that Linnell suggested that the Blakes should move to his town house in Cirencester Place, where they would be more comfortable and might live rent free. But Blake's weakness was growing upon him, and he could not face the removal:

> Am getting better every morning [he writes optimistically as ever], but slowly, as I am still feeble and tottering, though all the symptoms of my complaint seem almost gone. The fine weather is very beneficial and comfortable to me. I go on, as I think, improving my engravings of Dante more and more, and shall soon get proofs of these four which I have, and beg the favour of you to send me the two plates of Dante which you have, that I may finish them sufficiently to make show of colour and strength.
>
> I have thought and thought of the removal. I cannot get my mind out of a state of terrible fear at such a step. The more I think, the more I feel terror at what I wished at first and thought a thing of benefit and good hope. You will attribute it to its right cause—intellectual peculiarity, that must be myself alone shut up in myself, or reduced to nothing. I could tell you of visions and dreams upon the subject. I have asked and entreated Divine help, but fear continues upon me, and I must relinquish the step that I had wished to take, and still wish, but in vain. [*L.* 1136]

It is in this last year of his life that Blake annotates his copy of Dr Thornton's *New Translation of the Lord's Prayer*, published in the same year. The purpose of Dr Thornton's translation was to put fresh meaning into a devotional text which he felt had been rubbed smooth by centuries of unthinking repetition. Blake will have none of it. 'I look upon this', he writes on the title-page, 'as a Most Malignant & Artful attack upon the Kingdom of Jesus By the Classical Learned, thro' the Instrumentality of Dr. Thornton. The Greek & Roman Classics is the Antichrist. I say Is & not Are as most expressive & correct too.' Dr Thornton quotes Dr Johnson (always a bugbear of Blake's, 'winking & blinking') as saying that the Bible is the most difficult book in the world to understand without a commentary; which of course rouses Blake's indignation:

> Christ & his Apostles were Illiterate Men; Caiaphas, Pilate & Herod were Learned....The Beauty of the Bible is that the most Ignorant & Simple Minds Understand it Best—Was Johnson hired to Pretend to Religious Terrors while he was an Infidel, or how was it? [*T.L.P.* 1028]

Blake goes on to indulge in rather grim merriment about Dr Thornton's translation, which seemed to him to be purely materialistic in spirit. On the flyleaf he writes a parody:

> Doctor Thornton's Tory Translation, Translated out of its disguise in the Classical & Scotch languages into the vulgar English.
>
> Our Father Augustus Ceasar, who art in these thy Substantial Astronomical Telescopic Heavens, Holiness to thy Name or Title, & reverence to thy Shadow. Thy Kingship come upon Earth first & then in Heaven. Give us day by day our Real Taxed Substantial Money bought Bread; deliver from the Holy Ghost whatever cannot be Taxed; for all is debts & Taxes between Caesar & us & one another; lead us not to read the Bible, but let our Bible be Virgil & Shakespeare; & deliver us from Poverty in Jesus, that Evil One. For thine is the Kingship, [or] Allegoric Godship, & the Power, or War, & the Glory, or Law, Ages after Ages in thy descendants; for God is only an Allegory of Kings & nothing Else. Amen. [*T.L.P.* 1031]

It will be noted that Blake's *bêtes noires* are still the same: the Newtonian heavens, kings and priests, war and law, the classics and government. The emphasis may be distributed differently at various points of his works, but the underlying doctrines are constant. His own version of the Lord's Prayer, which he gives as a counterblast to Dr Thornton's 'Tory' version, is frankly communistic. He asks for money, tax and price to be taken away. His final annotations assert that Dr Thornton's real divinity is the Goddess Nature; the Doctor believes 'that God Creates nothing but what can be Touch'd & Weighed & Taxed & Measured'.

This was Blake's last flash of indignation. A letter to George Cumberland, dated 12 April 1827, tells that he has been 'very near the gates of death', and has returned 'very weak and an old man, feeble and tottering, but not in spirit and life, not in the real man, the imagination, which liveth for ever. In that I am stronger and stronger, as this foolish body decays.' In a letter to Linnell of the 25th April he is sanguine about recovery and profitable work; then we hear nothing more until July 3, when he speaks of a Sunday trip to Hampstead which 'brought on a relapse which is lasted till now'. It is the last of the series of letters still extant, and it is written only six weeks before his death.

Blake's last days, spent ill in bed, were taken up with the Dante engravings; but he broke off to draw a portrait of Catherine—'for you have ever been an angel to me', as he said. The end came on Sunday, 12 August 1827, and is best described in the language of a contemporary. George Richmond, an artist and friend of the Linnell group, writes to Samuel Palmer three days after the event:

> Lest you should not have heard of the Death of Mr Blake I have Written this to inform you—He died on Sunday Night at 6 Oclock in a most glorious manner. He said He was going to that Country he had all His life wished to see & expressed himself Happy hoping for Salvation through Jesus Christ—Just before he died His Countenance became fair—His eyes Brighten'd and He burst out in Singing of the things he Saw in Heaven. In truth He Died like a Saint as a person who was standing by Him Observed.

He was buried on Friday of the same week in Bunhill Fields and, according to his own request, with the rites of the Church of England.

Catherine survived her husband four years. For a time she was housekeeper for Linnell at Cirencester Place, as had previously been intended; then she looked after Frederick Tatham's chambers, and finally moved into 'humble lodgings at No. 17 Upper Charlotte Street, Fitzroy Square'. She lived on the proceeds of selling what remained of Blake's drawings and engravings. But she took little care of her health, and called in the doctor only when it was too late. She died on 18 October 1831, at the age of sixty-nine, and was buried at her husband's side in Bunhill Fields. A large number of his drawings and manuscripts were left to Tatham, who is suspected of destroying them on religious grounds.

II

THE EVERLASTING GOSPEL

A. MAN AND NATURE

CHAPTER XI

The Counterpoint of History

The British Antiquities are now in the Artist's hands; all his visionary contemplations, relating to his own country and its ancient glory, when it was, as it again shall be, the source of learning and inspiration. Arthur was a name for the constellation Arcturus, or Boötes, the keeper of the North Pole. And all the fables of Arthur and his round table; of the warlike naked Britons; of Merlin; of Arthur's conquest of the whole world; of his death, or sleep, and promise to return again; of the Druid monuments or temples; of the pavement of Watling-street; of London stone; of the caverns in Cornwall, Wales, Derbyshire and Scotland; of the Giants of Ireland and Britain; of the elemental beings called by us by the general name of Fairies; and of these three who escaped, namely Beauty, Strength, and Ugliness. Mr. B. has in his hands poems of the highest antiquity. Adam was a Druid, and Noah; also Abraham was called to succeed the Druidical age, which began to turn allegoric and mental signification into corporeal command, whereby human sacrifice would have depopulated the earth. All these things are written in Eden. [*D.C.* 796]

MAN, God, Nature—the objects of thought remain ever the same, though each succeeding epoch approaches them from a new angle and gives them a different emphasis. For the citizen of a small Greek state, eagerly working out the problems of government, Man is in the centre of the picture: Man as a political being, with his individuality largely subordinated to the claims of the commonwealth. For the medieval schoolman, the claims of the State are of small account in comparison with the claims of God; to know Him, to serve Him and to love Him are the supreme tasks. *Summa perfectio humani generis est visio divinae essentiae.* With the Renaissance the emphasis shifts again. The investigation of Nature absorbs the finest minds, and the task of the philosopher is somehow to fit the dignity of Man and the majesty of God into the changed world-picture. Of course there is no clear division. Each period leaves over for its successor unsolved enigmas and ill-assimilated points of view. Aquinas builds on the foundations of Aristotle, Bacon launches out into the ocean of truth with a kick at Aquinas. Epochs as well as individuals are 'great amphibiums', living in divided and distinguished worlds.

It is not only the philosophers for whom this metaphysical trinity is the norm. Art expresses in its own way the relations between God, Nature and Man of which philosophy is the more formal or intellectual *summa.* Expresses them, perhaps, more naturally and more completely. Art is the synthesis where metaphysics is the analysis. It springs from the whole man, and the whole man responds in an immediate faith. The happiest times have been those in which art and philosophy have worked together, as they have in the East, in Greece, and in the Middle Ages. But in these cases the philosophy has also been a theology.

There is a third voice which enters into the counterpoint of history. From the beginning there have been God-intoxicated men for whom the world has meant nothing in comparison with the vision of God. To know God, to be united with Him here on earth by an immediate sharing of His life, is the goal of the mystics. Their message has a strange unanimity, and so have the records of their experiences. Eastern or Western, Christian or Buddhist, they talk the same language. If we come to them after some reading in the philosophers, it is like entering a silence suddenly.

In some civilisations there is no division between mysticism and philosophy. The Orphic religion seems to have been of this unitive type; and the East has never separated the two roads to wisdom. But the general trends of mysticism and metaphysics in the West have been divergent, and sometimes widely so. The result has been a certain intellectual poverty in the mysticism, and a certain dryness in the metaphysics.

Art and mysticism have much in common. Blake makes no distinction between them. It is a truism to say that philosophy is a function of the reasoning, and mysticism and art an expression of the unreasoning part of Man—his emotions, his imagination, or his unconscious. We feel the identity of art and mysticism more in some arts than in others: in music, for instance, more than in painting or sculpture. The combination of the two non-representational arts of music and architecture is enormously potent in the service of religion.

Painting, since the Renaissance, has in Europe moved more and more away from its religious allegiance to become the humanistic art *par excellence*. But music, in the least mystical of centuries, could still convey 'thoughts beyond the reaches of our souls' because it was not bound down to representation. Bach and Handel continued to use the archetypal patterns of the dance for strikingly metaphysical ends.

In the same century William Blake presents the union of mystic, philosopher, painter and poet; and presents all of these in the supreme degree. There is, I think, no other mystic who has been so continually absorbed in the Divine Vision; and I know of none who can actually convey the taste of Eternity as he can, by some magic of his verse and his designs. He thought hard, too: the deeper we go into his metaphysical system the more evident appear the workings of an intensely active and powerful mind. He thought about the ultimate things, about Man, and God, and Nature. But not as separate entities. From the beginning he seems to have had no doubt that these three are one; and this unity he saw as Man.

How the primal unity became disrupted, and how it may be restored, is the theme of all his writings and almost all his paintings and engravings. To point the way to reunion was, he thought, the purpose for which he had been sent into the world; he was set apart, and inspired, as really as any prophet of Israel. In this second section of my study I shall examine the nature of his teaching and its meaning for life. But there is a preliminary task which must not be omitted. Blake's work is more than a summing up of history. It is also a criticism of history. What he wrote, and the way he wrote it, are influenced by his strong reaction to the spirit of his own age and of the centuries leading up to it. This criticism is not only implicit: it is often vigorously and uncompromisingly expressed. The Classics, the Druids, Judaism, the Renaissance, Bacon, Newton, and Locke—these meet us at every turn in his writings. Without at least an outline consideration of his attitude to these things we cannot hope to get very near his meaning, even in the early lyrics where overt reference to them does not appear.

In this chapter I have tried to give such an outline. Blake needs to be put in the context of the history of thought, and above all of English thought, if he is to be understood. He cannot be treated as a purveyor of 'pure' literature; the modern fetish of separating the 'poetry' from the 'belief' is even less applicable to him than it is to Milton or Wordsworth. His purpose is entirely and all the time religious, and as a religious writer we must take or leave him.

The counterpoint of history, then, is a double one. We have the three great strands of human thought: Man, Nature and God; and we have the three great looms of philosophy, religion and art for ever weaving their patterns. In the following pages I have had to destroy this counterpoint, for exposition can only deal with one thing at a time. This, Blake would say, is the primal sin of reason, which disrupts the unity of understanding.

For Blake, the counterpoint of history is between two forces, Reason and Imagination, Urizen and Los. Urizen is a terrible figure with his books of iron and his net of religion, binding down souls to the earth. Los is his opposite—the eternal spirit of prophecy, or the Poetic Genius, for ever struggling with Urizen to release the captive spirits of men. These are two aspects of the Human Fourfold, united in Eternity. The other two, Tharmas the body and Luvah the passions, are also perpetually in revolt against Urizen but would be powerless without the aid of Los. Sometimes, indeed, they are seduced into allegiance to their enemy. History thus becomes an exteriorisation of psychology: what is perpetually going on in the mind of Man manifests itself in the pattern of events. But for Blake the mind is the primary thing, apart from which the external scene has no existence. When we come to consider his thought in detail we shall see that he is the expounder of an idealism more thoroughgoing than Plato's or Berkeley's.

It is this counterpoint or tension between Urizen and Los which gives Blake's vast and varied work its unity and its peculiar grandeur. If we can keep it constantly in mind it will make plain much which otherwise seems confused and amorphous. We must always remember that Blake's writings are critical as well as constructive. They form a criticism of history and, we may add, a criticism of historians (such as Hume) who deliberately distort the facts to fit in with a philosophy of their own. In his historical paintings, for example, Blake tries to give

PLATE V

URIZEN REPELLING THE WAVES
(from *The Book of Urizen*)

PLATE VI

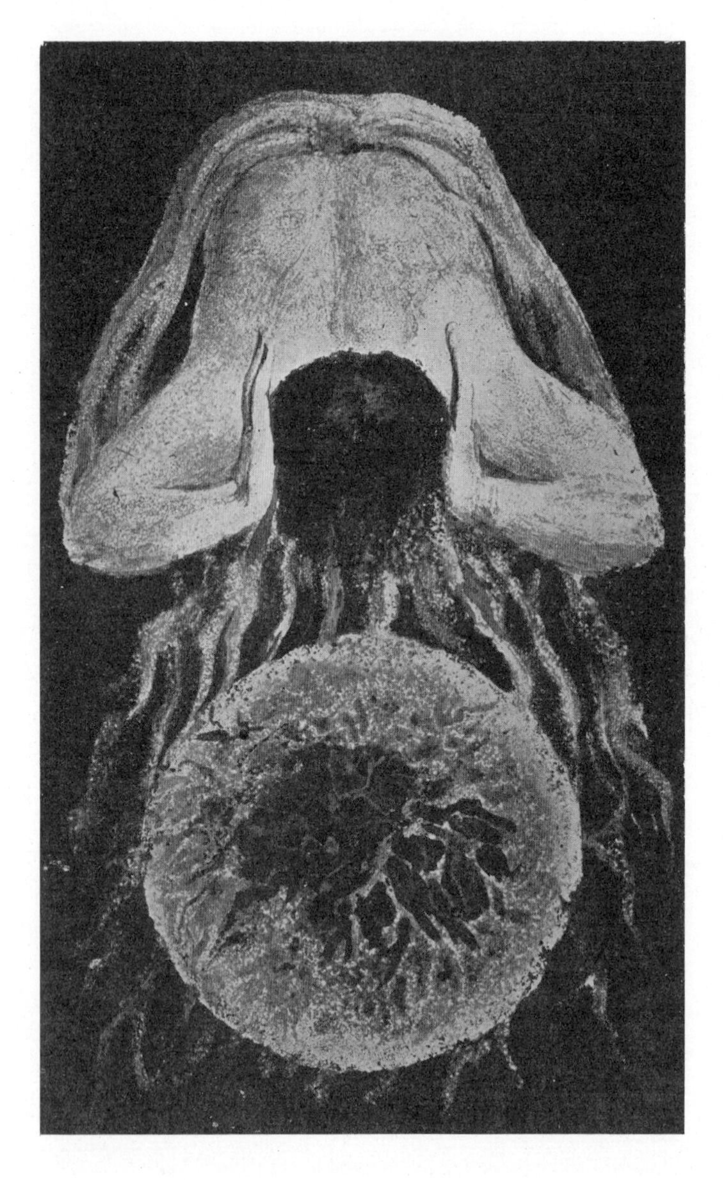

LOS BENDING OVER THE GLOBE OF LIFE BLOOD

(from *The Book of Urizen*)

the historical fact in its poetical vigour so as it always happens, and not in that dull way that some Historians pretend, who, being weakly organized themselves, cannot see either miracle or prodigy; all is to them a dull round of probabilities and possibilities; but the history of all times and places is nothing else but improbabilities and impossibilities; what we should say was impossible if we did not see it always before our eyes.... The reasoning historian, turner and twister of causes and consequences, such as Hume, Gibbon, and Voltaire, cannot with all their artifice turn or twist one fact or disarrange self evident action and reality. Reasons and opinions concerning acts are not history. Acts themselves alone are history, and these are neither the exclusive property of Hume, Gibbon, nor Voltaire, Echard, Rapin, Plutarch, nor Herodotus. Tell me the Acts, O historian, and leave me to reason upon them as I please; away with your reasoning and your rubbish! All that is not action is not worth reading. Tell me the What; I do not want you to tell me the Why, and the How; I can find that out myself, as well as you can, and I will not be fooled by you into opinions, that you please to impose, to disbelieve what you think improbable or impossible. His opinions, who does not see spiritual agency, is not worth any man's reading; he who rejects a fact because it is improbable, must reject all History and retain doubts only. [*D.C.* 797–8]

In these scornful words Blake rejects the sceptical histories current in his time, and affirms his own viewpoint. He does not, it is true, tell us how *any* historical fact or act can be reported without the why and the how creeping in; he does not note that the simple choosing of one fact to report rather than another implies a definite historical viewpoint (for no one can report all the facts) and is therefore prejudiced in some direction. But we know from these words that Blake himself, in what he has to say about history, will be prejudiced in the direction of postulating a 'spiritual agency' and accepting improbable facts or acts.

In spite of this, Blake's political and social attitude, as well as his philosophy, was realistic; it emerged from his observation of the 'minute particulars' of life in his own day and from his judgement on how these particulars had come about.

Thus, mystic as he was, he was also practical and wideawake in a sense that the rationalists, like Locke and Hume, complacently accepting their environment, were not. And this practicality, combined with an intense spiritual insight, is one of the great attractions of Blake. To whatever heights of vision his imagination may soar (and it is often breathtaking to follow him) he never loses sight of the common earth. It seems at first sight a paradox that this visionary, to whom the material world and the 'vile body' were 'as dust under his feet', should be so concerned for the sufferings of animals, for the right education of children, for the evils of the Industrial Revolution, and the proper remuneration of artists. This is not the way of the Eastern sage, who turns his eyes away from Nature and humanity to a sphere of abstraction; nor is it the way of the rationalist philosopher, existing in a world of formulae in which ethics themselves can be reduced to mathematical rules. But it is Blake's way, because it was his mission to show the world how it might redeem itself; and because he knew that all things are bound together in understanding:

> For not one sparrow can suffer & the whole Universe not suffer also
> In all its Regions, & its Father & Saviour not pity & weep. [*J.* 596]

The reader of Blake is soon left in no doubt that his philosophical *bêtes noires* are three: Bacon, Newton and Locke. Bacon comes at the beginning of the seventeenth century and gives the new experimental age its direction. Newton's masterpiece, the *Principia*, was published in 1687; while Locke's *Essay Concerning Human Understanding* appeared in its complete form three years later. Newton applies the inductive method to the stellar universe and discovers that God is a pure mathematician. Locke applies Newton's conclusions to psychology and discovers that human thought is a matter of mathematical combinations. Between Bacon and Locke come a variety of thinkers—Lord Herbert of Cherbury, Thomas Hobbes, and the Cambridge Platonists—who in one way or another rationalised religion and philosophy and paved the way for the triumphs of Deism and utilitarianism in the succeeding centuries. But Blake pays no attention to these intermediate figures. It is in Bacon, Newton and Locke that he sees (quite accurately) the essence of the things which he is to combat. In his own century, it is Voltaire, Gibbon and Hume who set the tone; while Pope introduces into poetry, and Sir Joshua Reynolds into painting, the vicious principles of these philosophers. No aspect of human life is free from the contagion of rationalism.

The course of history, for Blake, may be divided into three great periods. The first of these is the Golden Age, which may properly be said to stand outside history. In the Golden Age there is a complete unity of being; the present universe, with its distinctions of animal, vegetable and mineral, its men and trees and mountains, its earth and air and stars, did not exist. All things were included in the being of the Universal Man. But within the being of the Universal Man there was rebellion; one aspect of the Human Fourfold, reason, revolted against the whole and set himself up as sole lord. Being was disrupted, and in order to save Man from complete destruction the material universe was built. Urizen was the master-builder; but Los, the spirit of poetry, took part in the work that the way might still be open for a return to Eternity. Then followed a period of six thousand years, during which religions of mystery flourished: the strange cults of the East and of America, the Druids in Britain and elsewhere, and lastly the Catholic Church. These were finally overthrown by reason itself, but were followed by the imposition of an even falser and more terrible yoke: Natural Religion or Deism. This is the dispensation which extends from the Renaissance to Blake's own day.

Throughout the whole of history since the Fall, Los has been working like a ferment within the material world to point men's eyes to Eternity; and in the artists and poets and musicians mankind has never lacked prophets, voices crying in the wilderness of mystery or materialism. Blake's wholehearted condemnation of the Druids comes no doubt from the fact that they have left us no evidence of art; only the vast monoliths of Stonehenge which testify to the grossness of their materialism. The Druid religion is the first form taken by Urizen's tyranny after the Fall:

> In thoughts perturb'd they rose from the bright ruins, silent following
> The fiery King, who sought his ancient temple, serpent-form'd,
> That stretches out its shady length along the Island white.
> Round him roll'd his clouds of war; silent the Angel went
> Along the infinite shores of Thames to golden Verulam.
> There stand the venerable porches that high-towering rear
> Their oak-surrounded pillars, form'd of massy stones, uncut
> With tool, stones precious, such eternal in the heavens,
> Of colours twelve, few known on earth, give light in the opake,

> Plac'd in the order of the stars, when the five senses whelm'd
> In deluge o'er the earth-born man.... [*Eu.* 237]

There was a great deal of speculation about the Druids in the circles Blake frequented as a young man. What Blake saw was that Druidism, whatever else it might be, was a religion of mystery, of human sacrifice for sin, closely connected with astronomy. The oak and the rock become permanent symbols of cruelty and tyranny in his verse. In Druidism, indeed, lie the germs of both priestly religion and natural religion: mystery and human sacrifice on the one hand, and astronomical law and mathematic proportion on the other. It is no accident, too, that *Verulam*[1] should enter into Francis Bacon's titles.

Mystery and sacrifice were continued in Judaism. Blake was an assiduous student of the Bible, and he defends its inspiration against Bishop Watson. But he is no apologist for the religion of the Jews. It is a tissue of cruelty and oppression:

> To me, who believe the Bible & profess myself a Christian, a defence of the Wickedness of the Israelites in murdering so many thousands under pretence of a command from God is altogether Abominable & Blasphemous. Why did Christ come? Was it not to abolish the Jewish Imposture? Was not Christ marter'd because he taught that God loved all Men & was their father & forbad all contention for Worldly prosperity in opposition to the Jewish Scriptures, which are only an Example of the wickedness & deceit of the Jews & were written as an Example of the possibility of Human Beastliness in all its branches? [*W.A.* 954–5]

Judaism was a State religion, Moses a consummate statesman, and his code of laws the archetype of all oppressive codes, as the Jewish ceremonial is the archetype of all priestly imposture. The value of the Biblical text lies neither in its moral precepts nor in its historical accuracy, but in its symbolic meaning:

> If Moses did not write the history of his acts, it takes away the authority altogether; it ceases to be history & becomes a Poem of probable impossibilities, fabricated for pleasure, as moderns say, but I say by Inspiration. [*W.A.* 959]

But the spirit of Los worked within Judaism to produce the prophets. In *A Memorable Fancy* Blake tells that he asked Isaiah and Ezekiel

---

[1] See line 5 of the above quotation.

how they dared to assert that God spoke to them; and Isaiah replied that his perception of God was spiritual, a realisation of the infinite in all things. The history of Judaism is the record of a long struggle between the priestly and the prophetic elements.

The rational element of Druidism emerges in the classical civilisations of Greece and Rome. Greece, in Blake's view, bound down inspiration in the chains of reason. 'Greek philosophy...is a remnant of Druidism.' The Greeks had brilliant intuitions of wisdom, but they were at heart grammarians; they mixed up essential meaning with the laws of expression and gave equal validity to the thing said and the way it was said. But essential truth cannot be expressed in a formula exclusive of other formulae. It can only be expressed, in Keyserling's phrase, 'in profound contrapuntal opposition'. The legacy of rationalism which the Greeks bequeathed to the West included and indeed was based on an idea of the substantiality of names and formulae. It was believed that the totality of life could be grasped by the intellect and expressed in schematic form, in which contraries are mutually exclusive opposites: evil against good, truth against error, perfection against imperfection. The Western mind has been formed along these lines and now finds it impossible to think in other terms. Medieval scholasticism had the same foundations.

'The Greek and Roman Classics is the Antichrist.' With the solitary exception of Plato, Blake has nothing good to say of the great writers of Greece and Rome. The classical philosophers are bound in the chains of reason and grammar; and their morality is that of the law. Caesar is Virgil's only God. The Roman religion is State religion at its worst, and Jupiter is identified with Urizen. The Greek sages follow the Jews in teaching that to obey the moral code is the prime duty of life, but their writings lack the inspiration of the Bible:

The Stolen and Perverted Writings of Homer & Ovid, of Plato & Cicero,[1] which all men ought to contemn, are set up by artifice against the Sublime of the Bible; but when the New Age is at leisure to Pronounce,

---

[1] Blake found the idea that pagan learning and art were borrowed from the Hebrews in his favourite author, Milton (cf. *Paradise Regained*, IV). Berkeley, in *Siris*, also favours the theory of Greek borrowing from the East.

all will be set right, & those Grand Works of the more ancient & consciously & professedly Inspired Men will hold their proper rank, & the Daughters of Memory shall become the Daughters of Inspiration. Shakespeare & Milton were both curb'd by the general malady & infection from the silly Greek & Latin slaves of the sword.

The passage from which I quote the above (the *Preface* to *Milton*) goes on to urge the young men of the New Age to oppose those who 'would for ever depress Mental & prolong Corporeal War'. War, indeed, is Urizen's greatest weapon in his campaign to prevent Man from winning his way back to Eternity: he replaces mental by corporeal war. The Greeks and Romans are the prototypes of this; and Blake traces their wars directly to their mechanical morality and their apotheosis of law.

The Classics! it is the Classics, & not Goths nor Monks, that Desolate Europe with Wars. [*Homer & Virgil*, 767]

In a warlike state art can never flourish; there can only be appropriation and copying of the art of other nations.

The third age of the universe begins with the coming of Christ. He comes to bear emphatic witness against the moral code, against sacrifice for sin, and against rational philosophy. He is the summing up and the vital embodiment of all the prophetic energies that had gone before. He is truly the Word made flesh, for what before had been merely potential and exterior is made fully manifest in Him. The whole classical web of grammatical rationalism is torn asunder like the veil of the Temple by the paradox of His life, His teachings and His death.[1] What Blake recognised as the true genius of the Bible is its statement of the continual *tension* between Man and God. It is this tension, this interplay of contraries—the finite and the infinite, the sinful and the holy, tribal jealousy and the all-embracing love of God—which constitutes spiritual progress. The Bible is the record of a series of such tensions, developing on ever higher and higher planes, and culminating inevitably in the tension of the Cross, where

[1] Cf. W. B. Yeats, *Two Songs from a Play*:

'Odour of blood when Christ was slain
Made all Platonic tolerance vain,
And vain all Doric discipline.'

God, now identified *as Man*, resolves the series in Himself. All interplay of contraries, before and after Calvary, have reference to that central event and find in it their significance. Calvary is thus truly an Atonement.

Blake's root objection to paganism, to the perfection of Greek art, is thus explained. The Greeks failed to embody this tension, but sought instead to obtain fulfilment purely on the plane of this life. The cult of the Mean, of bodily and mental *ascesis* in preparation for this-worldly achievement, implies a blindness to the striving which is called spiritual. For spirit and matter are not principles on the same plane, nor can they be integrated on democratic terms. Spirit is the meaning, matter is the expression. The profound vein of pessimism which emerges again and again in Greek literature owes its origin to this attempt at a false balance. The Greeks tried—and their attempt was a magnificent one—to subdue the immortal spirit to an enjoyment of the beauty of this world; but they were unsuccessful. Plato, bound though he was in grammatical chains, constantly outpasses the limits of orthodox philosophy; the great dramatists cry with an anguish they cannot fully understand; and in the decay of Greek civilisation the Neo-Platonists are already on the mystic way.

The religion which Christ came to preach was the forgiveness of sins and the Kingdom of Heaven—the possibility of finding the way back to Eternity through vision and faith. He is fundamentally opposed to the Mosaic law and an arch-rebel in religion, politics, and morals. His teaching is simple:

> Jesus supposes every Thing to be Evident to the Child & to the Poor & Unlearned. Such is the Gospel. [*B.S.* 1022]

Indeed, it is too simple for the Scribes and Pharisees, who see that Christ's teaching of the forgiveness of sins overturns all their doctrines of sin and sacrifice. So they crucify Jesus, thereby unconsciously fulfilling His mission:

> Thus was the Lamb of God condemn'd to Death.
> They nail'd him upon the tree of Mystery, weeping over him
> And then mocking & then worshipping, calling him Lord & King.
> [*F.Z.* 411]

The Church, when Christ has passed from this earth, continues to worship the Cross—to worship the Crucifixion, which is Death, and not the Resurrection, which is Life.

> The Modern Church Crucifies Christ with the Head Downwards. [*V.L.J.* 842]

Priestcraft seizes upon and casts out the simplicity of the original gospel: the Catholic Church erects a new and elaborate ceremonial based upon the ancient pagan rites of sacrifice. Classical rationalism distorts the teaching of Man's sonship and participation in the eternal: the vast structure of scholasticism slowly grows up. But the spirit of Jesus could not wholly depart from the Church:

> The Divine Vision still was seen,
> Still was the Human Form Divine,
> Weeping in weak & mortal clay,
> O Jesus, still the Form was thine. [*J.* 599]

In its saints and mystics who sought communion with God, the Church harboured men of Christ-like character; in its art, the Gothic, the Church embodied 'living form'.

On the whole, however, medieval Christianity is antagonistic to the Gospel. The Church takes over precisely those moral statutes of Judaism which Jesus came to abolish, and she reinforces these with a code of sexual morals sterner than any the pagan world had known:

> As the caterpiller chooses the fairest leaves to lay her eggs on, so the priest lays his curse on the fairest joys. [*M.H.H.* 194]

As an organisation the Church did not understand the revolutionary nature of Christ's teaching but allowed it to be glossed and ceremonialised out of all recognition. Christianity was enslaved by the State when Constantine made it the official religion, and that moment marked its doom as a free power working for revolution. And with the fall of the Roman Empire another and spiritually more tyrannical Rome arose under the popes. The net of religion is spread across the world, and priestly imposture governs every energy of life.

With the Reformation Blake has no sympathy.[1] He sees the narrowness of its doctrines, and recognises in the revolt of Luther

---

[1] 'Remember how Calvin and Luther in fury premature
Sow'd War and stern division between Papists & Protestants.' [*M.* 507]

and Calvin not a movement towards spiritual freedom but an outburst of envy against the glory and power of Rome. The prose rhapsody, *Then she bore Pale desire* (written before 1777), makes clear Blake's feelings on this point. My quotation begins with pagan Rome:

> Rome, seated on seven hills, the mistress of the world, Emblem of Pride. She saw the Arts their treasures Bring, and luxury his bounteous table spread. But now a cloud o'ercasts and back to th' East, to Constantine's Great City, Empire fled, Ere long to bleed & die, A sacrifice done by a Priestly hand. So, once, the Sun his Chariot drew back to prolong a Good King's life. The cloud o'erpast & Rome now shone again, Miter'd and crown'd with triple crown. Then Pride was better Pleas'd. She saw the World fall down in Adoration. But now, full to the Setting Sun, a Sun arose out of the Sea; it rose, and shed Sweet Influence o'er the Earth. Pride feared for her City, but not long, for looking stedfastly, she saw that Pride Reign'd here. Now Direful Pains accost her, and still pregnant, so Envy came, & Hate, twin progeny. Envy hath a serpent's head of fearful bulk, hissing with hundred tongues; her pois'nous breath breeds Satire, foul contagion, from which none are free. [*M.Pr.* 862]

The piece continues in this vein to relate how the Church was disrupted and how the Wars of Religion deluged Europe in blood. It is yet another confirmation of Blake's thesis that priestly religion is an aspect of power politics and must resort from time to time to war which is power politics' inevitable weapon. Catholic and Protestant alike have completely overthrown the Gospel of Jesus, the gospel of love and forgiveness.

But worse is to follow. With all its faults, the medieval Church had at least paid lip-worship to Jesus and the medieval mystics had borne witness to *la primauté du spirituel.* The Renaissance is a second Fall. The rational man is set up as the type of perfection; the religious world-view is denied. But this does not mean freedom. A new mystery takes the place of the old, a mystery clothing itself in mathematic form. The priestly imposture had seemed to be consumed in the religious wars, but no:

> The Ashes of Mystery began to animate; they call'd it Deism
> And Natural Religion; as of old, so now anew began
> Babylon again in Infancy, call'd Natural Religion. [*F.Z.* 422]

The high priests of the new religion are Bacon, Newton and Locke: still derived from the Druids, for their mathematical reasonings are merely extensions of the rational principles which raised the monoliths of Stonehenge and connected their proportions with the motions of the stars. Sir Isaac Newton would have been astonished to hear himself denounced as the arch-Druid of history; but such, in Blake's view, he is. These three famous philosophers are seen as

> Three strong sinewy Necks & Three awful & terrible Heads,
> Three Brains, in contradictory council brooding incessantly,
> Neither daring to put in act its councils, fearing each-other,
> Therefore rejecting Ideas as nothing & holding all Wisdom
> To consist in the agreements & disagreements of Ideas,
> Plotting to devour Albion's Body of Humanity & Love....
> Three Forms named Bacon & Newton & Locke
> In the Oak Groves of Albion which overspread all the Earth. [*J.* 690]

The whole of Blake's system of thought constitutes, in effect, a criticism and a refutation of the philosophy of these three seventeenth-century thinkers.

It is time now to turn specifically to what we may call the root concept of history: the ways in which Man has regarded his own nature, for upon that depend his attitudes towards Nature and towards God.

Blake had the misfortune to be born into a century with grossly inadequate views of Man as a psychological, social or religious being. In place of the medieval antithesis of the sinner and the saint, based on the very realistic doctrine of the Fall, the philosophers had substituted a single abstract man corresponding in no way to reality. This strange figure was born without instincts, innate ideas or even capacity; he was perfectly amenable to education, which could transform him into a Michelangelo, a Newton or a Shakespeare at will; in a hypothetic 'state of nature' he lived strictly according to reason, but entered into a hypothetic 'social contract' for convenience; and by a further exercise of reason he could rid himself of prejudices which had been foisted on him by designing kings and priests. Individual men were of course equal, and should live together in a democracy.

This doctrine, in its pure state, recommended itself more to the logical French mind than to English common sense. Though it was John Locke who had assured his contemporaries that Man is 'by nature free, equal and independent' and born 'with a title to perfect freedom and uncontrolled enjoyment of all the rights and privileges of the law of nature', his fellow-countrymen during the hundred years between the *Essay* and the French Revolution continued to laud these sentiments in theory without in the least attempting to put them into practice or even develop their implications. That was left for the Encyclopédistes, for Helvétius and Voltaire and Rousseau. It was David Hume who delivered the really shattering blow not only against miracles but against the existence of a supreme being; but no one would have been more surprised (and I think we may say horrified) than he if he had seen Mrs Siddons enthroned as the goddess Reason on the high altar of Westminster Abbey. It is the English genius often to originate ideas, but never to push them to an extreme in theory or practice.

In England, though Locke was accepted as the philosopher *par excellence* and occupied, as Professor Willey has pointed out, a place not unlike that filled by Aristotle in the Middle Ages—though this was so, a hierarchical society continued to exist and showed no signs of exploding. In spite of Hume, natural religion flourished and the necessary hypothesis of a supreme being was everywhere accepted. It is characteristic, again, that Locke's two *Treatises Of Civil Government* were written to justify a revolution that was past, and not one that was to come. After the Glorious Revolution of 1688, Englishmen could settle down to live in peace and rational harmony, evil kings having been abolished with James II and presumptuous priests with the Non-jurors. Everything was now for the best in the best of all possible worlds.

The dominant characteristic of this chapter of our history seems to me its lack of energy. The great outburst of English vigour had come in the sixteenth century with the discoveries of Drake and Raleigh and the drama of Marlowe and Shakespeare. This vigour had degenerated in the succeeding age into religious bickerings, and the Civil War had disgusted all sensible men with its antitheses of Anglican and Calvinist, of Presbyterian and Independent. The eighteenth century wanted none of this; it preferred to call intellectual

14-2

energy enthusiasm and settle down into a calm *laissez-faire*. Man was considered solely as the rational animal; reason was the restrainer, the lid of Pandora's box. Once this lid is allowed to lift, who knows what horrors may not come flying out, never to be imprisoned again?

The honour of opening the box, if honour it be, we must give to William Blake. He was the first to be fully conscious of the wide disparity between fact and fiction in eighteenth-century psychology. He does not seem to have arrived at this understanding by slow and regular stages, but to have grasped the essential contradiction at once. He looked at men around him, and he looked into himself, and said: Men are not at all like that. They are not primarily rational, but emotional and imaginative. The mind is not a sheet of white paper at birth; it is scrawled over and blotted and illuminated by instincts and hereditary dispositions and innate talent. Men are not, moreover, confined to a mean position between hypothetical angels and ravening beasts. This 'isthmus of a middle state' may be crossed at will if only we have faith and vision.

CHAPTER XII

The Material Universe

> A murderous Providence! A Creation that groans, living on Death,
> Where Fish & Bird & Beast & Man & Tree & Metal & Stone
> Live by Devouring, going into Eternal Death continually! [*J*. 645]

BLAKE'S view of Nature derives from the highly personal fact of his own vision of the natural order *sub specie æternitatis*: that is to say, it is not a construction based on contemporary scientific theory. On the contrary, it is deliberately set against the scientific world-view. It has much in common, on the one hand, with the world-view of savages as set forth in the works of Lévy-Bruhl, and, on the other, with the simplifications of the artist. This 'double-vision' realisation of the world around him goes back, as with Wordsworth, to experiences of earliest childhood. But whereas, with Wordsworth, the experiences were vague and mysterious—

> Low breathings coming after me, and sounds
> Of undistinguishable motion—

in Blake's case they took precise theological forms: the figures of angels walking among the haymakers, and the face of God Himself looking out of the material frame of the universe.

We may suspect, of course, the influence of a Swedenborgian atmosphere in the Blake household. Later it is in his readings of Jakob Boehme that we must seek the more philosophic basis of his vision. Boehme, whose life in its obscurity and devotion to truth resembles Blake's at so many points, had also been engaged in constructing a system that should embrace Nature, and human history, and the nature of God, in a single synthesis. His work *Signatura Rerum* inspired much of Blake's thought on the double vision as applied to plants and animals and stones, in which the secret wisdom unattainable by the natural philosophers is opened to the enlightened imagination. However, with Boehme as much as with his other 'sources', we find Blake quietly leaving the track at some point where he meets a denial of his guiding principles of joy, forgiveness and the holiness of all that lives—and boldly striking out on his own. He is, at heart, the most independent of thinkers.

The natural philosophers—Bacon, Newton, Locke and their followers—believed that the key to the secrets of Nature lay in acute observation and experiment; and they believed that the Nature they were investigating was an ultimate. That is to say, they studied Nature to know Nature and have power over Nature. They wanted to wrest her secrets from her and so extend Man's glory and power as a denizen of this earth. But the aim of the theosophists (among whom, for our present purposes, we may class Boehme and Blake) was quite different. For them, Nature was not an ultimate, but a mask. It corresponded to something real, but that something was hidden. Nature can tell us about reality, but only after the fashion of a cryptogram. It has to be deciphered. We must have the key before we can begin to understand. To use another analogy, we may say that the message written in invisible ink has to be held in front of the fire before it can be read. This fire is the flame of understanding, or the love of God.[1]

Moreover, it is not for power over Nature that the theosophist seeks, but for understanding of the deep things of God. This understanding, which comes to him in its purest form in contemplation, may be widened and deepened through the study of the 'signatures of things' Boehme, in contrast to many of the saints of Catholicism, does not despise the beauty of the natural creation, but uses it as a window to the Divine. In this he is followed, especially in *Milton*, by Blake.

Many of the theosophists who were also alchemists did, in point of fact, seek for control over Nature and sometimes thought they had found it in the philosopher's stone or the elixir. But the more profound among them, such as Robert Fludd and Thomas Vaughan, gave even their alchemical speculations a spiritual meaning: and in Blake the beloved word 'gold' comes to lose its material sense entirely. In *magic*, again—that venerable tradition which also lends something to Blake's eclectic symbolism—the attempt to get at Nature's forces without experimentation is paramount. Obviously there is a close affinity between mysticism—the direct approach to

[1] The key to the cryptogram was held by Kepler and Galileo to be mathematics; but this of course was not accepted by the Hermetists.

God—and magic—the direct approach to Nature. If Man's body is a microcosm, as the Hermetic tradition down to Blake asserted, movements within it must be associated with and influential upon, as well as influenced by, movements in the macrocosm.[1]

Whatever the defects of the theosophical view of the universe, it did at least stress two points which orthodox Baconian doctrine tended to forget. First, the unity of all things. Second, the quality of life in all things. Nothing is dead, and there is no dualism of body and spirit, of Man and Nature, or of Man and God. There is, however, a balance of contraries—in the world, in Man, in the divine nature: and in this aspect theosophy forms as great a contrast to orthodox mysticism on the one hand as it does to orthodox science on the other. Orthodox mysticism insists that God is a unity, a *simplicity* inexpressible in any terms, even symbolic; the best we can do is to speak of Nothing, or Darkness; and we must not venture to suppose contradiction in the Divine Essence. Theosophy says No: there are contraries in the Divine Essence; through the interplay of these contraries Eternity becomes an ever-growing thing, not a static perfection. And through the doctrine of the contraries Boehme and Blake can explain what on the terms of orthodoxy are inexplicable: the creation of the world, and the existence of evil.

The data we note in the world around us may bring us to agree that this unorthodox view of God is more probable than the orthodox. The universe is what we would expect as the creation of a deity in whom darkness and light, good and evil, and even truth and error exist as a counterpoint of contraries. The universe as created by a metaphysically undifferentiated deity (if we can get over the crux of explaining why there should be any creation at all) would surely be infinitely more simple—a reflection of the divine of-a-pieceness. Moreover, the doctrine of evolution, so fatal to many mystical theories, fits in excellently well with the doctrine of a progressive eternity. The temporal order is quite neatly a mirror of the eternal order: or, as Blake would say, a distorted image of it.

The matter may be summed up by saying that God, in the theosophical view, is imagination; in the orthodox view, reason, eternally

---

[1] Blake gives this idea unwontedly Rabelaisian expression in the MS. verses beginning 'When Klopstock England defied' [*M.P.* 103].

contemplating itself. The eternal self-contemplative reason must remain pure and undefiled: its attention is fixed upon a point. But it is the function of imagination ever to burgeon out into new shapes, to create new ideas. There is no abstraction in the divine nature. The multifarious forms of things which we behold in this lower world are not pure illusion, even to the mystic insight: they are distorted formulations of existence in the noumenal world. It is only when we insist on seeing them as matter that we make them unreal, for matter has no existence, it is an abstraction of the rational faculty.

There is, therefore, a Nature or Pleroma in the eternal world: it is known to Blake as Jerusalem, the aggregate of minute particulars in the being of the Universal Man. As we have seen already, Man can cognise these particulars when he will, or, on the contrary, he can cognise unity in the form of Jesus. But on the temporal plane the minute particulars, torn from the body of Man at the Fall, are envisaged as Vala, a jealous cruel shadow opaque to the Divine Vision, Nature rejoicing in its separateness. We men are faced with the choice of seeing Vala or Jerusalem.

The shadow-nature, Vala, is cruel and jealous and hungry when separated from the divine. We should note how, often, Blake gives the attribute of *hunger* to Nature even in his most lyrical passages. Just as Urizen, the originator of the Fall, separated himself from Eternity, and withdrew into solitude, so Vala, his disciple, contracts herself and tries to draw all things into her maw and devour them. Matter is constantly seeking to destroy spirit. Albion himself shrinks, and only the Saviour's mercy in fixing the 'limit of contraction' saves him from being swallowed up altogether.

But working within Nature is Los, a principle of expansion, causing the minute particulars to grow in the sun's beams and 'look abroad' for the coming of the day of resurrection and unity. Hence the *tension* in Nature: the tension of life, or spirit, working against dead matter: achieving consciousness in stone, herb and beast, according to Blake's view, but the expression of consciousness only in Man, 'for the gate of the tongue is closed'. From this antagonism of the two principles of contraction and expansion motion arises: the Circle of Destiny begins to revolve, and the illusion of time and space presents itself to 'our mortal vegetative vision'. Los and

Enitharmon, who before the Fall 'contracted and expanded their all flexible senses' with the other immortals, now become fixed in the world of generation as time and space respectively. I shall have something to say about Blake's view of time and space in a moment.

The rotation of the Wheel of Destiny is accompanied with the keenest anguish. 'The whole creation groaneth and travaileth in pain together until now.' And the movement is an endless one: the creation has no power to free itself from the wheel: what is demanded is an intervention from above, i.e. from the order of Eternity. This intervention is granted with the coming of Christ. The creation groans for freedom, conscious of its enslavement; freedom is purely of the spiritual order. This freedom Jesus brings by pointing to the unconditioned, the Kingdom of Heaven, which is within. In spite of its anguish the creation is not willing to accept such a freedom: the remedy seems too simple and therefore 'chimerical'. The Four Zoas are not ready to resubmit themselves. It is hard to give oneself up to the second birth, especially as that birth is only attainable through the fire, i.e. the destruction of corporeal forms.

The theosophical view of Nature, in both its mystical and its alchemical aspects, was combated by Francis Bacon, whose position as the key figure standing at the parting of the ways between medieval and modern England has been sufficiently commented on.[1] It is unlikely that Jakob Boehme was known to Bacon even by name, nor does he refer directly to the great English cabbalist Robert Fludd, though there are strong indications that he was familiar with his writings (especially his account of the Creation) and was at some pains to refute his opinions. But there is no doubt that the mainspring of Bacon's 'Novum Organum', his *máchina technica* for the advancement of the sciences, was a turning away from the vitalistic universe of the theosophists to a mechanical universe: a manifold of material objects in space, dead matter analysable by dissection and experiment. We need not strive to understand: we need only investigate and manipulate. We are not concerned with the why, only with the how. This substitution of a mechanical world-scheme for

---

[1] The best general account will be found in the first two chapters of Professor Basil Willey's *The Seventeenth Century Background*.

the living universe of the cabbalists made Bacon the evil genius, the Urizen, of Blake's historical drama. Together with Newton and Locke, he is the supreme diverter of men's attention from their eternal salvation to the study of matter; and back to him may be traced most of the ills which Blake saw afflicting the society of his time. Among these we may note the brutalities of the Industrial Revolution, the decline of faith, and the mistaken psychology of human nature.

In what follows there is no attempt to give a synopsis of Bacon's argument in the *Advancement of Learning*. What I have done is to pick out those particular doctrines that must have irritated Blake most, and against which he explicitly turns his attack in his later writings. He tells us that he read 'Locke on Human Understanding & Bacon's Advancement of Learning' when he was 'very Young', and that his feeling was one of abhorrence.[1] 'They mock Inspiration & Vision. Inspiration & Vision was then, & now is, & I hope will always Remain, my Element, my Eternal Dwelling place; how can I then hear it Contemned without returning Scorn for Scorn?'

Bacon's main object in the *Advancement* is to divert men's minds from the search for final causes into a study of secondary causes, i.e. the laws of Nature, which have yet to be discovered and adequately commented on. This discovery can only be effected by observation and experimentation. Such was the felicity of Adam in Paradise, that he had no other work to do but consider and investigate the works of God. He was an experimentalist:

> After the Creation was finished, it is set down unto us that man was placed in the Garden to work therein; which work so appointed to him could be no other than work of contemplation;[2] that is, when the end of work is but for exercise and experiment, not for necessity; for there being then no reluctation of the creature, nor sweat of the brow, man's employment must of consequence have been matter of delight in the experiment, and not matter of labour for the use.[3]

---

[1] *Annotations to Reynolds' Discourses* (*R.D.* 1011). We find him quoting the *Advancement* in a letter to Dr Trusler, 23 August 1799: it is interesting to note that it is the original English version of 1605 that he uses, and not, as we might expect, a translation of the *De Augmentis*.

[2] The meaning of 'contemplation' for Bacon is very far from the received mystical sense: 'study' would come near the mark.

[3] *Advancement*, I.

This study of the external world is still the best use to which man can put his time, when he is freed from the sweat of the brow, for

> God hath framed the mind of man as a mirror or glass capable of the image of the universal world, and joyful to receive the impression thereof, as the eye joyeth to receive light; and not only delighted in beholding the variety of things and vicissitude of times, but raised also to find out and discern the ordinances and decrees which throughout all those changes are infallibly observed.[1]

The chief error of the mind, on the other hand, is to look into itself. Men must be humble and submit themselves to learn of nature:

> Another error hath proceeded from too great a reverence, and a kind of adoration of the mind and understanding of man; by means whereof men have withdrawn themselves too much from the contemplation of nature and the observations of experience, and have tumbled up and down in their own reason and conceits.[1]

Bacon suggests that even religion will benefit when the eyes of men are turned outwards upon the Creation; for the external world is nothing less than a second Scripture, declaring the power of God with no feeble voice.

This suggestion leads us straight into the realm of Natural Theology—the view of the relations of God, Nature and Man which held sway right up to Blake's day and found its most incisive voice in Thomas Paine. As the subject of Deism receives separate treatment in a later chapter, there is no need to discuss Bacon's elaboration of this thesis in the *Advancement*.[2] To Blake, who held that all deities reside in the human breast, and that we must seek God within us by a 'contemplation' very different from Bacon's, this is sheer error. True, he would agree that the footsteps of a creator can be traced in the universe: but this creator is precisely Urizen, the 'avenger', as Bacon calls him in an expansion of this section in the *De Augmentis*.[3]

Blake's frequent imagery of mines and furnaces in the symbolic books has been traced to various sources: the Industrial Revolution, the impedimenta of alchemy, and others; but it is interesting to find

---

[1] *Advancement*, I. [2] See below, Ch. XVIII.

[3] *De Augmentis*, III, 2 (p. 456 of the Ellis & Spedding one-volume edition of the Philosophical Works, ed. J. M. Robertson, 1905).

the hint here in the *Advancement*, with exactly Blake's application to the investigation and manipulation of the material universe:

If then it be true that Democritus said, 'That the truth of nature lieth hid in certain deep mines and caves'; and if it be true likewise that the Alchemists do so much inculcate, that Vulcan is a second nature, and imitateth that dexterously and compendiously which Nature worketh by ambages and length of time; it were good to divide natural philosophy into the mine and the furnace, and to make two professions or occupations of natural philosophers, some to be pioners and some smiths; some to dig, and some to refine and hammer.[1]

Blake took up this hint and expanded it in the machinery of *The Four Zoas*; but another suggestion of Bacon's, attacking the notion of a quaternary, was of course most obnoxious to Blake and he takes every opportunity of opposing it. Bacon is discussing 'the false appearances that are imposed upon us by the general nature of the mind'.

Hence it cometh, that whereas there are many things in nature as it were *monodica, sui juris*, yet the cogitations of man do feign unto them relatives, parallels, and conjugates, whereas no such thing is; as they have feigned an element of *Fire, to keep square with Earth, Water and Air*,[2] and the like: nay, it is not credible, till it be opened, what a number of fictions and fancies the similitude of human actions and arts, together with the making of man *communis mensura*, have brought into Natural Philosophy; not much better than the heresy of the Anthropomorphites, bred in the cells of gross and solitary monks, and the opinion of Epicurus, answerable to the same in heathenism, who supposed the gods to be of human shape. And therefore Velleius the Epicurean needed not to have asked, why God should have adorned the heaven with stars, as if he had been an Aedilis, one that should have set forth some magnificent shows or plays. For if that great work-master had been of an human disposition, he would have cast the stars into some pleasant and beautiful works and orders, like the frets in the roofs of houses; whereas one can scarce find a posture in square or triangle or straight line amongst such an infinite number; so differing an harmony there is between the spirit of Man and the spirit of Nature.[3]

---

[1] *Advancement*, II.

[2] My italics. Hence Blake's insistence (e.g. in *The Gates of Paradise*) on these four elements.

[3] *Advancement*, II. Blake picks up Bacon's phrase 'the great work master' and applies it to Urizen the demiurge at the beginning of the creation narrative from which the following quotation is taken. The phrase also occurs in a similar context in Spenser's *Hymne in Honour of Beautie*, stanza 5.

Blake's reaction to this passage is evident everywhere in his writings; in his defence of monks, in his insistence on the human form of the Divine, and not least in the wonderful passage of *The Four Zoas* in which every line seems to have been written in refutation of Bacon's thesis. Note the emphasis on square, triangle and straight line:

> Thus were the stars of heaven created like a golden chain
> To bind the Body of Man to heaven from falling into the
> Abyss.
> Each took his station & his course began with sorrow & care....
> Travelling in silent majesty along their order'd ways
> In right lined paths outmeasur'd by proportions of number,
> weight,
> And measure, mathematic motion wondrous along the deep,
> In fiery pyramid, or Cube, or unornamented pillar square
> Of fire, far shining, travelling along even to its destin'd end....
> Others triangular, right angled course maintain. Others obtuse,
> Acute, Scalene, in simple paths; but others move
> In intricate ways, biquadrate, Trapeziums, Rhombs, Rhomboids,
> Paralellograms triple & quadruple, polygonic
> In their amazing hard subdu'd course in the vast deep. [*F.Z.* 313–4]

By what alchemy Blake turns this odd collection of mathematical terms into great poetry we do not know; but it is still more curious to consider that we owe the whole splendidly vigorous passage to Blake's remembrance of a theory of Bacon's which he particularly disliked. Mathematical forms are commonly one of the evil things for Blake: here he uses them as a stick to beat Bacon.[1]

Bacon actually knew little about mathematics and less about astronomy. His world-picture is limited to this earth, to the terrestrial sciences, and to their application to the advancement of man's power and comfort. It is when we turn to the Newtonian world-picture that we find these studies attaining their supremacy, and 'living form

---

[1] Thus we find a curious inconsistency in Blake's use of mathematical imagery. When he is thinking of his beloved quaternary, or of Bacon's denial of it, he makes mathematical proportion an instrument of the creative Los. When he is thinking of the mechanical world-picture of Newton, mathematical proportion is seen as devilish.

destroyed by mathematic form'. Blake attacked Newton's vision, upturned to the stars—

> Innumerable, pitiless, passionless eyes,
> Cold fires, yet with power to burn and brand
> His nothingness into man....

—just as he had attacked Bacon's vision, directed downwards to plants and minerals. Both are divagations from the true way, the road back to Eternity.

Blake was concerned more with the consequences of Newton's theory, its meaning for ethics and theology, than with its scientific correctness, though we shall come in a moment to instances where he attacked the Newtonian time and space from a relativist standpoint. These consequences for theology are traced in a later chapter.[1] Meanwhile it may be noted that in all probability Blake derived a good deal of his ammunition against Newtonianism from the criticism of Bishop Berkeley, a philosopher we know he read and found, on the whole, congenial. Newton's direct influence on formal philosophy was very great. He set the tone for much of Locke's theorising, particularly in the direction of ascribing a soul to matter and positing space as the sensorium of God. In his third letter to Stillingfleet, Locke sees no reason why God should not have given matter a power of thinking as He has given it the power of moving in circles and ellipses. 'I am convinced by the judicious Mr Newton's incomparable book', he writes, 'that it is too bold a presumption to limit God's power in this point by my narrow conceptions.' Again, Locke's picture of a universe devoid of colour, sound, taste, odour, etc.—all the 'secondary' qualities—owes much to the *Principia*. No wonder Blake speaks in the *Descriptive Catalogue* of 'the Barren Waste of Locke and Newton'.

It was this barren waste, and the whole picture of reality dominated by Newton's law of gravitation, which Berkeley attacked in his *Treatise Concerning the Principles of Human Knowledge* (1710). Nowadays, he says, the great shibboleth by which everything is explained is 'gravitation', which explains nothing.

---

[1] See below, Ch. XVIII.

> The great mechanical principle in vogue is *attraction.* That a stone falls to the earth, or the sea swells towards the moon, may to some appear sufficiently explained thereby. But how are we enlightened by being told this is done by attraction?[1]

The scientists 'amuse themselves in vain' when they look for any cause apart from a mind; they should 'employ their thoughts (contrary to what some hold) about the *final causes of things*'.[2] We cannot know that the Author of Nature always works uniformly, 'in a constant observance of those rules we take for principles'. Berkeley terms scientists the *grammarians* of Nature, men who can very well distinguish the signs of the divine language without understanding its import:

> A wise man will choose to fix his thoughts on the sense and apply it to use, rather than lay them out in *grammatical remarks* on the language; so in perusing the volume of nature, it seems beneath the dignity of the mind to affect an exactness in reducing *each particular phenomenon to general rules*, or showing how it follows from them.[3]

There are nobler views than these to be had of Nature, views which will 'recreate and exalt the mind' and bring us to a closer or larger 'notion' of God.

It is interesting to see Berkeley returning here to what seems very like the old cabbalistic theory of the 'signatura rerum' with which we began this enquiry.

'The best grammar of the kind we are speaking of', Berkeley goes on, 'will be easily acknowledged to be a certain celebrated treatise of *mechanics*.' The reference is, of course, to the *Principia*. Berkeley could hardly ignore Newton; the completeness and success of his system stood directly in the way of his idealism, barring all approach for the world at large. He does not 'take upon him to make remarks on that extraordinary person', but he must consider 'some things he has advanced, so directly opposite to the doctrine we have hitherto laid down'. At the very beginning of that 'justly admired treatise' Newton makes certain propositions about time, space and

[1] *Principles*, 103. In fairness to Newton one must note that he never claimed or wished to 'explain' in this sense: his business was to record and classify observations.

[2] *Ibid.* 107. Berkeley's demand would, of course, entirely destroy science as we know it.

[3] *Ibid.* 109.

motion, which he distinguishes into absolute and relative, true and apparent, mathematical and vulgar; and all such distinctions suppose these ideas to have an existence 'without the mind'. These Berkeley proceeds to consider.

'Time, place and motion', he has noted a little earlier, 'taken in particular or concrete, are what everybody knows, but, having passed through the hands of a metaphysician, they become too abstract and fine to be apprehended by men of ordinary sense.'

> For my own part, whenever I attempt to frame a simple idea of *time*, abstracted from the succession of ideas in my mind, which flows uniformly and is participated by all beings, I am lost and embrangled in inextricable difficulties. I have no notion of it at all, only I hear others say it is infinitely divisible, and speak of it in such a manner as leads me to entertain odd thoughts of my own existence; since that doctrine lays one under an absolute necessity of thinking, either that he passes away innumerable ages without a thought, or else that he is annihilated every moment of his life, both which seem equally absurd....[1]

Now he proceeds with a similar criticism of Newtonian space, which is held to be absolute, in that it is imperceptible to sense; while there is also a relative space, which can be defined in relation to bodies. *Place* is that part of space occupied by any body, and may be absolute or relative according as the space is one or the other. Berkeley denies the existence of pure space in its absolute sense. It cannot exist 'without the mind', i.e. without being perceived. He does not even think that we can frame an idea of pure space exclusive of all body:

> When I speak of pure or empty space, it is not to be supposed, that the word *space* stands for an idea distinct from, or conceivable without body and motion. Though indeed *we are apt to think every noun substantive stands for a distinct idea*, that may be separated from all others: which hath occasioned infinite mistakes.[2]

Berkeley's endeavour all the time is to get rid of the tyranny of abstract ideas which in his opinion has vitiated philosophical thought for so long. By so doing, we are freed from 'that dangerous dilemma, to which several who have employed their thoughts on this subject

[1] *Principles*, 98. This passage has obviously inspired the Blakean diagram of time quoted below (p. 235). Note especially how Blake provides against 'annihilation every moment' by placing 'between every two Moments...a Daughter of Beulah'.

[2] *Ibid.* 116.

imagine themselves reduced, to wit, of thinking either that real space is God, or else that there is something besides God which is eternal, uncreated, infinite, indivisible, immutable'. This is directed at Locke and Dr Samuel Clarke, and to some extent at Newton, who, though he hesitated to identify space with God, thought it the 'boundless uniform sensorium' of the Deity.

Berkeley rounds off this section on the scientists with a criticism of mathematics. He does not deny the truth of mathematical principles or of deductions from them; but he thinks that erroneous views about quantity, common to both physics and mathematics, may lead to great errors in the *philosophy of mathematics.*

> To be plain, we suspect the mathematicians are, as well as other men, concerned in the errors (i) arising from the doctrine of abstract general ideas, and (ii) the existence of objects without the mind.[1]

He attacks the abstract idea of number, in a consideration of arithmetic, then deals in the same way with geometry and the idea of *extension.* Finally he criticises the idea of infinitesimals which is the basis of the calculus.

> Whatever the mathematicians may think of *fluxions* or the *differential calculus* and the like, a little reflection will show them, that in working by those methods, they do not conceive or imagine lines or surfaces less than what are perceivable to sense.[2]

Let us then get rid of these 'amusements' and employ our energies 'in the study of such things as lie nearer the concerns of life, or have a more direct influence on the manners'.

It would be possible to bring forward a great number of parallels between Berkeley and Blake to show how thoroughly the poet had read and pondered the philosopher. Certain passages, such as those on space and time which I am about to quote, may almost be considered versifications of Berkeley's ideas—though enormously extended and enriched by Blake's imagination. Enough has been said, however, to make it plain that Blake in painting his own world-picture in poems and designs was consciously relying on the support of Berkeley against the rationalist tradition of Bacon, Newton and Locke.

---

[1] *Principles*, 118.

[2] *Ibid.* 132. A remark which probably occasioned Blake's 'fluxions of an atom, a thing which does not exist'.

Yet there is a difference. Berkeley's revolt is itself consistently on the plane of *reason*, not on that of *imagination*: and that Blake perceived this difference is obvious in his comments on *Siris*.[1] On the plane of reason; and even, sometimes, on that of physiology. In the early treatise, the *Essay towards a New Theory of Vision*, he replaces Newton's abstract lines and angles by a muscular sensation in the eye. But Blake's revolt was all along on the plane of vision. We never hear of a moment when the universe appeared to him as anything but a cracked mask on the divine face. From his birth he *saw*—and saw with fierce intensity. God 'put his head to the window' and looked in at him when he was four; angels walked in the fields, and clustered in the branches of trees like golden birds. There was not a part of the great whole which was not alive with spirit. And when Blake says 'spirit', he does not mean rarefied matter, or a vague sensation of the numinous, a feeling or an intuition: he means *form*: a human form seen with most definite outline and in minutest detail:

Over Sea, over Land
My Eyes did Expand
Into regions of air
Away from all Care,
Into regions of fire
Remote from Desire;
The Light of the Morning
Heaven's Mountains adorning:
In particles bright
The jewels of Light
Distinct shone & clear.
Amaz'd & in fear
I each particle gazed,
Astonish'd, Amazed;
For each was a Man
Human-form'd. Swift I ran,
For they beckon'd to me
Remote by the Sea,
Saying: "Each grain of Sand,
Every Stone on the Land,
Each rock & each hill,

---

[1] See below, Ch. xviii.

Each fountain & rill,
Each herb & each tree,
Mountain, hill, earth & sea,
Cloud, Meteor & Star,
Are Men seen Afar." [*L.* 1051–2]

So, at moments, Blake saw the objects of the material universe. These moments came to Blake, and then they left him. And when they left him, he asked: Why? Why should they be so fleeting? In these moments Blake knew he was living a more real, because more intense, life than in the hours and days that came between. He knew, by an immediate intuition, that the forms he saw in vision were more truly alive than the men and women around him: for they were pure life, without mixture of mortality. He saw them far more clearly than he saw his father and mother and his brother James. And he knew the taste of Eternity.

His father and mother and brother, he found, were not like him. They did not see as he saw. They told him he should not see as he did—that he did not see these things, and hear them; that he was mistaken and wicked. It made no difference: he knew the truth and no one could take his knowledge away from him. But he saw the great cleavage that runs vertically down human society: the company of those that see, and the company of the blind. And the second are much more numerous than the first.

A lesser man—and there have been many seers who have fallen into this pit—would have been consumed with pride. 'We are the people, and wisdom shall die with us.' Blake was not like that. It is true that he was not a humble man: but his pride was in being a son of God. He believed that all men are the sons of God, that they have a right to be proud and to rejoice in their freedom. He looked around him, and he saw that men were not proud and happy. They were furtive and humble; they did not lift up their heads to see the things he saw. They did not share, they did not want to share in eternal life. They believed that they were 'worms of sixty winters', born to labour and procreate and die in the midst of a vast and soulless universe which was utterly indifferent to their fate. And their only hope, a hope growing fainter and fainter with the march of science, was a life after the grave 'in an allegorical abode where existence hath never come'.

Blake now turned to the teachings of wise men, to the books written by recognised instructors of humanity. It is the close of the eighteenth century. Pope is dead, Johnson is dead. Priestley, following Locke and Hartley, is denying the immateriality of the soul and preaching the doctrine of necessity. Godwin asserts human perfectibility. These, of course, are the rebels, the voices of an age which witnessed the American Revolt and the French Revolution. On the conservative side we have, apart from Burke, no spokesman of equal importance. But, rebel or reactionary, they built on the same foundations; or, if we prefer the metaphor, were carried along by the same stream—the stream that runs from Bacon to Locke.

Bacon, Newton, Locke—we have already had many a glimpse of the way in which these 'three sinewy necks' haunted Blake's mind like a kind of philosophical Cerberus. In at least a dozen places in his writings they are mentioned as an unholy Trinity—

> the Spectre, like a hoar frost & a Mildew, rose over Albion,
> Saying, "I am God, O Sons of Men! I am your Rational Power!
> Am I not Bacon & Newton & Locke who teach Humility to Man,
> Who teach Doubt & Experiment? & my two Wings, Voltaire, Rousseau?
> Where is that Friend of Sinners? that Rebel against my Laws
> Who teaches Belief to the Nations & an unknown Eternal Life?
> Come hither into the Desart & turn these stones to bread.
> Vain foolish Man! wilt thou believe without Experiment
> And build a World of Phantasy upon my Great Abyss,
> A World of Shapes in craving lust & devouring appetite?" [*J.* 651–2]

In this passage the Cerberus is identified with the Devil who tempted Jesus in the wilderness. Other passages, in which the three philosophers are referred to separately, are numerous. The above passage may be considered the *locus classicus*, for it gives us the main features of Cerberian philosophy to which Blake objected: the exaltation of reason as the sole means of attaining truth; the teaching of humility before Nature; the experimental method, and scientific doubt; the conception of rigid law; the picture of a world of matter, colourless, soundless, and scentless, in the abyss of time and space. But it is worth while to examine a few other references. At the very beginning of Blake's scheme, in the symbolism of the Fall, when 'a Philosophy of Five Senses was complete', 'Urizen wept & gave it into the hands of Newton & Locke'. 'Bacon's philosophy has ruin'd England', we are told in the annotations to Reynolds' *Discourses*; and in *Jerusalem* we have a striking picture of Albion under the threefold domination: first the sight of Bacon and Newton, 'sheath'd in dismal steel'; then

> I turn my eyes to the Schools & Universities of Europe
> And there behold the Loom of Locke, whose Woof rages dire,
> Wash'd by the Water-wheels of Newton: black the cloth
> In heavy wreathes folds over every Nation: cruel Works
> Of many Wheels I view, wheel without wheel, with cogs tyrannic
> Moving by compulsion each other, not as those in Eden, which,
> Wheel within Wheel, in freedom revolve in harmony & peace.
>
> [*J.* 574–5]

This picture of a mechanistic philosophy, with its imagery drawn from the Industrial Revolution, repressing and denying the natural visionary powers of Man is repeated over and over again, in different shapes, in Blake's writings. 'The minute articulations', the individual spirit in each man, are bruised by the abstractions and generalisations of Locke's system. Berkeley had protested against this in the name of Locke's own consistency: Blake denounces it in the name of humanity. And he is not without hope. Mankind, since the Fall, has been steeped in error; in Bacon, Newton and Locke this error has simply taken an extreme form—it has been 'defined'. Error defined can be cast out. At the close of *Jerusalem* Los calls to humanity to have done with 'this Satan, this Body of Doubt that Seems but Is Not':

> if Bacon, Newton, Locke
> Deny a Conscience in Man & the Communion of Saints & Angels,
> Contemning the Divine Vision & Fruition, Worshipping the Deus
> Of the Heathen, The God of This World, & the Goddess Nature,
> Mystery, Babylon the Great, The Druid Dragon & hidden Harlot,
> Is it not that Signal of the Morning which was told us in the Beginning?
>
> [*J.* 741–2]

The first step in defining error, the first gesture of the New Age, is to recognise the universe for what it is, a delusion. Here Berkeley had led the way; and in this negative approach Blake follows closely in his footsteps. 'The Satanic Space is a delusion', he echoes. His appeal to the microscope and telescope in *Milton*, Book I, in establishing the relativity of space, takes us back directly to Berkeley's criticism of the *Principia* in the *Principles of Human Knowledge*.

> As to that false appearance which appears to the reasoner
> As of a Globe rolling thro' Voidness, it is a delusion of Ulro.
> The Microscope knows not of this nor the Telescope: they alter
> The ratio of the Spectator's Organs, but leave Objects untouch'd.
> For every Space larger than a red Globule of Man's blood
> Is visionary, and is created by the Hammer of Los:
> And every Space smaller than a Globule of Man's blood opens
> Into Eternity of which this vegetable Earth is but a shadow. [*M.* 522]

But with the last four lines we have moved out of negative criticism into a mystical region alien to the early Berkeley. Note how skilfully Blake can, when he wishes, use reason to attack science. The microscope and the telescope do not make anything bigger: they simply alter the ratio in which objects are perceived by the organ of sight; in using them, the scientist tacitly admits the relativity of space. We are free then, Blake triumphantly concludes, to draw our own conclusions on the matter. If the microscope can show us an infinite world within the globule of blood, how much more reasonably may we employ our imagination, our power of vision, to the same end!

The essential idea of space is that of separation or separateness, a direct denial of the great law of unity which holds in Eternity. The material universe is so constructed that all experience must come to us *seriatim*, and not simultaneously. In concentrating upon one aspect of the whole, we lose all the others; and then our sense of possessiveness, or our pride, or our jealousy, leads us to acclaim that one aspect to be the whole, or at least the most important. Space, too, brings it about that aspects of reality, which in Eternity may themselves be seen as separate by the contracted senses, are still further subdivided: the androgynous Man, for example, becomes separated into male and female, and conflict results.

This separation from Eternity is also, of course, in Blake's philosophy a separation from the human consciousness. Space is simply the *form* taken by the internal universe when it is seen as external. In its reality, within the mind, the universe has no extension, and all events are simultaneous and all forms interpenetrative. In Eternity 'we enter into each others' bosoms'. Yet the denizens of Eternity are described by Blake as sharply delineated: they have a firm outline, they are not amorphous, and the interpenetration can never become a fusion. Just as the senses can contract or expand to see multiplicity or unity, so, we gather, can individualities lose their 'bounding line' at will and partake, not only of the consciousness of Universal Man, but also of the peculiar experience of each of their brothers.

Space then is illusory just as phenomena in space are illusory.[1] But, just as these objects may be used (seen not with but through the eye) to give us real knowledge of the forms of the eternal world, so space may be used to inform us of the *relations* of these eternal objects. Space may be described for our purposes as the manifold of the relations of objects. In what way, then, must we look at space if we are to perceive these eternal relations accurately?

The first thing we must learn is not to look at space in the way the 'philosophers' do. We must rid our minds of the concepts of infinity and absoluteness—concepts which belong to the eternal order, not to the temporal and physical one. The idea that space is infinite is a trick of Urizen's to humble us and confuse us so that we no longer think of looking inwards to find infinity. Space is not infinite: it is, in fact, something that we have made: it is the form of our looking outwards. The more we conceive that form as infinite, the more we shall be led away from our true infinity. In the end, we shall come to think of space as something divine in itself, or at least as the sensorium of God. This is one of the errors of Natural Religion.

The Sky is an immortal Tent built by the Sons of Los [*M.* 521]

we are told in *Milton*; and from *The Four Zoas* we learn further, in a description of the eternal world, how 'the wing-like tent of the Universe, beautiful, surrounding all', can be 'drawn up or let down at the will of the immortal man'. And even now, even in our mortal state, we must learn how to do this as a first step toward regaining our sense of reality. Ridding our minds of the notion of infinite space, we should observe carefully how space varies in its object-relations as we move about:

And every Space that a Man views around his dwelling-place
Standing on his own roof or in his garden on a mount
Of twenty-five cubits in height, such space is his Universe. [*M.* 521–2]

---

[1] Here for once Blake is in agreement with Hobbes, for whom space is 'the phantasm of a thing existing without the mind simply'. But in his *atomic* explanation of causality Hobbes stands in diametric opposition to Blake.

Obviously: since space is a creation of the mind, and since Man in his fallen state is no longer thinking as a unity, we can only have a number of personal universes. But let us, Blake begs, let us make them as real as possible! Let us clothe them in beauty and give them form. Let us keep the blue of the sky and watch the sunbeams darting from behind the clouds. Don't let us accept somebody else's universe, Sir Isaac Newton's or John Locke's—which are not even *theirs* in any personal sense, but abstract constructions of the reason. We don't know what Newton and Locke saw: we only know what they thought. We shall not get at the reality of space by examining abstractions; we have to use our senses first, and then our imaginations. Every man must see clearly his own private universe; and then he can begin to share.

> And on its verge the Sun rises & sets, the Clouds bow
> To meet the flat Earth & the Sea in such an order'd Space:
> The Starry heavens reach no further, but here bend and set
> On all sides, & the two Poles turn on their valves of gold;
> And if he move his dwelling-place, his heavens also move
> Where'er he goes, & all his neighbourhood bewail his loss. [*M.* 522]

Thus we are presented with the idea of variety, depending on 'the organ that beholds it', and the idea of definite form, preserved through all variety. These are the two aspects of eternal existence itself which we have learned from an observation of space unconditioned by scientific theory. We shall also be aware that God is not in space; for now we have realised that there is not one space, but a great number of spaces, and we cannot suppose God to be in each of them.

What Blake is trying to do, in fact, is to establish in his own way (i.e. by analogies and images, not by argument) the idea of the relativity of space; and, with space, motion in space is seen to be relative too. We have already seen how, in his myth of Los and Enitharmon who in the natural order are Time and Space, he imagines an original being, Urthona, in whom these two are one. Thus the idea of a fourth dimension, as well as of relativity,[1] may be discerned by the curious beneath Blake's symbols.

---

[1] It is interesting to find J. Y. Simpson, in *Nature: Cosmic, Human and Divine*, quoting the passage from page 522 of *Milton* with reference to 'the length of the radius of curvature of the universe' in Einstein's General Theory of Relativity. In

The idea of void space was so repulsive to Blake that we even find him, in *Milton*, reviving for a moment the Cartesian idea of vortices as against Newton's attraction of bodies. He utterly rejects the hypothesis that space is the sensorium of God, and that matter may have a soul of its own which is sufficient to explain the phenomenon of gravitation. With Berkeley, he opposes the scientific method of explaining effects by secondary causes:

> The Natural power continually seeks & tends to Destruction,
> Ending in Death, which would of itself be Eternal Death.
> And all are Class'd by Spiritual & not by Natural power. [*M.* 516]

It follows that we can learn nothing from a scientific study of the universe. Its laws are illusory. The moralist who points to the motions of the heavenly spheres as a symbol and pattern of divine law is binding down the spirits of his hearers to the most pitiful death-worship. Even Berkeley had erred in suggesting that Nature is a divine visual language through which God conveys his moral laws to Man. For Blake it is not in the law, the generalisation of the reasoning intellect, but in the minute particular, the eternal being of the particular phenomenon seen through imagination, that God speaks.[1] Nature is a system of ideas in the human imagination seen falsely as exterior. What we see around us in mountains, seas, birds, fishes, trees and flowers, are our own thoughts exteriorised at the Fall. It is Urizen—'your reason'—who makes what is inward appear outward. It is he who gives a material dress and a finite form to what is spiritual and infinite. What the prophet and poet has to do is to overthrow the weight of custom and restore the power of double vision

---

this, as in his doctrines of energy and organisation (with regard to physics) and in his doctrines of infant sexuality and inhibition (with regard to psychology), Blake's intuitive genius has hit upon truths which had to wait until long after him for rediscovery and development.

An anecdote from Gilchrist is also relevant: 'Some persons of a scientific turn were once discoursing pompously and, to him, distastefully, about the incredible distance of the planets, the length of time light takes to travel to the earth, etc., when he burst out: "It is false. I walked the other evening to the end of the earth, and touched the sky with my finger": perhaps with a little covert sophistry, meaning that he thrust his stick out into space, and that, had he stood upon the remotest star, he could do no more; the blue sky itself being but the limit of our bodily perception of the infinite which encompasses us!'

[1] Eighteenth-century admiration for the abstract *idea* of Nature is in striking contrast to the indifference to Nature *detail* in the writings of the time.

which will enable us to see the eternal form under the disguise of the temporal, of threefold vision which will enable us to reach unity through love, and of fourfold vision which destroys completely the doubting selfhood. 'May God us keep From Single vision & Newton's sleep!'

Everything depends on the senses. We have seen how, in the eternal world or Golden Age, men could expand or contract their senses at will—expanding, they beheld unity; contracting, diversity. At the Fall, contraction became permanent. When Urizen shrank the human form to a number of 'mortal worms' he gave them senses which 'distort the heavens from pole to pole'. When we look with our mortal eyes we are using a distorting medium. Everything seen through brown glasses looks brown. Similarly, everything viewed through the material eye looks material. Moreover, we appear to be looking outwards, when we are really looking inwards. We are observing our own thoughts, emotions, instincts, and so on, as though they were so many solid objects in motion outside us. And so far as we believe in the existence of these bodies, and so far as we occupy our minds in deducing their laws, we are living in a universe of death and error.

Time, like space, is an illusion of the vegetated intellect. Just as, in Eternity, there can be no idea of *extension*, so too there can be no idea of *succession*. Both these notions contain the principle of incompleteness. The *growth* which Blake postulates for his eternal world can hardly be made intelligible to our minds, because for us growth is a progress from incompleteness to completeness; but we note that when Blake and Boehme use this word they are careful to add the phrase 'from Eternity to Eternity'. The images of motion, of war and hunting which Blake uses should be handled with caution.

Our difficulties in talking about time spring largely from the fact that we have to use terminology drawn from space: a *long* time, a *short* time, *between* the hours ten and eleven, and so on. To measure time we must use spatial means: the circumference of a clock face, or the amount of sand running out of a glass. Again Blake refers us to a subjective conception:

> The hours of folly are measur'd by the clock; but of wisdom, no clock can measure. [*M.H.H.* 193]

Time may be conceived as the order of change in the objects of the phenomenal universe. It is the paradox of these objects 'fix'd into a frozen bulk' that being so fixed they are 'subject to decay and death'. Urizen's attempt to stabilise everything, to reduce the variety of Eden to uniformity, has resulted in a progressive chaos. Yet without time (which is 'the mercy of Eternity') the chaos would have been immediate and complete; and it is in time that the Incarnation, and the redemptive process that flows from it, have to manifest themselves.

Blake suggests a technique of deliverance from the illusion of time similar to that which he has devised for our deliverance from space. Each man, we saw, carries his own space about with him wherever he goes. And each man experiences his own time, in the intervals which separate his experiences of Eternity. This experience of Eternity Blake calls the *moment*; it is equivalent to 'a pulsation of the artery'. In it the visionary lives quite outside time.

Let us see what Blake has to say about the divisions of time:

> every Moment has a Couch of gold for soft repose,
> (A Moment equals a pulsation of the artery),
> And between every two Moments stands a Daughter of Beulah
> To feed the Sleepers on their Couches with maternal care.
> And every Minute has an azure Tent with silken Veils:
> And every Hour has a bright golden Gate carved with skill:
> And every Day & Night has Walls of brass & Gates of adamant,
> Shining like precious Stones & ornamented with appropriate signs:
> And every Month a silver paved Terrace builded high:
> And every Year invulnerable Barriers with high Towers:
> And every Age is Moated deep with Bridges of silver & gold:
> And every Seven Ages is Incircled with a Flaming Fire.
> Now Seven Ages is amounting to Two Hundred Years.
> Each has its Guard, each Moment, Minute, Hour, Day, Month & Year.
> All are the work of Fairy hands of the Four Elements:
> The Guard are Angels of Providence on duty evermore.
> Every Time less than a pulsation of the artery
> Is equal in its period & value to Six Thousand Years,
> For in this Period the Poet's Work is Done, and all the Great
> Events of Time start forth & are conciev'd in such a Period,
> Within a Moment, a Pulsation of the Artery. [*M.* 521]

Why is Blake going into this careful and elaborate description of the units of time? What is the point of his giving precise form and glorious ornament to the divisions of an illusion? We shall find the answer to this question when we understand the doctrine that in this passage he is tilting against: the Newtonian doctrine of absolute time. Just as, in considering Blake's ideas on space, we found him stressing the space-data given by our senses in opposition to the space-concept derived by abstraction, so here too he is telling us that while time itself is certainly unreal viewed *sub specie æternitatis*, it is *less* unreal in its *sensuous* aspects than in its formulation as an absolute. He is trying to give us a method of visualising ideas—hours, days, months, years—which undoubtedly have a meaning in the eternal world, though that meaning is not a temporal one. The concept of absolute time, however, like that of absolute space, is meaningless.

The passage from the *Principia* which was evidently in Blake's mind runs as follows:

> Absolute, true, and mathematical time, of itself, and from its own nature, flows equably without regard to anything external, and by another name is called duration: relative, apparent, and common time, is some sensible and external (whether accurate or unequable) measure of duration by the means of motion, which is commonly used instead of true time; such as an hour, a day, a month, a year.[1]

This passage would appear to Blake nothing more nor less than the description of an impious abstraction, Absolute Time, which conjoined with Absolute Space could be set up as God in the Temple of Nature. As his purpose is to break down all such idols, he exalts the relative aspects of time given by our sense-perceptions. For consider the consequences to Blake's redemption scheme latent in such a concept of absolute time. Time exists in this world of generation as 'the mercy of Eternity', that order in which the great drama of resurrection to unity is free to work itself out.[2] But if time is

---

[1] *Principia*, Definition VIII, *Scholium* I. Motte translation.

[2] Cf. William Law, *An Appeal to all who Doubt*: 'Had [the ancient sages] known that temporal nature, all that we see in this whole frame of things, was only the sickly, defiled state of eternal things put into a temporary state of recovery, that time and all transitory things were only in this war and strife to be finally delivered from all the evil that was brought into eternal nature, their hearts must have praised God for this creation of things as those morning stars did that shouted for joy when it was first brought forth.'

absolute, if it is there stretched out as it were through all Eternity, there can be no succession of events, for there can be no points in time with which any event can be correlated. Newton has ascribed to the temporal order, to this world of generation, the Eternity which belongs only to Eden.

This denial of the reality of absolute time enables Blake to get rid of causality. 'Everything is its own cause and its own effect.' In an Eternity where all things exist simultaneously, there can be no before and after, and consequently no cause and effect. Blake was concerned to show that cause and effect operate in time, in the material universe, but are not co-extensive with it. The cause, that is, operates in Eternity, the effect follows as we see it in time. His reason for wishing to prove this is of course his contempt for the natural order, which is *dead* so far as originating anything is concerned. This world, he said, is too poor to produce one seed. Even the digestive processes have to be carried on by spiritual agencies, or we should all starve to death!

> And every Natural Effect has a Spiritual Cause, and Not
> A Natural; for a Natural Cause only seems: it is a Delusion
> Of Ulro & a ratio of the perishing Vegetable Memory. [*M.* 516]

Hence, once again, the futility of scientific research, which seeks to discover causes of phenomena in the phenomenal multiverse itself and not in the noumenal world which lies behind. All that can be discovered so is a sequence of events: the so-called 'cause' is merely an incident in a series. And in considering this incident the investigator is pinning himself down to a fraction of time which becomes to him of absolute significance. The error of the astronomer —what we may call the space-error—is here reversed, and we get the time-error, the limitation to a point. Everything outside this point becomes irrelevant.

In other words, causation is meaningless apart from consciousness. Blake rejects efficient causes altogether and attributes everything to final causes, which he assigns to the world of Eternity. But where is this world of Eternity? As we already know, it is in the mind of Man. Thus we are led back to our familiar position that in the mind of Man lie the causes of our material universe.

Time, then, is the order of change; but this change, in so far as it is not mere decay, is a process having its causes in a consciousness superior to the temporal order. There are passages in Blake that suggest that he was familiar with the evolutionary speculations of Erasmus Darwin, but it is not necessary to make this assumption to explain his teleology. The note so often struck by St Paul, of 'the whole creation groaning and travailing in pain together until now', and elements in the Hermetic philosophy, are echoed in his writings.

Blake's is one of the few minds which have not been overawed, amazed and 'numinously' impressed by the stellar universe. The vast distances of the heavenly bodies, the sheer immensity of space—these thoughts easily browbeat the mind and put it into a docile and receptive mood. Gods and priests have always taken advantage of the fact. 'Canst thou bind the sweet influences of Pleiades, or loose the bands of Orion?' Job is asked, rhetorically, by a complacent Jehovah. And then the brightness of the stars, as they shine in the midst of infinite dark, provokes love and gratitude—'Without your light, how black and cold the universe would be!' And lastly the regularity of planetary motions, ordering our terrestrial day and showing forth the immutable laws of the Creator: it is almost impossible not to be impressed.

The numinous character of the stellar universe is thus well established. A vast temple with its lights, its ritual of ordered movement and dance, the burning altar of the sun—so it must have appeared to Man ages before the appearance of the great high priest, Sir Isaac Newton. And in this great temple who is the god, who the victim? The Druids and the Incas had their answer in human sacrifice offered to the sun, and the Greeks burned bulls to Apollo. For the Christian, however, it is the sacrifice of a broken and a contrite heart which is pleasing to the Architect of the Universe. God himself, the sublime Mathematician, demands worship because of the regularity of His diagrams, the logical beauty of His equations. The diversity of human imagination must learn to abase itself before an abstract and uniform perfection.

Was this really what Christ taught? If it was not, it was what the exponents of His religion taught in the eighteenth century. As the supernatural basis of Christianity slipped further and further into the sceptical abyss after the Renaissance, the numinous emotions were not destroyed but fixed themselves firmly on an abstract con-

From Golgonooza the spiritual Four-fold London eternal
In immense labours & sorrows, ever building, ever falling,
Thro Albions four Forests which overspread all the Earth,
From London Stone to Blackheath east: to Hounslow west:
To Finchley north: to Norwood south: and the weights
Of Enitharmons Loom play lulling cadences on the
winds of Albion
From Caithness in the north, to Lizard-point & Dover in the south

Loud sounds the Hammer of Los, & loud his Bellows is heard
Before London to Hampsteads breadths & Highgates heights To
Stratford & old Bow: & across to the Gardens of Kensington
On Tyburns Brook: loud groans Thames beneath the iron Forge
Of Rintrah & Palamabron of Theotorm & Bromion, to
forge the instruments
Of Harvest: the Plow & Harrow to pass over the Nations

The Surrey hills glow like the clinkers of the furnace: Lambeths Vale
Where Jerusalems foundations began; where they were laid in ruins
Where they were laid in ruins from every Nation & Oak Groves rooted
Dark gleams before the Furnace-mouth a heap of burning ashes
When shall Jerusalem return & overspread all the Nations
Return: return to Lambeths Vale O building of human souls
Thence stony Druid Temples overspread the Island white
And thence from Jerusalems ruins. from her walls of salvation
And praise: thro the whole Earth were reard from Ireland
To Mexico & Peru west, & east to China & Japan: till Babel
The Spectre of Albion frownd over the Nations in glory & war
All things begin & end in Albions ancient Druid roc-
-ky shore
But now the Starry Heavens are fled
from the mighty limbs of
Albion

Loud sounds the Hammer of Los, loud turn the Wheels of Enith-
armon
Her Looms vibrate with soft affections, weaving the Web of Life
Out from the ashes of the Dead; Los lifts his iron Ladles
With molten ore: he heaves the iron cliffs in his rattling chains
From Hyde Park to the Alms-houses of Mile-end & old Bow
Here the Three Classes of Mortal Men take their fixd destinations
And hence they overspread the Nations of the whole Earth & hence
The Web of Life is woven: & the tender sinews of life created
And the Three Classes of Men regulated by Los's Hammer, and
woven

'STONY DRUID TEMPLES'

(A page from *Milton*)

PLATE VIII

JERUSALEM REUNITED WITH GOD

(from *Jerusalem*)

ception of the universe. Whatever else might be illusory—the existence of a personal God, immortality, the soul, the divinity of Christ—this at least remained for the admiration and instruction of Man. Let us learn from the stars. Their distance from the earth and one another will teach us a Stoic calm, a remoteness from human desires and sorrows. Their orderly motions, Kant proclaimed, will inculcate obedience and the supremacy of law.

Natural Religion found its climax in Wordsworth and Matthew Arnold. In the early Wordsworth it is disguised and contaminated by animism and mysticism: but we find it strong in the *Ode to Duty* and the later lyrics:

> Stern Lawgiver! yet thou dost wear
> The Godhead's most benignant grace;
> Nor know we anything so fair
> As is the smile upon thy face:
> Flowers laugh before thee on their beds,
> And fragrance in thy footing treads;
> Thou dost preserve the stars from wrong;
> And the most ancient heavens, through Thee,
> are fresh and strong.

Arnold is still more explicit. We must learn from the stars, Wordsworth says. Arnold urges that we should become like them. Mankind is much too volatile, too emotional. The life runs too strongly in human veins, in all its fury and mire. Men love, and fight, and shout in a most unseemly fashion. But the stars, how much more gentlemanly! Let us do our best to imitate the stars:

> "Ah, once more", I cried, "ye Stars, ye Waters,
> On my heart your mighty charm renew:
> Still, still, let me, as I gaze upon you,
> Feel my soul becoming vast like you."
>
> From the intense, clear, star-sown vault of heaven,
> Over the lit sea's unquiet way,
> In the rustling night-air came the answer—
> "Wouldst thou *be* as these are? *live* as they.
>
> Unaffrighted by the silence round them,
> Undistracted by the sights they see,
> These demand not that the things without them
> Yield them love, amusement, sympathy.

And with joy the stars perform their shining,
And the sea its long moon-silver'd roll.
For alone they live, nor pine with noting
All the fever of some differing soul."

The austere beauty of these stanzas cannot make up for their lack of human warmth, their complete remoteness from life as it actually is to most men and women, a thing to be dealt with on the human plane. The 'joy' of the last stanza is quite inapposite. It is Arnold's longing to escape that is in evidence—his compulsion to ascribe superior merit to some construction outside 'the sphere of our sorrow', so that that sorrow shall not hurt him too deeply. What the mountains are for Wordsworth, the stars are for Arnold.

For the Newton-Locke picture of the universe as a complex of atoms moving in space, devoid of colour, sound and scent, Blake substituted a universe of living forms perceived by the imagination. He replaced the idea of matter by the idea of energy. He stressed the importance of organisation. Matter is a congealing of energy under the power of reason: it is an unreal abstraction. It is not even a datum of the fallible senses, but simply a dogma imposed by the reason which always continues with its vice of subduing diversity to static uniformity.

The secret lies in the right use of the senses:

This Life's dim Windows of the Soul
Distorts the Heavens from Pole to Pole
And leads you to Believe a Lie
When you see with, not thro', the Eye
That was born in a night to perish in a night,
When the Soul slept in the beams of Light. [*E.G.* 138–9]

In this vegetative universe the senses are confined and restricted; and the teachings of Bacon, Newton and Locke confine and restrict them still more. But the imagination is free. We must re-educate our senses, we must wipe away the dust which has fallen on the windows of the soul. And this is done not by using them less, as the ascetics say, but by using them more: with more energy, more intensity. The man who does not see truth is not the carnal man, but the rational man. So far as the body can see, what it sees is truth; it is the intellect that blinds. Push the enjoyment of the senses as far as it will go, and there is a transmutation of sense into spirit. The gates of perception open. 'The whole creation will be consumed and appear infinite and holy, whereas it now appears finite & corrupt. This will come to pass by an improvement of sensual enjoyment.'

And what is the world-picture presented to the regenerate man by his cleansed perceptions? The answer to this question is given by Blake in a multitude of forms. We may say that the greater part of his writing is an attempt to express what is ultimately inexpressible. The realities of Eternity cannot be conveyed through words evolved in time. Nevertheless we can get some insight into Blake's vision, so long as we constantly reinterpret his symbols and are not bound down by them. Let us remember that Eternity is free of time and space (instead of being, as Locke tells us, a catena of spatial and temporal units) and that we seek it inwards: inwards in the man, inwards in the flower, inwards in the stone.[1] The quality of vision is that it 'sees a World in a Grain of Sand And a Heaven in a Wild Flower'. Space and time disappear. The universe is penetrated with supernatural meaning.

> "Another Sun feeds our life's streams,
> We are not warmed with thy beams;
> Thou measurest not the Time to me,
> Nor yet the Space that I do see." [*L.* 1068]

In everything that is, the Eternal Humanity is perceived.

This viewpoint gives to Blake's passages of Nature description a quality of extraordinary immediacy. Far more than Wordsworth, he identifies himself with the things around him. He could stare at a knot in a piece of wood, he tells us, until he became frightened by the depth of significance that revealed itself. Even Keats's sympathy with the sparrow that 'picked about the gravel' outside his window seems *voulu* in comparison with the strange interiorness of Blake's Nature-poetry. There is something of the visionary understanding of the Old Testament prophet in his feeling for insects and birds and plants. He will break off his most central narratives to point to the instinctive joy of these 'narrow Engines'[2]:

---

[1] Cf. the quotation from *Jerusalem* given above, p. 161.

[2] 'What Reason may not go to School to the wisdom of Bees, Ants and Spiders? what wise hand teacheth *them* to do what Reason cannot teach *us*? Ruder heads stand amazed at those prodigious pieces of Nature, Whales, Elephants, Dromidaries and

> Seest thou the little winged fly, smaller than a grain of sand?
> It has a heart like thee, a brain open to heaven & hell,
> Withinside wondrous & expansive: its gates are not clos'd:
> I hope thine are not: hence it clothes itself in rich array:
> Hence thou art cloth'd with human beauty, O thou mortal man.
> Seek not thy heavenly father then beyond the skies.... [*M.* 498–9]

Solomon in all his glory is not arrayed like the lily or the little fly; the Kingdom of Heaven is within you. Blake conflates and modifies, but keeps always at the forefront of his mind the world-view of his Master. Not from beyond the skies, in the dim distances of interstellar space, nor in the general laws dear to Berkeley, but in the minute particulars God is always speaking. The dumb creation enjoys a bliss unknown to Man, for it is moved by instinct and not by reason, it remains true to the basic impulses of its being:

> How do you know but ev'ry Bird that cuts the airy way,
> Is an immense world of delight, clos'd by your senses five?[1]
> [*M.H.H.* 192]

And this, for Blake, is the meaning of 'holiness'—the wholeness of Being, which demands our reverence. For him, nothing is common or unclean. There is a great love and a great tenderness in his verses for every manifestation of life that is fragile and despised. Browne's precept to go to school to the ant and spider finds a ready hearer in him. He watches the spider weaving its web with diligent care, its 'little anxious heart' beating with anticipation of the trapped fly, and then sees how the passing bird snaps up the spider and 'leaves his Web all desolate'. His charity embraces all the forms of life, and his spiritual vision is far from blinding him to the minute particulars

---

Camels; these, I confess, are the Colossus and majestick pieces of her hand: but in these narrow Engines there is more curious Mathematicks; and the civility of these little Citizens, more neatly sets forth the wisdom of their Maker.' Sir Thomas Browne, *Religio Medici*.

[1] Compare what Lévy-Bruhl says of the mentality of the savage: 'Primitive thinking is underlaid with mysticism. The reality wherein the savage lives and has his being is in itself mystical. Neither a living creature, nor an inanimate object, nor a phenomenon of nature presents itself to the collective mind of the savage as it does to our individual mind. What we see in these things either escapes him altogether or else leaves him cold. But he sees much of which we have no inkling. Birds such as eagles and hawks which soar on mighty pinions see and hear everything; they are endowed with mysterious faculties which influence even the feathers of their wings.'

of plant and insect. He is when he wishes a closer observer than Wordsworth: he gives us the essential character of each creature with a few clean sweeps of his brush. In *Milton*, for example, there is a glorious Noah's Ark of creepers and crawlers and noisome weeds which no one else would think fit matter for poetry:

> the little Seed,
> The sportive Root, the Earth-worm, the gold Beetle, the wise Emmet
> Dance round the Wine-presses of Luvah: the Centipede is there,
> The ground Spider with many eyes, the Mole clothed in velvet,
> The ambitious Spider in his sullen web, the lucky golden Spinner,
> The Earwig arm'd, the tender Maggot, emblem of immortality,
> The Flea, Louse, Bug, the Tape-worm, all the Armies of Disease,
> Visible or invisible to the slothful vegetating Man.
> The slow Slug, the Grasshopper that sings & laughs & drinks:
> Winter comes, he folds his slender bones without a murmur.
> The cruel Scorpion is there, the Gnat, Wasp, Hornet & the Honey Bee,
> The Toad & venomous Newt, the Serpent cloth'd in gems & gold....
> There is the Nettle that stings with soft down, and there
> The indignant Thistle whose bitterness is bred in his milk,
> Who feeds on contempt of his neighbour: there all the idle Weeds
> That creep around the obscure places shew their various limbs
> Naked in all their beauty dancing round the Wine-presses. [*M.* 516–17]

In all their beauty! Yes, Blake sees beauty in everything, even in the louse and the tapeworm. Everything that lives is holy. How he rejoices in the idle weeds that creep around the obscure places, and applies the miraculously exact epithet to each insect and plant:[1] the *sullen* web of the spider, the *indignant* thistle, and so on; and makes the maggot an emblem of immortality, and the beetle, by giving to

---

[1] Once again Blake is *correcting*: correcting William Law here (and behind him Jakob Boehme), who can write as follows:

'All that is sweet, delightful, and amiable in this world, in the serenity of the air, the fineness of seasons, the joy of light, the melody of sounds, the beauty of colours, the fragrancy of smells, the splendour of precious stones, is nothing else but Heaven breaking through the veil of this world, manifesting itself in such a degree and darting forth in such variety so much of its own nature....'

—but makes a distinction between the weeds and flowers, between the thistle and the rose. Blake will have no distinctions, nothing cast out. Each manifestation of life has its beauty, and delights in its own *form*. So, too, we have seen him correcting the different exclusivenesses of Milton and Berkeley.

it his favourite adjective *gold*, a symbol of wisdom: the Egyptian scarabeus. Yet the man who wrote this ecstatic song of creation is the man who said: 'For My Self I do not behold the outward Creation & to me it is hindrance & not Action; it is as the dirt upon my feet, No part of Me.' A paradox? Yes: but not inexplicable when we remember the key of the double vision. If we look carefully at the lines just quoted, we see that all the time the inner character of the creatures is being conveyed through the outer description. The gold beetle is the spirit of wisdom; the indignant thistle is the same that appeared to him in 1801, as he walked across the Felpham fields to meet his sister, in the guise of 'an old Man grey'. The great triumph is that this double vision does not blur the minute particulars —it makes them more intense. The light must shine *outwards* before the glory of the windows of a Gothic church can be revealed. The spiritual meaning of creatures must be seen and felt before even their physical character can become apparent.

This inner life of the creation is revealed as joy. It is one of the virtues of Blake's poetry that it says so little about love: it concentrates on joy and energy and freedom. The idea of love has become very defiled and adulterated. When the Gospel proclaimed that God is love, and St Paul wrote his great panegyric of charity, the word still had a meaning. But Blake knew what crimes are committed in love's name: he knew for how many sentimentalities, cruelties, and smugnesses it is the excuse.

> Grown old in Love from Seven till Seven times Seven,
> I oft have wish'd for Hell for Ease from Heaven. [*M.P.* 125]

There speaks experience; and it was experience that led Blake to make joy and not love the vital principle of the universe:

> Arise, you little glancing wings & sing your infant joy!
> Arise & drink your bliss!
> For every thing that lives is holy; for the source of life
> Descends to be a weeping babe;
> For the Earthworm renews the moisture of the sandy plain.
> [*F.Z.* 317]

We have seen the procession, or rather the dance, of the insects and reptiles; next comes the dance of the flowers, 'whatever grows from its pure bud or breathes a fragrant soul'.

And again the note is joy:

> Thou percievest the Flowers put forth their precious Odours,
> And none can tell how from so small a center comes such sweets,
> Forgetting that within that Center Eternity expands
> Its ever during doors that Og & Anak fiercely guard.
> First, e'er the morning breaks, joy opens in the flowery bosoms,
> Joy even to tears, which the Sun rising dries; first the Wild Thyme
> And Meadow-sweet, downy & soft waving among the reeds,
> Light springing on the air, lead the sweet Dance: they wake
> The Honeysuckle sleeping on the Oak; the flaunting beauty
> Revels along upon the wind; the White-thorn, lovely May,
> Opens her many lovely eyes listening; the Rose still sleeps,
> None dare to wake her; soon she bursts her crimson curtain'd bed
> And comes forth in the majesty of beauty; every Flower,
> The Pink, the Jessamine, the Wall-flower, the Carnation,
> The Jonquil, the mild Lilly, opes her heavens; every Tree
> And Flower & Herb soon fill the air with an innumerable Dance,
> Yet all in order sweet & lovely. [*M.* 527–8]

It is Elizabethan in its humanism, yet more than Elizabethan, for the humanism is more deeply felt, the element of convention has vanished. Nevertheless here, as in his very Spenserian catalogue of trees, we glimpse what we are so liable to forget in Blake: his affinities with the Renaissance rather than with the Romantics, in putting Man at the very centre of the scheme, and making Nature subservient to Man. In every respect we find Blake taking the central position. He gives a spiritual meaning to Nature which no other poet approaches, but he makes Man the measure of all things. He deifies Man, but he is so far from the conventional humanist attitude that he stresses the fact of original sin and the necessity to be reborn continually. He is the supreme English mystic, who at the same time preaches an entire sexual liberty. He is a revolutionary, yet upholds the essentiality of order. And so on. We cannot fit him into our categories. He is the most catholic of poets.

The humanising tendency of Blake's mind is apparent in these lines on the flowers. The insects were seen as men, the flowers as women. Again the description is not a static one; it is alive with movement, the movement of the dance; and the lines themselves, exquisitely varied in stress and cæsura, seem to dance too.

We have had dance and scent and colour in Nature leading straight into the eternal world. Now, to end, it is the ministry of sound. The song of birds must often have wakened Blake at Felpham; it is heard throughout his later verses. 'The Lark is a mighty Angel', the 'messenger of Los'; and in *Milton* we are shown how all Nature listens attentive to his song.

> Thou hearest the Nightingale begin the Song of Spring.
> The Lark sitting upon his earthy bed, just as the morn
> Appears, listens silent; then springing from the waving Cornfield, loud
> He leads the Choir of Day: trill, trill, trill, trill,
> Mounting upon the wings of light into the Great Expanse,
> Reecchoing against the lovely blue & shining heavenly Shell,
> His little throat labours with inspiration; every feather
> On throat & breast & wings vibrates with the effluence Divine.
> All Nature listens silent to him, & the awful Sun
> Stands still upon the Mountain looking on this little Bird
> With eyes of soft humility & wonder, love & awe.
> Then loud from their green covert all the Birds begin their Song:
> The Thrush, the Linnet & the Goldfinch, Robin & the Wren
> Awake the Sun from his sweet reverie upon the Mountain. [*M.* 526–7]

It would seem, then, that Nature, in spite of her delusive materialism, can teach us many truths if we are careful to gaze at her with the cleansed eye of the imagination. There is a unity in Nature, which expresses itself as much in the 'struggle for life' as in the ministry of sun and rain. Blake does not, like Wordsworth, 'avert his ken' from the unpleasant facts: he sees beneath them to their eternal meaning and accepts them with joy. Tennyson and Hardy are horrified by the cruelty and waste in Nature; individuals, even types, vanish in the ocean of time. But for Blake there is no loss. Tree, insect, tapeworm, lion—all are individuals, forms of thought, and thought can never be destroyed:

> For every thing exists & not one sigh nor smile nor tear,
> One hair nor particle of dust, not one can pass away. [*J.* 572–3]

We are in a universe where the conservation of individualities is as true a law as the conservation of energy.

Now we can see more clearly the significance of the *Auguries of Innocence*. When referring to those verses in Part I of this book I suggested that Blake was doing something more than indulge in humanitarian sentiment when he wrote

> Each outcry of the hunted Hare
> A fibre from the Brain does tear, [*M.P.* 118]

and the rest of that series of intensely moving couplets. Yes: he is protesting against self-mutilation. The wild innocence of the hare, the liberty of the spider and the fly, are precious parts of the human totality, not brought wholly under the rule of reason.

Socrates' complaint, that he did not like to walk in the country because Nature taught him nothing about Man, thus becomes meaningless. Nature can teach us a good deal about Man if we look at her minute particulars with the eye of imagination, if we are ready to interpret and not to analyse. Science is not the way, for the analysis of the mechanism of illusion will leave us all the more deluded.

In animals, it was *instinct* that always aroused Blake's keenest admiration. It had been a great problem for the eighteenth century to explain how the bee wrought its cell and the bird built her nest, without introducing the abhorrent notion of innate faculties. We find the query in Locke, in Hume, and in the *Spectator* in much the same form as in Blake. They go to extraordinary lengths of non-observation in their attempts to prove that it is by practice and not by this forbidden innate idea that animals behave as they do. But for Blake the different instincts of animals form a shining example of freedom from reason's chains. It is by their participation in the world-soul that the 'dumb' creatures are able to perform their marvels of ingenuity:

> With what sense is it that the chicken shuns the ravenous hawk?
> With what sense does the tame pigeon measure out the expanse?
> With what sense does the bee form cells? have not the mouse & frog
> Eyes and ears and sense of touch? yet are their habitations
> And their pursuits as different as their forms and as their joys.
> [*V.D.A.* 208]

It is not, we gather, from any of the five senses that light the caverned man that the animals have this wisdom: it is from a sixth sense, or from vision itself. And this is why, in another place, Blake calls them 'the sons of Los', for they represent the art with which the Eternal Prophet moulded matter into minute particulars when he entered the vegetative world with Urizen, to save it from chaos. For them, morality has no fetters and law no punishment. The sole motives of their being are joy, energy and freedom in diversity.

The diversity of Nature is a very different thing from its disunity. It is disunited under the aspect of its separation from Man, and Blake gives expression to this disunity in a magnificent image in *The Four Zoas*.[1] But its diversity, which men perversely try to bring under the dominion of rational law, is a part of eternal being. Certainly Nature can teach man a lesson here. Blake saw the Satanic wheels of the Industrial Revolution joining forces with the Satanic wheels of Newtonian cosmology to crush the individuality out of men; and he pointed to the infinite variety of Nature:

> The pride of the peacock is the glory of God.
> The lust of the goat is the bounty of God.
> The wrath of the lion is the wisdom of God.
> The nakedness of woman is the work of God. [*M.H.H.* 193]

Those things which appear to us terrible in Nature are aspects of divine wisdom which, in our present fallen state, we cannot understand:

> The roaring of lions, the howling of wolves, the raging of the stormy sea, and the destructive sword, are portions of eternity, too great for the eye of man. [*M.H.H.* 193]

But we can, even now, understand the diversity of individuals. We can learn to grow and to work in our own way—and ignore the fool who wants to force everyone into one mould.

> The eagle never lost so much time as when he submitted to learn of the crow. [*M.H.H.* 194]

The great thing, as we shall see more fully in a later chapter, is to understand the main lines, the 'eternal lineaments', of one's own personality and follow them without deference to interfering busybodies.

To sum up. We have seen that Blake's objection to the current philosophy of science, the growth of which we have traced in other chapters of this book, was threefold. He repudiated the doctrine that Nature works by secondary causes, that time and space are real and are the theatre of motion in which only primary qualities are concerned, and that secondary qualities are less 'real' than primary ones. In the passages I have quoted we may note his stressing of

[1] Quoted, p. 95 above.

just those secondary qualities of colour, odour and sound above all the rest. It is not to Nature as the realm of universal law that he points (as Wordsworth and Arnold do) but to Nature in its creative aspect, alive with impulse and producing the most varied forms of beauty. For this reason he deliberately inverts the rôles which would have been given to lark and sun by most poets. It is not the lark which gazes up to the sun in gratitude and wonder, numinously impressed by the luminary's size and glory and regularity of motion, but the sun which interrupts his motion to look with 'eyes of soft humility & wonder, love & awe' at the lark in its burst of spontaneous song. At this moment it is recognised to be the living voice of Nature, and therefore 'all Nature listens silent to him'.

Nature, viewed as a closed system, is a postulate of the rationalistic mind. Abstract thought can speak of but cannot conceive an absolute space and an absolute time. The visionary faculty knows that eternity and infinity open inwards—into the corollas of flowers, into the grain of sand, and into the heart of Man. Seen from the current scientific angle, Nature is the great obstacle to understanding; and her daughter, Natural Religion, is as we shall see the supreme blasphemy. But as soon as we take another standpoint, looking 'not with but through the eye', everything is changed. We then see the universe, not as a 'fortuitous concourse of atoms' hurtling together in the void, but as the 'scattered parts of Man's immortal being': exquisitely varied minute particulars, rich in joy and energy. 'To the Eyes of the Man of Imagination, Nature is Imagination itself'—a dictum which exactly corresponds with the teaching of the Buddhist Lankavatara Sutra: 'In the transcendent sense there is no distinction between the Sangsāra and Nirvāna.'

In these minute particulars the wise man recognises thoughts and instincts which are akin to himself—which are, indeed, parts of himself in so far as he can view Man, Nature and God as one immortal being. It follows that nothing can be lost in Nature: there is no waste, and even the armies of disease have their place. From this understanding there spring a love and tenderness for flowers and birds and beasts and insects which forbid the possibility of hurting them. A loving and minute observation shows us that each is 'an immense world of delight', into which we can enter and from which we can learn the lessons of individuality, energy and joy.

B. MAN AND SOCIETY

CHAPTER XIII

The Proper Study

"O man, how great, how little thou! O man, slave of each moment, lord of eternity!" [*P.S.* 43]

THE psychology which dominated Blake's day was, like the current cosmology, the creation of Bacon, Newton and Locke. It was a view of Man which derived ultimately from classical theories, and in particular from Aristotle's doctrine of the mean; it had gone to Bacon for its categories of the human understanding, to Hobbes for its judgement of human potentialities, and to Locke for the final co-ordination and polishing of the whole synthesis. Its proudest achievement was the theory of the abstract Man, which pleased philosophers, educationists, theologians, and manufacturers alike.

Here, in the field of psychology, we come to the crucial point, the centre, of Blake's Instauratio Magna of the human totality. Man is the pivot on which all turns: as for Nature, society and theology, they are simply radiations, distorted reflexes, from this central light. It is of particular importance for our study of Blake, therefore, to get his doctrine on Man in its right place; and once again I introduce my comments on Blake's teachings with a short review of the situation from the Renaissance to the end of the eighteenth century.

The breakdown of the medieval system took a double form in the Reformation and the Renaissance. The Reformation was a revolt against the priestly system of the Catholic Church, a new insistence on the individual and his ability to find God without the aid of Church or sacraments. On the whole, we note, Protestantism merely substituted one kind of organised tyranny for another, and found a single fetish in the Scriptures to set up in place of saints, relics and pilgrimages. The Renaissance was more complex. On its intellectual side it was a revolt against reason; it stressed experiment in opposition to logic and turned men's minds to the external world.

In this it was greatly helped by the discoveries of the fifteenth and sixteenth centuries. On the emotional side it was a rebellion of the instincts against medieval oppression. The classics revealed a way of life which could be gracious and sensual at the same time. Morality was found to be an imposition of the Church to keep the people in awe. A free man could not submit to such bonds.[1]

The reaction against reason was only a temporary one. The 'reason' that was objected to was that founded on authority and deduced by logic. In the post-Renaissance years, under the tutelage of Bacon, a new reason came into vogue, based on experiment in the material world and applied to the mind of Man. When the sixteenth- and seventeenth-century philosophers discovered that the universe could be explained, little by little, on mechanical principles, they saw no reason why Man should not be explained in the same way. This technique reached its apogee in the age of Newton. Long before his day the philosophers had ceased to regard Man as a soul to be saved; they saw him as a machine governed by reason and the passions. How does this machine function best? they asked. If reason dominates and the passions are brought under control, came the answer. There was a considerable return to the classical standpoint. The unique value of the individual was lost sight of, and in such systems as that of Hobbes the State acquired despotic power. The seventeenth and eighteenth centuries were increasingly oligarchical periods in which the common man became a mere drudge for the benefit of the ruling classes and those writers who were so busily engaged in justifying the *status quo*.

In theory, however, the post-Renaissance philosophers insisted on the equality of men. Descartes comes right at the beginning of our period with his statement that 'what is called good sense or reason is equal in all men', Sir Joshua Reynolds towards its close with his belief that there are no born geniuses, only made ones. The authority of reason is supreme from beginning to end, through whatever modifications. The soul, on the other hand, which was the main thing for the Middle Ages, does not survive very long. It is still there in Descartes, but Hobbes abolishes it with everything else 'which is not body'. What survives the onslaught is a material frame

[1] As far as this aspect was concerned, Blake was himself a man of the Renaissance, and the Renaissance, like the French Revolution, was the work of the fiery Orc.

of greater or lesser density, the more rarefied part corresponding to the mind, on which the solid but imperceptible atoms thrown off by other parts of the universe impinge and produce sensations.

Once again, it is to Bacon that we must turn for the initial statement of the new psychology. He shows us three faculties in the human mind (not four, as with Blake), and these faculties are personified and represented as at war with one another. It is almost a picture of the Four Zoas, with Tharmas (the Instincts) left out. Bacon is discussing the functions of Rhetoric:

> The duty and office of Rhetoric is to apply Reason to Imagination for the better moving of the will...the end of Morality is to procure the affections to obey reason, and not to invade it; the end of Rhetoric is to fill the imagination to second reason, and not to oppress it....If the affections in themselves were pliant and obedient to reason, it were true there should be no great use of persuasions and insinuations to the will, more than of naked propositions and proofs; but in regard of the continual mutinies and seditions of the affections,
>
> *Video meliora, proboque,*
> *Deteriora sequor,*
>
> reason would become captive and servile, if Eloquence of Persuasions did not practise and win the Imagination from the Affection's part, and contract a confederacy between the Reason and Imagination against the Affections....[1]

It is precisely this division of the whole Man, this setting of one faculty against another, and the attempted domination by one of all the rest, that Blake is opposing in the whole of his work. Bacon's psychology depends on this division: there is no conception of faculties acting harmoniously together—instead we have coercion or persuasion, exactly as if the human totality were (as indeed Bacon consistently imagines it) a state or kingdom in which the reason is sole ruler and the affections errant subjects, with imagination performing the rather degrading rôle of 'agent or *nuncius* in both provinces, both the judicial and the ministerial'.

The imagination, Blake's faculty of vision, through whose fidelity to the human totality all the other faculties are ultimately redeemed,

[1] *Advancement*, II. Blake shows Urizen attempting to win Los over to this confederacy in Night II of *The Four Zoas*.

is in Bacon a mere element of persuasion, to be used but not honoured. All it has power to do is work upon the data of the senses, fashioning these into what fantastic shapes it may please. It has no insight into reality. In Bacon's division of the parts of human learning—history, poetry, and philosophy—each of these is assigned to a part of Man's understanding: reason takes charge of philosophy, memory deals with history, and imagination with poesy. Poesy is a very inferior branch of learning,

> in measure of words for the most part restrained, but in all other points extremely licensed, and doth truly refer to the Imagination; which, being not tied to the laws of matter, may at pleasure join that which nature hath severed, and sever that which nature hath joined, and so make unlawful matches and divorces of things...and is nothing else but Feigned History....[1]

Poetry has had special honour, says Bacon, 'in rude times and barbarous regions, where other learning stood excluded'. Blake could not fail to note the sneer in all this.

In the *De Augmentis* Bacon develops his account of the three parts of the understanding, and adumbrates the doctrine of ideas which was to receive its full statement at the hands of Locke, Hume and Hartley. Impressions first strike the senses, enter the understanding, are ruminated upon, and formed 'into certain classes by composition or separation':

> Thus it is clearly manifest that history, poetry, and philosophy flow from the three distinct fountains of the mind, viz., the memory, the imagination, and the reason; without any possibility of increasing their number.[2]

Yet another doctrine which was to be developed by later thinkers (this time especially by Hobbes) is that of the sensitive soul. Man has two souls, we are told, 'the one proceeding from the breath of God, the other from the elements'. Having thus saved appearances by mentioning the rational soul, Bacon proceeds to ignore it and concentrates his attention on the second or sensitive soul, to which all the faculties and functions of the understanding are attached. This sensitive soul is by no means immaterial. It 'must be allowed a

[1] *Advancement*, II.

[2] *De Augmentis*, II, 2.

corporeal substance, attenuated by heat and rendered invisible, as a subtile breath or aura, of a flamy and airy nature, having the softness of air in receiving impressions, and the activity of fire in exerting its action, nourished partly by an oily and partly by a watery substance, and diffused through the whole body'. In thus enduing matter itself with a thinking principle Bacon helped to give vogue to the doctrine of the mortality of the soul which was current in the seventeenth century and affected the beliefs of John Milton.

We come, finally, to Bacon's ethical ideas. What kind of morality confronted Blake as he read steadily through the *Advancement of Learning* and the *Essays*? Certainly not one which would appeal to his essentially Christian and mystical mind. Bacon's feet are set steadily on this earth. The tone of the *Advancement*, with all its allusions and examples, is classical; and it is the classical virtues, and especially Prudence and Justice, which are exalted. We know how often Blake correlates the classics with war; Bacon does the same, and praises the warlike states above all others. It is one of his main objects to prove that learning does not unfit a man or a state for war, but rather the contrary. In the *De Augmentis*[1] he gives advice on how to prepare for war, how to conduct one successfully, and how to use the arts of treachery. 'It is most conducive', he tells us, 'to the greatness of empire, for a nation to profess the skill of arms as its principal glory and most honourable employ.... No one body, whether natural or political, can preserve its health, without exercise; and honourable war is the wholesome exercise of a kingdom or commonwealth. Civil wars, indeed, are like the heat of a fever, but war abroad is like the heat of motion—wholesome; for men's minds are enervated and their manners corrupted by sluggish and inactive peace. And, however it may be as to the happiness of a state, it is doubtless best for its greatness to be as it were always in arms.' This is the dreary doctrine we have heard from the mouths of the dictators these last twenty years; Blake, too, lived in a world at war and knew its horror. 'What do these knaves mean by virtue?' he comments on a passage of the *Essays*. 'Do they mean

[1] *De Augmentis* II, 13; VIII, 3. It is probable, but not certain, that Blake knew the *De Augmentis* as well as the *Advancement*. In any case these passages simply expand doctrines of the earlier work, and show how well Blake understood Bacon's drift.

war and its horrors, and its heroic villains?... Bacon calls intellectual arts unmanly: and so they are for kings and wars, and shall in the end annihilate them.'

The Machiavellian spirit of so many of the essays and so much of the *Advancement* revolted Blake. Bacon teaches how to know people, how to use them: the arts of simulation and dissimulation. 'Good advice for Satan's Kingdom', Blake writes on the title-page of his copy of the *Essays*:

> Is it true or is it false that the wisdom of the world is foolishness with God? This is certain: if what Bacon says is true, what Christ says is false. If Caesar is right, Christ is wrong, both in politics and religion, since they will divide themselves in two. [*B.E.* 968]

Bacon's flattery of James I could not but be obnoxious to the republican Blake who hated kings and classed them with priests and wars among the things states could very well dispense with:

> Everybody knows that this is epicurism and libertinism, and yet everybody says that it is Christian philosophy. How is this possible? Everybody must be a liar and deceiver? No! "Everybody" does not do this; but the hirelings of Kings and Courts, who made themselves "everybody", and knowingly propagate falsehood. It was a common opinion in the Court of Queen Elizabeth that knavery is wisdom. Cunning plotters were considered as wise Machiavels. [*B.E.* 968]

No wonder, then, that Blake's final comment on Bacon in his annotations on Reynolds' *Discourses* is:

> Bacon's Philosophy has Ruin'd England. Bacon is only Epicurus over again. [*R.D.* 985]

John Locke, standing at the end of the 'century of genius' of which Bacon stood at the beginning, is still, we find, engaged in investigating and elaborating the problems raised by the *buccinator novi temporis*. The soul: is it material or immaterial? How do outside objects which are material manage to make an impression on the mind which is presumably immaterial? Locke, we note, is much more sceptical than Bacon. The fine glow of the Renaissance has cooled down considerably. He doubts whether the mind can really know very much about the outside world. At best, all our knowledge must be probable. We must know where to stop when our understanding 'is at the utmost extent of its tether, and to sit down in a quiet ignorance of those things which, upon examination, are found to be beyond the reach of our capacities'.[1] In Blake's view, 'less than All cannot satisfy Man', and all *can* be gained through the cultivation of the understanding; but Locke is well content with a moderate view of truth. He blames men for letting loose their thoughts into 'the vast ocean of being, as if all that boundless extent were the natural and undoubted possession of our understandings'. The great thing is to fix the 'horizon' accurately and then attend strictly to the territory on this side of the bounding line. Man's ignorance is great, and proceeds from three causes: our want of ideas, the want of a discoverable connection between the ideas we have, and a want of tracing and examining our ideas.

As to the first of these causes, Locke points out that our simple ideas are due to sensation; and how can we suppose that 'these few and narrow inlets' have any proportion to the immeasurable vastness of the universe? Other beings, in other parts of the universe, may have 'senses more and perfecter than we have, or different from ours....He that will consider the infinite power, wisdom and goodness of the Creator of all things will find reason to think that it was not all laid out upon so inconsiderable, mean, and impotent a creature as he will find man to be, who in all probability is one of the lowest of all intellectual beings.' This anti-humanism in Locke is, of course, a direct result of his domination by Newtonian physics. The universe is so vast, man is so small—and, consequently, so unimportant, so miserable, so impotent.

We are beginning to see, now, on what grounds Blake bases his objection to Locke. Locke is a colder, a more negative spirit than Bacon. The *Advancement of Learning* was an attempt to lead men in the wrong direction. The *Essay concerning Human Understanding* is an attempt to prove that they cannot go far in any direction. It is an attack on the dignity of the human spirit. Man is to be browbeaten into humility by the sight of the starry heavens—in Blake's eyes a stupid 'world of Cumbrous wheels, Circle o'er Circle'. Locke is doing his best to upset the scale of human values, the traditional scale of spirit, matter animate, and matter inanimate, by

---

[1] *Concerning Human Understanding*, Introduction.

which the greatness and pathos of Man's destiny have hitherto been measured. It is only vision and understanding, in Blake's sense of the word, which can restore this scale. For an antidote to Locke's argument here we should turn to Blake's tractate *There is No Natural Religion*, where a series of Lockean propositions are set side by side with a set of Blakean aphorisms.

This want of ideas, says Locke, also keeps us from any knowledge of spirits, whose existence we are aware of only by revelation. We do not know their powers, their degrees or their natures. But he begs leave to indulge in an 'extravagant conjecture' that spirits can frame and shape to themselves organs of sensation or perception so as to suit the object which they are considering. If, for example, they are engaged in studying the constitution of the blood, may not their eyes become highly efficient microscopes? Or suppose, following the example of the incomparable Mr Newton, they wish to penetrate into space, will not their eyes far exceed the optick glass of the Tuscan artist? Our own perceptions, unfortunately, are more limited:

> God has, no doubt, made them so, as is best for us in our present condition. He hath fitted us for the neighbourhood of the bodies that surround us, and we have to do with, and though we cannot, by the faculties we have, attain to a perfect knowledge of things, yet they will serve us well enough for those ends above-mentioned, which are our great concernment. I beg my reader's pardon for laying before him so wild a fancy concerning the ways of perception of beings above us; but how extravagant soever it be, I doubt whether we can imagine anything about the knowledge of angels, but after this manner, some way or other in proportion to what we find and observe in ourselves.[1]

Spirits, of course, like the human soul, are rarefied forms of matter. Our primary ideas of spirit are *thinking* and *motivity* (the power of putting something into motion). Spirits cannot operate except where they are; they are capable of motion, and do in fact move about from place to place. Locke shows impatience with all those who speak of spirit not existing in space and therefore as not subject to its laws:

> If it be said by anyone, that it cannot change place, because it hath none, for the spirits are not *in loco*, but *ubi*; I suppose that way of talking will

[1] *Ibid.* II, xxiii, 13.

not now be of much weight to many, in an age that is not much disposed to admire, or suffer themselves to be deceived by such unintelligible ways of speaking.[1]

Spirits move like anything else—except of course the eternal spirit we call God, to whom motion cannot be attributed, 'not because he is an immaterial, but because he is an infinite spirit'. Locke 'conjectures', in his cautious way, that created spirits are not totally separate from matter, because they are both active and passive.

It is against Locke's doctrine of ideas that we find Blake protesting with most vehemence—for example, in his comments on Reynolds' *Discourses*. By *idea* Locke means any kind of notion in the mind. His primary object in the first books of the *Essay* is to demolish the belief in innate ideas: notions imprinted on the mind without an origin in the outside world. No such things exist, he says; all our ideas come to us originally from outside, through our senses. At birth our mind is quite blank; sense-impressions produce our ideas as experience grows. These ideas, proceeding from sense-impressions or perceptions, Locke calls sensations. But the mind has the power of reflecting upon these ideas:

> The senses at first let in particular ideas, and furnish the yet empty cabinet; and the mind by degrees growing familiar with some of them, they are lodged in the memory, and names got to them. Afterwards the mind, proceeding further, abstracts them, and by degrees learns the use of general names. In this manner the mind comes to be furnished with ideas and language, the materials about which to exercise its discursive faculty: and the use of reason becomes daily more visible, as these materials, that give it employment, increase.[2]

Thus all our ideas can be traced to these two sources: *sensation*, and *reflection* on the operations of the mind itself.

How do outside objects impress the mind? Here we come to the permanent and apparently insoluble problem of epistemology. The mind, presumably, is immaterial; the object is material; where is the point of contact?[3] Locke only skates round the edge of the problem: he speculates on the means by which the impression of whiteness can

---

[1] *Op. cit.* II, xxiii, 21.
[2] *Ibid.* I, i, 15.
[3] Buddha's question to Ananda in the *Surangama Sutra*: 'If your mind has no substantiality of its own, how can it meet with any outer objects?'

affect the physical retina of the eye, for instance, but he makes no attempt to show how the vibrations of the retina are translated into mental terms. Nevertheless his own solution, though not fully expressed, is not left in doubt. As we should expect from a disciple of 'the incomparable Mr Newton' and a fellow of the Royal Society, he has no real belief in the immateriality of the mind. He conceives thought as a kind of vibration in a material substance:

> We have the ideas of matter and thinking, but possibly shall never be able to know whether any mere material being thinks or no; it being impossible to us, by the contemplation of our own ideas without revelation, to discover whether Omnipotency has not given to some systems of matter, fitly disposed, a power to perceive and think, or else joined and fixed to matter, so disposed, a thinking immaterial substance....And therefore it is not of such mighty necessity to determine one way or the other, as some, overzealous for or against the immateriality of the soul, have been forward to make the world believe....It is a point which seems to me to be put out of the reach of our knowledge: and he who will give himself leave to consider freely, and look into the dark and intricate part of each hypothesis, will scarce find his reason able to determine him fixedly for or against the soul's immateriality.[1]

The Lockean philosophy, with its doubt of the correspondence between exterior objects and ideas, pointed towards the scepticism which later emerged in Hume. Our perceptions are limited, our senses grossly inaccurate in their reporting of the data of the external world:

> There can be nothing more certain than that the idea we receive from an external object is in our minds: this is intuitive knowledge. But whether there be anything more than barely that idea in our minds, whether we can thence infer the existence of anything without us which corresponds to that idea, is that whereof some men think there may be a question made....[2]

While he protests he is far from sharing this doubt, we suspect Locke has not, really, much belief in the power of the human understanding to do more than deal adequately with the affairs of this life on a basis of probability. He is constantly warning his readers not to expect too much, and not to pry too far into metaphysics. When we turn

---

[1] *Op. cit.* IV, iii, 6. [2] *Ibid.* ii, 14.

to Berkeley, we see at once how unpleasant this negative attitude was to his eager Irish imagination. He paraphrases, at the beginning of the *Principles*, Locke's warning to 'the busy mind of man to be more cautious in meddling with things exceeding its comprehension, to stop when it is at the utmost extent of its tether, and to sit down in a quiet ignorance of those things which, upon examination, are found to be beyond the reach of our capacities' and expresses his disagreement.

> We may be too partial to ourselves in placing the fault originally in our faculties, and not rather in the wrong use we make of them....We should believe that God has dealt more bountifully with the sons of men than to give them a strong desire for that knowledge which he had placed quite out of their reach.[1]

No, the difficulty lies in our wilful blindness.

> We have first raised a dust and then complain we cannot see.

The dust is the doctrine of abstract ideas. This is the topic of a great part of the writings of philosophers, and is even thought to be the proper object of logic and metaphysics. Berkeley, as we have seen, has no belief whatever in abstract ideas—he considers them pernicious fictions. He had raised the question in the *Theory of Vision*, and now he returns to the attack. He is still a pupil of Locke, we note, in everything that concerns the doctrine of ideas apart from this question of abstraction. He accepts the threefold division into ideas of immediate sensation and ideas of reflection and compound ideas. But he finds abstract ideas inconsistent with the facts and with Locke's teaching in general. He pokes mild fun at the idea of an abstract Man—an idea which was in fact to become so popular in the eighteenth century and to rouse the particular wrath of William Blake:

> For example, the mind having observed that Peter, James and John resemble each other in certain common agreements of shape and other qualities, leaves out of the complex or compounded idea it has of Peter, James and any other particular man, that which is peculiar to each, retaining only what is common to all, and so makes an abstract idea wherein all the particulars equally partake—abstracting entirely from and cutting off all those circumstances and differences which might determine

---

[1] *Principles*, Introduction, 3.

it to any particular existence. And after this manner it is said we come by the abstract idea of *man*, or, if you please, *humanity*, or *human nature*; wherein it is true there is included colour, because there is no man but has some colour, but then it can be neither white, nor black, nor any particular colour, because there is no one particular colour wherein all men partake. So likewise there is included stature, but then it is neither tall stature, nor low stature, nor yet middle stature, but something abstracted from all these.[1]

And he returns, finally, to the evidence of his own mind. He does not know whether other men have the faculty of abstracting their ideas; but he does know that he has not. *General* ideas he can form: ideas, that is, which apply to any one of a number of particular ideas; and we must distinguish carefully between the two expressions 'general' and 'abstract'. General ideas are useful for the communication of knowledge. Abstract ideas, as we have heard, are simply dust.

Having thus cleared the dust, Berkeley begins to look about him. First a number of *things*—which for the mind are *ideas*—present themselves. Objects in a perpetual state of flux, of change of position and texture, and with every possible variety of shapes and colours—this is what Locke had seen, and which had so impressed him that he felt the human mind could never get behind these phenomena or receive enlightenment from any other source. But Berkeley sees something else—something which strikes him as of more importance than the flux of things. He sees the mind at work upon them, yet fundamentally separate from them. It is in the mind that they exist; and that which is not in the mind, i.e. cannot be imagined, has no real existence. Berkeley's expression of this comes at the very beginning of the *Principles*:

But besides all that endless variety of ideas or objects of knowledge, there is likewise something which knows or perceives them, and exercises divers operations, as willing, imagining, remembering about them. This perceiving, active being is what I call *mind*, *spirit*, *soul*, or *myself*. By which words I do not denote any one of my ideas, but a thing entirely distinct from them, *wherein they exist*, or, which is the same thing, whereby they are perceived; for the existence of an idea consists in being perceived.[2]

---

[1] *Ibid.* Introduction, 9.

[2] *Ibid.* 2.

Those last ten words are the gist of Berkeley's completed philosophy, and the rest of the *Principles* is simply an elaboration of them.

> It is indeed an opinion strangely prevailing amongst men,

he goes on,

> that houses, mountains, rivers, and in a word all sensible objects, have an existence, natural or real, distinct from their being perceived by the understanding.[1]

The root of this strange opinion is, as we might expect, the doctrine of abstract ideas. What could be 'a nicer strain of abstraction' than to attempt to distinguish 'existence' from 'being perceived'? Once again we have the philosophers coming to muddle the wits of the ordinary man. Nothing is more obvious, once we think about it without preconceptions, than that sensible objects can only exist so long as they are thought of by oneself, some other created spirit, or God himself. Spirit is that which perceives, that in which ideas exist; and it is thus the only *substance*. The natural philosophers, and Locke, give the name substance to an unknown thing called 'matter' in which all the qualities of motion, extension, and so on are supposed to inhere. But when we realise that it is in *mind* that these ideas exist, we get rid of the idea of matter altogether.

And what a gain this is, says Berkeley. The notion of matter has been an unmitigated nuisance to scientists and philosophers alike. It is contradictory, for it is supposed to be independent of the mind and yet, if we are to think of it at all, it must be an idea in the mind. It has troubled the philosophers and theologians with the problem of its eternity or non-eternity. It has given support to atheists and epicureans, and caused great difficulty in the acceptance of miracles. If, then, it can once be acknowledged that matter does not exist (and Berkeley does not see how anyone can fail to acknowledge this) a great source of error will have been removed from human thought.

To recognise the non-existence of matter, and the fact that ideas exist in the mind, does away at one blow with the long-standing problem: how can things, which are corporeal, impress the mind which is spiritual? Matter is inert, passive, unthinking; nor have

[1] *Op. cit.* 4.

the ideas themselves 'any power or activity'. They clearly cannot mpress themselves on the mind. But if, as has now been shown, they are in the mind all the time, the difficulty is resolved.

Finally, in this middle section of the *Principles*, Berkeley comes to the idea of God. A spirit, he has already told us, 'is one simple, undivided, active being—as it perceives ideas it is called the *understanding*, and as it produces or otherwise operates about them, it is called the *will*'. There can be no *idea* of a spirit; we can only know it by its effects. So it is with the supreme and uncreated Spirit; we can have no idea of Him[1] but through his works in Nature.

Berkeley's account of God may be left for a later discussion.[2] His account of the mind and its relation to things did nothing to hold up the sceptical cataclysm, and Man, in the succeeding century, came to be accounted nothing more than an automaton. As in Hobbes, the virtues and vices reduce themselves to reflexes. Perhaps the clearest expression of the Augustan view is given by Pope in the celebrated *Essay on Man*. This *Essay* is worth detailed analysis for our purposes. Before going on to consider it, however, let us glance at the key-passage from another account of Man, written in the later seventeenth century: by comparing the two poems we shall get a better picture of the change which was coming over psychology in the half-century which saw the triumph of the Newtonian synthesis.

The purely mechanistic psychology which Hobbes promulgated in the mid-seventeenth century proved rather too strong meat for an age still more than nominally Christian. His name became a bogy to frighten young free-thinkers. But he left his mark. He provided a philosophy for the courtiers of Charles II, who did not hesitate to take advantage of the doctrine that they were no more responsible for their actions than animals. The most interesting of his followers is the Earl of Rochester, whose *Satyr against Mankind* gives the *reductio ad absurdum* of Hobbism. The *Satyr* was written a year before Rochester's death at the age of thirty-three; it strikes one as being a disgusted reaction from a philosophy which sinks Man to the level of the beasts. If this is the result of your vaunted reason, it seems to say, let us have none of it; let us keep to the light of

[1] Berkeley of course uses the word 'idea' still in the Lockean sense; he does not deny direct knowledge of God.

[2] See below, Ch. XVIII.

Nature, the unerring guide of the senses and the instincts. Man, Rochester declares, is stupidly proud of being rational, he despises the senses, which are his real guides:

> The Senses are too gross; and he'll contrive
> A Sixth, to contradict the other Five:
> And before certain Instinct, will preferr
> Reason, which Fifty times for one does err—
> Reason, an *Ignis fatuus* of the Mind,
> Which leaves the Light of Nature, Sense, behind.
> Pathless, and dangerous, wand'ring ways it takes,
> Through Errour's fenny Bogs, and thorny Brakes:
> Whilst the misguided Follower climbs with Pain,
> Mountains of Whimsies, heapt in his own Brain,
> Stumbling from Thought to Thought, falls headlong down
> Into Doubt's boundless Sea, where like to drown
> Books bear him up a while, and make him try
> To swim with Bladders of Philosophy,
> In hopes still to o'ertake the skipping Light:
> The Vapour dances, in his dazzled sight,
> Till spent, it leaves him to Eternal Night.
> Then old Age and Experience, hand in hand,
> Lead him to Death, and make him understand,
> After a Search so painful, and so long,
> That all his Life he has been in the wrong.
> Huddl'd in dirt the reasoning Engine lies,
> Who was so proud, so witty, and so wise.

This anti-intellectualist reaction had no immediate effect; but it anticipates Swift in its *sæva indignatio* and Hume in its radical scepticism. The exaltation of 'nature' over reason points forward to the next century.

Let us now turn to our Augustan summing-up of this whole tradition from Bacon to Locke. The *Essay on Man* is a bad poem, an ill-knit patchwork of Bolingbroke's half-baked philosophy. Pope was not equipped to write a philosophical poem; when he glances at moral ideas in passing, as in his superb verse *Epistles*, he is admirable; but he should not have attempted a long discussion. As it is, the very commonplaceness of Pope's treatment here suits our purpose well enough. Blake's own teaching was addressed to the common man, not the philosopher; Pope shows us what the common man was thinking. Pope was always in the fashion, whatever else he might not be; and his *Essay on Man* had an immense reputation on the Continent as well as in England.

Pope challenges comparison with Milton at the beginning of his poem. Milton opens *Paradise Lost* with a statement of his purpose, which is to

> assert Eternal Providence
> And justify the ways of God to men.

In this high argument he calls upon the Holy Spirit to aid him. Pope calls on no spirit holier than Bolingbroke; together they will examine the 'mighty maze' of man's being:

> Eye Nature's walks, shoot folly as it flies,
> And catch the manners living as they rise:
> Laugh where we must, be candid where we can;
> But vindicate the ways of God to man.

There is, of course, no possible comparison with Milton. No one would call Milton a philosopher, but his intellect was both serious and energetic to a degree that Pope never knew; and in the impossible task that he set himself he depended on his own thinking. Pope's thinking had been done for him by Locke, Clarke, Shaftesbury and Bolingbroke; all he has to do is to simplify and to vulgarise. His scheme falls into four parts: (i) of the nature and state of Man with respect to the universe; (ii) of the nature and state of Man with respect to himself as an individual; (iii) of the nature and state of Man with respect to society; (iv) of the nature and state of Man with respect to happiness. We notice at once an important omission—there is no discussion of the nature and state of Man with respect to God. That topic comes up in the second section, only to be dismissed as presumptuous. 'Presume not God to scan.'

Pope begins his argument by saying that we can only reason about God or Man from what we know; and knowledge, we remember, is to Pope and his age only sense-perception. We cannot know why Man has been formed 'so weak, so little and so blind'; we can only surmise that he fits into his place in the universal scheme of things. He must not ask to outpass the bounds of humanity:

> The bliss of man (could pride that blessing find)
> Is not to act or think beyond mankind;

> No powers of body or of soul to share,
> But what his Nature and his state can bear.
> Why has not man a microscopic eye?
> For this plain reason, man is not a fly.
> Say what the use, were finer optics given,
> To inspect a mite, not comprehend the heaven?
> Or touch, if tremblingly alive all o'er,
> To smart and agonise at every pore?
> Or quick effluvia darting through the brain,
> Die of a rose in aromatic pain?

The argument is repeated from Locke's *Essay*.[1]

Next Pope speaks of the wonders of instinct—the hound sagacious, the nice bee, the grov'ling swine and the half-reasoning elephant, all have their several powers: but all these powers are distinct from reason. A vast chain of being extends from gross matter up through insects, beasts and Man to spirit:

> All matter quick, and bursting into birth

and no link can quit its place without the ruin of the whole:

> All are but parts of one stupendous whole,
> Whose body Nature is, and God the soul;
> That, changed through all, and yet in all the same;
> Great in the earth, as in the ethereal frame;
> Warms in the sun, refreshes in the breeze,
> Glows in the stars, and blossoms in the trees;
> Lives through all life, extends through all extent;
> Spreads undivided, operates unspent!
> Breathes in our soul, informs our mortal part,
> As full, as perfect, in a hair as heart;
> As full, as perfect in vile man that mourns,
> As the rapt seraph that adores and burns:
> To him no high, no low, no great, no small;
> He fills, He bounds, connects and equals all.

We note the pervading influence of the Newtonian synthesis; and the corollary which Newton, Locke and Clarke dared not append overtly, that God is simply the soul of the universe, is here calmly accepted. We gather that this is now a part of the religion of all sensible men. What we call God is just life itself, the unifying power

[1] *Concerning Human Understanding*, II, xxiii, 12.

of the universe; no longer even the celestial mechanic, but the principle of the mechanism.

The second epistle of the *Essay* is still more illuminating. It begins with the famous epigrammatic lines in which Pope defines the limits of human understanding. Compare this passage with Rochester's *Satyr* (by which it is obviously inspired) and note the decreased tension and more polished rhetoric of Pope's lines:

> Know then thyself, presume not God to scan,
> The proper study of mankind is man.
> Placed on this isthmus of a middle state,
> A being darkly wise, and rudely great:
> With too much knowledge for the sceptic side,
> With too much weakness for the stoic's pride,
> He hangs between; in doubt to act, or rest;
> In doubt to deem himself a god, or beast;
> In doubt his mind or body to prefer;
> Born but to die, and reasoning but to err;
> Alike in ignorance, his reason such,
> Whether he thinks too little, or too much:
> Chaos of Thought and Passion, all confused;
> Still by himself abused, or disabused;
> Created half to rise, and half to fall;
> Great lord of all things, yet a prey to all;
> Sole judge of truth, in endless error hurl'd:
> The glory, jest, and riddle of the world!

It is worth while to study the differences between Pope's passage and Rochester's a little more closely. Besides the decreased intensity, and the replacement of a colloquial by a didactic style, we note a significant shift of emphasis. In Rochester the contrast is between a life according to reason and a life according to instinct or sense. Man is a pilgrim, an adventurer in search of truth, but he follows a false guide. In Pope, on the other hand, there is no suggestion of a search. Placed on this isthmus of a middle state, he is a passive being. The contrast is a dichotomy in the nature of things, unalterable by Man. Rochester implies that Man can live well if he will: provided he follows the light of Nature and not his erring reason. Pope is completely pessimistic. Life is just like that: we can do nothing about it. Even Newton's achievement is limited and partial.

Superior beings, when of late they saw
A mortal man unfold all Nature's law,
Admired such wisdom in an earthly shape,
And show'd a Newton as we show an ape.

Having fixed Man's position in the scheme of things to his own satisfaction, Pope now proceeds to generalise about his psychology. There are two principles in human nature: the one is self-love, which provides the motive power; the other is reason, which guides and restrains. Man is seen as a watch:

Self-love, the spring of motion, acts the soul;
Reason's comparing balance rules the whole.
Man, but for that, no action could attend,
And, but for this, were active to no end.

Both these principles have one end in view, the attainment of pleasure and avoidance of pain.

The passions are all modes of self-love, and are governed by reason. But each man has one ruling passion, to which even reason is subservient; and this is as it should be, for the ruling passion is the child of Nature:

Yes, Nature's road must ever be preferr'd;
Reason is here no guide, but still a guard;
'Tis her's to rectify, not overthrow,
And treat this passion more as friend than foe.

How then shall we judge between vice and virtue? By conscience, is the reply. Conscience never deceives us.

Pope begins his third epistle with a thoroughly mechanistic picture or rather diagram of the universe. Atom gravitates to atom, matter thereby rises to life:

See plastic Nature working to this end,
The single atoms each to other tend,
Attract, attracted to, the next in place
Form'd and impell'd its neighbour to embrace.
See Matter next, with various life endued,
Press to one centre still, the general good.
See dying vegetables life sustain,
See life dissolving vegetate again:
All forms that perish other forms supply;

> (By turns we catch the vital breath, and die)
> Like bubbles on the sea of Matter borne,
> They rise, they break, and to that sea return.
> Nothing is foreign: parts relate to whole;
> One all-extending, all-preserving soul
> Connects each being, greatest with the least;
> Made beast in aid of man, and man of beast;
> All served, all serving: nothing stands alone:
> The chain holds on, and where it ends, unknown.

'And where it ends, unknown.' If, then, Man cannot know God, if he cannot govern his ruling passion or make any change in his station between god and beast, what is there left for him to do? To live, the eighteenth century would reply, to live agreeably together in society. This is the end towards which education must be directed, and education can work wonders.[1] Man is a political animal; his tendency, like the atoms', is towards unity. Pope does not believe with Hobbes that men are driven unwillingly into a social contract by their own savagery. They enter such a contract by their nature; first, in the marriage tie and the family, then in the tribe. Nature here is wiser than reason. A patriarchal state is followed by city-states, then by confederations under a monarch. Tyranny next arises, priest-craft, and human sacrifice. The circle—or rather spiral—is completed when the sage appears

> but to restore
> The faith and moral Nature gave before;
> Relumed her ancient light, not kindled new,
> If not God's image, yet his shadow drew.

Thus, Pope ends, self-love and social are the same: Man finds strength and completion in society.

The fourth and last epistle investigates the question of happiness. This is Man's supreme good, but there is complete disagreement about where it is to be found. The best way is to 'take Nature's path, and mad opinions leave'. Let us use our common sense. But we must note that happiness lies not in the good of one but in the good of all.

---

[1] "Why," said Quid, "I think that any natural fool would make a clever fellow, if he was properly brought up." [*I.M.* 873]

Happiness does not consist in riches, wisdom, or anything but three possessions: health, peace and competence. These are dependent on temperance and virtue. There is really no such thing as evil. All is for the best in the best of all possible worlds:

> What makes all physical or moral ill?
> There deviates nature, and here wanders will.
> God sends not ill, if rightly understood;
> Or partial ill is universal good.

Pope ends this sorry catenation of commonplaces with the crowning cliché: 'Virtue alone is happiness below'. This is the 'sole bliss' which Heaven can bestow upon all men, rich and poor, wise and stupid. We can all be good, and we can all love our neighbours and even our enemies. 'True self-love and social are the same.'

Pope's portrait of Man, with small modification from Hume, held the field in the popular mind up to the end of the eighteenth century. It is obviously an artificial picture. We behold, not the rich diversity of individual human beings, but an enormous abstract Man, holding a place in Nature between the brutes and the spirits; limited by his nature to a knowledge of his immediate environment, and quite unfit to explore metaphysical problems; animated by exactly two principles, reason and self-love. A single ruling passion dominates all the others and governs the man from birth to death. Man is thus a being in whom free-will has no real existence. In spite of this, however, Man is somehow capable of using his reason to direct himself along the path of happiness, which is the real object of his existence. Happiness lies in the attainment of pleasure and avoidance of pain. The great rule is: 'Follow Nature'.

From Bacon to Pope we have now followed the course of English psychology in those points to which we shall find Blake's attack most consistently directed. We have seen Berkeley focusing his own criticism on the doctrine of abstract ideas rather than on any particular *moral* deviation in the rationalist position. Blake takes up Berkeley's anti-abstract dialectic, but goes far beyond him in scrutinising the ethical basis of the whole system. Morality, in his view, was evil if it was not rooted in freedom; and it is against the current ideas of liberty that he first aims his shafts.

CHAPTER XIV

Morality

Active Evil is better than Passive Good. [*L.A.* 917]

IF the later eighteenth century had a single dominant ideal, it was that of liberty. Liberty from exploitation by tyrannical governments, supernatural religions, nationalism, social classes and conventions. It was the dream of Voltaire, Rousseau, and the Encyclopédistes. Washington and Mirabeau tried to make it a reality. The revolutionary movement blossomed into a thousand shapes throughout Europe and America. Politically, the French Revolution echoed in England as well as in the Continental states; in literature, we have the Romantic movements in France, England and Germany; architecture flung off classical shackles to plunge into a debauchery of Gothic. Religion itself had a belated awakening, in England at least, and found its soul again in the Catholic Revival.

The word liberty has, for Blake, a double reference. There is liberty, first, from the group; whether it be the tyranny of the family, the class, society as a whole, the nation, or the Church. The individual instinctively believes that this freedom from his environment is necessary before he can achieve another freedom: the freedom from himself, from his own fears, weaknesses and desires. It is for this reason that the hermit leaves society to live in the woods and mountains, that the *guru* wanders the roads of India with his bowl and staff. But not all can have this detachment from society. Most of us have to live and work within the framework in which we were born. And this framework binds and constricts us.

The instruments of constriction are many. The State demands our allegiance, our money, and, on occasion, our life. The family demands our support and affection. The Church demands belief and the observance of ceremonial ordinances. But, working behind and through all these instruments, we can see one supreme instrument of constriction: morality. As members of a group, we support morality, believing it necessary to the preservation of the group. As individuals, we feel its weight at every critical moment of our lives, and constantly we rebel. Hence hypocrisy, cruelty and all the ills which spring from a double standard, a divided mind. Morality is for the group against the individual. The individual wishes to lead his own life, to fulfil himself, without the chains of morality. But he cannot fling off these chains, because he is afraid. He is not only afraid of what society would do to him if he rebelled; he is also afraid of what would happen if *all* rebelled. Morality is the product of each man's fear of his neighbour.

Thus men, when they fling off one morality, accept another. They merely exchange slaveries. The men of the French Revolution abandoned Christian morality, but they acclaimed the classical virtues. Wordsworth substituted a belief in the moral character of Nature for a belief in organised religion: he deduced ethical laws from the strength of the mountains, the ordered motions of the stars. These taught him, day by day, to improve in virtue and character, to *become* wise and prudent and temperate, to *become* a true child of Nature. 'Thus build we up the being that we are.'

For Blake, too, the supreme word is liberty. But liberty is gained not by the will but by the understanding. Understanding springs from faith—faith in the power of the intellect to attain truth. This understanding is the free exercise of the mind in the present moment.

The morality of Blake, then, springs not from the idea of becoming but from that of being. All morality which is based on will, on discipline, and imitation, looks to the future and the past. If yesterday one acted thus and thus, to-day one takes a resolution that to-morrow one will not act thus and thus, but in another way.

> [And] tasks in hours of insight will'd
> Can be through hours of gloom fulfill'd.

Thus we proceed from day to day postponing life, postponing fulfilment until some mirage of a day when we shall be perfect.

> With aching hands and bleeding feet
> We dig and heap, lay stone on stone;
> We bear the burden and the heat
> Of the long day, and wish 'twere done.[1]

---

[1] Matthew Arnold, *Morality*. This short poem deserves careful study for its expression of a doctrine the very antithesis of Blake's: it forms a good point of comparison.

Whether our ideal of life is in some far-distant day when our will shall have perfectly conquered our impulses, or in the world after death, at any rate it is not *now*. But life is *now*: what is past is dead, what is future is not yet born. All ideals are in themselves dead, for they are of the past, they do not deal with the life that is now in a pulsation of the artery, they are not adapted to the minute particulars of the present situation. We cannot imitate anyone in the past, and continue to live in the present. To imitate Christ, in that sense, is to cease to be myself. I cannot will myself to be Christ, passing judgement on my past deeds which are no longer part of me, and looking forward to the emergence of a fictitious person in the future who is not and never will be myself.

Life in the 'eternal now' is the essence of Blake's teaching. Here and now 'eternity expands its everduring doors'. Only by entering this life can we be free from fear and desire. But this living in the present moment does not mean idleness, freedom from thought, a false Quietism. On the contrary, it means intense activity of the intellect. Life, to Blake, was understanding, 'the burning fire of thought'. To live in the moment is to understand the moment: to understand it by being it, in complete freedom from fear and from seeking, not asking what it sprang from or what it will bring. This is what Blake meant by vision. It is full and complete consciousness. And here, we note, Blake's teaching sets itself rigorously apart from all teaching that exalts the unconscious at the expense of the conscious mind. Blake is no Lawrence, no denigrator of the mind or eulogist of the instincts. He does, as we have seen, stress the importance of the instincts in an age when they were hardly recognised to exist. He admits the subconscious world, and builds on its foundations. But the building itself stands high and clear in the rays of the sun of intellect—in full consciousness.

The subconsciousness is in its right place precisely where it is: in darkness. There it is the root of the whole tree, feeding its life day by day. It is foolish to dig it up. Blake shows himself entirely opposed to over-analysis—to a fingering of the delicate roots of a man's being in the interest of morality. And if he were living to-day he would, I believe, have the same objection to psycho-analysis. 'Wilt thou stretch out the fibres of my soul like stalks of flax to dry in the sun?' The root has its natural existence in the earthy darkness; to drag it out is to destroy it. Even if the analyst succeeds in what he sets out to do, even if he eliminates those tensions which are the cause of suffering, has he accomplished anything valuable? In the fact of *tension* lies the whole possibility of progress in Man. Through suffering his nature becomes deeper and broader. To understand tension is not, as the psycho-analyst says, to get rid of it: it is to use it consciously for the passage to another plane of being.

Blake knew pain and the value of pain. 'Joys impregnate. Sorrows bring forth.' He knew how easily joy passes into sorrow, and sorrow into joy. 'Excess of sorrow laughs. Excess of joy weeps.' And he knew how dearly experience is bought:

> What is the price of Experience? do men buy it for a song?
> Or wisdom for a dance in the street? No, it is bought with the price
> Of all that a man hath, his house, his wife, his children.
> Wisdom is sold in the desolate market where none come to buy,
> And in the wither'd field where the farmer plows for bread in vain.
>
> [*F.Z.* 318]

This experience passes into the unconscious, though its fruits remain. It is no longer thought about, or worried over; for to live in memory is, as we have seen, contrary to Blake's gospel of life. The tension remains, active in the unconscious. And above, on the plane of intellect, the imagination is perpetually flowering from these solved tensions. There is no gap between the life of the intellect and the life of the instincts and the animal functions.

For this reason Blake rejected every form of ascetic morality, and in this he is wellnigh unique among the great religious thinkers. He believed that tensions can never be resolved by destruction. He believed that the lower earthy part of Man has to remain there as a soil from which the higher sunlit flowers may spring. Good and evil are permanent in every man. Blake expresses this in the *Vision of the Last Judgment* in his usual uncompromising style:

> The Combats of Good & Evil is Eating of the Tree of Knowledge. The Combats of Truth & Error is Eating of the Tree of Life; these are not only Universal, but Particular. Each are Personified. There is not an Error but it has a Man for its Agent, that is, it is a Man. There is not a Truth but it has also a Man. Good & Evil are Qualities in Every Man, whether a Good or Evil Man. These are Enemies & destroy one another

by every Means in their power, both of deceit & of open Violence....
Satan thinks that Sin is displeasing to God; he ought to know that
Nothing is displeasing to God but Unbelief & Eating of the Tree of
Knowledge of Good & Evil. [*V.L.J.* 841–2]

Asceticism is based on the idea that good and evil should not exist in fruitful tension side by side in a man. Its ideal is calm and uniformity. One half of a man's being must be destroyed in favour of the other half. Thus all will be peace and tranquillity. But such an ideal is sponsored by the reason, ever at enmity with the passions and instincts, ever analysing and separating and judging. Can the human totality permit one part of itself to usurp command?[1] Or, looking now at humanity as a collection of individuals, can a single standard of conduct be imposed on such varied personalities? 'One Law for the Lion & Ox is Oppression.'

Hence Blake's insistence on the Four Zoas, which express the vital complexity of Man and therefore of the universe. Body—which we call matter or the instincts—reason, emotion, imagination: these are the four dominant aspects of life, and these are also the instruments which the mind uses to deal with life. We cannot get beyond these four principles. Nor can we analyse them into something simpler. They are ultimates.

What are the Natures of those Living Creatures the Heav'nly Father only
Knoweth. No Individual knoweth, nor can know in all Eternity. [*F.Z.* 278]

The Fall itself resulted from the attempt to disturb the fluid balance of these contraries: Urizen's sin was, in fact, morality.

When Urizen, the primeval priest, set up his religion of 'one King, one God, one Law' against the diversity of Eden, he retired to 'a place in the North' where he drew up a code of morality. The

[1] The attitude of André Gide, in our own generation, strangely resembles Blake's in this respect. 'Je n'ai jamais rien su renoncer', he remarks in his *Journal*, 'et protégeant en moi à la fois le meilleur et le pire, c'est en écartelé que j'ai vécu. Mais comment expliquer que cette cohabitation en moi des extrêmes n'amenât point tant d'inquiétude et de souffrance, qu'une intensification pathétique du sentiment de l'existence de la vie? Les tendances les plus opposées n'ont jamais réussi à faire de moi un être tourmenté; mais perplexe—car le tourment accompagne un état dont on souhaite de sortir, et je ne souhaitais point d'échapper à ce qui mettait en vigueur toutes les virtualités de mon être; cet état de dialogue qui, pour tant d'autres, est à peu près intolérable, devenait pour moi nécessaire.

essence of that code is uniformity. The blessed diversity of Eden is destroyed; reason is the sole arbiter of human life. This root conception of Blake's thought is expressed in many places and in many ways. Perhaps the concisest statement is in *Jerusalem*:

> The Spectre is the Reasoning Power in Man, & when separated
> From Imagination and closing itself as in steel in a Ratio
> Of the Things of Memory, It thence frames Laws & Moralities
> To destroy Imagination, the Divine Body, by Martyrdoms & Wars.
> [*J.* 699]

Note the significant emphasis on memory. The great sin of Urizen was his looking into futurity; his great opaque defence against the Divine Vision was formed of 'the Things of Memory'. Backward looking and forward looking are alike evil.

The most complete and systematic exposition of the doctrine of liberty comes in *The Marriage of Heaven and Hell.* We have already glanced at this, but now we must turn back to it again. Here the theme of diversity is expressed under the form of 'contraries', a word which Blake also uses in the sub-title of the *Songs of Innocence and Experience.*

First, the general statement:

> Without Contraries is no progression. Attraction and Repulsion, Reason and Energy, Love and Hate, are necessary to Human existence.
> From these contraries spring what the religious call Good & Evil. Good is the passive that obeys Reason. Evil is the active springing from Energy.
> Good is Heaven. Evil is Hell. [*M.H.H.* 191]

Blake thus stresses at the outset the dynamic quality of his vision. The marriage is to be a true marriage, with no absorption of one partner into the other; and it is to be fruitful.

But in this world we do not see this marriage. Why? Blake gives the answer in his next section, *The Voice of the Devil* (and we must note that 'the Devil' here is not the Satan who is later identified with Urizen, but the spirit of energy). He attacks the idea of a codification of wisdom:

> All Bibles or sacred codes have been the causes of the following Errors:
> 1. That Man has two real existing principles: Viz: a Body & a Soul.
> 2. That Energy, call'd Evil, is alone from the Body; & that Reason, call'd Good, is alone from the Soul.
> 3. That God will torment Man in Eternity for following his Energies.

But the following Contraries to these are True:

1. Man has no Body distinct from his Soul; for that call'd Body is a portion of Soul discern'd by the five Senses, the chief inlets of Soul in this age.

2. Energy is the only life, and is from the Body; and Reason is the bound or outward circumference of Energy.

3. Energy is Eternal Delight. [*M.H.H.* 191]

To begin with, then, Blake abolishes the false dualism of soul and body. The physical body is not a true part of Man: like all the material things which seem outside him, it is a portion of soul whose real spirituality is distorted by the shrunken eye, touch, smell and taste of vegetated Man. Thus, to say that 'Energy is alone from the Body' has no meaning; it is 'the only Life'—that is, it is life itself, manifesting itself through the body because in this world reason has dominated the other modes of expression. And for energy, in whatever way it manifests itself, there can be no punishment, no hell. Hell, as Blake tells us in another place, is the inhibition of energy: the possession of passions which cannot be released. 'I do not believe there is such a thing litterally, but hell is the being shut up in the possession of corporeal desires which shortly weary the man, *for* ALL LIFE IS HOLY.'

Hell is built by the restrainer, reason, so far as we consider it under the guise of a prison. In *The Marriage of Heaven and Hell*, of course, Blake is using the idea 'hell' in its contrary sense. Heaven is the abode of reason, and reason is the restrainer, the Jehovah who cast recalcitrant energy out of Paradise. Restraint is by no means a virtue. It is a symptom of weakness:

Those who restrain desire, do so because theirs is weak enough to be restrained; and the restrainer or reason usurps its place & governs the unwilling.

And being restrain'd, it by degrees becomes passive, till it is only the shadow of desire. [*M.H.H.* 191]

We cannot restrain energy without killing it; for freedom is of its essence. Give it freedom, allow it excess, and it will develop and combine into a whole world of forms. Beginning in the body, it will not rest there. It will revolutionise the mind also.

Blake's position is plainly anarchism. He believed that a man is the greater, the richer the nature he possesses. He did not want any authority in this commonwealth of impulses and desires. If a man is dominated by reason, if he lives the life of a human turnip, it is because his vitality is low. It is not hard to be 'good' when there is so little incentive towards 'evil'. Few of the 'good' people we come across are notable for their dynamism, though they may display a henlike fussiness. We note that the great creative minds—the artists and poets—have rarely been good in the moral sense; through understanding, not through reason, through acceptance of their totality, not through destruction, they have let their energies flow into creative channels. The watchword—so frequent throughout Blake—is *Organisation.* To organise one's energies through intuitive vision, not through the will, is the great art. It is not difficult for the half-alive to destroy their more dangerous impulses for the sake of social, religious or physical security. It is a far greater task for the fully alive to order their lives without the cramping of any impulse, good or evil. This is a question for the intellect, not the reason: and by intellect Blake means a complete awareness, by the whole man, of the facts of his being. 'Thy own eternal lineaments explore....' Not being shut up in itself, the imagination is open to an influx from the whole of human consciousness which will prevent any one-sided development:

> Men are admitted into Heaven not because they have curbed & govern'd their Passions or have No Passions, but because they have Cultivated their Understandings. The Treasures of Heaven are not Negations of Passion, but Realities of Intellect, from which all the Passions Emanate Uncurbed in their Eternal Glory. The Fool shall not enter into Heaven let him be ever so Holy. Holiness is not The Price of Enterance into Heaven. Those who are cast out are All Those who, having no Passions of their own because No Intellect, Have spent their lives in Curbing & Governing other People's by the Various arts of Poverty & Cruelty of all kinds. Wo, Wo, Wo to you Hypocrites. Even Murder, the Courts of Justice, more merciful than the Church, are compell'd to allow is not done in Passion, but in Cool Blooded design & Intention.
>
> The Modern Church Crucifies Christ with the Head Downwards.
>
> [*V.L.J.* 842]

It is very interesting to note Blake's insistence on intellect. This marks him off from the usual religious and mystical mind in the West, which is almost blatantly naïve, emotional and non-intellectual. How many Catholic saints are famous for their childishness, their complete want of brains! Protestantism, too, has often appealed to the emotions and blind faith of its converts, rarely to their understanding. The kind of faith that Blake wants is very different from this. It is a penetrating faith, an awareness which is as far removed from blind adherence to dogma on the one hand as it is from rational doubt on the other. Doubt and dogma, indeed, are two faces of the same error, the dominance of the rational faculty. Blake insists that faith shall be built on experience, the experience that he called vision; and on acceptance, which is a recognition of every aspect of the human totality.

> "How can one joy absorb another? are not different joys
> Holy, eternal, infinite? and each joy is a Love." [*V.D.A.* 210]

The characteristic of energy is that it branches out into infinite forms of life; and that it is indestructible. The view of current morality is that there is only one joy, that of 'goodness'; and this is defined as abstention from the energies called 'sin', together with the performance of acts of kindness, humility and justice, and practice of the worship of God. But there are various kinds of joy, both in ourselves and in the several 'characters' of men; and energy loves to pass from one to another of them. This is the dance of contraries which each man perceives in himself, by which lust is followed not only by satiety but by a spiritual awakening, which in its turn may pass into the energy of art; and in art the tension is resolved. 'Art is the forgiveness of sins.' We should not think that by art here Blake meant only poetry or painting or music—he meant any kind of creative activity. But when he claims freedom it is always the freedom of the artist—that freedom from 'peace of mind', that antithesis to tranquillity, which is essential to creative work. The interests of the artist are not concentrated on the making and preserving of a personality, but fly off in all directions. This is why artists may rightly be described as 'dissipated'.

But we must beware that we do not confuse the evil springing from energy with the evil that comes from weakness. This latter should properly be called vice:

> But as I understand Vice it is a Negative. It does not signify what the laws of Kings & Priests have call'd Vice; we who are philosophers ought not to call the Staminal Virtues of Humanity by the same name that we call the omissions of intellect springing from poverty. [*L.A.* 932]

This negative quality always issues as cruelty, the most terrible of the vices. Unwilling to see energy and joy in another—more especially, it would seem, in animal or child (though it may simply be defencelessness that brings opportunity)—the restrainer binds down the victim for the satisfaction of his own pleasure in frustration. Thus reason produces an evil more horrible than that which it seeks to restrain.

The ideal of the free and harmoniously developed individual which Blake advocates in and out of season might appear to be a self-evident one; but this is far from being the case. It is too difficult for the great majority. Most people prefer to mutilate themselves, to 'disarm the tempter', to simplify their natures. That they henceforth lead only a half-life does not matter. They have chosen the easier path; and, to compensate themselves for what they have lost, they turn with glee to the task of mutilating others and persecuting those eccentric individuals who prefer to lead a complete life.

A code of *morality* is the first instrument which the reason devises for the enslavement of energy. Blake shows in the *Book of Urizen* that he is aware that morality precedes religion. A code such as the Decalogue is a typical set of prohibitions directed against the infinite diversity and changefulness of life—'stern demands of Right & Duty instead of Liberty'—or, in a splendid image,

> The fiery joy, that Urizen perverted to ten commands
> What night he led the starry hosts thro' the wide wilderness. [*A.* 220]

Such law is based on an altogether static conception of life in the individual; and in the sphere of society, it seeks to subdue all individuals to the one pattern. As with the Mosaic code of ten commandments, so too with the four classical virtues:

> the four iron pillars of Satan's Throne,
> (Temperance, Prudence, Justice, Fortitude, the four pillars of tyranny).
> [*M.* 523]

This spiritual strait-jacket cramps all the energies of life. Instead of growth in understanding, we have frustration under the influence of the will.

In his doctrine of the will, Blake anticipates the findings of modern psychology, and perhaps goes beyond them. For him, the will is a function of memory, rooted in time; and it is always evil. 'There can be no Good Will', he tells us. 'Will is always Evil; it is pernicious to others or suffering.' All that can be accomplished by the will is suppression, never discovery. The more we exercise the will, the further back we are driven by the law of inverse effort. The will is only acquainted with that part of total knowledge which derives from the past and is interpreted by reason; it is therefore never in possession of a body of facts complete enough to make a valuable decision. The vast corpus of facts left out of account in its decisions rises up against it and nullifies all efforts to obey it. Suicidal in its results within ourselves, it is devilish when imposed on others. It is the antithesis of understanding, for it seeks to apply a limited personal standard to a totality which it neither comprehends nor seeks to comprehend.

A second or auxiliary instrument of restraint is found in *religion.* Urizen, when he had promulgated his moral code, wandered about among his sons and daughters to see how well his laws were being kept. He was quickly disappointed:

> no flesh nor spirit could keep
> His iron laws one moment. [*B.U.* 256]

He found that men were not pure reason, like himself; they had other faculties, less amenable to discipline: imagination, senses, passions. How were these to be perverted? Urizen wept with hypocritic tears over the cities of mankind:

> And wherever he wander'd, in sorrows
> Upon the aged heavens,
> A cold shadow follow'd behind him
> Like a spider's web, moist, cold & dim,
> Drawing out from his sorrowing soul,
> The dungeon-like heaven dividing,...
> And all call'd it The Net of Religion. [*B.U.* 257]

Thus religion springs from Urizen's hypocritic pity; and soon the Tree of Mystery grows from under his foot—Mystery, which includes dogmas, ceremonies, rites, to ensnare the imagination of Man:

> And he commanded his Sons to form a Center in the Deep;
> And Urizen laid the first Stone, & all his myriads
> Builded a temple in the image of the human heart.
> And in the inner part of the Temple, wondrous workmanship,
> They form'd the Secret place, reversing all the order of delight,
> That whosoever enter'd into the temple might not behold
> The hidden wonders, allegoric of the Generations
> Of secret lust, when hid in chambers dark the nightly harlot
> Plays in Disguise in whisper'd hymn & mumbling prayer. The priests
> He ordain'd & Priestesses, cloth'd in disguises beastial,
> Inspiring secrecy; & lamps they bore: intoxicating fumes
> Roll round the Temple.... [*F.Z.* 386–7]

The light of Eternity is the light of day, the 'golden porches of the Sun', but religion loves mystery, darkness and disguise. Men are offered an idol to worship, and promised bliss in a life to come; they are given strange doctrines to bemuse their minds; or, on the other hand, they are threatened with terror in a life after death if they do not keep the moral and ceremonial law.

> "Thy purpose & the purpose of thy Priests & of thy Churches
> Is to impress on men the fear of death, to teach
> Trembling & fear, terror, constriction, abject selfishness," [*M.* 541]

Milton tells Urizen. Thus the priestly caste is kept in power and battens on the labours of the poor. Blake is a staunch anti-clerical.

Religion, in its attempt to curb the spirit of Man, develops systems of *discipline*, holding up models to which the individual is expected to conform, outlining plans of action, detailing virtues he should cultivate and vices he should avoid. Asceticism, in its extreme form, aims at killing the original man and replacing him with another built on approved sacerdotal lines. The natural instincts must all be rooted out and destroyed. A single pattern is prescribed. This pattern is Christ, if the system be Christian, but a Christ interpreted and remodelled by the Church. For Blake, however, Christ in every man is the realisation of human unity, not a collection of moral virtues or dogmatic attributes. So far as we develop within us the conviction of solidarity with other men and with animals and plants and stones, so far we are 'organising' Christ within us. We cannot imitate Christ in the sense of following a prescribed pattern; and whatever pattern we set consciously before ourselves must come through the narrowing brain of another man. For the Roman Catholic, it is true, this problem is solved by his belief that the Gospel picture of Christ is accurate in every detail; and further, that the ecclesiastical picture, where it differs from the Gospel picture (as it does at many points), is a development or elaboration guided by the direct inspiration of the Holy Ghost. But all men have not this belief in verbal or ecclesiastical inspiration.

If there is a meaning in the idea 'the imitation of Christ' it is not a meaning which involves the will. In many passages of Blake's writing we find the phrase 'We become what we behold': an epitome of the now much-exploited if not newly-discovered truth that the unconscious tends to carry into effect the ideal held before it by the conscious mind. If we are to grow 'into the measure of the stature of the fullness of Christ', it will be by contemplation, effortless and individual. No one can prescribe spiritual rules for anyone else. St Paul in the third chapter of II Corinthians gives us the text we require. 'We all, with open face beholding as in a glass the glory of the Lord, are changed into the same image from glory to glory, even as by the Spirit of the Lord.' Note that 'as in a glass'. It is our own reflection, but glorified, Christ shining through us, the perfection of our own nature in Christ, into which we are changed. There is no standardised model.

Blake expresses this truth with great vigour:

> No discipline will turn one Man into another, even in the least particle, & such discipline I call Presumption & Folly. I have tried it too much not to know this,[1] & am very sorry for all such who may be led to such ostentatious Exertion against their Eternal Existence itself, because it is Mental Rebellion against the Holy Spirit, & fit only for a Soldier of Satan to perform. [*L.* 1130–1]

For each man there is only one road to Eternity, the path of his own individuality. To attempt to follow another man's path is stultification and eventual despair. 'One Law for the Lion & Ox is

[1] No doubt he is thinking of his unfortunate experience with Hayley in the old Felpham days.

Oppression.' To restrain desire is stultification and despair. 'Enjoyment & not Abstinence is the food of intellect.' And while we are concentrating on our mechanical ideal of perfection we fall into the most colossal egotism. Seeking to create an 'abstract Man' in ourselves, we see only an abstract Man in others. The minute particulars of the living beings around us are hidden from us. Hence arises that pernicious type of benevolence and philanthropy which seeks to succour mankind in the mass, and to do it without the expense of emotion or understanding:

> "Till pity is become a trade, and generosity a science
> That men get rich by." [*A.* 223]

The voice of the Living Creatures in *Jerusalem* preaches another gospel:

> "He who would do good to another must do it in Minute Particulars:
> General Good is the plea of the scoundrel, hypocrite & flatterer."
> [*J.* 655]

At this point we may consider Blake's analysis of the virtues. (i) Charity. Blake's century, the eighteenth, has rightly been called the century of philanthropy, for at no previous time had more, and more concentrated, efforts been made to relieve human misery. But the curse of abstraction lay upon it all. The English saying which is so strange to the Latin races, 'as cold as charity', is eloquent of the depths to which St Paul's great virtue has fallen. Charity for us is too often a matter of organisation, by which we mean mechanisation: the relief of poverty and sickness, not because we care for the poor and sick as human beings, but because poverty and sickness, if allowed to go to extremes, are a menace to our social security.

Charity itself is used as a means of exploitation. 'The parson claims the labour of the farmer', then uses his helplessness to tyrannise over him. Again and again in his discussion of this subject Blake's dislike for the clergy comes out. He hated the 'deadly black' of clerical garments, a symbol of repression and opposition to the glowing energies of life. Priestcraft is hypocrisy and villainy. And it is the priests who are most closely associated with the giving of charity. He describes their technique:

> "Compell the poor to live upon a Crust of bread, by soft mild arts.
> Smile when they frown, frown when they smile; & when a man looks pale
> With labour & abstinence, say he looks healthy & happy;

And when his children sicken, let them die; there are enough
Born, even too many, & our Earth will be overrun
Without these arts.[1] If you would make the poor live with temper[ance],
With pomp give every crust of bread you give; with gracious cunning
Magnify small gifts; reduce the man to want a gift, & then give with pomp.
Say he smiles if you hear him sigh. If pale, say he is ruddy.
Preach temperance: say he is overgorg'd & drowns his wit
In strong drink, tho' you know that bread & water are all
He can afford. Flatter his wife, pity his children, till we can
Reduce all to our will, as spaniels are taught with art. [*F.Z.* 370]

There is close observation there. It is a perfect picture of 'charity', in its cold calculations on how best to break the spirit, its hypocrisy, its brutal disregard of the dignity of another's personality; and how well, in 'gracious cunning', Blake has caught the accents of Lady Bountiful!

(ii) Duty. The blessed word 'Service', by which Big Business to-day ennobles its activities, was reserved in Blake's day for minor purposes such as helping one's neighbour. The word 'duty' took its place: the statesman's duty to govern his country, the parson's duty to guide and guard the morals of his flock, the soldier's duty to kill and be killed. While the word 'duty' was applied in a large and magnanimous sense to the governors, it was applied in quite another sense to the governed. Urizen reads to his children from the Book of Brass—the brazen code of hypocrisy:

Listen to the Words of Wisdom,
So shall [you] govern over all; let Moral Duty tune your tongue,
But be your hearts harder than the nether millstone. [*F.Z.* 370]

Such is the creed of the exploiter. But for the exploited, there is duty too: the duty taught them as children in their Catechism. 'To love, honour and succour my father and mother. To honour and obey the King and all that are put in authority under him. To submit myself to all my governors, teachers, spiritual pastors and masters. To order myself reverently to all my betters.' It is a rather negative conception, but useful for the pastors and masters. In such a conception there is no room for that liberty which is alone creative. The

[1] I.e. of Malthusianism. The first edition of the *Essay on Population* appeared in 1798, three years after Blake had begun writing *The Four Zoas*.

status quo must be preserved at all costs; and individual energy is petrified.

(iii) Humility.

> Was Jesus Humble? or did he
> Give any Proofs of Humility? [*E.G.* 135]

The orthodox Christian says Yes, Blake answers No. The inculcation of humility is yet another device of the exploiter. The man who realises his sonship with God cannot be humble. There is none to whom he is subordinate:

> God wants not Man to Humble himself:
> This is the trick of the ancient Elf.
> This is the Race that Jesus ran:
> Humble to God, Haughty to Man,...
> And when he Humbled himself to God,
> Then descended the Cruel Rod.
> "If thou humblest thyself, thou humblest me;
> Thou also dwell'st in Eternity.
> Thou art a Man, God is no more,
> Thy own humanity learn to adore,
> For that is my Spirit of Life." [*E.G.* 138]

Humility, indeed, is only doubt: doubt of one's eternal being, doubt of everything beyond the scope of the vegetated eye. And it is cowardice. 'Sneaking submission can always live': it takes courage to affirm, to oppose and to rebel.

Religion has always placed humility high in the list of virtues, for it is an excellent safeguard against rebellion. Orthodoxy constantly stresses the greatness, majesty, and power of God, in contrast to the littleness, misery and weakness of Man. God is incomprehensible, and the wretched faculties of Man are unable to attain knowledge of Him. Faith is a great mystery. Only by bowing the intellect can we 'mortal worms' attain heaven. Humility in fact is the spiritual counterpart of sacrifice for sin. But to sacrifice one's sonship with God is even more terrible than to sacrifice one's body. 'Compell'd to pray repugnant & to humble the immortal spirit', Man renounces his true nature.

(iv) Purity. Considered in its negative aspect, as it is by priests and moralists, the idea of purity is also used for the purposes of exploitation. The sexual urge is one of the most powerful; the exploiter has only to find a formula in which it can be fixed to have a splendid weapon against his victim. I leave for the next chapter the positive side of sex, with all the related questions of love and marriage. Suffice it here to link the moral virtue of purity with what I have already said of morality as a repressive code. We have seen how charity and humility are closely connected with the material exploitation of the poor: charity is the giving back to the worker of an infinitesimal part of what has been stolen from him, and the payment for that is humility and gratitude. But it is not often realised that the sexual problem too, as we have it so widespread and so deep to-day, springs also from the conditions of employment. It is a by-product of the unnatural divorce of work from creative activity, on which I shall touch more fully in my last chapter. For what, in its essence, is the inordinate preoccupation with sex but a craving for fulfilment and, however denied, for creation—a craving which would not arise in this anguished form if the individual could find in his work a real satisfaction, such as was possible in former ages? We seek in physical union with another being, then another and another, a relief and security which is only to be found on the basis of individual understanding. Exploited, in our turn we wish to exploit.

CHAPTER XV

Desire, Love and Marriage

"What may Man be? who can tell! but what may Woman be
To have power over Man from Cradle to corruptible Grave?" [*J.* 614]

THE theme of liberty and exploitation, which we considered in the last chapter, applies as closely to the personal as to the social sphere. For the gospel of energy which is Blake's, sex must be of prime significance. The symbolic books are, among other things, a sustained effort to deal with the relations of man and woman on a higher plane than the merely physical or sentimental. That is not to say that Blake's treatment is intellectualist or detached. Very far from it! A deep indignation burns through his mythological conflicts, an intensely personal note; and more than once we are tempted to see the figures of William and Catherine Blake under the disguises of Los and Enitharmon.

Blake's indignation is directed against the possessiveness of love. In Eternity there is no sex, no division into man and woman. Such a division, as we have seen, was the result of the Fall. And it is destructive of liberty. For both sexes, being divided, feel their incompleteness, and seek to achieve a full reunion which is actually impossible on the plane of sex. The former unity of the self can only be regained on the plane of understanding. Nevertheless, the instinctive feeling that a large measure of unity can be gained is correct. The body—Tharmas—is the most innocent of the Four Zoas, the one who at the Fall sinned only by doubting his own holiness. Through the senses we still have an access to the eternal world; and the sense of touch is the most perfect of the five. As Blake teaches in the brilliant prelude to *Europe*,[1] it is by the sexual act that Man can most easily 'pass out' of his temporal limitations. But only in the light of understanding. If our idea of love is 'stolen joys' and 'bread eaten in secret', our action has the opposite effect. It shuts us

[1] Quoted above, p. 56.

up all the closer in our cavern. Finally the moment must we have envisaged love rightly, when we shall say

> Till I turn from Female Love,
> And root up the Infernal Grove,
> I shall never worthy be
> To Step into Eternity. [*M.P.* 106]

Blake's doctrine of free love has been seized upon by a number of people to justify promiscuity. These people do not take the trouble to read very deeply in Blake, or they would discover that he condemns the pursuit of sensation as sternly as the severest moralist. 'Hell is the being shut up in the possession of corporeal desires.'[1] The teaching of promiscuity is mainly justified from the *Songs of Experience* and the *Visions of the Daughters of Albion*, both early writings, in which Blake is more concerned with the problems of inhibition and jealousy than with the question of understanding. We have seen how the emphasis in his work changes after the revelation at the Truchsessian exhibition. Blake was never a sensationalist, an epicure; but a careless reading of these early poems does seem to give some authority for sensationalism.

The *Songs of Experience* illustrate the wrongs done by society to the individual, and especially to the young, in the way of repressing or perverting desire. This is their dominant theme. The *Songs of Innocence* had conveyed in an extraordinary variety of ways the instinctive joy of childhood: had conveyed this joy by metres which seem to escape from the formalism of prosody, by borrowing a kind of irresponsible baby language, by images of freedom. The child comes into the world a creature of impulse, delighting in its instincts and unaware that there can be anything wrong in them. From the beginning the sexual instinct is dominant. But the child is soon taught that these impulses are to be restrained. Parents, schoolmasters and priests combine to instil the sense of sin and the desire

[1] *L.A.* 913. Blake's annotations to Berkeley's *Siris* are not supposed to have been written until 'about 1820': but surely his thought here is influenced by paragraph 104 of that work: 'The soul of man was supposed by many ancient sages to be thrust into the human body as into a prison...the worst prison is the body of an indolent epicure...whose nerves are mutually affected by the irregular passions of his mind. This ferment...stimulates the soul with mad desires, which, not being natural, nothing in nature can satisfy.' See also Ch. XVIII, p. 337, n. 3.

for secrecy into the young mind. The conflict with parents[1] begins from the first moments of life.

> My mother groan'd! my father wept.
> Into the dangerous world I leapt:
> Helpless, naked, piping loud:
> Like a fiend hid in a cloud.
>
> Struggling in my father's hands,
> Striving against my swadling bands,
> Bound and weary I thought best
> To sulk upon my mother's breast. [*S.E.* 77]

This short poem, *Infant Sorrow*, sums up a whole psychology of childhood. The pain of birth, the father's resentment at his wife's having to suffer, the mingling of helplessness and self-assertiveness in the child, the immediate binding of the struggling limbs, the realisation of impotence. Blake's vision has penetrated deeply into the origins of future mental conflicts. And this analysis he continues, for the older child, in *The Schoolboy*.[2]

Blake loved children. 'The best in the book!' he comments on Lavater's aphorism: 'Keep him at least three paces distant who hates bread, music, and the laugh of a child.' But he never sentimentalises them. He never ascribes to them a factitious 'innocence'. Because he thought all that lives holy, and because sex is to him the purest form of energy, he had no need to put blinkers on when he looked at a child.

Parents and priests do their worst to give children a sense of sin and distort their minds. In *A Little Girl Lost*, it is the child's father who brands her love as infamous; while religion, in *The Garden of Love*, plays its part in the educative process, turning impulse into secrecy and affection into jealousy. Jealousy itself is the theme of *My Pretty Rose-tree*. The whole purport of the *Songs of Experience* is epitomised in the four intense lines:

> Children of the future Age,
> Reading this indignant page,
> Know that in a former time
> Love! sweet Love! was thought a crime. [*S.E.* 79]

---

[1] Fuller treatment of this subject will be found in the next chapter.

[2] I comment on this in the following chapter.

The hatred of secrecy in love is expressed in many of the MS. poems which Blake never intended for publication. All his writings show clearly his worship of the sun, his exultation in golden light and his welcome for the dawn. He is not a poet of night or twilight. And his mind seems to have been particularly oppressed by the convention that sexual enjoyment is a thing for the night, something to hide away and gloat over in secret with a kind of guilty pleasure. The story of his being found naked with his wife in the summer-house at 13 Hercules Buildings is a practical expression of what he felt about all this—an expression which has met with shocked comment from his biographers. For Blake there was nothing to be ashamed of.

> Are not the joys of morning sweeter
> Than the joys of night?
> And are the vig'rous joys of youth
> Ashamed of the light?
>
> Let age & sickness silent rob
> The vineyards in the night;
> But those who burn with vig'rous youth
> Pluck fruits before the light.[1] [*M.P.* 93]

This, it seemed to him, was the sane and sensible view; and above all things he strove, amid the mad conventions of morality, to be sane and sensible.

If we now turn to the *Visions of the Daughters of Albion*, that charter of sexual liberty, we find the various aspects of the theme as treated in *Songs of Experience* caught up and knit together in a connected whole. The poem is a lament over the possessiveness of love and the impossible demand for purity. Its characters are three: Oothoon, 'the soft soul of America', the pure sexual instinct (we remember that Tharmas, in the symbolic West, is both 'body' and 'freedom'); Bromion, religion and morality; and Theotormon, jealous desire. Oothoon plucks the 'bright Marygold', the sunflower which in *Songs of Experience* is already a sexual symbol, and runs to meet Theotormon; but she is enslaved by Bromion and made his harlot—instinct in servitude to religion; and Theotormon, her

[1] 'Before the light' means 'in front of, in the presence of, the light'.

true lover, is consumed with jealousy. Oothoon is at first convinced by Bromion that she is stained with sin, and she calls on Theotormon's eagles to rend her breast; but intuition soon displaces morality, and she sees that there is no permanent state in life, only a continual rebirth. She sings the praises of instinct in animals, and blames Urizen for the confusion that morality introduces into the simplicity of love:

> "How can one joy absorb another? are not different joys
> Holy, eternal, infinite? and each joy is a Love." [*V.D.A.* 210]

She describes the innocence of desire, first in the child—

> "Infancy! fearless, lustful, happy, nestling for delight
> In laps of pleasure: Innocence! honest, open, seeking
> The vigorous joys of morning light; open to virgin bliss,"
> [*V.D.A.* 212]

—then in the youth. But this innocence is quickly corrupted by morality, which teaches the arts of modesty and hypocrisy. Desire cannot be destroyed, but it can be driven underground, with the flock of perversions which this brings in its train.

> "The moment of desire! the moment of desire! The virgin
> That pines for man shall awaken her womb to enormous joys
> In the secret shadows of her chamber: the youth shut up from
> The lustful joy shall forget to generate & create an amorous image
> In the shadows of his curtains and in the folds of his silent pillow.
> Are not these the places of religion, the rewards of continence,
> The self enjoyings of self denial? why dost thou seek religion?
> Is it because acts are not lovely that thou seekest solitude
> Where the horrible darkness is impressed with reflections of desire?"
> [*V.D.A.* 213]

This is plain speaking indeed, yet the dignity and seriousness of Blake's treatment of this ostracised theme are remarkable. Apart from a few lines of Lucretius, I can recollect no comparable reference. 'The self enjoyings of self denial' is a brilliant and penetrating criticism of the ascetic ideal.

In contrast to all this, Oothoon cries 'Love! Love! Love! happy, happy Love! free as the mountain wind!'

> "Can that be Love that drinks another as a sponge drinks water,
> That clouds with jealousy his nights, with weepings all the day,

To spin a web of age around him, grey and hoary, dark,
Till his eyes sicken at the fruit that hangs before his sight?
Such is self-love that envies all, a creeping skeleton
With lamplike eyes watching around the frozen marriage bed.

But silken nets and traps of adamant will Oothoon spread,
And catch for thee girls of mild silver, or of furious gold.
I'll lie beside thee on a bank & view their wanton play
In lovely copulation, bliss on bliss, with Theotormon:
Red as the rosy morning, lustful as the first born beam,
Oothoon shall view his dear delight, nor e'er with jealous cloud
Come in the heaven of generous love, nor selfish blightings bring."
[*V.D.A.* 214]

Let us now examine the conclusions of this poem. In the first place we are informed once more that sexual desire is born with the infant, and that innocence properly means freedom from the sense of shame, not ignorance. The sense of shame is infused into the child by parents and priests, who are enraged by the sight of an instinctive delight they themselves have lost. Thus boy and girl are driven to the 'enormous joys' of secrecy, turning the expansive generative force into 'self enjoyings'. Then, when the time for marriage comes, this is found to be either a matter of the exploitation of the woman by the man—'bound in spells of law to one she loathes'—or of the shackling of the man's polygamous desires by the jealousy of the woman. Blake does not call this love, he calls it possessiveness.

The contrast in Blake is between 'love', which is 'lawless, wing'd & unconfin'd', and 'deceit', which is 'lawful, cautious, & refin'd'. The one breaks all chains, the other forges fetters. Free love is celebrated in a number of MS. lyrics and in passages of the symbolic works. It is 'Nobodaddy', the Father of Jealousy, who is anxious that men shall not know the liberation that comes in the frequent and perfect consummation of desire. He throws darkness and secrecy over sex. But the wise disregard his laws and gratify their desires:

Abstinence sows sand all over
The ruddy limbs & flaming hair,
But Desire Gratified
Plants fruits of life & beauty there. [*M.P.* 99]

We must trap the moment while it is ripe, or we shall never cease to regret it. Those who have resisted love become old maids and wish they had been whores.

There is no doubt as to what Blake is preaching: an absolute freedom of desire from any restraint, either inner or outer. But he knew as well as anyone else the impossibility of this ideal in society as it is now constituted. On this, the most vital and instinctive of all acts, Urizen has laid his cold and heavy hand. Man is denied the liberty which the very animals enjoy, to love when and where he will. Instead of being the great highway into Eternity, desire has been constituted the supreme fetter, the most galling of chains. 'The Wild Flower's Song' of pure instinct meets with nothing but scorn.

Unfortunately, woman is only too ready to agree with the priests and moralists that desire and fruition are evil. In the symbolic books it is Enitharmon's conviction of sin, her belief that the Son of God can only descend to condemn and not to forgive, that postpones the resurrection into unity. And she has a subtler reason for believing this. Regarded as the purveyor of a forbidden pleasure, she obtains dominion over the male. Deceit brings power. She is even concerned to convince the man that he is only a worm, that he has no eternal life; for she knows that once he fully realises his divinity he will escape from her toils:

She cries: "The Human is but a Worm, & thou, O Male! Thou art
Thyself Female, a Male, a breeder of Seed, a Son & Husband: & Lo,
The Human Divine is Woman's Shadow, a Vapor in the summer's heat.
Go assume Papal dignity, thou Spectre, thou Male Harlot! Arthur,
Divide into the Kings of Europe in times remote, O Woman-born
And Woman-nourish'd & Woman-educated & Woman-scorn'd!" [*J.* 673]

Scorned most of all, we note further, when chivalrous and respectful. Blake like many other poets noticed that it is the cheap and flashy qualities in a man which most impress women; they despise intelligence, gentleness, and any unusual power.[1] Again, perhaps, they are fundamentally afraid that intelligence in the man may rob them of their dominion and so they feel it safer to stick to the stupid: they

[1] Cf. the lyric 'The look of love alarms' in *M.P.* 100.

prefer the man who is rooted in earth, with no vision beyond the narrow physical environment:

> "The Man who respects Woman shall be despised by Woman,
> And deadly cunning & mean abjectness only shall enjoy them.
> For I will make their places of joy & love excrementitious,
> Continually building, continually destroying in Family feuds.
> While you are under the dominion of a jealous Female,
> Unpermanent for ever because of love & jealousy,
> You shall want all the Minute Particulars of Life." [*J*. 730]

Urizen's cynicism is expressed at the Fall by uniting the organs of love and of excretion. Blake often exclaims against the limitations of the sexual act:

> "Why a tender curb upon the youthful burning boy?
> Why a little curtain of flesh on the bed of our desire?" [*B.Th.* 173]

In Eternity embraces are not localised: they are an interpenetration of the whole being:

> Embraces are Cominglings from the Head even to the Feet,
> And not a pompous High Priest entering by a Secret Place. [*J*. 689]

And this 'deceit' is a woman's chief quality. It is her unwillingness openly to acknowledge the physical basis of love, while at the same time tying down the man to the purely physical. By thus creating division and perplexity in his mind, she prevents his ever living in that eternal moment which is his true life and to which love, above everything else, should be the gateway. She constantly sets her will against the man's. She creates an unreal situation in which the man is forever lustful and she forever chaste and coy—a kind of Grecian Urn existence. And this brings her enormous pleasure:

> "The joy of woman is the death of her most best beloved
> Who dies for Love of her
> In torments of fierce jealousy & pangs of adoration." [*F.Z.* 316]

Thus her image usurps the 'throne of God' in man, and his humanity is destroyed anew on the stems of generation.

In this 'deceit' she has her natural allies, the priests. Or, to put it more accurately, her folly is exploited by the priests for their own ends. It is really to the advantage of the woman as well as the man that love should be free, natural, spontaneous; but she easily lets herself be persuaded into a perverse delight in modesty. She delivers herself over to morality, and in so doing she delivers up the man as well. For his happiness is dependent on her. She is consoled for the loss of delight by the mysteries of religion, by the pomp and ceremonies which act so efficiently upon her weaker intelligence. But man has no such compensation, if he is virile and impatient of humbug. Instead of piety, he chooses destruction. The creative force, perverted, is turned to the uses of war:

> "I am drunk with unsatiated love,
> I must rush again to War, for the Virgin has frown'd & refus'd.
> Sometimes I curse & sometimes bless thy fascinating beauty.
> Once Man was occupied in intellectual pleasures & energies,
> But now my Soul is harrow'd with grief & fear & love & desire,
> And now I hate & now I love, & Intellect is no more.
> There is no time for any thing but the torments of love & desire."
> [*J*. 687]

So long as desire is not gratified, it occupies the mind to the exclusion of everything else. This is the fallacy at the base of all systems of asceticism. And it is for this reason that Blake always links together religion and war.

The sin of woman is thus precisely the original sin of Urizen: the exercise of will against humanity, the will to restrict the multiplicity of joys, the denial of eternal life:

> "Calling that Holy Love which is Envy, Revenge & Cruelty,
> Which separated the stars from the mountains, the mountains from Man
> And left Man, a little grovelling Root outside of Himself." [*J*. 580]

If Urizen is the Father of Jealousy, women are indeed his daughters. They are jealous of a man's intelligence, which seems to threaten their empire over him; and, moreover, each woman is afraid and jealous of other women. Instead of 'giving their maidens' to their husbands, they cruelly drive them away. The wife seeks to monopolise her husband. This struck Blake as indescribably shocking. How can one joy absorb another? he asks. How can love be bound in the fetters of law? If it is not free, it ceases to be love. If it cannot exercise itself on a variety of objects, it loses its spontaneity and freshness. Married love, confined to a single object, grows stuffy and decays. If the man wants other women (and Blake did not think it natural to be satisfied with *one*), will his instincts be changed by the fact that their satisfaction is forbidden? On the contrary, his desire will be exacerbated. It is the sexual code which creates the Don Juans and the Casanovas. 'Prisons are built with stones of Law, Brothels with bricks of Religion.' Prostitution, disease and perversion are among the fruits of repression.

At this point I would like to digress for a moment. In everything that Blake says about sex we must remember that he is talking about real sex, real desire, and not the caricature which passes for it nowadays. He is not speaking of the modern itch for sensation. The widespread sexual neurosis of the present day was unknown to him. The sexual appetite of twentieth-century man is kept in a constant state of stimulation by every possible means of advertisement, from the films down to advertisements for toothpaste. It is so incessantly stimulated that it has largely become meaningless, a simulacrum of desire. The nerve has been titillated too often. The vice which worries us has largely ceased to be a vice—it is a habit only. We accept the heavy sex-atmosphere of our towns and cities as we accept their ugliness and dirt, because it has become a part of our lives, not because we actually *feel* anything. It is not for the gratification of this kind of habit-itch, this self-titillation of a senile society, that Blake is pleading. He is concerned with nothing but the energy of youth.

To return to our consideration of 'woman's triumph'. Marriage is the device adopted by society to bind a man down to a single joy, which by its monotony soon becomes misery. It is the greatest triumph of the priests, who now, through the woman, gain power over a man's most intimate life, over his goings-in and his comings-out, over his family. Blake married Catherine because he found she pitied him; but he soon discovered that 'pity divides the soul'. Imprisoned in a 'golden cage' he longed for liberty. We cannot ignore an autobiographical significance in lines such as these:

> To a lovely mirtle bound
> Blossoms show'ring all around,
> O, how sick & weary I
> Underneath my mirtle lie.
> Why should I be bound to thee,
> O, my lovely mirtle tree? [*M.P.* 97]

and there are many other lyrics and passages in the longer poems where the rebellious, personal note breaks through. Catherine was a good wife, but the best of wives is intolerable if she wars obstinately against a man's individuality. Blake bore the intolerable to the end.

The mockery of marriage (springing largely from the early education of 'the little female') is that it often restrains desire within marriage as well as outside it. False modesty and an acutely unreal attitude to the body persist. And the priests are at work again, persuading the wife that pleasure in the sexual act is evil, that it must be resisted, and, when submitted to, only with distaste. This horrible doctrine, which in a Puritan country like England is only too common in the middle and lower classes, finds a bitter condemnation in Blake.

> "Have you known the Judgment that is arisen among the
> Zoas of Albion, where a Man dare hardly to embrace
> His own Wife for the terrors of Chastity that they call
> By the name of Morality? their Daughters govern all
> In hidden deceit! they are Vegetable, only fit for burning.
> Art & Science cannot exist but by Naked Beauty display'd."
>
> [*J.* 618]

In the experience which drew from him the above incredulous lines, Blake comes very close to D. H. Lawrence.

The male, too, gets his share of condemnation in submitting to the institution of marriage. He too is an exploiter, anxious to have what he wants entirely to himself. He wants to feel secure, to feel more real as mirrored in an *alter ego*: he does not realise that we feel more secure in proportion as we sink deeper and deeper into the understanding of our own natures, and in no other way. In marriage, in any case, a new type of insecurity is achieved, binding the man more tightly down to the world of time and space, with its anxiety for past and future. Fear is doubled and quadrupled with the added responsibilities of a wife, children and possessions. Blake does not say that this ought to be so; in an ideal marriage it would not be so; but he points out that it is so. As the relations of man and woman are now legally constituted, marriage cannot but be an intolerable burden to one or other of the partners, if not to both. If they are sufficiently well-off to be free from the economic insecurity, there are other forms of fear and anxiety from which they cannot be released. Jealousy, possessiveness, indifference—unless love is free these conditions must inevitably arise.

The motives that operate in the family dominate the State too. The national policy reflects in its magnified way the jealousies, envies, ambitions and snobberies of its component groups. Just as the husband and wife think any stratagem is justified if it is 'for the children's sake', so too the statesman permits himself villainies for the sake of his country from which he would shrink in disgust as a private individual. Morality, which intervenes at every moment of the individual's life to cramp his creative activities, is absolutely non-operant in the field of international relations. The whole force of law pursues through life the individual's efforts to find himself in the satisfaction of love; but the satisfaction of hate, on an enormous scale, is held to be praiseworthy. Morality surrenders her sceptre to the big battalions with a smile.

Dilige et quod vis fac. Augustine's motto, taken in a sense which the saint would certainly have repudiated, is Blake's key to Eternity. His idea of love is not romantic, spiritual or chivalrous. It is rooted, like all his notions, in the senses. In the sexual act, free from fear, jealousy, and possessiveness, we have our nearest way to Eden. 'The woman lives from the life of the male': she must not set her will up against him. Jealousy is her besetting sin. Love must be free, and man needs to know the diversity of love if he is to be happy. As it is the wife's duty to see that her husband is happy, it follows that she will help him to find his diversity of loves. Thus satisfied, man will be free to bend his thoughts on Eternity, on the understanding of his own being, and on creative work. But if his desires are frustrated, he rushes into war to get rid of his pent-up energy. Women ally themselves with the priests in this frustration, and the priests bless war and its instruments. The energies which cannot be diverted into war (and which spring up in a distorted form during war) are wasted in brothels and in perversions.

> 'Twas the Greeks' love of war
> Turn'd Love into a Boy,
> And Woman into a Statue of Stone—
> And away flew every Joy. [*M.P.* 126]

CHAPTER XVI

Education

> There is no use in education. I hold it wrong. It is the great sin.
> [W. Blake as quoted by H. Crabb Robinson, 10 Dec. 1825.]

THE chief link between the training given by the family and that given by the State is, of course, education. Here parents and State divide responsibility. Parents are concerned to mould the growing spirit to their own likeness. The child is regarded as a miniature edition of father or mother. The State is at pains to infuse the doctrines of duty, patriotism and citizenship. In the eighteenth century, and well on into the nineteenth, it was considered natural and right that the child should put childish things behind him as quickly as possible and take up the burden of adult responsibilities. He was not to linger in any fairyland. Life, real life, lay ahead, not in the present moment. Childhood was a tiresome chrysalis state to be got over at full speed.

Not that childhood was much of a fairyland for the eighteenth-century boy and girl! Whether they belonged to the rich class or the poor, their lives were regimented at every turn. To 'scourge off all youthful fancies from the new-born man' was considered to be the first duty of the parent who had his child's welfare at heart. And this duty was taken over from the parents by the teacher when schooldays began. Blake himself never went to school:

> Thank God, I never was sent to school
> To be Flog'd into following the Style of a Fool. [*Ep.* 854]

It is difficult to imagine what an orthodox teacher would have made of William Blake. As it was, by staying away from school he discovered things for himself, things very different from what he would have learned 'under a cruel eye outworn'. He learned, for example, to look critically at the various forms of education and their aims.

He looked, first, at the education of the poor. There was not much of this. Just enough of reading in the parish schools for a child to get through his catechism. Just enough arithmetic for him to add up a simple sum. And even this was not universal. The lad who was destined to work in the fields all his life until rheumatism crippled him so that he must be removed, at fifty or so, to the poor-house, had no need of booklearning. Parson and farmer would give him all the knowledge necessary for his welfare in this world and his salvation in the next. Or the chimney-sweep, the little boy sold to a master for unlimited exploitation: what need had he of the three R's when he spent all his waking life in the pitch-black interiors of chimneys?

The educational treatises of this period make curious reading—especially those dealing with the schooling of the poor. Isaac Watts, in 1728, addressing 'the Generous Supporters of the Schools of Charity' on 'your most desirable Ends, that is, to keep the Poor from being a nuisance to the *State*, to render them some way useful to the World, and to put their Feet into the Path that leads to their own happiness here and hereafter', spends most of his pains in attempting to persuade the sceptical that the poor should be given *some* education—if not much. He draws up a set of propositions which are to govern the policy of the Dissenting Charity Schools:

Proposition I. The Great God has wisely ordained in the Course of his Providence in all Ages, that among Mankind there should be some Rich, and some Poor: And the same Providence hath allotted to the Poor the meaner Services, and hath given to the Rich the superior and more honourable Businesses of Life: Nor is it possible, according to the present Course of Nature and human Affairs, to alter this Constitution of Things, nor is it our Design to attempt any Thing so unreasonable.

Proposition II. As the Children of the Rich in general, ought to enjoy such an Education as may fit them for the better Businesses of Life, so the Children of the Poor (especially such as need the Charity of their Neighbours) should not be generally educated in such a Manner as may raise them above the Services of a lower Station....

Proposition VI. And if it were possible, I would have every Charity School so constituted, that the Children of the Poor both in City and Country, might be employed in some Work and Labour, generally one Half of the Day; that it might have partly the Nature of a *Work-House*, as well as of a *School*, for all those who are to live by their hard Labour, rather than by their Learning.[1]

[1] Isaac Watts, *An Essay towards the Encouragement of Charity Schools* (1728).

Charity Schools, whether Dissenting or Church of England, were in fact constituted on this system. A little learning, the ability to read and write, was mixed with a good deal of labour, the preparation for adult manual work. Their ideal, as Birchenough points out in his excellent *History of Elementary Education*, was 'training the poor to poverty'. By Blake's time they had developed into 'Houses of Industry', where the children, in return for board and education, were worked hard enough to pay for their keep and something over: hence the strict accuracy of the second epithet in Blake's line,

> Babes reduc'd to misery,
> Fed with cold and usurous hand. [*S.E.* 70]

The annual service to which Blake refers in this poem, *Holy Thursday*, was held in St Paul's on the Thursday in Whitsun Week. All the London Charity children attended, and a sermon was delivered, usually eloquent enough of the spirit in which these little ones were received. Preaching in 1706, the Archdeacon of Huntingdon, afterwards Bishop of Peterborough, affirmed that 'the greatest disorders in any neighbourhood do most commonly proceed from the folly of children' (a remarkable statement enough!) and that without the Charity Schools 'the poor ragged children would swarm like locusts in our streets and by playing about, with lies, and oaths, and filthy language in their mouths, they would corrupt the children of the better sort'.[1] It was from these London schools that apprentices were farmed out to local tradesmen and later carted off to the industrial towns of the north. What they suffered there will be described in the next chapter.

The exploitation of the poor and defenceless always aroused Blake's fiercest indignation—and it was no abstract passion. Tatham, one of the men who knew Blake best, tells us of a revealing incident when Blake actively intervened to prevent injustice and cruelty:

> Blake was standing at one of his windows, which looked into Astley's premises (the man who established the theatre still called by his name), and saw a boy hobbling along with a log to his foot, such an one as is put on a horse or ass to prevent their straying. Blake called his wife and asked her for what reason that log could be placed upon the boy's foot.

[1] I owe this reference to W. K. Lowther Clarke, *Eighteenth Century Piety* (S.P.C.K.).

She answered that it must be a punishment for some inadvertancy. Blake's blood boiled, and his indignation surpassed his forbearance. He sallied forth, and demanded in no quiescent terms that the boy should be loosed, and that no Englishman should be subjected to those miseries, which he thought were inexcusable even towards a slave. After having succeeded in obtaining the boy's release in some way or other, he returned home. Astley by this time, having heard of Blake's interference, came to his house and demanded, in an equally peremptory manner, by what authority he dare come athwart his method of jurisdiction. To which Blake replied with such warmth that blows were very nearly the consequence. The debate lasted long, but like all wise men whose anger is unavoidably raised, they ended in mutual forgiveness and mutual respect. Astley saw that his punishment was too degrading, and admired Blake for his humane sensibility, and Blake desisted from wrath when Astley was pacified.[1]

Blake desisted from wrath because he had got his own way; but in the larger field of man's inhumanity to children the battle was not to be won in a day or a generation. There could be no ceasing from mental strife for Blake. His life's work was, among other things, one long battle for the poor against their exploitation by society, against the cruelty of which Astley's log was a not unfitting symbol.

Among the many puzzles with which organised religion presents the earnest enquirer not the least is the cleavage between the practice of religion and the teaching of its Founder. The Church, one cannot help feeling, has never taken Jesus seriously except as the convenient focus for a cult. The most striking of His doctrines, and perhaps the only one besides 'forgiveness' which cannot be paralleled in the other great religions, is concerned with the divine nature of the child's consciousness. In a flash Jesus raised the child to a height he had never attained in the long centuries that had gone before. 'And Jesus called a little child unto him, and set him in the midst of them, and said, Verily I say unto you, Except ye be converted, and become as little children, ye shall not enter the kingdom of heaven.' 'Of such is the kingdom of heaven', He says again; and affirms that their angels always behold the face of the heavenly Father.

[1] Tatham, *Life of William Blake* (published 1906), pp. 23–4.

Nothing could be plainer! The child is set in the midst of the disciples, for they have something to learn from the child, something essential. But the disciples showed no consciousness of understanding this lesson. We can imagine their puzzled glances at one another as their Master spoke. What is He driving at now? why doesn't He get on with restoring the Kingdom to Israel? Nor has the later Church paid any greater attention. Far from having anything to teach the adult, in the eyes of pastors and masters the child has everything to learn. To many orthodox teachers there is something peculiarly sinful and unregenerate about a child. That gaiety, that spontaneous delight in living—horrible! The child must be taught that it is not here 'to feel its life in every limb', but to shoulder the bitter burdens of life. The utmost severity has to be employed to drive this home. It is even wicked, as Dr Watts pointed out, to feel love for one's children. Such love is stolen from a jealous God and given to sinful creatures.

Nature has soft and powerful hands,
   And Reason she controls;
While children with their little hands
   Hang closest to our souls.

Thoughtless they act th' old Serpent's part;
   What tempting things they be!
Lord, how they twine about our heart,
   And draw it off from thee!

What did Jesus, herein differing from His followers, see in the child to make Him accord it so high a place? The answer is not hard to find, from Blake's standpoint. The great characteristic of Jesus Himself was that He 'acted from impulse and not from rules'. The child, too, is all impulse. He lives in a pre-logical world. He has a sublime confidence in the goodness of the universe and has to be taught the arts of doubt and suspicion. They do not come to him naturally. He has to be taught, moreover, the duty of loving his elders and betters.

To begin with, the child loves only himself. He feels pleasure in his own being, in the movements of his limbs and in his immediate physical sensations. In many of the lyrics of the *Songs of Innocence* Blake gives expression to this infant spontaneity. Then, starting from the contact with his mother's breast, the child comes to 'love' his environment: but only in so far as that environment ministers to his own safety and well-being. There is no greater folly than to talk about a child's 'affection', and no worse crime than to demand such affection from a child. The young child is incapable of affection. Yet how many parents, and especially mothers, do we see busily engaged in making emotional demands of even the smallest children! By these methods the young mind becomes hopelessly confused. In *A Little Boy Lost* Blake shows his insight into this truth. The child who speaks in the first two verses is expressing the fact that for him the environment is subsumed into the ego.

> "Nought loves another as itself,
> Nor venerates another so,
> Nor is it possible to Thought
> A greater than itself to know:
>
> And Father, how can I love you
> Or any of my brothers more?
> I love you like the little bird
> That picks up crumbs around the door." [*S.E.* 78]

The sequel to this plain speaking, the burning of the little boy by the priests of Albion, suggests that it was the Fifth Commandment that Blake had in mind when he wrote the poem. There is no doubt that the existence of this particular commandment had a great deal to do with his life-long aversion for the Mosaic code. The injunction to 'honour thy father and thy mother' has been a powerful weapon in the hands of those whose mission it is to crush the spirit of children.

We can be sure that frequent appeals to the Fifth Commandment had their part in the educational system pursued by such as Susanna Wesley at the beginning of the century. 'I insist on conquering the will of children betimes....' After the spirit has been broken, reason and precept can be relied on to continue the good work. The great aim is to bring about conformity to a standard. The unique nature of each child is overlooked. It is assumed that a perfectly blank page (except for some blots of original sin) is provided on which the educator may write what he pleases. Again we note the ill effects of that doctrine of acquired ideas which Locke handed on to the eighteenth century. In the details of his educational system, Locke himself is often enlightened and just; but it was the most mechanical parts which his admirers seized upon.

The process of standardisation begins early. Children like to play: it is their way of expressing the world they live in, the world of imagination. From that world they body forth modes of creative activity. These activities often appear meaningless to the adult mind, which is capable of perceiving significance only in terms of formulae or in pre-established routine. But the child, without routine, loses itself completely in its play. It attains a concentration which an adult mind cannot understand. It is completely *aware*.

Now this awareness is by no means 'bird-wittedness'. It is not the fluttering mental instability of so many half-alive people, but precisely the opposite. It is, in the first place, openness to a wealth of impressions, and then absorption in one of them so complete that everything else is forgotten. Past and future disappear, and only the present exists. In this eternal moment the child lives in the pure imagination; and out of the imagination he will create, with bits of string, with paper, with pebbles, with mud, or with nothing at all, a new world.

This capacity of the child for absorption is naturally so obnoxious to the adult that he is constantly concerned to break it. He will call it stupidity, insanity, daydreaming, laziness. From behind rustling pages of *The Times*, frowning, he will rebuke the silent child in its corner. And he will call upon education to carry his rebuke into effect.

It is quite clear why there should be this antagonism. The child, lost in its thoughts and visions is at liberty—perfect liberty. Liberty from parents, from time and place, from law. To the adult's eye this is a terrifying spectacle. Blake put his finger on the root of the matter. The adult is 'offended with the innocence of a child...because it reproaches him with the errors of acquired folly'. At the bottom of the adult's annoyance there is both jealousy and fear. Dr Edward Glover tells us that 'grown-ups may be physically stronger than children, but they are, nevertheless, secretly afraid of them or, rather, of their minds.'[1] It is the fear of the dweller in a cave when he sees the strange wild graceful creatures dancing outside. It is the fear and hatred which the savages felt for Rima in Hudson's masterpiece.

---

[1] From the essay *Man–the Anachronism* in the collection, *This Changing World.*

Better any kind of conventional activity, even destructive, than this silent freedom: that is what the adult thinks. So the child is taken from his play and forced into games.

Games, of course, differ from play in that they have to be learned. The faculties of imitation and memory are called into action. Play is the spontaneous creation of meaning, whereas games are obedience to a formula. They are stereotyped, and deviation from the rule entails a penalty. As moral training, they are indeed excellent from the adult point of view. The boy is glad to be running about, and he learns to co-operate with others. He sinks his own individuality in that of the crowd. His creative powers are destroyed, and he comes to look on play as an activity fit only for babies.

I have said that the child is forced into games: 'forced' not only in the physical sense but also in the hot-house sense, into an exteriorisation of energies which at that particular stage of development should be left largely interior. The personality suffers. Everyone has known children who from five to ten years of age have been delightfully intelligent, natural and creative, and have come back from their first term at a boarding-school with all the charm and individuality gone. And it is accepted as quite natural, altogether right and good. They have conformed to what is expected of them. It is odd that parents, in spite of the hideous mess most of them get their own lives into, are blissfully confident that they know exactly what sort of men and women their children ought to become. But no one can know the potentialities of a child. Each must grow according to the subtle pattern of his own being. 'Leave it alone' should be the great motto. 'Schoolmaster' is one of the titles Blake gives to Urizen, the Evil One. 'Schoolmaster of souls', the Eternal Man cries to Urizen,

> "O how couldst thou deform those beautiful proportions
> Of life & person; for as the Person, so is his life proportion'd."
>
> [*F.Z.* 428–9]

The great fetish is character—a word whose original meaning is an *image*. By character is meant a fixed or centralised personality, around which revolve a limited number of virtues largely classical in tone. This is the solar system within man. The idea of education for 'the better sort', the well-to-do, is to produce a type which will be able to deal with situations as they arise, not on the basis of understanding, but on that of will and habit. The child is inculcated with a limited set of attitudes which can be drawn upon without thought at any moment. Without thought—for thought implies indecision, the possibility of choice between two or more ways of acting; and this is a weakness. Action must be immediate, determined, irrevocable: the law of the Medes and Persians. The *quality* of the action is of little importance: it is the strength of character behind it that counts. The man of character never hesitates, never considers alternatives. He goes straight forward and 'gets things done'. His moral code is rigid and of the simplest. It includes conformity to the team—the machine of which he is a part—and the old stoic virtues of fortitude, prudence, temperance and justice.

The man of genius, said Keats, has no character. Character is a façade built over hollowness and insufficiency. Face your man of character with an unusual situation, or with a personality outside the reach of his mind, and he will collapse or bluster. True, he 'gets things done': but what sort of things? Without understanding there can be no right action. The chaos of the modern world should demonstrate the bankruptcy of this ideal.

For the individual, character is a simple defence against life, a mask so early and so skilfully constructed that he may wear it to the end. Elderly gentlemen perfectly protected against thought may be seen any day in London's clubs. The movement of life passes them by. Impervious, they are only too anxious that others should share their blessed state. As chairmen of committees, as governors of schools, they pass on the apostolic succession.

It is not altogether an easy thing, however, to turn the naturally impulsive being of a child into the stereotyped pattern required. He is born without experience of suffering or deceit, he acts from his whole being. The mind-forged manacles are still non-existent. But soon the parents begin to worry about this spontaneity. They think it high time the child should begin to realise the seriousness of life. Absorption in the imagination is construed as laziness:

> The father forms a whip to rouze the sluggish senses to act
> And scourges off all youthful fancies from the new-born man.
>
> [*T.* 166]

And next comes the period of schooling. The child has to acquire knowledge—the conventional, dead knowledge of the educationists: Latin, Greek, history, mathematics, and the rest. For the immediate intuition of the living universe which he possessed as a child, he has to substitute a lifeless memory-framework. And he has to acquire character. The world is evil, is cruel and deceitful. The boy must be broken in to this realisation. He must be taught to be hard in his turn, to be suspicious and aggressive and selfish. Thus the vicious circle is perpetuated, and there is no possibility of new principles entering the circle with the new generation. He has to acquire morality, to learn to distrust and curb his instincts, and to see that other people curb theirs. He is taught that he may expect to find one woman whom he may love and make his wife and the mother of his children; and that there are other women who will appeal to his senses and whom he may use as playthings so long as he is not open about it. Religion consists in attendance at church, the giving of charity, and a vague belief in God and immortality which may be expected to grow dimmer with the years: but which may profitably be replaced by a belief in the divinity and immortality of the social system or the State.

In *Songs of Innocence* we are shown the nature of the child before it has been perverted by education. The state of innocence is closeness to the world of vision. Vision sees the eternal forms of things behind their physical appearances. It sees the world as a unity full of joy and freedom. The child is unique as an individual and has not had that uniqueness educated out of him. In all his actions and thoughts he is uninhibited: the whole world is an 'Ecchoing Green' to him, with no envious nurse to call him home. Between the nature called animate and that called inanimate he makes no distinction: nor between his own nature and that of insect or bird. To him nothing is common or unclean.

When he enters school all this is ended. On innocence follows experience. For hours on end he is shut away between four walls from the sun and the wind and the blue sky; he is taught to sit still; he is compelled to be silent; dead knowledge is stuffed into his brain.

Blake, as we know, never went to school; but he felt most keenly the misfortune of those who do. His poem *The Schoolboy* is the most poignant expression in our literature of the folly which turns the happy spontaneity of childhood (which, left to itself, would bring forth the fruits of wisdom in riper years) into misery and hopeless boredom. The first stanza is a most musical evocation of the child's delight in living:

> I love to rise in a summer morn
> When the birds sing on every tree;
> The distant huntsman winds his horn,
> And the sky-lark sings with me.
> O! what sweet company. [*S.I.* 66]

The child's joy is identified with the joy of the lark—the little bird, we remember, which sang so sweetly that the 'awful sun' itself paused on the mountain top to listen. But this picture of delight is immediately followed by the contrast—the miserable slavery of school:

> But to go to school in a summer morn,
> O! it drives all joy away;
> Under a cruel eye outworn,
> The little ones spend the day
> In sighing and dismay.
>
> Ah! then at times I drooping sit,
> And spend many an anxious hour,
> Nor in my book can I take delight,
> Nor sit in learning's bower,
> Worn thro' with the dreary shower. [*S.I.* 66]

The young spirit rebels against these unnatural conditions, thinking of the sunlit freedom outside the four walls of the prison, the golden hours fleeting away ungarnered. The dreary shower of useless knowledge beats upon the brain, so numbing it that never in later life will the unhappy victim be able to take delight in books. How can the wild heart of a child bear such a burden of tedium and fear?

> How can the bird that is born for joy
> Sit in a cage and sing?
> How can a child, when fears annoy,
> But droop his tender wing,
> And forget his youthful spring? [*S.I.* 66]

In Blake's time fear was considered an essential part of education, as it is to-day in all but advanced circles of educational thought.

And with fear, its concomitant punishment: the solemn daily beating of a child of two is recorded, if I remember rightly, by J. S. Mill. Anyone objecting to these methods of education would have been considered crazy. And Blake was, one remembers, considered crazy; but he stuck to his point:

> O! father & mother, if buds are nip'd
> And blossoms blown away,
> And if the tender plants are strip'd
> Of their joy in the springing day,
> By sorrow and care's dismay,
>
> How shall the summer arise in joy,
> Or the summer fruits appear?
> Or how shall we gather what griefs destroy,
> Or bless the mellowing year,
> When the blasts of winter appear? [*S.I.* 66]

Blake's penetrating questions still confront parents. He is not speaking as a sentimentalist about childhood, but as a psychologist concerned for the harmonious and progressive development of the whole Man. He looks beyond the period of childhood, and he sees the repressed struggling spirit, with its load of useless mental furniture, its inability to take delight any more in the natural goods of life, or even in the books that have been thrust upon it too early and by the wrong method. He asks for an education that shall be an education in living—and that is something that the young personality has to give itself, in the open air, in the company of other children and of the life of Nature. Education as it was in Blake's day and as it has largely remained, alas! in spite of the teachings of Rousseau and Pestalozzi and others who have thought like Blake, was hideously repressive. Then and to-day State education bludgeons away the precious quality of uniqueness in each child—those 'minute particulars' of personality that give it its eternal station in the Land of Life. In school a class of children ceases to be a number of living entities: the individual is subsumed in the herd.

Again we are faced with the monster of abstraction, the Cerberus with which Blake was fighting all his life long. We have seen how the eighteenth century was dominated by the idea of the abstract Man—an idea that had been growing up since Bacon's day. We find it well developed in Locke. Though individuals may differ through the influence of environment and education, they are essentially the same, and this essence can be abstracted in thought. Thus the study of Man becomes a science. Ignore the minute particulars of personality, concentrate on the abstraction, and you are well equipped to deal with any man in any situation. 'The proper study of mankind is man.' Not *men*—man. Now the child, said the philosophers, can be considered in the abstract with even more advantage. He comes into the world without a thought, without an idea, with no element of that tiresome stuff, personality. His mind is a sheet of white paper. All we have to do is write on it. If the child revolts—what can it be but original sin which had better be flogged out of him?

Blake's view was the contrary. Let the young spirit develop, not only for its own sake but for society's. 'We live not for ourselves'—true: but the most precious gift we can give to others is the contribution of our personal quality. Unfortunately society will never recognise this truth, in spite of the glaring fact that whatever mankind has accomplished in the course of centuries has always been the work of individuals, recalcitrant to the herd, preferring implacably the guidance of their own *daimons*. The so-called consciousness of the mass is always retrograde.

Again the nature of Blake's teaching is not in doubt. It is anarchism. We have seen anarchism applied to the personal life of love and marriage: here it is applied to the education of the child. And of course society, so long as it is not built up on anarchist principles, cannot accept such a view of education. The two races of men, the exploiters and the exploited, must be prepared from earliest childhood for their destiny. What that destiny is, viewed through the eyes of Blake, we go on to see in the next chapter.

CHAPTER XVII

Society

> There souls of men are bought & sold,
> And milk-fed infancy for gold;
> And youth to slaughter houses led,
> And beauty for a bit of bread. [*M.P.* 96]

BLAKE was a Londoner born and bred, and in spite of his three years at Felpham he remained a Londoner to the end. In this he differs radically from his Romantic successors of the Lake School and from the cosmopolitan Byron and Shelley. The framework of London's streets and districts, Lambeth and Islington and Primrose Hill and 'ever-weeping Paddington', wove itself into the pattern of his symbolism. But in the midst of all his visions he never lost sight of the human London of commerce and misery and vice.[1] He saw the daily scene with the keenest of eyes.

> I wander thro' each charter'd street,
> Near where the charter'd Thames does flow,
> And mark in every face I meet
> Marks of weakness, marks of woe.
>
> In every cry of every Man,
> In every Infant's cry of fear,
> In every voice, in every ban,
> The mind-forg'd manacles I hear. [*S.E.* 76]

On this detailed observation he constructed his social thinking. Rousseau's proclamation is not forgotten in these verses. 'Man is born free, and everywhere he is in chains'—the mind-forged manacles. And he analyses the complexity of enslavement.

> How the Chimney-sweeper's cry
> Every black'ning Church appalls;
> And the hapless Soldier's sigh
> Runs in blood down Palace walls. [*S.E.* 76]

---

[1] Alas, in cities where's the man whose face is not a mask unto his heart? [*M.Pr.* 864]

There it is, the accusation. You, minister of religion, are responsible for the torture of the child against whose exploitation you raise not a word of protest;[1] you, the King, are responsible for the wretchedness of the soldier snatched away from his home by the press-gang. Most horrible of all is beauty prostituted 'for a bit of bread':

> But most thro' midnight streets I hear
> How the youthful Harlot's curse
> Blasts the new born Infant's tear,
> And blights with plagues the Marriage hearse. [*S.E.* 76]

That, as Mr T. S. Eliot comments, is the naked vision.

Blake lived through the development of the Industrial Revolution, but because his home was London and not Lancashire or Yorkshire, it is the woes of the climbing-boys and the harlots that occupy him, rather than those of the young miners and factory-hands. He is not indifferent to the hardships of the farmers and country labourers at a time when the agricultural communities were in violent transition; but his criticism of such anomalies as tithes—

> "With what sense does the parson claim the labour of the farmer?" [*V.D.A.* 211]

—has not the same immediacy as his attacks on prostitution and militarism.

With time his view widened. Blake was always keenly interested in social matters, and he was from the beginning on the side of the working-classes against their exploiters. The latter half of the eighteenth century and the first decades of the nineteenth mark as profound a change in the economic order as the Renaissance had brought in the wider sphere of philosophy and theology and nationalism. Of course we cannot delimit the Industrial Revolution within the period 1760–1830. The Renaissance itself might be considered the genesis of the change-over from the feudal economic system to a capitalistic one. But it is during these years, Blake's lifetime we may say, that a unique combination of circumstances made it possible for industry to take unparalleled strides forward in England. These factors—the commercial expansion of England

[1] The compression of thought is brilliant: the very walls of the church are *appalled* by a misery to which the hearts of the clergy are quite apathetic.

in the eighteenth century, the growth of the woollen industry, the enclosures of common land which drove the country people into towns, the improved methods of mining coal and the new inventions in power-machinery—it does not fall within the scope of this book to discuss. Their effects, however, in shaping the pattern of society in Blake's day, must be briefly described.

The outstanding fact is the triumph of the machine. There had been machines before 1760, of course, but these had been employed mainly in cottage industry. Lombe's 'fully fledged textile factory' at Derby—a silk mill—existed since about 1719, and became the model for Arkwright's cotton-spinning factories; but this was an exception.[1] It was worked by water-power, and the real development of the factory system only became possible with the advent of steam. Before 1750–60 spinning had been carried on in cottages by skilled workers on hand-operated looms. But in the great new factories which began to spring up unskilled women and children could be employed to look after the machines; and the skilled workers were thrown out of their jobs.

What Blake thought of machines is perfectly clear from many a reference in his writings. He laments the destruction of the old rural crafts, and sees in the dominance of machinery the end of art. 'A Machine is not a Man nor a Work of Art; it is destructive of Humanity & of Art.' He recognised that industrialism, with its concomitant migration of a rural population into the towns, meant the replacing of human life governed by the natural rhythms of the seasons by a robot life based on the rhythms of the machine. In consequence, the sense of values by which mankind has previously lived is reversed:

And all the Arts of Life they chang'd into the Arts of Death in
  Albion.
The hour-glass contemn'd because its simple workmanship
Was like the workmanship of the plowman, & the water wheel
That raises water into cisterns, broken & burn'd with fire
Because its workmanship was like the workmanship of the shepherd;
And in their stead, intricate wheels invented, wheel without wheel,
To perplex youth in their outgoings & to bind to labours in Albion

[1] I owe these facts to Mrs M. D. George's *England in Transition.*

Of day & night the myriads of eternity: that they may grind
And polish brass & iron hour after hour, laborious task,
Kept ignorant of its use: that they might spend the days of wisdom
In sorrowful drudgery to obtain a scanty pittance of bread,
In ignorance to view a small portion & think that All,
And call it Demonstration, blind to all the simple rules of life.

[*J.* 675–6; *F.Z.* 393]

The clauses of this indictment are worth analysing in detail. First Blake condemns the replacement of the life standard by the death standard: the rhythm of organic growth by the rhythm of the machine. This standard imposes itself in every aspect of life: the hour-glass in its primitive simplicity is superseded by the intricate mechanism of a clock. Secondly, he condemns the thwarting of the individual's life-aims, the enslavement to the machine: and we note how he puts his finger on an aspect of this which modern psychologists have stressed—the evil effect of piece-work, of specialisation. The worker who spends his whole time polishing or grinding one bit of brass, say a rivet, without understanding the broad design of which his rivet is a minute part, soon collapses through boredom. This for Blake is a symbol of the whole tendency of the machine to shut the meaning of the universe out from Man.

The final point of the indictment lies in the wretched conditions of labour and the starvation pay. The mill-labour of the eighteenth and early nineteenth centuries was provided largely by women and children. This was nothing new in English industry. The charity schools were based on the notion that children should be taught to earn their own bread (and frequently their parents' too) and earn it at the earliest age possible. These schools from the outset provided instruction in wool-spinning, shoe-making, knitting and so on, to fit the boys for apprenticeship and the girls for domestic service. With the coming of the factories in the mid-century such schools declined, for more and more children were required for factory labour which needed no training. Moreover, the orphan children in workhouses, who used to be farmed out to tradesmen situated at sufficient distance from the locality in which the workhouse stood, were now sold to mill-owners, still farther away and with still less sense of responsibility. An endless supply of these children was available. There was an enormous increase in the population. The following figures are given by G. D. H. Cole in his *History of the British Working Class Movement*:

> The first census was not taken until 1801, and no accurate figures exist for earlier times. But, though estimates differ, they agree on this point. Between 1500 and 1600, and again between 1600 and 1700, the growth of population did not exceed a million in the century. Between 1700 and 1800, the increase was nearer three millions, and between 1801 and 1831 another five millions were added. These figures, moreover, are for England and Wales alone. Thus, to the greater productivity of the individual worker, to the greater intensity of labour, and to the increased industrial employment of women and young children, was added a most powerful fresh factor—the immensely rapid increase of population.

From the point of view of labour-supply, as Mr Cole points out, the Industrial Revolution falls into two parts. In the first period, up to about 1800, there is a surplus of workers in the country but a shortage in the factory districts. This shortage was made up partly by the employment of workhouse children. But by the beginning of the nineteenth century migration from the country had taken place in sufficient numbers to enable factory owners to draw on local supplies of children. These were abundant enough to displace adult workers. They were of course paid a minimum wage. The standard of living fell still more, and the conditions of labour for the children deteriorated to a frightful extent.

When Blake wrote in *The Four Zoas* his denunciation of child labour, the picture he drew, far from being exaggerated, erred on the side of moderation and, for once, of over-generalisation.

> children are sold to trades
> Of dire necessity, still laboring day & night till all
> Their life extinct they took the spectre form in dark despair.
>
> [*F.Z.* 386]

The fact is, Blake had no personal experience of the conditions in the northern factory towns: he wrote from hearsay, and from his intuitive understanding. Very few of the great writers of the time suspected these horrors; had they done so, we should have had a chorus of denunciation. It was not, indeed, until 1842, fifteen years after Blake's death, that the public was fully enlightened by a document called the First Report of the Children's Employment

Commission. Fully enlightened, that is, as far as the coal mines were concerned. The Commission, set up two years before, dealt only with this aspect of the problem. The Report showed that the usual age for children to start work in the mines was seven or eight. In some cases it was much earlier.

Some were employed as 'trappers', others for pushing or drawing coal trucks along the pit tunnels. A trapper, who opened the ventilation doors on which the safety of the mines depended, would often spend as much as sixteen hours a day crouching in solitude in a small dark hole. 'Although this employment scarcely deserves the name of labour,' ran the Commission's report, 'yet as the children engaged in it are commonly excluded from light and are always without companions, it would, were it not for the passing and repassing of the coal carriages, amount to solitary confinement of the worst order.'[1]

Girls as well as boys were employed, 'harnessed like dogs in a go-cart', to crawl on all fours down eighteen-inch high passages, or stood ankle-deep in water for twelve hours working the pumps at the pit-bottoms. 'One child who was cited, only six years of age, carried or dragged half-a-hundredweight every day up a distance equivalent to the height of St Paul's Cathedral.' The most sickening cruelty accompanied this slavery. One witness described how he had seen a boy beaten with a pick-axe. 'Lord Ashley in a speech in the Commons mentioned another whose master was in the habit of thrashing him with a stick through which a nail had been driven: the child's back and loins were beaten to a jelly, his arm was broken and his head covered with the mark of old wounds.'[2]

These things were nothing new. They had been going on for years, and they had been defended on the grounds of economic necessity both by the mine-owners and by the economists. The children were kept working their sixteen hours a day till they died of exhaustion or fell into the machinery and so perished. It did not matter: there was always a fresh supply. The African slave was a valuable commodity for the American slave-owner; he had to be treated with as much consideration as a good horse. It is interesting

---

[1] Arthur Bryant, *English Saga* (pp. 51–2), to which I am indebted for many of my facts in this chapter.

[2] *Ibid.* p. 52.

to note that Wilberforce, so enthusiastic for freeing the slaves in America, was a bitter opponent of reform in the factories.

The factories were run mainly, as has been pointed out, by women and children. The father of the family, often a skilled worker in some trade now rendered useless from any of a variety of causes, remained idle at home. It was a tragic situation—tragic not only in its immediate misery, but in the long chain of evils which flowed from it. Generations cooped up in the horribly dark and insanitary towns of the North could not be expected to produce a race of healthy Englishmen. We are still paying to-day for those generations that never saw the sun.

For an account of the conditions in the factories, again I cannot do better than quote Mr Bryant's narrative. He shows us the situation of the mother who is working twelve or thirteen hours a day in the mill and has no time to bring up her children. Immediately after childbirth she is forced back to the mill.

The effect on the children can be imagined. The home to which they returned at night, often too weary even to eat, was an untended hovel. The machines to which they hurried back before dawn never tired as they did. In the country which had abolished slavery and was vigorously opposing the slave trade in every corner of the world, 'strappers' were kept to flog drowsy factory children lest they dropped asleep at their work, and groups of pallid mites could be seen supporting each other home as they dragged their limbs up the dark cobbled lanes of the Lancashire and Yorkshire valleys.

Many were crippled for life: few grew to mature and healthy manhood or womanhood. Long, monotonous and unnatural working positions resulted in permanent curvature of the limbs. Whole families went about with crooked legs or twisted shoulders. Knees bent inwards and backwards, ankles were thickened and deformed and spinal columns pressed forward or to one side. Every street had its company of cripples, of prematurely aged and arthritic youths bent double and limping, of hag-like girls with deformed backs and hips....The factory population of Lancashire and the West Riding was discoloured and stunted and seemed more like some ill-fated race of pigmies than normal human beings. A Leeds surgeon testified that but for the constant new recruits from healthy country stock, the race of millhands would soon be wholly degenerate.[1]

[1] *Ibid.* p. 60.

Blake had no need to look as far as the northern towns for examples of the horrors to which the machine condemned women and children. Mrs George points out in her exhaustive survey of London life[1] that the metropolis differed in many respects from the rest of England in its reaction to the Industrial Revolution; and not least in its freedom from the more obvious forms of mechanisation. The small workshops which were driven out of existence by the factories in the North held their own in London. The condition of the poor improved progressively from about the middle of the eighteenth century onwards; and it is indeed at the very time that the status of the poor apprentice in London is being bettered that the iniquitous system of carting pauper children from the metropolis to the cotton towns of the North begins. Nevertheless, the peculiar evils of the Spitalfields weaving community and of the infant chimney-sweepers persisted in London throughout the whole of this period. Neither these, nor the hordes of prostitutes, nor the terrible conditions of the prisons, can be ascribed to the Industrial Revolution.

The conditions of the Spitalfields weavers might even suggest that Blake's references to 'children sold to trades of dire necessity' were directed simply to local evils.[2] The details of these conditions may be found in Mrs George's book. 'Quite young children', we read, 'worked at filling quills for the weaver's shuttle.' Drawing the threads in the looms was a task given to older boys; it is described as fearfully exhausting, and the children were sometimes taken ill after as little as five or six hours of it. The close, cramped labour brought on disease, and contemporary observers comment on the stunted physique of the weavers.

Blake himself belonged to the small-shopkeeper class which in London was fairly prosperous and managed to hold its own through the period of transition. Within this class the apprentice system was firmly established. The original idea of apprenticeship was, of course, the protection of a trade against the competition of unwarranted intruders, and the training of successors. But by the eighteenth century the apprentice system had come to be for the parish authorities

[1] Mrs M. D. George, *London Life in the Eighteenth Century.*

[2] The craft must have been familiar which supplied Blake with an image for his own decrepitude: 'only bones & sinews, All strings & bobbins like a Weaver's Loom', and dominated so much of the symbolism of the prophetic books.

a useful means of getting rid of unwanted children. The children were virtually sold to their masters and no notice was henceforth taken of them. The way was open to unlimited exploitation.

The most shameful treatment was meted out to these unfortunates. And public indifference cannot be excused by ignorance in the case, let us say, of the little chimney-sweeps or 'climbing-boys' who prowled the cold streets of London. Blake focusses his readers' attention on this evil in his early lyrics. Amid all the joy of the *Songs of Innocence* this grim note is sounded. The child who speaks in *The Chimney Sweeper* is so young—'milk-fed infancy'—that he cannot pronounce his words without a lisp.

> When my mother died I was very young,
> And my father sold me while yet my tongue
> Could scarcely cry "'weep! 'weep! 'weep! 'weep!"
> So your chimneys I sweep, & in soot I sleep. [*S.I.* 58]

Poetic exaggeration? Not a bit of it. There were parents, we are told, who were 'ready to dispose of their children under the influence of a glass of gin'. Others carried their little ones about and sold them to the highest bidder. Children of four were apprenticed. The smaller the child the better, for the flues were narrow and tortuous; and often the little boy had to be stripped of his rags and sent up naked. It has been calculated that there were about five hundred of these climbing boys in London in the year 1817:

> They started with a period of extreme misery, mental and physical, until they became inured to their trade. Their terror of the pitch-dark and often suffocating passage had to be overcome by the pressure of a greater terror below. In order to induce them to climb up, the more humane masters would threaten to beat them, or perhaps only promise them plum-pudding at the top; the less humane would set straw on fire below or thrust pins into their feet. A careful master would send an experienced child up behind to show the newcomer how to place his feet and to catch him if he fell. Sometimes the seasoned boy would bring up pins to prevent halts in mid-chimney. When the 'repugnance' of ascending the chimney, as it was euphemistically called, had been overcome, there followed many months of acute physical suffering from the sores on elbows and knees. Gradually these parts would grow insensible. "Some boys' flesh", said a master in 1817, "is far worse than others, and it takes

more time to harden them." He estimated that it took six months, as a rule, for the parts affected to grow 'cartilaginous'.[1]

These affected parts became cancerous and the disease was fatal unless surgically treated at an early stage.

The children not only worked among soot, they slept among it too, in a cellar; Blake's '& in soot I sleep' is strictly accurate. They had to be up early in the morning, crying for hire in the streets:

> we rose in the dark,
> And got with our bags & our brushes to work. [*S.I.* 59]

They worked chiefly in the winter, and were hardly ever washed. Often they were forced to go up chimneys which were on fire, and some were thus burned to death. Others were suffocated by falling into the great heaps of soot which collected in the horizontal passages of the flues. In summer the climbing-boys were compelled to go out on the streets and beg for their masters.

It is clear that Blake's indignation was powerfully excited by the misery of these children. He returns to the attack in *Songs of Experience*:

> A little black thing among the snow,
> Crying "'weep! 'weep!" in notes of woe!
> "Where are thy father & mother? say?"
> "They are both gone up to the church to pray.
>
> Because I was happy upon the heath,
> And smil'd among the winter's snow,
> They clothed me in the clothes of death,
> And taught me to sing the notes of woe.
>
> And because I am happy & dance & sing,
> They think they have done me no injury,
> And are gone to praise God & his Priest & King,
> Who make up a heaven of our misery." [*S.E.* 71]

Yes, religion has its heavy share in the blame, as Blake does not fail to remind us in the contrasted pictures of *Holy Thursday* in the two books of *Songs*. These chimney-sweepers were largely recruited from the same class of charity-children, 'fed with cold and usurous hand',

[1] J. L. and Barbara Hammond, *The Town Labourer*.

that every year on Thursday in Whitsun-week were herded into St Paul's to thank God for all his benefits.

Yet, essentially, it was neither the Church nor the hard-heartedness of parents, but 'the wretched State of Political Science, which is the Science of Sciences' [*P.A.* 819], that wrought the misery of the poor. A system in which the masses were regarded as having 'no interest in the country except the interest of breathing'[1] yet were pressed into that country's armed forces, could be called neither just nor wise. The workmen of the northern manufacturing towns were kept in awe by having the militia quartered upon them. The revolutionary theorists of London were threatened, silenced or imprisoned. A vast network of government espionage ran through English society. With the rise of new conditions in industry much of the country's legal machinery had become obsolete, but there was no attempt at reform: on the contrary, repressive legislation was tightened up and implemented. By the eighteenth century there were over 200 capital offences on the Statute Book, and the death penalty was actually invoked for thirty of them. Boys of fourteen were hanged for stealing a loaf of bread.

The inevitable result of these conditions was a great increase in vice of all kinds. 'Prisons are built with stones of Law, Brothels with bricks of Religion.'

> "They mock at the Labourer's limbs: they mock at his starv'd Children:
> They buy his Daughters that they may have power to sell his Sons:
> They compell the Poor to live upon a crust of bread...." [*J.* 606]

London was thronged with prostitutes and its prisons with debtors. 'The Harlot's cry from Street to Street Shall weave Old England's winding Sheet', Blake warned. In the Fleet prison whole families were lodged and brought up to vice; and the process was helped on by the sale of drink, and especially of gin, within the prison walls. This surrounding world of misery and suffering pressed in upon Blake, and takes shape in the violent imagery of the symbolic books.

These unpleasant facts about the conditions of the labouring poor have been quoted at some length to give the background to Blake's

---

[1] Ireton, speaking in the Council of the Parliamentary Army in 1647 (quoted by J. L. and Barbara Hammond, *op. cit.*).

social thinking. What was his reaction? Did it go any further than indignation?

> The voice of slaves beneath the sun, and children bought with money

re-echoes through his verses; and though he could do little in a practical way, he was the first great poet of the nineteenth century to give unmistakable expression to the misery of the urban poor. Moreover, he associated himself from the beginning with the revolutionary movement, and celebrated in verse the fall of tyranny in France.

The theme of liberty appears early in Blake's writings. At first it is patriotic, nationalistic. There is the influence of Shakespeare in the background, the Shakespeare of *Henry V* and *Richard II.* In the dramatic piece *Edward III* (from the *Poetical Sketches*) the Prince remarks of Dagworth:

> "He is a genuine Englishman, my Chandos,
> And hath the spirit of Liberty within him," [*P.S.* 30]

words followed almost immediately by the King's:

> "O Liberty, how glorious art thou!
> I see thee hov'ring o'er my army, with
> Thy wide-stretch'd plumes; I see thee
> Lead them on to battle." [*P.S.* 31]

But this association of liberty with kings and wars rapidly dissolves. A growing realisation of social distress, evident in the *Songs of Experience*, persuaded Blake that liberty was not to be achieved on foreign battlefields. The American revolt showed him where tyranny lay—in oppressive government—and the way to be free:

> Why should I care for the men of thames,
> Or the cheating waves of charter'd streams,
> Or shrink at the little blasts of fear
> That the hireling blows into my ear?
>
> Tho' born on the cheating banks of Thames,
> Tho' his waters bathed my infant limbs,
> The Ohio shall wash his stains from me:
> I was born a slave, but I go to be free. [*M.P.* 90]

Already the West is become the symbol of freedom. In the *Song of Liberty* that ends the *Marriage of Heaven and Hell*, it is in the West that red Orc, the spirit of revolution, is seen. He comes to bring freedom from the chains of religion, marriage, greed, race, and war:

> Golden Spain, burst the barriers of old Rome!
> Cast thy keys, O Rome, into the deep down falling, even to eternity down falling,
> And weep.
> In her trembling hands she took the new born terror, howling.
> On those infinite mountains of light, now barr'd out by the atlantic sea, the new born fire stood before the starry king!...
> Look up! look up! O citizen of London, enlarge thy countenance! O Jew, leave counting gold! return to thy oil and wine. O African! black African! (go, winged thought, widen his forehead.)

Orc is cast down into the deep by Urizen, but in his fall he arouses the nations, he stamps Urizen's stony law to dust, and proclaims the end of empire and conquest. A Chorus ends the Song:

> Let the Priests of the Raven of dawn no longer, in deadly black, with hoarse note curse the sons of joy. Nor his accepted brethren—whom, tyrant, he calls free—lay the bound or build the roof. Nor pale religious letchery call that virginity that wishes but acts not!
> For every thing that lives is Holy. [*M.H.H.* 203–4]

Already, we see, Blake conceives of revolt on every plane: not only on the political, but on the racial and the intellectual and sexual. In *America* (1793) this wider connotation is emphasised:

> "The morning comes, the night decays, the watchmen leave their stations;
> The grave is burst, the spices shed, the linen wrapped up;
> The bones of death, the cov'ring clay, the sinews shrunk & dry'd
> Reviving shake, inspiring move, breathing, awakening,
> Spring like redeemed captives when their bonds & bars are burst.
> Let the slave grinding at the mill run out into the field,
> Let him look up into the heavens & laugh in the bright air;
> Let the inchained soul, shut up in darkness and in sighing,
> Whose face has never seen a smile in thirty weary years,
> Rise and look out; his chains are loose, his dungeon doors are open;
> And let his wife and children return from the oppressor's scourge.
> They look behind at every step & believe it is a dream,

> Singing: 'The Sun has left his blackness & has found a fresher morning,
> And the fair Moon rejoices in the clear & cloudless night;
> For Empire is no more, and now the Lion & Wolf shall cease.'"
>
> [*A.* 219]

Blake's conception of liberty has widened and deepened. His verse is proceeding on a variety of planes, contrapuntally. The mystical note has been introduced: the resurrection is to be in Christ. Then, ostensibly, the Industrial Revolution is brought in: 'the slave grinding at the mill', and the man who is in a still worse plight, whose wife and children are toiling in mine or factory while he lies idle. But it is not only of these outer servitudes that Blake is speaking. There is the inner enslavement to the ego, and we shall not understand him fully until we remember that he is primarily concerned with the release from this.

When the French Revolution disappointed its English adherents, Blake, because he had seen the cataclysm from the first as a symbol, was able to go on to a more radical revolutionism embracing the whole Man and beginning with the individual. He came to see that politics is not the place to begin:

> I am really sorry to see my Countrymen trouble themselves about Politics. If Men were Wise, the Most arbitrary Princes could not hurt them. If they are not wise, the Freest Government is compell'd to be a Tyranny. Princes appear to me to be Fools. Houses of Commons & Houses of Lords appear to me to be fools; they seem to me to be something Else besides Human Life. [*P.A.* 819]

Is Blake throwing up the sponge here? Is he retiring into an ivory tower and leaving the poor and oppressed to shift for themselves? I believe not. I believe that Blake is simply shifting his emphasis. He has seen that rebellion and change must come first within the individual, and then within a group of individuals, the 'young men of the New Age', before any general movement could be successful. He believed in the invulnerability of wisdom, and the contagiousness of goodness. He did not find this belief, or anything approaching it, in the teachings of Paine and Godwin. They denied the world of vision, in which he lived, as flatly as did the reactionaries. They based their plans for the amelioration of society on the dogma of human perfectibility. Their faith admitted no Fall and no supernatural world.

The virtues they proposed to inculcate were the old classical virtues which always lead to war. The goddess Reason was to be enthroned in place of the goddess Superstition; but for Blake this was no improvement.

Thus Blake moved away from external revolutionism, and found in the teachings of Christ a more radical reversal of accepted values, penetrating deep into the nature of Man, and giving birth to a new creature. The figure of Jesus is never absent from his earliest pages; but with deepened meditation on His thought Blake comes to give Him more and more prominence until in *Jerusalem* he can exclaim: 'Be thou all my life!' It is Blake's version of the Christian message that we shall consider in the following pages.

C. MAN AND GOD

CHAPTER XVIII

Deism

If God is anything he is Understanding. [*S.D.L.* 933]

NATURAL Religion or Deism appears in its earliest form (like so much else in his age's 'climate of opinion' that Blake objected to) in Francis Bacon's *Advancement of Learning*. He sought 'the dignity of knowledge in the arch-type or first platform, which is in the attributes and acts of God, as far as they are revealed to man and may be observed with sobriety'. The Creation shows forth God's power and wisdom. He made the universe *ex nihilo*, and 'in a moment'; His amazing power is still displayed in this His second scripture. 'As concerning Divine Philosophy or Natural Theology, it is that knowledge or rudiment of knowledge concerning God which may be obtained by the contemplation of his creatures; which knowledge may be truly termed divine in respect of the object, and natural in respect of the light.'

The course of the tradition of Deism through Lord Herbert of Cherbury, the Cambridge Platonists, and other minor figures does not concern Blake: he concentrates his gaze on Bacon, Newton and Locke, and reserves his arrows for them. It is clear that he knew the *Principia* and the *Opticks*: and from these works he had read the character of their author pretty accurately; Newton's abstract intelligence, his disdain of art (he spoke of his friend the Earl of Penmore's interest in sculpture as 'a love for stone dolls'), his indifference to the pleasures of the senses, his moralisings, his absorption in the details of Jewish ceremonial religion and in the chronology of Biblical history and prophecy: all these traits together go to make up a personality which may almost be equated with Blake's Urizen.

The Newtonian synthesis was triumphant because it worked. It did provide a satisfactory and impressive picture of the scheme of things: and into its framework there was not a subsidiary problem in physics or stellar mathematics which could not be fitted and find its solution. Nor was the benefit confined to the realm of pure thought. Moralists and theologians found a friend and a pattern in the regular motions of the stars, to which they could point as exemplars of human life. Throughout the eighteenth century there is a strong tradition both in theology (sermonising) and in literature (e.g. Addison's 'The spacious firmament on high' and much of Thomson) of what we may call 'astronomical morality'. We shall find the tradition reaching its apogee—and its final vulgarisation—in Paine's *Age of Reason.*

Nor was the application in the least accidental or adventitious. Newton himself was a most devout man. He told Bentley that he had a religious motive in writing the *Principia*:

> When I wrote my treatise about our system I had an eye upon such principles as might work with considering men, for the belief of a Deity; and nothing can rejoice me more than to find it useful for that purpose.

He believed that his demonstration of law in the planetary system would strengthen the argument from design which in his day was the main 'proof' of the existence and wisdom of God. A convinced Deist, he read the Bible diligently, and would have been horrified to think that his picture of the universe as a vast machine would soon come to be one of the best weapons in the atheist's arsenal. But this time was not yet. At first, the *Principia* was accepted as a valuable contribution to religious apologetics. When Bentley, in 1692, was appointed the first lecturer on Robert Boyle's foundation he chose for his subject 'A Confutation of Atheism', and he ended his course of lectures with a demonstration of Divine Providence based on the nature of the physical universe as described by Newton. Bentley was an acute thinker but of course he had not the mathematical knowledge to understand the *Principia*; he therefore applied to Newton to give him the essence of his teaching. Newton replied in five interesting letters, in which he presents the First Cause as a mathematician:

> To make such a system with all its motions, required a cause which understood, & compared together the quantities of matter in the several bodies of the sun and planets and the gravitating powers resulting from

thence...and to compare and adjust all these things together in so great a variety of bodies, argues that cause to be not blind and fortuitous, but very well skilled in mechanics and geometry.

In the *Opticks*, too, Newton speaks plainly of his belief that natural philosophy will contribute to the improvement of ethics.

And if natural philosophy in all its parts, by pursuing this method, shall at length be perfected, the bounds of moral philosophy will also be enlarged. For so far as we can know by natural philosophy what is the first cause, what power he has over us, and what benefits we receive from him, so far our duty towards him, as well as that towards one another, will appear to us by the light of nature.

Newton was always keenly interested in the preservation of a moral code. Locke's repudiation of innate ideas gave him some concern, and he wrote to Locke on the subject, saying that this doctrine struck at the root of all morality and brought its author under suspicion of being a Hobbist. The alarmed philosopher expressed his willingness to have Newton look through the *Essay Concerning Human Understanding* and mark the offending passages. Newton was perfectly right, of course, in thinking that Locke's repudiation of innate ideas tended in the long run to atheism; but a little consideration should have shown him that what Locke had done in psychology was simply a reflection of his own achievement in astronomy when he replaced the innate 'virtues' and 'appetites' of bodies by an external law.

If the laws of the universe could be found within the universe itself, the origin and cause of all things were revealed directly in Scripture. Newton accepted the Bible as an inspired book—inspired not only in its theology, but in its morals, its history, and its ceremonial teaching too.[1] For him, the Church of God is a continuous entity existing from the Creation until now. The divine truth was given to the patriarchs, continued in the Jewish religion and handed on *unchanged* to the Christian Church. When Christ appeared, His teaching was no new revelation: it was a confirmation of the truth delivered to Moses. In Thesis VI of his *Irenicum: or Ecclesiastical Polity tending to Peace*, Newton gives a clear statement of his belief

[1] Cf. Blake's view of the Bible and of the new dispensation brought by Jesus Christ (see below, Chs. XIX and XX).

that under different names the Jewish system was continued in the Christian Church:

The same government was propagated from the Jews to the converted Gentiles, the name of synagogues being changed to that of churches, & the name of Chief Rulers and Princes of the Synagogues into that of Presidents & Bishops, the Bishop being the President of the Council of Elders....

What place is there, in this picture of Christianity as the continuation of Judaism, for the person of Christ? None, certainly, for Christ the Son of God, the Second Person of the Trinity. The doctrine of the Trinity was mysterious to Newton: that is, it required the exercise of faith. The other kind of mystery, which we may call ceremonial mystery, he accepted easily; but he would not accept the carpenter's son of Nazareth as the eternal God by whom all things—including Sir Isaac Newton's universe—were made. Jesus was a man, nothing more. Of course these views could not be published in the seventeenth century; but the posthumous *Two Notable Corruptions of Scripture*, attacking the Trinitarian texts I John v. 7 and I Timothy iii. 16, makes it clear that Newton was a Socinian.

From these rapid glances at Newton's theology we get a consistent picture of a mind dominated by the idea of mathematical law, religious not in a mystical but in a ceremonial and moral sense. His conception of God is of a Being of great power and wisdom, who has created the universe according to immutable laws, and has continued these laws in the moral and religious spheres for the guidance of His creature, Man. Newton's mind is so dominated by ideas of time and space that he often comes perilously near to positing these as attributes of God, although he denies this position in the *Opticks*. He does, at any rate, see the stellar universe as a place destined to be inhabited by Man after the Last Judgement, as the following passage from a MS.[1] demonstrates:

God made & governs the world invisibly, & hath commanded us to love & worship him, & no other God; to honour our parents & masters, & love our neighbours as ourselves; & to be temperate, just & peaceable, & to be merciful even to brute beasts. And by the same power by which

[1] Quoted by Sir David Brewster, *Newton*.

he gave life at first to every species of animals, he is able to revive the dead, & hath revived Jesus Christ our Redeemer, who hath gone into the heavens to receive a kingdom, & prepare a place for us, & is next in dignity to God, & may be worshipped as the Lamb of God, & hath sent the Holy Ghost to comfort us in his absence, & will at length return & reign over us, invisibly to mortals, till he hath raised up & judged all the dead, & then he will give up his kingdom to the Father, & carry the blessed to the place he is now preparing for them, & send the rest to other places suitable to their merits. For in God's house (which is the universe) are many mansions, & he governs them by agents which can pass through the heavens from one mansion to another. For if all places to which we have access are filled with living creatures, why should all those immense spaces of the heavens above the clouds be incapable of inhabitants?

Here, with a vengeance, we have the 'Substantial Astronomical Telescopic Heavens' in which, in Blake's paraphrase, Dr Thornton's God dwells.[1] With Newton, the very idea of spirit is in danger of disappearing from Christian thought: we are left with nothing but matter in varying degrees of rarefaction. The logical consequences of the Newtonian philosophy, which issued in nineteenth-century materialism, are quite apparent in Sir Isaac's own writings. They were apparent to Blake: and to some clear minds in Newton's own time. The foreign mathematicians, who were still wedded to the Cartesian system of vortices, pointed out that in effect Newton had banished God from the universe. Newton replied to these criticisms in the famous *Scholium Generale* which concludes the *Principia*. But in 1715 a philosophic mind of the first order renewed the attack. Leibniz questioned Newton's orthodoxy in a letter to Princess Caroline which contains the following propositions:

(i) *Natural religion itself* seems to decay [in England][2] very much. Many will have human *souls* to be material; others make *God himself* a corporeal being.

(ii) *Mr Locke* & his followers are *uncertain* at least whether the soul be not material & naturally perishable.

(iii) *Sir Isaac Newton* says that *space* is an *organ*, which God makes use of to perceive things by; it will follow that they do not altogether depend upon Him, nor were produced by Him.

---

[1] See above, p. 192.

[2] Parenthesis added by the Princess or possibly by Dr Samuel Clarke, whom Newton persuaded to answer the challenge for him.

(iv) Sir *Isaac Newton* & his followers have also a very odd opinion concerning the Work of God. According to their doctrine, God Almighty wants to *wind up* his watch from time to time, otherwise it would cease to move. He had not, it seems, sufficient foresight to make it a perpetual motion. Nay, the machine of God's making is so imperfect according to these gentlemen, that he is obliged to clean it now & then by an extra-ordinary concourse, & even to mend it as a clockmaker mends his work; who must consequently be so much the more unskilful a workman, as he is oftener obliged to mend his work, & to set it right. According to *my* opinion the same force & vigour remains always in the world, & only passes from one part of matter to another, agreeably to the laws of nature & the beautiful *pre-established* order. And I hold that when God works miracles, he does not do it in order to establish the wants of nature, but those of grace. Whoever thinks otherwise, must have a very mean notion of the wisdom & power of God.

Leibniz's reference to Locke reminds us how decisively that philosopher was influenced by his friendship with Newton (whom he had met in 1689) and by his study of Newton's cosmology. It was Locke who applied the Newtonian temper to psychology and carried one step further the materialisation of mental processes. In Blake's frequent allusions to Locke he is often coupled with Newton in a way which shows that Blake had deeply considered and perfectly understood the relation between the two thinkers:

"O Satan, my youngest born, art thou not Prince of the Starry Hosts
And of the Wheels of Heaven, to turn the Mills day & night?
Art thou not Newton's Pantocrator, weaving the Woof of Locke?"[1]
[*M.* 468–9]

To come to Berkeley after Locke and Newton is like entering another world. The familiar landmarks, to which we have grown accustomed in our travels from Bacon up to the 'barren waste' of the two later thinkers, disappear. The ballast which has been fastened to our feet is shaken off,[2] and we seem to fly rather than walk. Objects, too, are strangely different; they have reassumed the colours and sounds and scents of which they had been deprived by Locke, but they have lost solidity.

[1] Cf. Newton, *Principia*, Scholium Generale: [Ens intelligens] omnia regit non ut anima mundi, sed ut universorum dominus. Et propter dominium suum, dominus deus παντοκράτωρ dici solet.

[2] See Blake, *Letter* 19 in Nonesuch edition.

Together with these secondary qualities of matter Berkeley brings back the understanding in which they, in harmony with the primary qualities, exist. God is neither space nor a celestial watchmaker: He is pure being, in Whom all things live and move. From Him all effects proceed:

But you will say, Hath Nature no share in the production of natural things, and must they be all ascribed to the immediate and sole operation of God? I answer, if by 'Nature' is meant only the visible *series* of effects or sensations imprinted on our minds, according to certain fixed and general laws, then it is plain that Nature, taken in this sense, cannot produce anything at all.[1] But, if by 'Nature' is meant some being distinct from God, as well as from the laws of Nature, and things perceived by sense, I must confess that word is to me an empty sound without any intelligible meaning annexed to it. Nature, in this acceptation, is a vain chimera, introduced by those heathens who had not just notions of the omnipresence and infinite perfection of God. But it is more unaccountable that it should be received among Christians, professing belief in the Holy Scriptures, which constantly ascribe those effects to the immediate hand of God that heathen philosophers are wont to impute to Nature. "The Lord He causeth the vapours to ascend; He maketh lightnings with rain; He bringeth forth the wind out of His treasures. . . ." But notwithstanding that this is the constant language of Scripture, yet we have I know not what aversion from believing that God concerns Himself so nearly in our affairs. Fain would we suppose Him at a great distance off, and substitute some blind unthinking deputy in His stead, though (if we may believe St Paul) "He be not far from every one of us."[2]

The one great objection to Berkeley's view—the existence of evil in the non-human universe—he hardly touches upon, either in the *Principles* or elsewhere. His one comment is feeble:

The very blemishes and defects of Nature are not without their use, in that they make an agreeable sort of variety, and augment the beauty of

[1] Cf. Blake, 'This world is too poor to produce one seed'.

[2] *The Principles of Human Knowledge*, 150. The whole of this passage expresses pure Blake doctrine, and is probably the source of many of Blake's ideas. The same ideas are to be found in Boehme, and, following him, in William Law: 'This world, with all its stars, elements, and creatures, is come out of the invisible world; it has not the smallest thing or the smallest quality of anything but what is come forth from thence, and therefore every quality of everything is what it is and worketh that which it worketh by a secret power in and from the invisible world.' W. Law, *The Way to Divine Knowledge*.

the rest of the creation, as shades in a picture serve to set off the brighter and more enlightened parts. We would likewise do well to examine whether our taxing the waste of seeds and embryos, and accidental destruction of plants and animals, before they come to full maturity, as an imprudence in the Author of Nature, be not the effect of prejudice contracted by our familiarity with impotent and saving mortals. In man indeed a thrifty management of those things which he cannot procure without much pains or industry may be esteemed wisdom. But we must not imagine that the inexplicably fine machine of an animal or vegetable costs the great Creator any more pains or trouble in its production than a pebble does....[1]

Blake's 'To create a little flower is the labour of ages' has a more gracious and a wiser ring than that; and I believe it was with this coldly inhuman passage of Berkeley in his mind that he drew his tender pictures of the little seed looking out to see if the winds were abroad 'with their invisible array' to bear her to her earthy bed, and the spider snatched away by the 'famish'd Bird':

> "His Web is left all desolate that his little anxious heart
> So careful wove & spread it out with sighs and weariness."[2]
>
> [*F.Z.* 297]

Even Berkeley's pebble, he shows us, is more wonderful than the mind of the philosopher can comprehend:

> the poor indigent is like the diamond which, tho' cloth'd
> In rugged covering in the mine, is open all within
> And in his hallow'd center holds the heavens of bright eternity.
>
> [*M.* 520]

---

[1] *Principles*, 152.

[2] Here we find Blake actualising, particularising, and thus giving tremendous poignancy to, the tragedy of waste and suffering in Nature which Berkeley dismisses so airily. Berkeley has become the victim of the vice he attacks so constantly—abstraction: he has here been transformed into Urizen by want of understanding; and thus we find Blake performing the redemptive function which he gives to Milton in his epic of that name: he clothes Berkeley's abstract conception in flesh and blood and lets us see what it really entails. In his picture of the little seed, however (*F.Z.* 420), he would seem to have in mind Berkeley's own description in *Siris*, paragraph 141: 'The seeds of things seem to lie latent in the air, ready to appear and produce their kind, whenever they light on a proper matrix. The extremely small seeds of fern, mosses, mushrooms, and some other plants are concealed and wafted about in the air, every part whereof seems replete with seeds of one kind or other. The whole atmosphere seems alive.'

There was, indeed, much in Berkeley which Blake found it impossible to accept. Even his most mystical work, *Siris, a Chain of Philosophical Reflections and Enquiries concerning the Virtues of Tar-water* (1744), contains doctrines such as the opposition of body and spirit and the denial of the senses which were anathema to the preacher of excess and the holiness of all life. Yet *Siris* marks a great step forward for Berkeley. Between his last philosophical work of importance (*Alciphron*, 1732) and *Siris*, a great, a revolutionary book had been given to the world in the shape of Hume's *Treatise of Human Nature*. There can be no doubt that Berkeley read the *Treatise*; and the change of direction in *Siris* suggests that he now realised that the basis of Locke's ideas of sense-perception led too directly to scepticism of the Hume type to be used fruitfully for idealistic ends. Some new approach was needed; and in years of private meditation his thought had passed from the narrow bounds of Locke into the *largior æther* of Platonism.

There is a well-known dictum to the effect that Plato and Aristotle divide between them the empire of the human mind. It could only have been said by someone calmly ignorant of the East; but for European thought it has a certain relevance. Berkeley was a born Platonist in a century which, for all its rejection of the Schoolmen, was Aristotelean in tone. He happened, in his youth, to come under the then dominant influence of Locke, the English Aristotle; and he did not shake himself free until near the end. All through his long series of expositions of an idealist philosophy he was labouring under the dead weight of Locke's crypto-materialism. It was a losing battle, and perhaps Berkeley's message would have taken a firmer hold on the English mind if he had come out in the beginning as a Platonist in the succession of Cudworth, More and the rest of the Cambridge school. Now, only nine years before his death, he tacitly acknowledges his error.

Siris is a eulogy of the virtues of 'tar-water', a curious panacea in which Berkeley had great faith, illustrated by metaphysical truths which take us to the farthest extent of his thought. The sensible world, from which Berkeley had started in the *New Theory* and the *Principles*, sinks into the background; the very word, *idea*, which he had formerly used in its Lockean signification, is replaced by the word *phenomenon*. A certain dogmatic note to be found in the earlier controversial works has vanished; *Siris* is calm, tolerant and unassertive. Berkeley is content to suggest approaches to truth rather than affirm that he has found the key. He does not desert his previous convictions, but he realises that the formula *esse est percipi* is the first step and not the last on a road which clearly is widening from the philosophic grove into the mystic way.

Siris is not a logically developed treatise like the *Principles* and the mystical reflections have to be dug out of a mass of pseudo-medical detritus. The starting-point is that old axiom of Berkeley's, a denial of the term 'cause' to anything material. There are instrumental motions, or 'second causes', necessary for the regular course of Nature, without which Man could not live on this planet. But God is not bound to such instrumentality.[1] We must not think that gravitation explains anything about causes. Nothing in Nature can be accounted for on merely mechanical principles. Nor does Leibniz's 'pre-established harmony'[2] account for deviations from the norm or for freaks in Nature. 'We cannot make even one single step in accounting for the phenomena, without admitting the immediate presence and immediate action of an incorporeal agent, who connects, moves, and disposes all things, according to such rules, and for such purposes, as seem good to Him.'

The idea of *force* cannot be reduced to mathematical principles:

> Sir Isaac Newton asks, Have not the minute particles of bodies certain forces or powers by which *they* act on one another, as well as on the particles of light,[3] for producing most of the phaenomena in nature? But, in reality, those minute particles are only agitated, according to certain laws of nature, *by some other agent*, wherein the force exists, and not in them, which have only the motion.[4]

---

[1] See above, Ch. XII.

[2] See above, p. 333.

[3] Blake's notes on *Siris* are supposed to have been written about 1820. The conflation of 'Newton' and 'particles of light' in the following lines written about 1800–3 suggests that he read the book much earlier: the name Democritus, too, comes on the same page of *Siris*.

> The Atoms of Democritus
> And Newton's Particles of light....

[4] *Siris*, 250.

In *Siris*, Berkeley develops his idea of Nature as a divine visual language, with some help from Plotinus:

> Plotinus observes, in his third Ennead, that the art of presaging is in some sort the reading of natural letters denoting order, and that so far forth as analogy obtains in the universe, there may be vaticination. And in reality, he that foretells the motions of planets, or the effects of medicines or the results of chemical or mechanical experiments, may be said to do it by natural vaticination.[1]

Since Nature forms a sort of Rational Discourse, we can understand that it proceeds from an Intelligence; and the fact that we cannot perfectly understand the discourse shows that the Intelligence is profounder than our own. Orpheus and Empedocles styled this first Cause *Love*: 'Intellect enlightens, Love connects, and the Sovereign Good attracts all things.' The ancient philosophers were no fools, although 'the successful curiosity of the present age, in arts, and experiments, and new systems, is apt to elate men, and make them overlook the Ancients'. The Pythagoreans and Platonists 'had a notion of the true System of the World'. Plotinus 'acknowledgeth no place but soul or mind, expressly affirming that the soul is not in the world, but the world in the soul. And farther, the place of the soul, saith he, is not body, but soul is in mind, and body in the soul.'[2]

Berkeley discusses the ancient belief that the world is an animal. The Egyptians thought all things partake of life. There is no chasm in Nature—all things exist as links in a chain of being stretching up from the stones at our feet to pure spirit. Here we have expressed the dominant theme in *Siris*: the unity and continuity of being which Blake was to stress in *Auguries of Innocence* and many other parts of his writings. 'Intellect is the very life of living things', according to the Platonists; 'which doctrine implies that all the faculties, instincts, and motions of inferior beings, in their several respective subordinations, are derived from, and depend upon Mind and Intellect.' It is all very well for scientists to consider nothing but

---

[1] *Op. cit.* 252.

[2] In the remarkable paragraphs 177–87 Berkeley considers the East as the source of metaphysical knowledge: he cites the Egyptians, Hermes Trismegistus, the Chaldeans, the Persians and even the Chinese. All this would be most agreeable to Blake. 'The philosophy of the east taught the first principles of human perception.' [*M.H.H* 196]

the material appearances of things for the purposes of their experiments:

> But those who, not content with sensible appearances, would penetrate into the real and true causes (the object of Theology, Metaphysics, or the *Philosophia Prima*), will rectify this error, and speak of the world as contained by the soul, and not the soul by the world.[1]

We may, without impiety, consider the universe as an animal; but we must not consider God to be the sentient soul of the animal. There is no sensorium in God, for that would imply that He is dependent on sense:

> God knoweth all things, as pure mind or intellect; but nothing by sense, nor in nor through a sensory. Therefore to suppose a sensory of any kind, whether space or any other, in God, would be very wrong, and lead us into false conceptions of his nature.[2]

Here Blake makes the first of his marginal comments, with reference to the last word of this passage: 'Imagination or the Human Eternal Body in Every Man.' I need hardly point out that Berkeley would not have accepted this gloss.

Body is the opposite of spirit. Our bodies are impediments, weighing us down and hindering us at every turn. But there is no resistance to the Deity. Hence we should not imagine Him tied down to a body, even if that body is the universe. We must remember that natural phenomena are only natural appearances. They have the advantage over reality in that they present themselves first to the mind and find an easy foothold there; we cling to them and forget the eternal forms of which they are mere shadows:

> They and the phantoms that result from those appearances, the *children of imagination* grafted upon sense, such for example as pure space, are thought by many the very first in existence and stability, and to embrace and comprehend all other beings.[3]

We see how far Berkeley has moved from his early respect for sense-impressions towards a Platonic doctrine of innate ideas. Blake underlines the words italicised, and comments:

> The All in Man. The Divine Image or Imagination.
>
> The Four Senses are the Four Faces of Man & the Four Rivers of the Water of Life. [*B.S.* 1021]

---

[1] *Op. cit.* 285. [2] *Ibid.* 289. [3] *Ibid.* 292.

In other words, he cannot approve of an idealism which rejects the senses or the imagination. In vindicating the senses against Berkeley he is of course quite in line with his constant vein of thought; but he does not realise that Berkeley is giving the word 'imagination' a very different meaning from his own. It is important to note that while Blake welcomes Berkeley as an ally in some respects, he is cautious not to give his approval to any kind of asceticism or life-denial masked as idealism. Blake agrees that the body is an impediment; but the senses are true 'inlets of soul' if we exercise the imagination through them.

Berkeley develops his thesis that the senses have the first lien on our interest. At first we look no farther, until the dawn of intellect which casts 'a ray on this shadowy scene', and then the objects of sense come to appear no more than 'fleeting phantoms'. The vulgar are occupied purely with the 'outward form of gross masses'; the mechanical experimentalist examines the 'inward structure and minute parts' and discovers the laws of their motions; but the philosopher must take a step higher from the sensible into the intellectual world:

> he will then change his system, and perceive that what he took for substances and causes are but fleeting shadows: that the mind contains all, and acts all, and is to all created beings the source of unity and identity, harmony and order, existence and stability.[1]

And intellectual truths are so remote from those conveyed by the sense that they 'may well be excluded from vulgar speech and books, as abstract from sensible matter'.[2]

The next passage on which we find Blake commenting discusses the relation of God and Nature:

> Plato and Aristotle considered God as abstracted or distinct from the natural world. But the Egyptians considered God and Nature as making one whole, or all things together as making one Universe. In doing which

---

[1] *Op. cit.* 295.

[2] Berkeley here uses the term 'abstract' in a different sense from that which he criticised in Locke; the relation is rather of the Platonic 'idea' to its concrete form. Note the aristocratic tone of all Berkeley's argument here: he seems to have quite given up his early naïve faith that the 'vulgar' could understand him so long as they were not debauched by false philosophy. This exclusiveness is another point which would displease Blake.

they did not exclude the Intelligent Mind, but considered it as containing all things. Therefore, whatever was wrong in their way of thinking, it doth not, nevertheless, imply or lead to Atheism.[1]

Blake, of course, has no quarrel with Plato and Aristotle for considering God as distinct from Nature; but, he points out, they also considered God as a Being distinct from the human mind. 'They also considered God as abstracted or distinct from the Imaginative World, but Jesus, as also Abraham and David, considered God as a Man in the Spiritual or Imaginative Vision. Jesus considered Imagination to be that Real Man & says I will not leave you Orphaned, I will manifest myself to you; he says also, the Spiritual Body or Angel as little Children always behold the Face of the Heavenly Father.' Blake will have none of a philosophy, however 'spiritual', which removes God from the immediate knowledge of men into an abstract heaven, to be reached only by efforts of the reason. Man is face to face with God at every moment if he will but renounce moral virtue and cleanse the doors of perception which are the senses.

In *Siris* there is a constant line of attack on the senses—in reaction, I think, from the excessive deference to them in the earlier books. Berkeley shows no inkling of Blake's distinction of seeing not with but *through* the eye, of recognising the senses for what they are, windows into the 'eternal world which ever groweth'; and yet, if he had followed up his own doctrine, that what we seem to see outside is really inside the mind, he must in the end have come to this truth. Blake always says that the body is evil—so long as we are content to regard it as a material thing and rest in it. The cure for this blindness is not less sensual enjoyment, is not asceticism: it is more and intenser sensual enjoyment, so great that the husk of flesh is burnt away and feeling and thought are one in vision. Berkeley allows the senses an acquaintance with only the lowest kind of knowledge:

By experiments of sense we become acquainted with the lower faculties of the soul; and from them, whether by a gradual evolution or ascent, we arrive at the highest. Sense supplies images to memory. These become

---

[1] *Op. cit.* 300.

subjects for fancy to work upon. Reason considers and judges of the imaginations. And these acts of reason become new objects to the understanding. In this scale, each lower faculty is a step that leads to one above it. And the uppermost naturally leads to the Deity; which is rather the object of intellectual knowledge than even of the discursive faculty, not to mention the sensitive.[1]

For Blake this will not do at all. Berkeley seems here to have slipped back again into Locke's threefold division of ideas, and reason again becomes the arbiter of truth. 'Knowledge is not by deduction,' Blake comments, 'but Immediate by Perception or Sense at once. Christ adresses himself to the Man, not to his Reason. Plato did not bring Life and Immortality to Light. Jesus only did this.' It is a magnificent vindication of the rightness of the whole Man against all partial theories. Our insight into truth, our participation in the Kingdom of God, is gained instantaneously. 'Between two moments bliss is ripe.' And again Blake declares his allegiance to Christ alone as the revealer of life and Eternity.

Blake's next comment is addressed less to the actual paragraph he is reading than to the spirit of the Bishop's whole discourse. He clearly feels in *Siris*, for all its idealism, the heavy hand of eighteenth-century morality and snobbery. The Bishop is a mental aristocrat writing for other aristocrats, not for the common folk for whom Christ died. This conviction evidently grew on Blake the deeper he read into *Siris*. His comment, 'Jesus supposes every Thing to be Evident to the Child & to the Poor & Unlearned. Such is the Gospel', has not really much relevance to Berkeley's:

There is according to Plato properly no knowledge, but only opinion concerning things sensible and perishing, not because they are naturally abstruse and involved in darkness: but because their nature and existence are uncertain, ever fleeting and changing.[2]

As a matter of fact, what Berkeley says here agrees very well with Blake's repeated assertion that the forms of the imagination are much clearer and more real than any form in Nature. And Blake continues with even less appositeness to the text under consideration: 'The whole Bible is fill'd with Imagination & Visions from End to End

[1] *Op. cit.* 303.

[2] *Ibid.* 304.

& not with Moral Virtues; that is the baseness of Plato & the Greeks and all Warriors. The Moral Virtues are continual Accusers of Sin & promote Eternal Wars & Dominency over others.' What has happened is that the name of Plato cropping up in Berkeley's text at this moment has released, automatically, the flood of anger against the classics which we know was seething in Blake's mind around 1820.[1] 'The Classics! it is the Classics, & not Goths nor Monks, that Desolate Europe with Wars' he cries in his pamphlet *On Homer's Poetry* (1820). The inscriptions around the engraving of the Laocoon Group, in the same year, are still more eloquent. 'If Morality was Christianity, Socrates was the Saviour', and 'The Gods of Greece & Egypt were Mathematical Diagrams—See Plato's Works'. The last remark is repeated in a note to *Siris*. 'God is not a Mathematical Diagram', Blake protests when Berkeley, quoting Aristotle, says 'Theology [is conversant] about Being abstracted and immovable; which distinction may be seen in the ninth book of his *Metaphysics*'.

Nor will Plato's support of innate ideas (as explained by Berkeley) satisfy him. He does not believe that sensible occasions are absolutely necessary for 'exciting into act what was already pre-existent in the soul'. This gives too great a rôle to the body. 'The Natural Body is an Obstruction to the Soul or Spiritual Body.' Again one feels that Blake is irrationally prejudiced against Plato; and much of the account of Platonism which follows in *Siris* could not but appeal to him. Unfortunately, where he agrees he is content to pass by without comment, and we have only the irascible notes to guide us.

When he does express agreement, it is cautiously. Themistus, a Peripatetic of the fourth century A.D., opines that all beings are in the soul. 'For, saith he, the forms are the beings. By the form everything is what it is. And, he adds, it is the soul that imparteth forms to matter.' Blake notes: 'This is my Opinion, but Form must be apprehended by Sense or the Eye of Imagination. Man is All Imagination. God is Man & exists in us & we in him.' He will not give licence for the reason to be considered the faculty by which God is apprehended; and he is afraid that both Platonists and Peripatetics—and the Bishop—are of this opinion. Much, of course, depends on the sense given to the word 'reason'. Plato's *nous* is

[1] This is discussed in the chapter on art, Ch. XXIII below.

very different from Hobbes' or Locke's *reason*: 'intellect' might be a better translation; and Berkeley himself had travelled far from his Lockean origins on this point. But Blake is obstinate in his distrust of the classics; and his last note is uncompromisingly adverse: 'What Jesus came to Remove was the Heathen or Platonic Philosophy, which blinds the Eye of Imagination, The Real Man.'

> Human souls in this low situation, bordering on mere animal life, bear the weight and see through the dusk of a gross atmosphere, gathered from wrong judgements daily passed, false opinions daily learned, and early habits of an older date than either judgment or opinion. Through such a medium the sharpest eye cannot see clearly. And if by some extraordinary effort the mind should surmount this dusky region, and snatch a glimpse of pure light, she is soon drawn backwards, and depressed by the heaviness of the animal nature to which she is chained. And if again she chanceth, amidst the agitation of wild fancies and strong affections, to spring upwards, a second relapse speedily succeeds into this region of darkness and dreams.[1]

Berkeley himself made no 'extraordinary effort'; his theory of vision and its idealist consequences seem to have come to him as something obvious and very simple. But his importance in the history of English thought *is* extraordinary, and can hardly be exaggerated. He asserted the dependence of the universe upon mind in a predominantly materialistic century. He was understood by only a few; but he made possible the step forward taken by Hume, and he gave food for thought to Blake and the Romantics. His originality is beyond question. Locke built up his philosophy, patiently, on the old foundations of Hobbes and Bacon, with a great deal of help from the Newtonian world-picture. He hardly contributed a new idea of his own. Berkeley stepped straight outside the Bacon-Newton-Locke picture and looked at the world afresh. His rejection of materialism in the very heyday of Newtonian physics is supremely courageous. His penetrating mind adumbrated criticisms of the Newtonian system which are more fully expressed at the present day. He saw quite clearly that the scientific approach to reality is a partial one, and in its abstraction an unreal one, for it seeks to analyse its perceptions of the external world apart from the mind perceiving them. He saw

[1] *Op. cit.* 340.

that science could not, in the long run, get on without a philosophy. And the world-view professed by some modern scientists, as for instance J. S. Haldane in his *Philosophy of a Biologist*, is remarkably close to Berkeley's. I cannot do better than close this chapter with his description of the relation of Man to the universe:

> We are at present accustomed to assume as self-evident the existence of a purely physical world. But this assumption has not only been ruled out by the development of modern philosophy: it is also ruled out by the fact that the world of our conscious experience is a world, not merely of life, but of personality in the sense already explained. In the constitution of the world we as persons are intimately involved, and the conception of a world which, though it comes to be perceived, exists independently of perception of it, has no real meaning, however convenient it may be for certain purposes.

CHAPTER XIX

The Bible

Both read the Bible day & night,
But thou read'st black where I read white. [*E.G.* 133]

THE man who was proud to call himself 'English Blake' was not least English in his devotion to the Bible. Of the three great literary influences on his writing—Ossian, Milton and the Bible—the last was the deepest and most pervasive. His conception of his own mission is that of the Hebrew prophets, and his symbolic works have the genuine ring of Isaiah and Ezekiel. His imagery has the combined immediacy and universality of Scripture. He believed himself to be inspired in exactly the same sense as the sacred writers.

But in comparison with the Old Testament prophets, he claims to have a larger charter in that he writes under the new dispensation of Jesus Christ. In the exordium to *Jerusalem*, indeed, he asserts that it is the Saviour Himself who bends over him at sunrise,

Spreading his beams of love & dictating the words of this mild song. [*J.* 552]

Therefore he can criticise the Old Testament from a vantage-ground higher than its writers possessed. He grants it no blind allegiance. He distinguishes the divine character of its purpose from the all-too-human means through which that purpose is expressed. He points to the Jews themselves as the most awful example of disobedience, wilful blindness and cruelty that history has to show. The whole Bible is the record of their resistance to the light which was brought to them by the prophets, their clinging to a religion of laws and ceremonies in preference to the pure religion of the spirit.

Moreover, from the beginning he adopts the mystical mode of interpretation of the Scriptures which was so much used by the early Fathers of the Church, as well as by the Gnostics; and thus he escapes any callow fundamentalism. He treats the Bible as a storehouse of esoteric knowledge. How is this knowledge to be interpreted? By the light within, Blake would answer. 'All deities reside in the human breast.' Since the coming of Christ, priestly intervention between God and Man has been done away: 'every man is priest and king in his own house'. In this respect Blake is a Protestant of the Protestants.

He is not at all Protestant, however, in his strenuous denying of any *moral* value to the Bible. In this, he considers that the Reformers went wide astray. The Bible is not a moral code and a commentary on it: it is a series of visions. It is by stressing the moral code and by ignoring the visionary quality of Scripture that wars are brought about:

> The Whole Bible is fill'd with Imagination & Visions from End to End & not with Moral Virtues; that is the baseness of Plato & the Greeks & all Warriors. The Moral Virtues are continual Accusers of Sin & promote Eternal Wars & Dominency over others. [*B.S.* 1022]

His attitude defines itself early in his writings. In Principles 5th and 6th of *All Religions are One* (*c.* 1788) he tells us:

> The Religions of all Nations are derived from each Nation's different reception of the Poetic Genius, which is every where call'd the Spirit of Prophecy.
>
> The Jewish & Christian Testaments are An original derivation from the Poetic Genius; this is necessary from the confined nature of bodily sensation. [*Did.* 149]

Blake, we note, is making no exclusive claim for the Hebrew and Christian Scriptures. The sacred writings of all nations are equally inspired, in so far as they are a product of the poetic genius, the imagination, and not of the reason or 'moral sense'. Moreover what is valuable in any literature, sacred or profane, derives from participation in this original insight into the poetic genius. Blake objected to the Greek and Roman classics, not because they were (as he thought) imitations from Hebrew originals and other sacred writings of the East, now lost: but because they had adulterated the primal inspiration with reason and morality.

This is not to say that the inspiration of the Bible itself is unmixed. There is no mechanical infallibility. It is the task of understanding to sift the true from the false. In *The Marriage of Heaven and Hell* (*c.* 1793) 'the voice of the Devil' informs us that

> All Bibles or sacred codes have been the causes of the following Errors:
> 1. That Man has two real existing principles: Viz: a Body & a Soul.
> 2. That Energy, call'd Evil, is alone from the Body; and that Reason, call'd Good, is alone from the Soul.
> 3. That God will torment Man in Eternity for following his Energies.
> [*M.H.H.* 191]

How have these corrupt dogmas found their way into the inspirational writings? Obviously through the priests, who have seized upon the Scriptures (written by poets) and use them for their own purposes. Blake states the contraries of these dogmas and brings forward Biblical grounds for his assertions.

In the same early work Blake describes *A Memorable Fancy*, in which he converses with the prophets Isaiah and Ezekiel. He questions them on the nature of inspiration, and especially on their statements that God spoke directly to them. This is an important locus in Blake's work, not only for his general Biblical criticism, but also for the light it throws on the much-debated question of what he meant when he spoke of his own conversations with supernatural visitors:

> Isaiah answer'd: "I saw no God, nor heard any, in a finite organical perception; but my senses discover'd the infinite in everything, and as I was then perswaded, & remain confirm'd, that the voice of honest indignation is the voice of God, I cared not for consequences, but wrote."
> [*M.H.H.* 195–6]

Then Ezekiel takes up the thread, and after making the important pronouncement that "The philosophy of the east taught the first principles of human perception",[1] he explains that Israel held the first principle to be the poetic genius 'and all the others merely derivative'. This is a bold assertion. Revelation is given to mankind through poets and artists, not through priests and philosophers. It is to this idea of revelation, then, that we must return if we wish to regain the Golden Age.[2]

---

[1] By which we must understand, I think, the art of perceiving the human in all things through the development of spiritual consciousness.

[2] Hence Blake's emphasis on art: see the concluding chapter.

A second *Memorable Fancy* shows that Blake had already reached the conclusion that Christ, far from giving 'his sanction to the law of ten commandments', deliberately broke them all as an example to His followers. *The Marriage of Heaven and Hell* anticipates all the teaching of *The Everlasting Gospel* written a quarter of a century later. It is hardly possible to speak of Blake's thought as evolving: he emphasised first one point and then another, but the whole can be found in epitome in his earliest works.

That does not mean, of course, that in the expression of his thought Blake escaped outside influence. We must remember that he was in contact with a group of thinkers—Paine, Priestley, Price—who were particularly interested in Biblical criticism. Tom Paine's *The Age of Reason* is a sustained attack on the credibility of Scripture. And it is in his marginal comments on Bishop Watson's *Apology for the Bible in a Series of Letters addressed to Thomas Paine* that we get Blake's clearest views on the whole question. Here he really lets himself go in defence of Paine (whose ideas he detested) against Bishop Watson (whose ideas he detested still more). It is not Paine's thesis he supports, but his honesty.

The first part of *The Age of Reason* was published in 1794, the second in 1795. Written in Paine's straightforward hard-hitting style, it is an attack on the authority of the Bible as history and as morality. Paine was a sincere Deist; he saw the revelation of God in the universe, and the Bible seemed to him nothing but a tissue of blasphemous fables and revolting anecdotes of human cruelty. The basis of Paine's attack is the contention that the Bible contradicts itself so constantly in point of chronology that no unprejudiced person can put any faith in its accounts. Moreover, the picture of God as a petty and malevolent tyrant which it presents accords not at all with the majestic nature of the Supreme Being as revealed to us in the universe. We must give up the Bible if we wish to worship God worthily.

Paine's book is an onslaught upon everything that Blake held dear: the inspiration of the Bible, the divinity of Christ, the imagination itself; and an assertion of everything that he most detested: Natural Religion, Newtonian nature, reason. Yet his comments are all for Paine and against Bishop Watson. Why? Because he saw in

Paine honesty fighting the good fight of liberty, and in the Bishop hypocrisy, State religion, fighting to continue the enslavement of the human mind. Paine is therefore nearer to the Kingdom of God than the Bishop.

It is worth while, I think, to go through *The Age of Reason* in some detail, with the Bishop's comments so far as they are re-commented by Blake. Paine gives an excellent statement of the extreme position in Deism at the close of the eighteenth century. It involved a rejection of the Bible and Christianity which the more respectable Deists would not bring themselves to make; and they pursued with their undying hatred, both in England and America, the man who did not hesitate to go to the extreme point. It expresses the complete satisfaction which the keenest minds of that time felt in the mechanistic view of the universe and of life. And it presents a picture of 'the Almighty lecturer' which vividly recalls Blake's presentation of Urizen as the 'schoolmaster of souls'.

Moreover, Paine has a good title to be considered the father of modern Biblical criticism in England. Without a knowledge of Hebrew and Greek, he had not the equipment which the later 'higher critics' handled so perilously. But the things which could be seen by the naked intelligence he did see: he refused to be blinded by tradition or imposture. And he set down his conclusions with a force and directness which cost him the popularity he had won in many parts of the world by his defence of civil liberties.

The first part of the book is not included in Bishop Watson's criticism: but as it is necessary to an understanding of the second part, and as it is the best short account of Deism in existence, I shall give a brief analysis. Let us bear in mind that these were the very arguments for Deism that Blake must have heard and combated at Joseph Johnson's literary evenings. In this way we shall get the diatribes against Natural Religion in the prophetic books into their proper perspective.

The sub-title of *The Age of Reason* is 'An investigation of true and fabulous theology'. It is important to note that Paine believes that there is a true theology; and the first sentences of his book make it plain that his object is to define this, 'lest in the general wreck of superstition, of false systems of government, and false theology, we lose sight of morality, of humanity, and of the theology that is true'.

This general wreck of falsehood he expects to result from the French Revolution, which has already abolished the 'whole national order of priesthood and everything appertaining to compulsive systems of religion' in France.

Paine begins with a personal profession of faith, which he makes 'with all that sincerity and frankness with which the mind of man communicates with itself'.[1] This profession relates to God and Man:

> I believe in one God, and no more; and I hope for happiness beyond this life.
>
> I believe in the equality of man, and I believe that religious duties consist in doing justice, loving mercy, and endeavouring to make our fellow-creatures happy.

He does not believe in the creed of any Church, for 'my own mind is my own church'. As for national Churches, they appear to him 'no other than human inventions set up to terrify and enslave mankind, and monopolise power and profit'. He has no wish to force others to hold his opinion on this point. The essential thing is sincerity. 'It is necessary to the happiness of man that he be mentally faithful to himself. Infidelity does not consist in believing or in disbelieving; it consists in professing to believe what he does not believe.' Here we seem to catch the very accents of Blake; and it may occur to us to wonder how far Blake's direct prose style was formed in listening to Paine's arguments for human liberty, and how far his apocalyptic verse style arose out of his violent disagreements with that philosopher on the subject of Natural Religion. It is difficult to judge which was most influenced by which. Both were men of sturdy independence of mind and of original views.

Following his *confessio fidei*, Paine goes on to attack the claim to a particular divine revelation made by the Jews, the Christians and the Mohammedans. He points out that nothing can truly be called a revelation that comes to a man at second-hand, as the Bible comes to us. No one is obliged to believe, for instance, the account of the Virgin Birth, simply because he is told it in a book. The only true revelation must be an immediate one. The first Disciples, if we accepted the Gospel record as accurate, might be said to have received such a revelation.

---

[1] A remarkable, and indeed Blakean, expression of the spiritual unity of mankind.

Taking the Nativity story as an example of how 'revelations' arise, Paine observes that such legends were very current in the pagan mythology of the time, and he has the wit to observe that Mary and the saints, with the Trinity, took the place of the heathen Pantheon, 'and Rome was the place of both'.

Christ Himself, Paine remarks, 'was a virtuous and amiable man'.

> The morality that he preached and practised was of the most benevolent kind,

though very similar teachings had been given by Confucius and some of the Greek philosophers. He wrote no account of Himself, and the miraculous narratives of the New Testament are fabulous. He opposed the 'corruptions and avarice of the Jewish priests...and it is not improbable that the Roman Government might have [had] some secret apprehension of the effects of his doctrine....Between the two, this virtuous reformer and revolutionist lost his life.'

The mythology which the Christian Church has erected upon the life and teachings of Jesus now comes in for destructive analysis. Paine has no difficulty in showing the incredibility of the fable and its unworthiness to be considered an account of the workings of the Divine Mind. It is true there have been some very good men who have believed it,

> enthusiastically enraptured by what they conceived to be the infinite love of God to man, in making a sacrifice of himself....But, if objects for gratitude and admiration are our desire, do they not present themselves every hour to our eyes? Do we not see a fair creation prepared to receive us the instant we are born—a world furnished to our hands that cost us nothing? Is it we that light up the sun, that pour down the rain, and fill the earth with abundance? Whether we sleep or wake, the vast machinery of the universe still goes on.

Paine proceeds to a consideration of the books of the Old and New Testaments, which he maintains are full of worthless fables. 'When the Church mythologists established their system', they decided by vote which scriptures should be admitted into the canon. To the books so admitted they gave the name of Revelation. They were the word of God, ratified by the vote. But, says Paine,

> whenever we read the obscene stories, the voluptuous debaucheries, the cruel and torturous executions, the unrelenting vindictiveness with which

more than half the Bible is filled, it would be more consistent that we called it the word of a demon that the word of God. It is a history of wickedness, that has served to corrupt and brutalise mankind; and, for my own part, I sincerely detest it, as I detest everything that is cruel.

Only in the Book of Job, and to a less degree in the Psalms, do we find anything worthy of the majesty of God. As for the prophets, they are simply poets (the word poet, Paine notes, does not occur in the Bible), and by a misunderstanding of the name their wild utterances are taken as having a profound meaning:[1]

It is altogether unnecessary after this to offer any observations upon what those men, styled prophets, have written. The axe goes at once to the root by showing that the original meaning of the word has been mistaken, and consequently all the inferences that have been drawn from those books, the devotional respect that has been paid to them, and the laboured commentaries that have been written upon them, under that mistaken meaning, are not worth disputing about. In many things, however, the writings of the Jewish poets deserve a better fate than that of being bound up, as they are now, with the trash that accompanies them under the abused name of the word of God.

Turning to the New Testament, Paine points out that the four Evangelists give no biography of Jesus, but merely a chain of 'detached anecdotes'. Jesus, like Moses and Mahomet, was a poor man; but whereas they were genuine founders of new religions 'Jesus Christ founded no new system. He called men to the practice of moral virtues and the belief of one God. The great trait in his character is philanthropy.' As to the degree of genuineness of the Gospels and the other parts of the New Testament, nothing certain can now be known:

One thing, however, is much less equivocal, which is that out of the matters contained in those books, together with the assistance of some old stories, the Church has set up a system of religion very contradictory to the character of the person whose name it bears. It has set up a religion of pomp and of revenue in pretended imitation of a person whose life was humility and poverty.

The result of the doctrine of sin, reprobation and justification by the blood of Christ has been to deny Man that immediate access to

[1] Here we have the obverse of Blake's contention in *The Marriage of Heaven and Hell.*

his Creator that he can achieve through a contemplation of God's revelation in the universe:

> It is by his being taught to contemplate himself as an outlaw, as an outcast, as a beggar, as a mumper, as one thrown, as it were, on a dunghill, at an immense distance from his Creator, and who must make his approaches by creeping and cringing to intermediate beings, that he conceives either a contemptuous disregard for everything under the name of religion, or becomes indifferent, or turns what he calls devout. In the latter case he consumes his life in grief, or the affectation of it. His prayers are reproaches. His humility is ingratitude. He calls himself a worm, and the fertile earth a dunghill, and all the blessings of life by the thankless name of vanities. He despises the choicest gift of God to man—the GIFT OF REASON; and having endeavoured to force upon himself the belief of a system against which reason revolts, he ungratefully calls it *human reason*, as if man could give reason to himself.

The true revelation is the universe, the Bible of Nature. It speaks a universal language; it can neither be forged nor suppressed. It tells Man of the power of God, of His wisdom, His munificence, and His mercy. By our reason we arrive at a knowledge of the First Cause: by reason exercised on a consideration of the visible creation. We find nothing of this in the Bible, except it be in the Book of Job and the 19th Psalm. And here Paine quotes Addison's paraphrase of that psalm: a poem that had become the metrical charter of English Deism.

> The Spacious Firmament on high,
> With all the blue Etherial Sky,
> And spangled Heav'ns, a Shining Frame,
> Their great Original proclaim.

'What more does man want to know', cries Paine as he comes to the end of Addison's six melodious verses, 'than that the hand or power that made these things is divine, is omnipotent? Let him believe this, with the force it is impossible to repel if he permits his reason to act, and his rule of moral life will follow of course.'[1]

It appears, then, that Christianity is a false theology, giving a totally wrong idea of the nature of God. Having established this,

[1] Bacon's second Scripture (Nature) has thus, at the end of the long rational tradition, come to be accounted the only one.

Paine comes to the question: What is the true theology? He gives the answer which the course of science from Bacon to Newton had made inevitable, but which had never been enunciated so precisely before. 'That which is now called natural philosophy, embracing the whole circle of science, of which astronomy occupies the chief place, is the study of the works of God, and of the power and wisdom of God in his works, and is the true theology.' Science, the study of the material universe, and theology, the study of the divine, are one and the same thing.

Paine demonstrates why this must be so. He points to the immutability of natural law, by which, for example, we can find out the date of eclipses. This law is not a human invention. It springs from the Divine Mind. But it is codified by Man chiefly in the science of trigonometry, which Paine calls 'the soul of science. It is an eternal truth; it contains the *mathematical demonstration*[1] of which man speaks, and the extent of its uses is unknown.' Man does not make a triangle: he merely represents one on paper; and so with the lever and the mill-wheel:

> It is the structure of the universe that has taught this knowledge to man. That structure is an ever-existing exhibition of every principle upon which every part of mathematical science is founded. The offspring of this science is mechanics....The man who proportions the several parts of a mill uses the same scientific principles as if he had the power of constructing a universe; but as he cannot give to matter that invisible agency by which all the component parts of the immense machine of the universe have influence upon each other, and act in motional unison together without any apparent contact, and to which man has given the name of attraction, gravitation, and repulsion, he supplies the place of that agency by the humble imitation of teeth and cogs. All the parts of man's microcosm must visibly touch. But could he gain a knowledge of that agency, so as to be able to apply it in practice, we might then say that another *canonical book* of the word of God had been discovered.[2]

It is interesting to note how in the Bible of nature Paine reads white where Blake reads black. The mill-like structure of the universe is

---

[1] Paine's italics. 'Mathematical demonstration', in morals, in politics, and in art, was, as we have already seen, the Mecca of eighteenth-century thought.

[2] How delighted Paine would have been to know the principle of 'remote control' by which ships and aeroplanes can now be steered!

roof that the god of reason built it: that god is Urizen, r of our woe.[1]

acher of true theology is God Himself, Paine declares. Why go to priests and sacred books for what is written plain ...ore our eyes?

> The Almighty lecturer, by displaying the principles of science in the structure of the universe, has invited man to study and to imitation. It is as if he had said to the inhabitants of this globe we call ours: "I have made an earth for man to dwell upon, and I have rendered the starry heavens visible, to teach him science and the arts. He can now provide for his own comfort, AND LEARN FROM MY MUNIFICENCE TO ALL TO BE KIND TO EACH OTHER."

If this didactic purpose were not in the universe, it would be to no end that God gave man eyesight good enough to observe the stars. Everything must have a use. 'A less power of vision would have been sufficient for man if the immensity he now possesses were only given to waste itself, as it were, on an immense desert of space glittering with shows.'

Let us then have done with all the nonsense of dead languages which is forced into the heads of unwilling children and teach them instead the 'true theology' of natural science. Paine is convinced there will be no difficulty in this. The little brains will drink it in:

> The human mind has a natural disposition to scientific knowledge, and to the things connected with it. The first and favourite amusement of a child, even before it begins to play, is that of imitating the works of man. It builds houses with cards or sticks; it navigates the little ocean of a bowl of water with a paper boat; or dams the stream of a gutter, and contrives something which it calls a mill; and it interests itself in the fate of its works with a care that resembles affection. It afterwards goes to school, where its genius is killed by the barren study of a dead language, and the philosopher is lost in the linguist.

Why, then, is not science taught in the schools? Because, Paine answers, its conclusions are so obviously incompatible with the doctrines of 'revealed' religion. This is why the Middle Ages were

---

[1] 'cruel Works
Of many Wheels I view, wheel without wheel with cogs tyrannic
Moving by compulsion each other....' [*J.* 574–5]

so barren of science, and Galileo was persecuted. The classical philosophers began well, but their tradition was interrupted by the 'long interregnum' of Catholicism. 'The Christian system laid all waste; and if we take our stand about the beginning of the sixteenth century, we look back through that long chasm to the times of the ancients as over a vast sandy desert in which not a shrub appears to intercept the vision of the fertile hills beyond.'

Glancing back at his own childhood, Paine sees that 'the natural bent of my mind was to science. I had some turn, and, I believe, some talent, for poetry; but this I rather repressed than encouraged, as leading too much into the field of imagination.'[1] He attended mathematical lectures and studied the globes. While he had no disposition for politics he saw that 'I had to form a system for myself in accordance with the moral and philosophical principles in which I had been educated'. He followed closely what was going on in America and wrote his *Common Sense* in support of American independence. As for religion, 'from the time I was capable of conceiving an idea, and acting upon it by reflection, I either doubted the truth of the Christian system or thought it to be a strange affair'. A sermon upon 'Redemption by the Death of the Son of God' which he heard when he was seven or eight so revolted him that he 'could not see for what purpose they preached such sermons'. This was not a thought which had in it anything of childish levity, says Paine: he still thinks in the same way; 'and I moreover believe that any system of religion that has anything in it that shocks the mind of a child cannot be a true system'.[2]

> How different is this from the pure and simple profession of Deism! The true Deist has but one Deity; and his religion consists in contemplating the power, wisdom and benignity of the Deity in his works, and in endeavouring to imitate him in everything moral, scientific, and mechanical.

And in all this, we note, there is not a word of the problem of evil, of the cruelty of Nature, or of the divine discontent in the heart of Man!

---

[1] An echo of Locke's advice in his treatise on education. A Lockean statement of the nature of ideas follows a few sentences further on.

[2] This sentence, in its tender and quiet wisdom, seems to me the best Paine ever wrote.

Dr Watson, Bishop of Llandaff, described by Professor Basil Willey[1] as 'a sort of third-rate Burke', was a great friend of the British Constitution and had written a tract against the French Revolution which drew a reply from William Wordsworth—in the days before he became a friend of the Constitution too. In this statement of revolutionary principles Wordsworth denounces the Bishop's inhumanity and hypocrisy, and accuses him of having 'aimed an arrow at liberty and philosophy, the eyes of the human race'. In 1797 the Bishop is up to his old tricks again, this time pretending to defend the Bible ('I did not know it needed any apology', muttered old George III) against Paine's criticism in the second part of *The Age of Reason*. Blake's comments are written on the title-page and in the margins of the text. He first animadverts with some bitterness on Watson's claim to 'defend' the Bible, 'in this year 1798'. It was a year of Government prosecutions and imprisonments, a year in which anyone really defending the New Testament ideal of 'all things common' and liberty and contempt for power and wealth would quickly have found himself in gaol:

To defend the Bible in this year 1798 would cost a man his life.

The Beast & the Whore rule without control.

It is an easy matter for a Bishop to triumph over Paine's attack, but it is not so easy for one who loves the Bible.

The Perversions of Christ's words & acts are attack'd by Paine & also the perversions of the Bible; Who dare defend either the Acts of Christ or the Bible Unperverted?

But to him who sees this mortal pilgrimage in the light that I see it, Duty to his country is the first consideration & safety the last.

Read patiently: take not up this Book in an idle hour: the consideration of these things is the whole duty of man & the affairs of life & death trifles, sports of time. But these considerations [are the] business of Eternity.

I have been commanded from Hell not to print this, as it is what our Enemies wish. [*W.A.* 949]

Bishop Watson's Preface, dated 10 May 1796, remarks on the dangerous nature of Mr Paine's writings, which have circulated 'amongst the unlearned part of the community, especially in large manufacturing towns'. We can well understand how dangerous this

---

[1] *The Eighteenth Century Background*, p. 261.

would appear to the Bishop and his instigators! Watson's 'Defence of Revealed Religion' will, his friends hope, 'be efficacious in stopping that torrent of infidelity which endangers alike the future happiness of individuals, and the present safety of all Christian states'. Blake underlines the last three words in his copy, and comments: 'Paine has not attacked Christianity. Watson has defended Antichrist.' And his eye hits on a list of books written by the Bishop, printed at the front of the *Apology*. One of them is 'The Wisdom and Goodness of God, in having made both *Rich and Poor* [underlined by Blake]: a Sermon, preached before the Stewards of Westminster Dispensary.'

Read the xxiii Chap. of Matthew & then condemn Paine's hatred of Priests if you dare [Blake remarks]. God made Man happy & Rich, but the Subtil made the innocent, Poor. This must be a most wicked & blasphemous book.[1] [*W.A.* 950]

To return to *The Age of Reason*. It will not be necessary for me to analyse the Second Part in such detail as the First, for here Paine simply applies the principles he has already established to the end of destroying the authority of Scripture. His patient undermining of each canonical book in turn is both interesting and intelligent. Our concern, however, is with the larger issues raised. Paine begins his Preface to Part II by confessing his disappointment with the course of the French Revolution towards the end of 1793:

The just and humane principles of the revolution, which philosophy had first diffused, had been departed from. The idea, always dangerous to society as it is derogatory to the Almighty, that priests could forgive sins, though it seemed to exist no longer, had blunted the feelings of humanity, and callously prepared men for the commission of all manner of crimes. The intolerant spirit of Church persecutions had transferred itself into politics; the tribunals, styled Revolutionary, supplied the place of an Inquisition; and the Guillotine of the State outdid the fire and faggot of the Church. I saw many of my most intimate friends destroyed, others daily carried to prison, and I had reason to believe, and had also intimations given me, that the same danger was approaching myself.[2]

Under these circumstances it seemed to Paine that a refutation of Biblical claims was more urgent than ever.

---

[1] Paine too noted the title of this sermon and wrote his *Agrarian Justice* to refute it.

[2] The Second Part of *The Age of Reason* was written in a French prison and Paine escaped the guillotine by a miracle.

Bishop Watson's treatment of the Preface is severe. He wishes that Paine's life had not been spared to write the Second Part of his book, for 'it would have been fortunate for the Christian world, had your life been terminated before you had fulfilled your intention'. Blake is horrified at this. 'Presumptuous murderer', he comments. 'Dost thou, O Priest, wish thy brother's death when God has preserved him?'

In accomplishing your purpose [the Bishop continues] you will have unsettled the faith of thousands; rooted from the minds of the unhappy virtuous all their comfortable assurance of a future recompense; have annihilated in the minds of the flagitious all their fears of future punishment; you will have given the reins to the domination of every passion, and have thereby contributed to the introduction of the public insecurity, and of the private unhappiness usually and almost necessarily accompanying a state of corrupted morals.

Blake sees in this First Letter 'the sting of the serpent...as well as [its] glittering Dissimulation'. And there is indeed a strange contrast, even to our eyes, between Paine's open and honest attack and Watson's tongue-in-cheek defence. 'If such is the characteristic of a modern polite gentleman', Blake says with some justice, 'we may hope to see Christ's discourses Expung'd. I have not the Charity for the Bishop that he pretends to have for Paine. I believe him to be a State trickster.' And that probably hits the nail on the head.

The Bishop goes on to an attack on Paine's competence to discuss Biblical subjects. What does he know of exegesis? Is he well up in the commentators? Has he examined every side of the question? Blake sweeps all this aside. Dissenting completely from Paine's views, he yet sees that Paine is a *force*, an embodiment of energy, and therefore to be acclaimed:

Paine is either a Devil or an Inspired man. Men who give themselves to their Energetic Genius in the manner that Paine does are no Examiners. If they are not determinately wrong they must be Right or the Bible is false; as to Examiners in these points they will be spewed out. The Man who pretends to be a modest enquirer into the truth of a self evident thing is a Knave. The truth & certainty of Virtue & Honesty, *i.e.* Inspiration, needs no one to prove it; it is Evident as the Sun & Moon. He who stands doubting of what he intends, whether it is Virtuous or Vicious, knows not what Virtue means. No man can do a Vicious action & think it to be Virtuous. No man can take darkness for light. He may pretend to do so & may pretend to be a modest Enquirer, but he is a Knave.

[*W.A.* 953]

Paine attacks the authority of the Bible first on humanitarian grounds. It ascribes to God's commands actions which are cruel and treacherous. It cannot therefore be a trustworthy guide. The Bishop counter-attacks by calling this an exploded argument of Morgan, Tindal and Bolingbroke (all prominent Deists). How can Paine maintain a belief in the God of Nature, who sends earthquakes, famine and pestilence? Does not his argument lead to disbelief not merely in the God of Revelation but in any kind of righteous God?

When Catania, Lima and Lisbon, were severally destroyed by earthquakes, men with their wives, their sons and their little ones, were swallowed up alive:—why do you not spurn, as spurious, the book of nature, in which this fact is certainly written, and from the perusal of which you infer the moral judgment of God?

Now here the Bishop does seem to have got hold of a good argument—not his own, incidentally, but taken from Butler's *Analogy of Religion*. The evil inherent in the natural order is the Achilles' heel of the Deistic position. No amount of faith in human perfectibility and the wickedness of priests and kings will explain away the cancer cell, the earthquake and the malaria-bearing mosquito. Human beings may possibly develop into saints, but Nature will carry on in her old wicked ways.

Blake of course has an answer:

The Bible says that God formed Nature[1] perfect, but that Man perverted the order of Nature, since which time the Elements are fill'd with the Prince of Evil, who has the power of the air. [*W.A.* 955–6]

But as for Watson's contention that God ordered the massacres in Palestine, this really is blasphemy. 'The Earthquakes at Lisbon etc. were the Natural result of Sin, but the distruction of the Canaanites by Joshua was the Unnatural design of wicked men.'

To me, who believe the Bible & profess myself a Christian, a defence of the Wickedness of the Israelites in murdering so many thousands under

[1] The Pleroma, *natura naturans*, not 'physis', *natura naturata*.

pretence of a command from God is altogether Abominable & Blasphemous. Why did Christ come? Was it not to abolish the Jewish Imposture? Was not Christ marter'd because he taught that God loved all Men & was their father & forbad all contention for Worldly prosperity in opposition to the Jewish Scriptures, which are only an Example of the wickedness & deceit of the Jews & were written as an Example of the possibility of Human Beastliness in all its branches? Christ died as an Unbeliever & if the Bishops had their will so would Paine: see page 1: but he who speaks a word against the Son of man shall be forgiven. Let the Bishop prove that he has not spoken against the Holy Ghost, who in Paine strives with Christendom as in Christ he strove with the Jews.

[*W.A.* 954–5]

It is clear enough now in what light Blake regards Paine. He is Orc, the spirit of Revolution, the refiner's fire sweeping everywhere to destroy the rubbish of centuries. The fire blazes its way through truth and falsehood alike, for it is not the function of fire to 'examine', but to burn. The truth will stand, and will emerge purer from the flames. Paine's rôle is not an individual, but a universal one; for he is not speaking from interest, or from policy, or from weakness. Therefore he is serving inspiration and imagination even when he seems to be destroying them. In this Paine differs from such materialists as Bacon, Newton and Locke, and their imps, Burke and Watson, who dare not speak out and who support a system in which they do not believe.

The Bishop now turns his attention to Paine's attack on the credibility of the miraculous events of the Old Testament, such as Joshua's arresting the course of the sun and moon. He owns that it appears strange that God should have acted thus,

and should have so far demeaned himself, as to give to that people a burdensome ritual of worship, statutes and ordinances, many of which seem to be beneath the dignity of his attention, unimportant and impolitic ...[*The Bible or Peculiar Word of God, Exclusive of Conscience or the Word of God Universal*, Blake puts in, *is that Abomination, which, like the Jewish ceremonies, is for ever removed & henceforth every man may converse with God & be a King & Priest in his own house.*]...but what is there that is not strange? It is strange that you and I are here—that there is water, and earth, and air, and fire—that there is a sun, and moon, and stars—that there is generation, corruption, reproduction.

To which Blake replies that 'It is strange that God should speak to man formerly & not now, because it is not true;[1] but the Strangeness of Sun, Moon, or Stars is Strange on a contrary account'.[2] And when the Bishop puts forward the argument that the plan of Providence, though strange, is so complex and so obviously wise and good that it can only have proceeded from a divine source, Blake points out that 'The Bible tells me that the plan of Providence was Subverted at the Fall of Adam & that it was not restored till Christ'. He differs from both Paine and Watson in holding that [true] 'Natural Religion is the voice of God & not the result of reasoning on the Powers of Satan'—which is the typical activity of the scientist.

Paine argues in the Second Part that Moses could not possibly have written the books ascribed to him. He gives a number of reasons—Moses is spoken of in the third person, events are mentioned that occurred hundreds of years after his death, and so on. Yet these books relate thoughts and words and acts of Moses which, if genuine, could only have been known to himself. This contradiction is good evidence that the books were written long after Moses' time; and there is internal evidence that they are a priestly compilation. The Bishop tries to counter this by urging that the genuineness of the books does not depend on the point of authorship: 'they may still contain a true account of real transactions, though the names of the writers of them should be found to be different from what they are generally esteemed to be'. This seems a poor argument. We may accept the main lines of Livy's history as true, so far as it is not miraculous: but the speeches he puts into the mouths of his actors we take to be inventions. Why should we not adopt this course with the Pentateuch? Blake's comment here is apposite:

> He who writes things for true which none would write but the actor (such are most of the acts of Moses), must either be the actor or a fable writer or a liar. If Moses did not write the history of his acts, it takes away the authority altogether; it ceases to be history & becomes a Poem of probable impossibilities,[3] fabricated for pleasure, as moderns say, but I say by Inspiration. [*W.A.* 959]

[1] I.e. it is not true that conversation of Man with God has now ceased.

[2] I.e. while Man has always been able to talk with God, the sun, moon and stars have not always existed—and that is why they appear strange.

[3] Note the Aristotelean phrase—from the *Poetics*.

Again Blake makes his view of inspiration clear. Inspiration does not consist in the literal accuracy of the events recorded in the Bible. The mere *event* has no importance, for it takes place in time which is itself an illusion. The event is simply the stuff with which significance clothes itself. Salvation does not depend on swallowing every word of the Bible, but on an effort of the understanding by which, among other things, the meaning of Scripture becomes clear. The Bible is the record of God's dealings with ungrateful and rebellious Man. The medium through which those dealings are described—the written word—while it communicates, also distorts, for it is a construction of that same Man who is the object of judgement.

The Bishop is just as misguided in his view of miracles. He blames Paine for denying the miracles wrought by Jesus, but himself holds that miracles have now ceased. He considers them to have been arbitrary exhibitions of force. Blake opposes this mechanical conception with a more vital idea which fits in with the words of the Evangelists:

> Jesus could not do miracles where unbelief hindered, hence we must conclude that the man who holds miracles to be ceased puts it out of his own power to ever witness one. The manner of a miracle being performed is in modern times considered as an arbitrary command of the agent upon the patient, but this is an impossibility, not a miracle, neither did Jesus ever do such a miracle. Is it a greater miracle to feed five thousand men with five loaves than to overthrow all the armies of Europe with a small pamphlet?[1] Look over the events of your own life & if you do not find that you have both done such miracles & lived by such you do not see as I do. True, I cannot do a miracle thro' experiment & to domineer over & prove to others my superior power, as neither could Christ. But I can & do work such as both astonish & comfort me & mine. How can Paine, the worker of miracles, ever doubt Christ's in the above sense of the word miracle? But how can Watson ever believe the above sense of a miracle, who considers it as an arbitrary act of the agent upon an unbelieving patient, whereas the Gospel says that Christ could not do a miracle because of Unbelief?
>
> If Christ could not do miracles because of Unbelief, the reason alledged by Priests for miracles is false; for those who believe want not to be confounded by miracles. Christ & his Prophets & Apostles were not Ambitious miracle mongers. [*W.A.* 960–1]

[1] Paine's *Rights of Man* (1791–2).

Blake in this passage gives what seems to me a perfectly cogent and worthy explanation of miracles. As for the prophets, he supports Paine's thesis (which he had already suggested in *The Marriage of Heaven and Hell*) that prophecy did not mean fortune-telling. A prophet is a man who *speaks out*, who utters 'his opinion both of private & public matters. Thus: If you go on So, the result is So. . . . A Prophet is a Seer, not an Arbitrary Dictator.'

Watson spends a lot of time over this question of the authenticity of the Pentateuch. He tries to prove that Moses did write the books that bear his name; and if he did not, then they are 'public records' and therefore accurate statements of facts. Blake laughs sarcastically at the naïve idea of public records being true. He points out that Watson is dealing all the time with Paine's lesser, more technical, objections and quietly ignoring the main arguments against the Bible, which are not textual but moral:

> One, for instance, which is that the books of the Bible were never believ'd willingly by any nation & that none but designing Villains ever pretended to believe—That the Bible is all a State Trick, thro' which tho' the People at all times could see, they never had the power to throw off. Another Argument is that all the Commentators on the Bible are Dishonest Designing Knaves, who in hopes of a good living adopt the State religion; this he has shewn with great force, which calls upon His Opponent loudly for an answer. I could name an hundred such.
>
> [*W.A.* 959]

The conclusion of the whole discussion is, as Blake puts it: 'The Bishop never saw the Everlasting Gospel any more than Tom Paine.' Both stress the moral precepts of the Bible and of Natural Religion, but 'The Gospel is Forgiveness of Sins & has No Moral Precepts; these belong to Plato & Seneca & Nero'. The Bishop deliberately distorts the doctrine of forgiveness of sins to suit the policy of governments:

> Two precepts you particularize as inconsistent with the dignity and the nature of man—that of not resenting injuries, and that of loving enemies [*Well done, Paine!*]. Who but yourself ever interpreted literally the proverbial phrase—'If a man smite thee on thy right cheek, turn to him the other also?'—Did Jesus himself turn the other cheek when the officer of the high priest smote him? [*Yes, I have no doubt he Did.*] It is evident, that a patient acquiescence under slight personal injuries [*O Fool! Slight*

Hippocrite & Villain!] is here enjoined; and that a proneness to revenge, which instigates men to savage acts of brutality, for every trifling offence, is forbidden.

Savage acts of brutality were to be reserved, it would seem, by Christ's law, for more serious offences: e.g. those offered against the rights of property. Watson speaks scornfully of 'the ignorant and immoral' who are unfitted to understand the meaning of Scripture. 'Are they the Publicans & Sinners that Christ loved to associate with?' asks Blake. 'Does God Love the Righteous according to the Gospel, or does he not cast them off?' And on the last page of his copy he writes:

> It appears to me Now that Tom Paine is a better Christian than the Bishop.
>
> I have read this Book with attention & find that the Bishop has only hurt Paine's heel while Paine has broken his head. The Bishop has not answer'd one of Paine's grand objections. [*W.A.* 967]

Blake did not modify the conclusions about the nature of the Bible and inspiration which he had come to in *The Marriage of Heaven and Hell* and the notes on Watson's *Apology*. His later writings contain even more frequent allusions to the Scriptures. The *Vision of the Last Judgment* stresses the contrast between fable or allegory and vision, the Greek and Roman classics being examples of the one and the Bible of the other. 'The Hebrew Bible & the Gospel of Jesus are not Allegory, but Eternal Vision or Imagination of All that Exists.' In 1810 Blake was increasingly concerned with the antithesis of states and individuals, and he sees the main personages of the Old Testament narrative as emblems of states. He links this up with his other dominant idea that Jesus is the One Man under the form of whom mankind sees itself when expanding the senses in vision. 'These various States I have seen in my Imagination; when distant they appear as One Man, but as you approach they appear Multitudes of Nations.' The references to the Bible scattered through the prophetic books develop this conception still further. The meaning of the Old Testament, as also the meaning of all later history, is made plain only in the person and acts of Jesus Christ.

CHAPTER XX

The Son of Man

I am not a God afar off, I am a brother and friend;
Within your bosoms I reside, and you reside in me:
Lo! we are One, forgiving all Evil, Not seeking recompense. [*J.* 552]

BLAKE'S is a Christianity from which the Father is left out. The Son is the central, dynamic figure, operating in the world order; the Holy Ghost is the indwelling spirit through whom we attain understanding. It is not as sons, but as brothers, that Blake envisages the human family.

The word 'father' plainly has unpleasant associations for him. Father, tyrant, king, priest—the group holds together and expresses all those ideas of repression and hypocrisy that Blake abhorred. It is Urizen to whom, most commonly, he applies the title 'father': 'Father of jealousies', 'cruel Father of men'. Tiriel, in the earlier myth, is the wicked old man who curses his sons and daughters. And to the idea of God as Father Blake applies the ludicrous term 'Nobodaddy' in a particularly scurrilous poem.

In his religious views, as in his social views and his conception of Nature, Blake shows himself an anarchist. He will not have the order of domination: he insists on a free working together of autonomous agencies. All evil springs from the belief in an hierarchy, or rather a monarchy, a system in which *one* commands and many obey. Men are brothers: and if it is asked how men can be brothers without also being sons, Blake replies that we must not think in terms of time, but of eternity, in which there is neither fore nor after, neither generation nor death. We may use the idea of sonship, as Christ Himself used it, only if we give up the notion of begetter and begotten. When Crabb Robinson asked Blake what he thought of the Divinity of Christ, Blake warmly replied that Christ was in truth the Son of God: and then added, 'And so am I and so are you'. For Jesus was pre-eminently the Son of God simply because He realised, to a degree unknown before, the unity of Man in God—and so made it possible for all other men to realise that unity.

Thus, though Blake sometimes uses the idea of sonship, and the terms 'father' and 'family', he is never quite at ease with them. The idea of brotherhood, and the idea of membership of a living organism, come more naturally to his mind. At times, indeed, he sets Jesus up in contrast to Jehovah.

> Thinking as I do that the Creator of this World is a very Cruel Being, & being a Worshipper of Christ, I cannot help saying: "the Son, O how unlike the Father!" First God Almighty comes with a Thump on the Head. Then Jesus Christ comes with a balm to heal it. [*V.L.J.* 844]

In consequence, we find him stressing those parts of Christ's message —the forgiveness of sins, the refusal to judge, the kingdom within, the insight of children—which are opposed to the idea of authority.

Blake's interpretation of the Christian Gospel, it may be objected, is a very partial one. He emphasises the things in the canonical text that he likes, that fit in with his private beliefs, and he ignores or combats the things that are contrary to those beliefs. And this objection may be admitted—with the proviso that Blake only does what everyone else does. We all make our own selections from the reported sayings of Jesus, and form a picture of His life and acts which omits many of the data. We do this for the simple reason that we must, if we are to form any picture and produce any coherent body of doctrine at all. The four Gospels are not of the nature of straightforward narratives, all saying the same things in much the same way. Quite apart from the Johannine account, the three Synoptic Gospels show great variations in their presentation of Christ's teaching; there are incoherences, discrepancies, contradictions. There are divergencies of attitude and tone. Matthew is obviously writing for a Jewish audience; he tries to show that Christ's good news is a fulfilment of the law, not an abrogation of it. Luke addresses the Greeks and Romans; his tone is gentle and his teaching has a sweet reasonableness. Mark, on the other hand, emphasises the revolutionary and eschatological sides of the Messianic message.

The selection that each of us makes, or that one Church makes in contrast to another, depends on a number of factors. The early Church still preserved a revolutionary fervour, and its teachings incorporated pacifism, a sort of communism and the expectation of a speedy second coming of the Lord Jesus. But as the generations wore on, and the Day of Judgement still delayed, these aspects tended to disappear. Church and State drew together under Constantine: the resultant hybrid emphasised morality, ceremony and ecclesiastical organisation; the wilder spirits went out into the desert, or, later, founded monasteries, or became preaching friars. The original impulse was lost. Christ's religion, the Everlasting Gospel of forgiveness and anarchy, had become State religion, the code of judgement and obedience. With Luther a new revolutionary movement began, and a neglected aspect of the doctrine—justification by faith—was emphasised. But always, within the ecclesiastical organisation, the conservative attitude gained the upper hand and it was the more obvious ethical precepts that got all the limelight. It was left to individuals here and there to bring out the fundamentally revolutionary nature of the Gospel.

Blake was one of these individuals. His point of view was something like this. 'In the recorded sayings of Christ we have a number of contradictions. The contradictions on the whole are between *revolutionary* utterances in morals, politics, psychology and religion, and *conservative* pronouncements in the same fields. Now the revolutionary sayings seemed extremely queer to Christ's disciples—who were often far from grasping their Master's train of thought. But He reiterated them so persistently, and the disciples were so convinced by their contact with Him that He was indeed the Son of God, that they wrote them down as they had received them. Christ's personality was strong enough to ensure that the main outlines of His teachings did not perish. With these highly original pronouncements, however, they incorporated a number of conservative dicta which made the Gospel more palatable to converts and especially to new Jewish disciples. We need not suspect the evangelists of any wilful fraud in this: it is very probable that many of Christ's more outrageous sayings became unconsciously distorted in their memories, and appeared in a more conventional guise. The marvel is that we still have in the Gospels so many obviously original sayings—words which bear the impress of an individual mind. It is these sayings, differing generically from any other recorded words of man, that we should accept as conveying the true message of Christ.'

We may imagine Blake as thinking along these lines when he writes, for instance, in *The Everlasting Gospel*,

> Both read the Bible day & night,
> But thou read'st black where I read white. [*E.G.* 133]

But the matter may be put in yet another way. Here is a great religious teacher whose doctrine was considered dangerous enough, by the State and ecclesiastical authorities, to make His liquidation imperative. He is crucified, but a band of simple and ignorant men carry on His work and found a world-wide Church. We expect, in examining His recorded sayings, to find evidence of the revolutionary character of this teacher. We do find such evidence; but it is embedded in a mass of non-revolutionary material which fails to amalgamate with it. What do we do, if we are honestly seeking the truth? Do we take the ethical precepts which, however lofty they may be, can be paralleled in both Jewish and classical morality, and would certainly never have brought Jesus to the Cross? Or do we take the outrageous, queer, revolutionary sayings, and set to work to see whether they fit together and make a pattern—however unlikely that pattern may be?

The Churches have taken the first course. They have given Christ's name to a religious system which incorporates the ceremonial and social laws of the ancient Jews with the ethical code of the Greeks and the philosophy of Aristotle. The revolutionary teaching of Jesus they have either quietly ignored or interpreted as allegory, Oriental hyperbole or 'counsels of perfection'. The book in which this teaching is contained they have embalmed in a dead language inaccessible to the common people. The Catholic Church has been violently opposed to the translation of this subversive matter into the vernacular. 'The Bible was regarded by Church and State in England as being of such a dangerous and incendiary character that long after the invention of printing no translation into the vernacular was permitted.'[1] Nevertheless, surreptitious translations did appear—the Wycliffe Bibles, Tyndale's New Testament and Coverdale's complete version. 'Once more the ruling classes awoke to the revolutionary implications of the Bible, and in 1543 a law was passed that "no woman (unless she be noble or gentle woman), no artificers,

[1] *The Bible designed to be read as Literature* (ed. E. S. Bates), p. 1232.

apprentices, serving-men under the degree of yeomen. . .husbandmen, or labourers" be allowed to read this radical literature. With the persecution of the reformers under Queen Mary the new translators were either executed, as was Rogers, or fled to the Continent, as did Coverdale.'[1]

Blake did not take the same course as the Church. He chose the second alternative. He saw that what we should expect of a revolutionary is revolt: and he found in the Gospels a great deal which chimed in with his own deep convictions. The more he pondered these sayings, the more they came to form an organic pattern in which he recognised the image of his own inner life. The person of Christ became very real to him. And if we trace this figure through Blake's writings, we find it becoming ever clearer, richer in detail and more central, till in the end it absorbs every other thought. Blake *knew* Christ; and he felt no hesitation in rejecting those distortions of the Gospel which hide His face. His reinterpretation is vital and far-reaching; and to return to a reading of the New Testament after a prolonged study of Blake is to feel a revelation. The well-known sayings take on a richer meaning, are more closely knit. What had been obscure is now crystal-clear. And the figure of Jesus, no longer vague and church-windowy, stands out in firm and full proportions.

It is the Christ-child who is most in evidence in Blake's early writings. He is the patron of the *Songs of Innocence*, from the child on the cloud in the *Introduction* to the 'infant small' of *On Another's Sorrow*. Blake lays the emphasis on His gentleness and care for children. The miseries of the poor and helpless are known to Him because He was once poor and defenceless Himself. Again, in *Europe* (1794), the Miltonic imitation recalls the Nativity:

> The deep of winter came,
> What time the secret child
> Descended thro' the orient gates of the eternal day:
> War ceas'd, & all the troops like shadows fled to their abodes.
>
> [*Eu.* 234]

The Four Zoas (1795–1804) shows a continuation of the interest in the Nativity theme, especially in its early pages; but now the

[1] Bates, *loc. cit.*

conception is deepened through a study of St John's Gospel. Blake puts in a marginal reference at the beginning of his poem: 'And the Word was made flesh, and dwelt among us (and we beheld his glory, the glory as of the only begotten of the Father), full of grace and truth.' It is an easy transition from Christ the Child, the Lamb of God, to Christ the Good Shepherd, and it is this typically Johannine conception that we find dominating *The Four Zoas*. Albion is the sheep that has gone astray, Jesus is the pitying shepherd:

> He is the Good Shepherd, He is the Lord & Master
> To Create Man Morning by Morning, to give gifts at Noon day.
>
> [*F.Z.* 285]

But already Christ is identified with the Divine Vision, mankind conscious of its unity, who must descend to redeem Albion, mankind unconscious of its unity. Here the influence of St Paul rather than of St John becomes apparent, and particularly of the Epistle to the Ephesians, which Blake quotes in the original Greek for his motto to *The Four Zoas*: 'For our contention is not with the blood and the flesh, but with dominion, with authority, with the blind world-rulers of this life, with the spirit of evil in things heavenly.' Translated thus, and not in the misleading version of the King James Bible, the revolutionary and anarchical principles of Blake's poem become boldly defined.

Ephesians, with its dwelling on the idea of Christ as the 'gathering together in one' of all things, was evidently a favourite epistle of Blake's: it is perhaps the most mystical and certainly the freest from that morbid asceticism which was so distasteful to the great preacher of excess. We see its influence throughout *The Four Zoas*, and not least in Los's warning to Enitharmon that the Eternals must

> survive by stern debate
> Till we have drawn the Lamb of God into a mortal form.
> And that he must be born is certain, for One must be All
> And comprehend within himself all things both small & great.
>
> [*F.Z.* 289]

The repeated phrase, 'the Divine Image', which Blake probably got directly from Jakob Boehme, also derives ultimately from St Paul. The Second Epistle to the Corinthians speaks of 'Christ, who is the image of God'. And as *The Four Zoas* proceeds it steadily develops the theme that Christ is the whole human family seen as One Man:

> those in Great Eternity met in the Council of God
> As one Man, for contracting their Exalted Senses
> They behold Multitude, or Expanding they behold as one,
> As One Man all the Universal family; & that One Man
> They call Jesus the Christ, & they in him & he in them
> Live in Perfect harmony, in Eden the land of life.... [*F.Z.* 298]

Thus it becomes clear that Blake believes in the Divinity of Christ in the most transcendental, the most Pauline sense. Jesus is the Divine Lamb ordained from the beginning of the world to redeem the world. He is divine because He is the epitome of all things in heaven and earth, and understands all things to be one. He is, in short, incarnate understanding. He is God; for, says Blake, 'if God is anything he is Understanding'. Jesus perfectly understood His mission and His own nature; there was no division in Him and He wore no masks. When He invites us to follow Him it is an invitation to 'cultivate our understandings'. And this is the reason He spoke in parables. He knew that wisdom and truth cannot be poured into men as we pour water into a jar. There must be a mental effort. He wanted men to think. 'Will, Desire, Love, Pain, Envy...are Natural, but Understanding is Acquir'd.'

It is by understanding that we 'imitate' Christ. Understanding ourselves, seeking the divinity within us through contemplation; understanding other men, which is true worship;[1] understanding the message of art, by which we penetrate into the eternal world; understanding the signature of things in Nature, by which we renew that intercourse with the Pleroma that we held in Eternity. Thus throughout the poem *The Four Zoas* we see Christ as light shining in darkness; He rends the veil of mystery; He separates the spiritual from the corporeal, and sets a limit to opacity and contraction; He illuminates art:

> the Divine Countenance shone
> In Golgonooza. Looking down, the daughters of Beulah saw
> With joy the bright Light, & in it a Human form,
> And knew he was the Saviour, Even Jesus: & they worshipped.
> [*F.Z.* 400]

[1] This idea is developed in the following chapter.

And the Jesus who is the Lord of Light in *The Four Zoas* is to be presented as the God of Fire[1] in *Jerusalem*: the more intellectual vision has passed into the ecstatic union.

In the letters which Blake wrote at the time he was working on *The Four Zoas* we have abundant evidence of his devotion to Christ and to the cause of Christ. The beautiful vision described in a letter (1800) to Thomas Butts is an apprehension of Christ as the unity of all things.[2] In 1802, again, he tells Butts:

> The Thing I have most at Heart—more than life, or all that seems to make life comfortable without—Is the Interest of True Religion & Science, & whenever any thing appears to affect that Interest (Especially if I myself omit any duty to my Station as a Soldier of Christ), It gives me the greatest of torments. [*L.* 1061]

Another letter to Butts, in the same year, describes a period of intense unhappiness, which has at last been overcome:

> I am again Emerged into the light of day; I still & shall to Eternity Embrace Christianity and Adore him who is the Express image of God; but I have travel'd thro' Perils & Darkness not unlike a Champion. I have Conquer'd, and shall Go on Conquering. Nothing can withstand the fury of my Course among the Stars of God & in the Abysses of the Accuser. [*L.* 1065]

We know from a letter of 1803 that he was reading the Testament in Greek and comparing it with the Authorised Version. In the same year he tells Butts that he does not intend to bury his talents in the earth, 'but do my endeavour to live to the Glory of the Lord & Saviour'.

This resolution bore fruit in the intensely Christian poem, *Milton*, written between 1804 and 1808. The *Preface* urges the 'Young Men of the New Age' to abandon Greek and Roman models and follow Blake in being 'just & true to our own Imaginations, those Worlds of Eternity in which we shall live for ever in

---

[1] Cf. W. Law, *An Appeal to all who Doubt*: For the strength and vivacity of fire must be both the majesty of light and the ardour of love. It is the glorious out-birth, the true representative of God the Father eternally generating His only Son, Light and Word.

[2] See below, pp. 407–8.

JESUS OUR LORD'—words which are followed immediately by the famous lines beginning

> And did those feet in ancient time
> Walk upon England's mountains green? [*M.* 464]

—a magnificent expression of Blake's devotion to the cause of Christ. In the First Book of the poem he gives himself up wholly:

> thou, O Lord,
> Do with me as thou wilt! for I am nothing, and vanity.
> If thou chuse to elect a worm, it shall remove the mountains.
> [*M.* 498]

Milton is the one of the three great symbolic poems which is more especially the Gospel of Renunciation. Milton renounces his selfish happiness in Paradise and descends again into the world of generation to annihilate his selfhood and redeem the sexual aspect of himself which he had despised. This is an image, a particular form, we might say, of the Saviour's descent into the world and His taking on the body of sin in the Virgin's womb; and *Milton* stresses

> "Faith in God the dear Saviour who took on the likeness of men,
> Becoming obedient to death, even the death of the Cross." [*M.* 505]

Besides these Pauline echoes, we find more reference to the Confessors and Martyrs, and praise of the self-sacrifice of such men as Wesley and Whitefield, than we have in the other symbolic books. Blake shows plainly here that, whatever his hatred of conventional religion, he has the greatest respect for true devotion and evangelical zeal, whether in the Church or out of it.

Jerusalem (1804–20) might be called the epic of Jesus, as *The Four Zoas* is the epic of Los and *Milton* the epic of Blake in his identification with Milton. But the distinction is hardly more than superficial, for now Blake views the Saviour under an aspect which brings Him close to identity with Los—and the identification is actually made at the close of the book. In *Jerusalem* Jesus becomes the sun-god, the God of Fire, and Blake makes this clear in his Preface addressed *To the Public*: 'I...hope the Reader will be with me, wholly One in Jesus our Lord, who is the God of Fire and Lord of Love to whom the Ancients look'd and saw his day afar off, with trembling &

amazement.' The antithesis: Sheep . . . Goats, written at the head of the Preface suggests the refining fire of judgement which blazes out in the conclusion of the poem, while the motto Μόνος ὁ Ἰησοῦς states the criterion of that judgement.

Blake's view of inspiration was declared, we remember, in *The Marriage of Heaven and Hell*, and we must keep in mind the terms of the discussion between Isaiah and the poet when we read at the beginning of *Jerusalem* that Jesus 'dictates' the words of 'this mild song'. The message is addressed to the fallen Albion. Why should he be so stubborn? The Saviour pleads with him to seek union, to 'expand':

> "I am not a God afar off, I am a brother and friend;
> Within your bosoms I reside, and you reside in me:
> Lo! we are One, forgiving all Evil, Not seeking recompense."
>
> [*J.* 552]

Christ is shown as 'the bright Preacher of Life', the giver of all mental gifts. He is crucified by those whose will it is that Man shall not have more abundant life; but He rises again to manifest His power over death:

> "I am the Resurrection & the Life.
> I Die & pass the limits of possibility as it appears
> To individual perception." [*J.* 669]

We can only understand Christ, that is to say, when we contemplate Him from our imagination, from our state of unity with all humanity. Viewed from the standpoint of the narrow selfish individuality, Christ's meaning 'passes the limit of possibility' and must be disbelieved.

By His death and resurrection He destroys this separative standpoint, which is identical with the rationalism of Urizen, and appears before Albion in His aspect of the sun-god:

> Then Jesus appeared standing by Albion as the Good Shepherd
> By the lost Sheep that he hath found, & Albion knew that it
> Was the Lord, the Universal Humanity; & Albion saw his Form
> A Man, & they conversed as Man with Man in Ages of Eternity.
> And the Divine Appearance was the likeness & similitude of Los.
>
> [*J.* 745]

Jesus teaches Albion the law of renunciation; Albion throws himself into the Furnaces of Affliction, which immediately become

> Fountains of Living Waters flowing from the Humanity Divine. [*J.* 746]

Suffering and evil are seen to be a dream, and all things are finally gathered together into one in Christ.

Side by side with this current of mystical interpretation, and from time to time mingling with it, there is another stream of more personal realisation of Jesus as man and teacher. We find it expressed in its most direct and superficially absurd aspect in the MS. note: 'I always thought that Jesus Christ was a Snubby or I should not have worship'd him, if I had thought he had been one of those long spindle nosed rascals', and in its fullest form in *The Everlasting Gospel. The Marriage of Heaven and Hell* shows Him as a revolutionary, come to bring not peace but a sword—by forcing men to think and so make distinctions, not between right and wrong, but between truth and error. He is not a moralist, but a man living from His impulses. He mocked the Sabbath and the Sabbath's God, opposed the Fifth Commandment, and 'stole the labours of others to support him'. His clearness of vision is emphasised by Blake's comment, *This was Christ*, on Lavater's aphorism: 'The greatest of characters, no doubt, was he who, free of all trifling accidental helps, could see objects through one grand immutable medium, always at hand, and proof against illusion and time, reflected by every object, and invariably traced through all the fluctuation of things.' Blake notes again, *This is our Lord*, on another aphorism which describes the man who 'harmoniously unites each variety of knowledge and of powers'. Thus early—i.e. by 1788—had Blake come to ponder deeply the character of Jesus and discern in it the qualities of freedom from accidents, visionary power and harmonious development of varied gifts.

In his annotations to Berkeley's *Siris*, written some thirty-two years later, Blake shows why Christ was the supreme teacher. He appealed to the whole of a man's personality. 'Christ addresses himself to the Man, not to his Reason.' He did not assume that children and simple folk were incapable of receiving His message;

on the contrary, He addressed Himself specially to them, as being least biassed by the distorting reason. 'Jesus supposes every Thing to be Evident to the Child & to the Poor & Unlearned. Such is the Gospel.' In this He showed His understanding of the human heart and His superiority to the pagan philosophers:

> What Jesus came to Remove was the Heathen or Platonic Philosophy, which blinds the Eye of Imagination, The Real Man. [*B.S.* 1023]

This, then, is the figure that moves through Blake's writings, vivid though drawn with so few strokes, full of revolutionary energy and as far removed as may be from the 'Gentle Jesus, meek and mild' of conventional religion.

> I am sure this Jesus will not do
> Either for Englishman or Jew, [*E.G.* 141]

he confesses somewhat ruefully. He was right; the Blakean Jesus has not been installed side by side with the Pauline Jesus, the Augustinian Jesus, the Thomist Jesus, the Anglican Jesus, the da Vinci Jesus, the Burne-Jones Jesus and all the little Jesuses of the stained-glass window designers, in the ecclesiastical pantheon.

The Everlasting Gospel was written about 1818—in a blaze of indignation at the parodies of Christ which were being held up for worship by the Christian Churches. We cannot know what the particular monstrosity was that Blake had in mind when he wrote:

> Seeing this False Christ, In fury & Passion
> I made my Voice heard all over the Nation, [*E.G.* 141]

for the context is lost, and this couplet remains fragmentary like so much else in *The Everlasting Gospel*, which is not a complete poem but a collection of passages thrown together with no certain order. But the fragment marked (*a*) in the Keynes edition gives us some idea of what this false Christ must have been like: a hook-nosed demagogue, preaching philanthropy and Natural Religion instead of the gospel of discriminating understanding and imagination:

> The Vision of Christ that thou dost see
> Is my Vision's Greatest Enemy:
> Thine has a great hook nose like thine,
> Mine has a snub nose like to mine:

Thine is the friend of All Mankind,
Mine speaks in parables to the Blind:
Thine loves the same world that mine hates,
Thy Heaven doors are my Hell Gates. [*E.G.* 133]

The conviction that Jesus was not an indiscriminate philanthropist had already been expressed in a MS. sentence written between 1808 and 1811: 'Jesus does not bear...he makes a Wide distinction between the Sheep & the Goats; consequently he is Not Charitable.' The distinction is, in fact, between sin and error. Sin disappears in face of forgiveness; but the stubbornness of error can only be removed by 'the burning fire of thought'.

Thus we find Jesus full of tenderness towards sinners, and full of anger towards those who persist in error through pride, cruelty and hypocrisy. When He said to the man sick of the palsy, "Son, thy sins be forgiven thee", the scribes charged Him with blasphemy.

Loud Pilate Howl'd, loud Cai[a]phas yell'd,
When they the Gospel Light beheld.
It was when Jesus said to Me,
"Thy Sins are all forgiven thee." [*E.G.* 132]

But Christ cursed the Scribes and Pharisees; He scourged the money-changers from the Temple, and

Used the Elders & Priests like Dogs.

From these and other signs Blake concludes that Jesus was not 'gentle'. He was rude to His parents when they found Him in the Temple. His voice is loud as thunder when He defies Satan, refusing to worship him:

Thunders & lightnings broke around,
And Jesus' voice in thunders' sound:
"Thus I seize the Spiritual Prey.
Ye smiters with disease, make way.
I come your King & God to sieze.
Is God a smiter with disease?" [*E.G.* 134]

Thus He denies the dogma that disease is God's method of punishing sin.

Nor is Jesus humble, any more than gentle. He is too proud to take a bribe, and Blake does not believe that He really told His disciples to love their enemies.

> he acts with triumphant, honest pride,
> And this is the Reason Jesus died.
> If he had been Antichrist, Creeping Jesus,
> He'd have done anything to please us. [*E.G.* 135]

In the miracles Blake sees Jesus' wrath burning through the land—His wrath against the false doctrine of disease. When He is finally lifted up on the Cross He refuses to pray for the world; He had done so in the Garden, but now He recognises this for a mistake.

Jesus gives no lessons of chastity. On the contrary, He protects the woman taken in adultery from the punishment of stoning to which she is liable under the law; and by so doing He proclaims its abrogation:

> Jesus was sitting in Moses' Chair,
> They brought the trembling Woman There.
> Moses commands she be stoned to death,
> What was the sound of Jesus' breath?
> He laid His hand on Moses' Law:
> The Ancient Heavens, in Silent Awe
> Writ with Curses from Pole to Pole,
> All away began to roll:
> The Earth trembling & Naked lay
> In secret bed of Mortal Clay,
> On Sinai felt the hand divine
> Putting back the bloody shrine,
> And she heard the breath of God
> As she heard by Eden's flood:
> "Good & Evil are no more!
> Sinai's trumpets, cease to roar!" [*E.G.* 139]

Jesus tells the woman that she need fear nothing, for no one has dared to condemn her. But she must confess her sin, and so obtain forgiveness. And what is this sin, in Jesus' eyes? Not, we note, that she has given her body to many: but that she has done so without love.

> "What was thy love? Let me see it;
> Was it love or dark deceit?"

And the woman answers:

"Love too long from Me has fled;
'Twas dark deceit, to Earn my bread;
'Twas Covet, or 'twas Custom, or
Some trifle not worth caring for;
That they may call a shame & Sin
Love's temple that God dwelleth in,
And hide in secret hidden shrine
The Naked Human form divine,
And render that a Lawless thing
On which the Soul Expands its wing."

This then was her sin: to give her body through covetousness, or through habit, or with levity: and this sin has been forced upon her by 'them', the moralists with their 'dark pretence to Chastity', whence 'Secret Adulteries' inevitably arise. And now we realise that it was not in fact her *sin* that Jesus was asking her to confess, for sin needs no confession. He was leading her to realise her *error*: and in the light which He radiates, she did realise it. Her error was that through the perverted counsels she had received from the teachers of her youth, she had considered love evil and made a 'dark pretence to Chastity'. Could this too be forgiven her, she pleads?

"My sin thou has forgiven me,
Canst thou forgive my Blasphemy?
Canst thou return to this dark Hell,
And in my burning bosom dwell?" [*E.G.* 140–1]

Jesus does forgive her, for by recognising her error she has already driven it out; but in doing so He arouses the wrath of the Scribes and Pharisees.

The final section of *The Everlasting Gospel* shows us Jesus as the complete revolutionary. He mocked the Sabbath, He turned fishermen into divines and so upset the social order, He destroyed the idea of sin. He attacked war and justice. He scorned His parents, and sent His seventy disciples into the world 'against Religion & Government'. He was a vagrant and a friend of prostitutes and publicans. He died on the gibbet as a common criminal.

Such is the portrait of Christ the Man which emerges from the pages of Blake. The degree of credence which the reader is prepared to give to this portrait must depend largely on taste. If the traditional hazy picture has not too strong a hold on the sentiments, there is much in this vivid and colourful presentation to attract. There is, of course, a good deal which Blake has left out, and a good deal he has put in. But it is significant, I think, that the Blakean Jesus agrees in essentials with the Jesus of St Mark more than with the Jesus of the other Gospels. Blake was not aware that Mark is the earliest of the Gospels, a fact established by modern scholarship. But what is more important than the verisimilitude of Blake's portrait of Christ is his digest of His teaching—and particularly the claim that his own work is devoted to preaching the Everlasting Gospel which Christ brought into the world. How far, in fact, does Blake's teaching correspond with Christ's message as set forth in the New Testament? This is the question which I try to answer in the following pages.

CHAPTER XXI

The Everlasting Gospel

There is not one Moral Virtue that Jesus Inculcated but Plato & Cicero did Inculcate before him; what then did Christ Inculcate? Forgiveness of Sins. This alone is the Gospel, & this is the Life & Immortality brought to light by Jesus, Even the Covenant of Jehovah, which is This: If you forgive one another your Trespasses, so shall Jehovah forgive you, That he himself may dwell among you; but if you Avenge, you Murder the Divine Image, & he cannot dwell among you; because you Murder him he arises again, & you deny that he is Arisen, & are blind to Spirit. [*E.G.* 131]

THE New Age which Blake expected to dawn with the triumph of the French Revolution was frustrated. The forces of conservatism within the hearts of men were still too strong. The hierarchical system of society stood firm in the rest of Europe, and was speedily set up again in France. The prestige of the moral law and of the State organisation was not really shaken: for it was based on two powerful factors—the inertia of the individual, and the persistent belief in a divine sanction for the structure of society.

To-day the situation is quite different. The sanctions on which society was based in Blake's time have quite vanished. The hierarchical structure of society is a mere shell, ready to topple over at any moment. Only the *vis inertiae* of human nature keeps the thing in position, and it is only upon this *vis inertiae* that the rulers of men can now count. For men no longer believe, as they did in Blake's day, that the universe is itself a monarchical system, which the State quite naturally reflects. They no longer believe that there is a personal God spying out all their ways and commanding obedience to governors, pastors and masters. They no longer believe that there is an eternal code of morals whose validity is guaranteed by a Supreme Being, and whose infraction is punished by misery in this world or the next.

One by one the old gods have crumbled, or been dynamited. The Old Testament God went first, with the Darwinian revolution; then the loving Father of the New Testament, also discredited by Darwin and finally pushed over by the shock of war. In his place a religion of humanity was set up, but the course of events in Russia has now quietly deflated *that*, except for a few fundamentalists. And finally the ancient idolatry of Caesarism, polished up to look brand-new in Italy and Germany, has gone up in smoke too.

What is left? Men are faced with chaos, unless they begin to look where the sages have always told them to look: *into their own minds*.

There are only two alternatives now: either the steep road down into chaos and annihilation, or the leap of faith towards the unity of mankind. And this unity must be based on the human imagination, because there is nothing else left to base it on.

It was Blake's faith that the thing men have in common was more important than their differences. This thing is *consciousness*. Blake's prescription for unity was the development of consciousness: consciousness of that larger Self which lies behind the fretful individual self, and in which all men share.

And when we have found that, Blake said, we shall have found God.

The Kingdom of Heaven is within you. So Jesus taught, and because He taught this truth He was for Blake the supreme guide of humanity—the Light of the World. Blake knew little of Hindu philosophy, nothing of Buddha, nothing of Lao-Tzu. He knew that 'the philosophy of the east taught the first principles of human perception'. Had he known more of the great religious systems other than Christianity, it is likely that he would have found them in some ways more congenial than were certain aspects of that faith. Taoism is more clearly anarchistic, Buddhism lays more stress on self-annihilation; both these systems omit the nauseous doctrine of hell. But he would still have acclaimed Jesus as the great Master, and His gospel as the everlasting gospel. For Jesus taught the forgiveness of sins. 'The Glory of Christianity is to Conquer by Forgiveness.'

The Kingdom of Heaven is no other than the inner world of understanding, the imagination, which Blake also calls vision and Eternity. 'The Kingdom of Heaven is within you', Christ tells His disciples. It is attained by trust in Him: 'I am the Way, the Truth and the Life'; by abiding in Him: 'I am the Vine, ye are the branches: he that abideth in me, and I in him, the same bringeth forth much fruit: for without me ye can do nothing.' Christ, as we have seen, is the consciousness of the unity of Man. This living in Christ is the constant realisation of the divine humanity in oneself, in one's fellow-men and in the world of Nature. This is the only way to the true life, the life which Man forfeits when he falls into the Ulro of materialism, doubt and fear; and therefore Christ can rightly say, 'I am the Way, the Truth and the Life: no man cometh unto the Father, but by me'. For Christ is the perfect realisation of all the partial understanding which till His coming had lain scattered in the ages of the world.

The first step upon the way of understanding is also the last. There is no progressive revelation for the individual. There is an initial recognition of the need for salvation—'repentance', a change of mind. The soul recognises its own *détraquement*, its need for cleansing from a lifetime's accumulation of error. It is as though a man had fallen drunk into a ditch and wakes up the next morning to find himself covered with slime. His urgent need is for a bath. It is a luxury to get the wet, smelly, clinging clothes off. He steps into the bath and is clean. So the soul turns to the cleansing truth of Christ and immediately it is renewed.[1] 'He that hath seen me hath seen the Father.' In this recognition of the Christ within, the personality for the first time understands its own being, its own nature: and is free. There are no more masks. The struggle henceforth is not to win virtues, or avoid vices (which will drop away of themselves if they are really incompatible with the revealed personality) but to 'keep the divine vision in time of trouble'. Now, and only now, comes the effort of the will: not to destroy, but to create.

Blake's teaching about the will is very significant. 'There can be no Good Will', he tells us uncompromisingly. 'Will is always Evil.' By will he means here the faculty with which we try to change ourselves according to a pattern prescribed by the reason, by moral codes, and by religious organisations. This attempt must always end in disaster (even if the victim does not recognise it as disaster) for the reason has no faculties for understanding the whole of personality. It is concerned with a very limited portion of the human totality. Only the understanding, drawing its life from the senses, the instincts, the obscure physical processes, as well as from the reason and the

[1] Instantaneous conversion was of course an important feature of the theory and practice of Wesley's and Whitefield's revivalist movements. With them it was associated with an overwhelming conviction of *sin*, whereas with Blake it was *error* that was understood as error and cast off.

intuition, is fitted to deal with that whole. The imposition of the will ends in disaster in one of two ways.

The less serious catastrophe is that the totality rejects the pattern proposed to it by the reason, and there is what the religious used to call a backsliding, which may be repeated over and over again if the will is persistent and the personality strong. This happens in the case of men of decided intellect and powerful passions; and the result is a worse chaos than before. Much more serious, however, is the case of the man of weak passions and intellect (the two always go together) who does allow his personality to be crushed into an alien mould, and goes through life thenceforth as a mutilated being. There is always a feeling of frustration: and the cripple will in compensation spend the rest of his life seeing that other and more vigorous spirits conform to the same rules as himself. These are the men who are eternally opposed to the man of genius, denying his inspiration and ascribing his energies to the powers of evil. They are the forces of reaction and the impediment to every step forward in Man's evolution.

That will is evil must remain true so long as will is a function of the reason. But when directed by the understanding—which never criticises or judges, remember—it takes on another meaning. To attain the Divine Vision is one thing, and it is a transforming thing. To keep it is another. The soul liberated by a flash of pure intuition is still imprisoned in flesh, is subject to the laws of the flesh, and has to fight against a host of enemies. Therefore Jesus told His disciples to watch and pray, that they enter not into temptation. It is *after* a man has entered into the Kingdom of Heaven that the exercise of the will becomes appropriate: and this Blake recognises when he says, 'The Will must not be bended except in the Day of Divine Power'. The day of divine power is the moment of recognition. The truth is only understood in this moment. Now comes the effort of concentration: to keep the eye fixed on the truth—concentration on attaining the fullest possible understanding of one's being and of clearing that being from the accumulation of false selves.

Thus we see that 'goodness' does not come first: it is a result, not a condition, of entering the Kingdom of Heaven. We must see what the truth is before we begin to strive towards truth: and truth can only be seen in the spirit. We must know our goal before we can set out—or we shall go in the wrong direction. We must keep our gaze fixed on the divine light.

Only in this sense is an 'imitation of Christ' possible. Christ is the Universal Humanity in every man; as we behold Him we 'come in the unity of the faith, and of the knowledge of the Son of God, unto a perfect man, unto the measure of the stature of the fullness of Christ'. In Blake's terms, 'we become what we behold'. This concentration is the necessary discipline which the regenerate man must go through. It is not a moral discipline, but a training of the intelligence and the imagination. It is not painful: on the contrary, it is pure delight. For by it a man renews his fellowship with those eternal forms from which he was separated at the Fall, he knows once more the taste of Eternity.

Even after entrance into God's kingdom there can be no *moral* effort. There is no room for such an irrelevance. If we try to get rid of what seem to us to be sins we shall simply be falling back into our old selfhood, our old reliance on moral codes, our old habit of judging between right and wrong. No: our energy must be guided solely in a positive direction: towards fuller and closer union with Christ. What are really vices are negatives which will vanish of themselves, as the shadows flee away at sunrise. It is Urizen who seeks to deflect our purpose from its positive goal:

> Serpent Reasonings us entice
> Of Good & Evil, Virtue & Vice. [*G.P.* 761]

As soon as we begin to think about good and evil, we forget Eternity. Our warfare must be intellectual, not moral. Urizen tries to persuade us that sin is displeasing to God, that we cannot be saved until we have got rid of our sins. This is a counsel of despair. 'He who waits to be righteous before he enters into the Saviour's kingdom, the Divine Body', Blake warns, 'will never enter there.' Christ's counsel is more to the point than Urizen's: let the tares grow up with the wheat until the day of harvest, for in trying to pull up the tares we shall certainly uproot the good corn too.

Christ was born into a society where two great heresies about human nature met. There was first the heresy of ceremonial and sacrificial religion, based on the doctrine that Man was to be saved by following a minutely articulated moral code, that he was a criminal living under the eternal wrath of God. The other was the classical heresy of the mean: Man is a creature of this earth, who lives best by balancing the claims of his body and his spirit so that neither gets the upper hand.[1] If the first doctrine produced gloom and cruelty, the second could produce nothing but mediocrity. Spirit and flesh do not exist on the same plane; there is a tension and a warfare between them. They cannot be reconciled as equal partners. Only when the body is regarded as the instrument of spirit can a right relation be reached. And that relation itself is still a state of tension. For it is through tensions, as Blake so often points out, that the personality passes on to new realisations.

The tension of the Cross is at the centre of Christ's teaching. 'Whosoever will come after me, let him deny himself, and take up his cross, and follow me. For whosoever will save his life shall lose it; but whosoever shall lose his life for my sake and the gospel's, the same shall save it.' Hence the whole necessity for an Incarnation—that spirit and flesh may know their true relationship. And as long as the spirit is tied to the flesh there must be anguish, even for those who have passed into the Kingdom:

> Many Persons, such as Paine & Voltaire, with some of the Ancient Greeks, say: "we will not converse concerning Good & Evil; we will live in Paradise & Liberty." You may do so in Spirit, but not in the Mortal Body as you pretend, till after the Last Judgment; for in Paradise they have no Corporeal & Mortal Body—that originated with the Fall & was call'd Death & cannot be removed but by a Last Judgment. While we are in the world of Mortality we Must Suffer. The Whole Creation Groans to be deliver'd; there will always be as many Hypocrites born as Honest Men, & they will always have superior Power in Mortal Things. You cannot have Liberty in this World without what you call Moral Virtue, and you cannot have Moral Virtue without the Slavery of that half of the Human Race who hate what you call Moral Virtue. [*V.L.J.* 842–3]

There is an irreconcilable dualism in the nature of Man which must cause strife while Man is in the flesh. Orthodox religion urges

---

[1] In Aristotle the mean is found midway between the excess and defect of certain *qualities*: e.g. the golden mean between rashness and cowardice is courage. But the antithesis of soul and body, and the necessity of reconciling the two, will be found at the basis of this system.

Man to resolve this strife by destroying some part of his nature; and unfortunately this part, the evil, is the source of all energy. Blake, on the other hand, advocates neither destruction nor an impossible harmony, but an acceptance of the fact of tension and a transmutation of evil continually into good through the power of understanding:

> Man is a twofold being, one part capable of evil & the other capable of good; that which is capable of good is not also capable of evil, but that which is capable of evil is also capable of good. [*L.A.* 921]

Why this should be so Blake explains in *The Marriage of Heaven and Hell*,[1] which gives the first clear expression to the doctrine of the contraries. If we try to destroy evil, which is energy, we destroy life itself. Blake thoroughly accepted the fact of original sin—indeed his whole theology is based on the Fall—and he goes so far as to say that 'Man is born a Spectre or Satan, & is altogether an Evil'; but this is followed by the solution, that Man 'requires a new Selfhood continually, & must continually be changed into his direct Contrary'. This changing into the contrary comes with understanding and a complete willingness at any moment to give up everything that one is, every attitude, every belief, in obedience to the Divine Vision.

This is the repentance and the rebirth that Jesus taught. He called upon His disciples to leave all and follow Him: to abandon their old selves, their cherished traditions and beliefs. 'Except a man be born again, he cannot see the kingdom of God.' Unless there is a real change of heart, going far deeper than the moral sense, a man cannot even begin to understand the existence of an eternal world. And this rebirth means a sacrifice of the selfhood. This is never a sacrifice of the Self, but a discovery of the Self. We put off our beloved masks only to find, at last, our real face. Hence the feeling of ecstasy that accompanies self-annihilation. At the end of *Jerusalem* Albion throws himself voluntarily into the furnaces—and finds, not torment, but delight.

This willingness to be reborn, not once but many times, is the condition for remaining *alive*. Man's nature is not one which should remain imprisoned in any of the truths which take possession of him, for he is able to go forward to ever newer truths, stepping out

[1] See above, Ch. XIV.

of the old ones as a butterfly emerges from its chrysalis. There can be no static condition in the mind of a being who is compounded of contraries. Even in Eternity the investigation of reality remains the great pursuit of Man.

What this means in practice is that the man who wishes to remain truly alive will not rest content with any formulation of truth. There must come a time when new vistas open and call to be explored. Then comes the testing-time: it is so fatally easy to cling to the old, beloved formulation, the truth which has now become an error, and reject the new and relevant truth. That is what the Jews did in rejecting Christ; and that is the condemnation of all Churches and codes of spiritual and moral wisdom. Truth is paradoxical; it cannot be codified; it contains within itself the germ of its own disintegration. 'Except the seed die [as a seed]', said Christ, 'it abideth alone: but if it die, it bringeth forth much fruit.' All the words of men are seeds; their fruit is in living. And this explains why the great masters of human thought, Christ, Buddha, Lao-Tzu, left only parables and aphorisms, gnomic sayings capable of germinating afresh for new generations of men, patient of ever-renewed interpretations. They produced no codes. Their aim was to suggest, to rouse the imagination, to make men think for themselves. Their words 'come home to men's businesses and bosoms' in application to the minute particulars; and it is this fact that gives them their unique and perennial value.

For it is to the individual that Jesus addresses Himself. More than any teacher who had gone before, He stresses the importance of the individual, the unique value of one human soul in the sight of God. The parable of the lost sheep, of the pearl of great price, of the lost coin, and many a direct piece of teaching brought this truth home to His hearers. There is only the individual man: there is no general man to be treated in the abstract. Between the individual man and the Universal Man, Christ, nothing intervenes. Thus the teaching of Jesus sets itself against the politics of the Greeks, and the art theory of the eighteenth century, the philosophy of Locke and the social science of Hobbes. It is 'these little ones' who are the representatives of Christ on earth, not a Church of pomp and ceremonies. 'The whole of the New Church is in the Active Life & not in Ceremonies at all.'

The nature of the individual lies, as we have seen, in the tension of the contraries. The task is, not to suppress this tension, but to make it fruitful. This can only be done by recognising that each component of the personality has its right to exist. Blake went far beyond the current psychology of his time in recognising the instincts and asserting their holiness. More than that, he realised that it is on their free play that the health of the personality depends. A man is only free when he can view every aspect of his being as an historic product which is not fixed but has every right to existence: the result of an energy which may at any moment transmute the 'evil' manifestation into 'good'. There is no question of accepting any manifestation as permanent:

> I do not consider either the Just or the Wicked to be in a Supreme State, but to be every one of them States of the Sleep which the Soul may fall into in its deadly dreams of Good & Evil when it leaves Paradise following the Serpent. [*V.L.J.* 841]

But there can be no tampering with the facts of the personality that we find within us. This is the sin of sins, for it is an interference by the meddling intellect with depths and subtleties it is utterly unequipped to deal with. The intellect, or rather the reason, is essentially analytic and destructive, not creative; and in dealing with evil we are concerned all the time with creative forces which will not submit to rules:

> No discipline will turn one Man into another, even in the least particle, & such discipline I call Presumption & Folly. I...am very sorry for all such who may be led to such ostentatious Exertion against their Eternal Existence itself, because it is Mental Rebellion against the Holy Spirit, & fit only for a Soldier of Satan to perform. [*L.* 1130–1]

Within the human fourfold—the conception which is the basis of Blake's psychology—the body has its honoured place: and the manifestation of the body is the instincts. Their place is in the depths, in what is nowadays called the subconscious, and Blake gives repeated warnings that they are not to be dragged out into the light of day. In the depths they are the foundation of the whole structure. Even in their most evil guise, they are the dung-hill from which the flower of consciousness springs, and without which it would die. Our grossest desires, and the fleeting lusts and cruelties which we dare not admit even to ourselves as from time to time they rise to the surface of the mind's ocean, are as indispensable to the soul's health as the intestines are to the body's. Blake does not invite us to draw up these deep-sea monsters and gloat over them, but he does tell us not to try to destroy them. We are to leave them in peace. 'Every thing that lives is holy.'

The whole trouble with orthodox morality on this point is that 'holiness' is not regarded as a property which all life has by the mere fact of being, but as a thing to be striven after: the goal of an impossible purity. The moralists simply will not look at the facts of Man's being as they are: they set up an image and require all men to conform to it. Now this aiming at sinlessness is precisely the error of Satan the Accuser, for which he is cast out. Blake makes this quite plain in talking of the forgiveness of sins:

> Forgiveness of Sin is only at the Judgment Seat of Jesus the Saviour, where the Accuser is cast out, not because he Sins, but because he torments the Just & makes them do what he condemns as Sin & what he knows is opposite to their own Identity.
>
> It is not because Angels are Holier than Men or Devils that makes them Angels, but because they do not Expect Holiness from one another, but from God only....Angels are happier than Men & Devils because they are not always Prying after Good & Evil in one another & eating the Tree of Knowledge for Satan's Gratification. [*V.L.J.* 843–4]

In fact, 'holiness' in the sense of freedom from sin is not a goal to be striven after at all. In the first place no real moral progress is possible without rebirth, even if it were desirable; and the man who is born again does not bother his head about moral progress. He has put a new meaning into life, and he can now leave it to the meaning to transmute the facts. This meaning, for the Christian, is Christ: 'not I live, but Christ liveth in me'. All the things which to the unregenerate man were impossible, the perfection to which he could never attain along the old road of moral effort, are attainable in Christ. A new direction is given to living, energy pours into new channels, and what is excessive in the realm of desire finds its way into the deeper well of love and understanding. The jettisoning of morals does not lead to chaos. An outer artificial rule is replaced by an inner organic pattern.

We are now in a position to grasp the lines along which Blake estimates his virtues and vices. Once again it must be stressed that in Blake's view (as, incidentally, in Shakespeare's) sin is nothing other than the destruction of *order*, and that reason divorced from imagination is the agent of that destruction. The problem is always to reorganise the chaos which reason has produced by its insistence on uniformity. There can be no question of restoring the old order, for Eternity is not static; nor can there be any question of reason, the author of the Fall, being the agent of renewal. We are left, then, with the three other components of personality: the instincts, the affections, and the intuition; and of these the intuition, aided by the other two, is the only possible choice. The ideal is to organise the good and the evil qualities within us into a harmonious but not a static whole.

How are we to set about this? The moralists will draw up for us a list of virtues and vices, and tell us to create a consummate tranquillity by eliminating the vices and cultivating the virtues. But we now know that the virtues are passive qualities deprived of all capacity for act, while the so-called vices are store-houses of energy. We shall be well advised to abandon the moralists' standard list of vices and virtues, based on the ideal of static perfection, and adopt the division suggested by Blake, in which the qualities springing from energy are classed as virtues, and the qualities arising from weakness are classed as vices:

> As I understand Vice it is a Negative. It does not signify what the laws of Kings & Priests have call'd Vice; we who are philosophers ought not to call the Staminal Virtues of Humanity by the same name that we call the omissions of intellect springing from poverty. [*L.A.* 932]

A new classification must be made: on one side the staminal virtues, on the other the omissions of intellect. Or we may make a threefold division: Evil, Good, and Vice: evil being the crude manifestations of energy, good the finished product when these manifestations have been restrained and refined, vice the simple negation of energy. Among evils we may class lust, anger, pride, extravagance, and unrestrained desires of all kinds. Among goods, humility, mercy, charity, pity, and other accepted virtues. Among vices, murder, theft, slander, treachery, cruelty, timidity, and all manner of weakness.[1]

[1] See above, Ch. XIV, from which the present chapter carries on, with some unavoidable repetition, in relating morality with the teaching of Christ.

Since energy is the supreme fountain of evils and goods, idleness may be expected to be, in Blake's moral system, the great sin. And so it is. He calls it the sin of Sodom. In this, there is no principle of renewal, as there is in evil. In fact, what is called sin is only reprehensible when it means sloth. When, on the contrary, it means freedom and energy (and sexual enjoyment means both) it is the root of all new flowering in the individual. Blake saw through to the truth that the vices—sadism, repression of others, negative attitudes towards life—are the expression of a profound *emptiness*, a need to be reassured, an insatiate feeding on the life of another human being. These vices can all be included under the category of idleness, for they are impossible where real creative activity exists.

Blake's rule, then, is *pecca fortiter*, so long as it is really evil and not vice you are dealing with: and in the midst of the sin *understand it*, penetrate beyond the act to the significance of the act. Become conscious. Then, if the sin is really to be outgrown, the understanding will take over the job of transmutation. But the operative word is *fortiter*—with energy, no half measures. 'The road of excess leads to the palace of wisdom. If the fool would persist in his folly, he would become wise.' It is not by impoverishment, but by enrichment, that the inner harmony is to be achieved. This alone is *organisation*: the moral technique is stultification.

Organisation is one of the key words in Blake's thought. He applies it to every one of the many aspects of life he is concerned with: to literary technique, to art, to psychology, to the religious life. It means the living pattern as opposed to incoherence, to amorphousness on the one hand and to mechanical rigidity on the other. And at its root is *impulse*, the free workings of a liberated spirit. That which springs from impulse, he knows, must be good, *on that plane on which the spirit is liberated.* The man who is liberated on the highest plane, the imagination, can do nothing but good; the man who is liberated on a lower plane (let us say the untutored savage on the physical plane) can do nothing but good on the physical plane, though he may do evil on the spiritual. For impulse is freedom: the capacity to act rightly without reference to the bonds of right and wrong.

In place of the mechanical list of virtues and vices Blake thus puts a perfectly organic conception. We may envisage it as a plant, in which the instincts and passions are the soil, impulse is the root, energy is the life-sap, and free action is the flower. Organisation is the directing of every inner faculty so that it obeys the deepest impulse unhesitatingly. This is true freedom, and chaos is as far away from it as is mechanical regimentation. But the freedom must come from within, from understanding. It must come from excess, not from deprivation. And understanding must come in the very moment of action. It means an acceptance of the facts. 'You never know what is enough till you know what is more than enough.' The criterion is the test of fruitfulness.

'By their fruits ye shall know them.' This was the counsel Jesus gave His disciples when they were puzzled about the *bona fides* of other teachers. It is Blake's criterion too. His ethic is an ethic of energy and fruitfulness. He found in history that the most fruitful men had been those most given over to their *daimon*—not the 'good' men who followed the rules, but the 'bad' men who followed nothing but their own identity, the great artists and writers who were, in his view, the real Christians. He noted the paradox that these men, following their identity and obeying their impulses, gave the truly Christian example of single devotion to their art and complete indifference to their own worldly welfare, while the moral Christians were concerned with nothing other than the salvation of that very selfhood which Christ said they must lose. And he observed another and more sinister fact: that they were bitterly opposed to the men of genius.

In this they were guilty of the great sin, the sin against the Holy Ghost.

CHAPTER XXII

Worship

Go, tell them that the Worship of God is honouring his gifts
In other men & loving the greatest men best, each according
To his Genius which is the Holy Ghost in Man; there is no other
God than that God who is the intellectual fountain of Humanity.
He who envies or calumniates, which is murder & cruelty,
Murders the Holy-one. Go, tell them this, & overthrow their cup,
Their bread, their altar-table, their incense & their oath,
Their marriage & their baptism, their burial & consecration. [*J.* 736–7]

CHILDREN worship God best, for their angels behold His face continually. Their minds, as we know, are full of vivid images of a world which adults have lost: they are in direct intuitive contact with reality. Next to them come the artists, who *are* artists simply because by some miracle they have retained the image-making faculty. And last come the common run of mankind, who are not artists themselves, but can value great art, and give honour where it is due. This is their form of worship.

But this is not enough. Blake believed that all men are artists, though the majority do not know it. They have the image-making faculty, buried away beneath a debris of logic and morality. Only remove that debris and the faculty will reassert itself. But let us begin by 'loving the greatest men best'. Let us see what art really is, and then we shall love it so much that we shall all wish to practise it.

This is Blake's idea of worship, and he believed it was Christ's too. What led him to this belief?

At the coming of Christ it was the ceremonial religions of mystery that were in full swing, and against them He turned His condemnation. When He is accused of gluttony and winebibbing, He denies that the old rules and ordinances have any power over the New Man that He is and that He means His followers to be. The Everlasting Gospel cannot be expressed in the old forms, will not combine with Judaism. To attempt such a combination is to put new wine into old bottles—the bottles will be split with the energy of the fermenting wine and the wine will be spilt. 'New wine must be put into new wine-skins.'

The new religion is a religion of liberty. Observance of the Sabbath cannot continue as a fetish for His disciples. 'The Sabbath was made for man, and not man for the Sabbath, therefore the Son of Man is Lord also of the Sabbath.' Even the natural ties of kinship are broken for the New Man. 'Who is my mother, or my brethren?', He asks, when the crowd tell him they are looking for Him. 'Whosoever shall do the will of God, the same is my brother, and my sister, and mother.'

He teaches that true worship is spiritual. When the Samaritan woman reminds Him of the difference between her people and the Jews—'Our fathers worshipped in this mountain; and ye say, that in Jerusalem is the place where men ought to worship'—Jesus shows that Samaritans and Jews are both in error. 'Woman, believe me, the hour cometh, when ye shall neither in this mountain, nor yet at Jerusalem, worship the Father. But the hour cometh, and now is, when the true worshippers shall worship the Father in spirit and in truth: for the Father seeketh such to worship Him. God is [a] spirit: and they that worship him must worship him in spirit and in truth.'

This spiritual worship is in Blake's view nothing more nor less than *art*. What did Jesus mean when He said that the children's angels continually behold the face of God? Most of us take that to be a pretty saying. To Blake it meant something definite. Blake knew, as psychologists have now found out, that children have a faculty for seeing images which most adults have lost. And he identified this faculty with the phrase of Jesus. This seeing of images *is* the beholding of the face of God.

Now the artist not only sees, he expresses what he sees. The child does the same. He is a true artist. His normal form of expression is play, which I have already discussed in a previous chapter.[1] *Play is the art of the child.* It is the expression of his perception of the noumenal world, and his delight in and thankfulness for what he perceives. That is, play is worship.[2] When we watch a child at play,

---

[1] See above, Ch. XVI, pp. 306–12.

[2] That Blake realised this is perfectly clear from what Palmer tells us. Blake 'loved to be with little children and to talk about them. *That is heaven*, he said to a friend, leading him to the window, and pointing to a group of them at play. Declining, like

we are in the presence of a religious act: an act far more religious than any the adult can produce, with his rigid forms and ceremonies, or his vague aspirations. Play is a child's homage to reality, as well as his symbolic participation in it.

So, too, with the adult artist. If he is an artist of the type envisaged by Blake—that is, not a copier of Nature but a vehicle for the expression of visionary images—his work has a profound religious significance. It is an act of worship. It was Blake's belief that Christ Himself was an artist—and he seems to be referring to plastic art, and not to the literary perfection of the Parables. 'Jesus & his Apostles & Disciples were all Artists,' he declares. 'Their Works were destroy'd by the Seven Angels of the Seven Churches in Asia, Antichrist Science.' And he insists that a man who is not an artist is not a Christian. 'The unproductive man is not a Christian, much less the Destroyer.'

Art and Christianity are the same. For art means the forsaking of everything which comes in the way of the Divine Vision: it cannot live with money, secrecy, ambition, war, or any selfish emotion. Taking this standpoint, Blake makes worship a creative thing, not a mere performance of mechanical rites.

Before going on to consider Blake's views on art in detail, we must try to find out exactly what he meant by vision. For this is the foundation of his philosophy of life and art and worship. There is a wealth of references in poems, letters and miscellaneous prose to this mystical state in which he lived more continuously, perhaps, than any other man of whom we have record—the great founders of religions apart. Some of the clearest of these references come in his letter of 23 August 1799, to Dr Trusler, which I have already quoted.[1] The essence of vision, we learn there, is to see not with but through the eye: to accept the material medium as an instrument, but not as an interpreter. Hence the paradoxical character of much of Blake's writing about Nature: he can praise it and curse it in the

---

Socrates...the common objects of ambition, and pitying the scuffle to obtain them, he thought that no one could be truly great who had not humbled himself "even as a little child". This was a subject he loved to dwell upon, and to illustrate.' Quotation in Gilchrist's *Life*.

[1] See above, Ch. VI.

same breath. 'Imagination is my world; this world of dross is beneath my notice', he affirms; and then, 'Nature is Imagination itself'. Seen with the Newtonian eye, Nature is indeed dross to Blake; but seen with the eye of the imagination, which recognises every exterior form as a true part of itself rent away at the Fall, it is the Jerusalem of Great Eternity.

As soon as we cease to behold the Creation as material, it is burnt up, Blake tells us in the *Vision of the Last Judgment*. This is how he himself was able to live so continuously in Eternity even while he was still in the body:

> I assert for My Self that I do not behold the outward Creation & that to me it is hindrance & not Action; it is as the dirt upon my feet, No part of Me. "What," it will be Question'd, "When the Sun rises, do you not see a round disk of fire somewhat like a Guinea?" O no, no, I see an Innumerable company of the Heavenly host crying, 'Holy, Holy, Holy is the Lord God Almighty'. I question not my Corporeal or Vegetative Eye any more than I would Question a Window concerning a Sight. I look thro' it & not with it. [*V.L.J.* 844]

This last sentence is the basis of Blake's theory of vision—one more radical than Berkeley's. 'The eye altering alters all.' To regain the power of contracting and expanding the senses at will is the aim of his teaching. When this is achieved all outside objects will appear *humanised*, no longer alien to Man but a part of his very being.

The distinction between single and double vision, then, is in the first place the difference between seeing reality as material and seeing it as spiritual. But this depends on a further distinction: between seeing the outside world as a generalisation and seeing it as an organism made up of minute particulars. The regenerate man sees Nature in its minutiae—'every lineament distinct'—or sees it as a human unity, the Universal Man, Jesus Christ. These are the two permissible alternatives; and natural philosophy adopts neither. Newton's 'single vision' makes an abstract of Nature. Matter is robbed of its particulars of colour, sound and scent and reduced to algebraic formulae. The mind which has invented these formulae worships its creations as divine, and the abstraction turns back upon the mind itself: intellect is governed by mathematical rules in the forms of logic, morality, politics and even theories of art.

Blake's way of regeneration, through the understanding, is the unique escape from the cul-de-sac. Give impulse its head, exercise the intellect in the moment of action, bend the double vision inwards and see your action in its minute particulars and its relation to the Divine Humanity.

Blake always insists on the *clarity* which marks real vision. There is nothing vague or misty about it. Every form is well defined. Spiritual forms are not less but more distinct than material ones. Modern psychologists who have investigated the images called up by children have found this to be the case with them also. Blake points to the example of the prophets:

> The Prophets describe what they saw in Vision as real and existing men, whom they saw with their imaginative and immortal organs; the Apostles the same; the clearer the organ the more distinct the object. A Spirit and a Vision are not, as the modern philosophy supposes, a cloudy vapour, or a nothing: they are organized and minutely articulated beyond all that the mortal and perishing nature can produce. He who does not imagine in stronger and better lineaments, and in stronger and better light than his perishing and mortal eye can see, does not imagine at all. The painter of this work ['The Bard'] asserts that all his imaginations appear to him infinitely more perfect and more minutely organized than any thing seen by his mortal eye. Spirits are organized men. [*D.C.* 794–5]

This important paragraph makes a number of things clear in Blake's theory of vision. Note the emphasis on *organisation*, with the suggestion that the grossness of matter inflicts a certain amorphousness on natural forms from which spirits are fortunately free. Seen without the 'muddy vesture of decay', their lineaments are more clearly perceived, in all their connections and ramifications. Again, we note that the imagination possesses *organs* or senses distinct from those of the body, by which it perceives truth; the corporeal ones are merely windows. Just as one can do without windows by walking out through the door, so the mystic 'steps into Eternity' at will. But in the spiritual sphere all is reversed: freedom is not outwards, but inwards:

> What is Above is Within, for every-thing in Eternity is translucent:
> The Circumference is Within, Without is formed the Selfish Center,
> And the Circumference still expands going forward to Eternity,
> And the Center has Eternal States.... [*J.* 691]

Now this gift of seeing eternal forms in the clearest precision is one which is confined to children, artists and mystics: but Blake believed that it should not be so confined. He believed that all men should have this power. It is lost at the close of childhood through the anxiety of parents and teachers that the child should give up its images and begin to deal with the 'real world'. The great art of life for the man who has realised the illusory character of this world, is to recover his childhood vision. Blake had to teach Catherine how to see the same heavenly visitants that he saw. The faculty did not come to her naturally, or rather she had lost it long ago. One wishes that Blake had described more exactly his technique of re-education. Perhaps he felt that the necessary conditions—purity of heart, freedom from mercenary motives, rejection of the lusts for power and possessions, simple faith—were sufficiently well known, sufficiently stressed by all the great religious teachers, to need no elaboration. One fact emerges, from an anecdote of George Richmond's, recorded by Gilchrist—that the visions sometimes vanished in the dark night of the soul, and that the necessary tranquillity and faith for their reappearance had to be sought in prayer:

> Once, the young artist, finding his invention flag during a whole fortnight, went to Blake, as was his wont, for some advice or comfort. He found him sitting at tea with his wife. He related his distress; how he felt deserted by the power of invention. To his astonishment, Blake turned to his wife suddenly and said: 'It is just so with us, is it not, for weeks together, when the visions forsake us? What do we do then, Kate?' 'We kneel down and pray, Mr Blake.'

Yet one important and unique aspect of Blake's technique of re-education we do know, and that is his emphasis on art as an exercise in vision; and we may well imagine that he made much use of this, in addition to contemplation and silent prayer, in his training of Catherine. It is in his theory of art that he stands apart from the other great mystics, who have tended to neglect the aesthetic approach altogether. This is not true, of course, of Plato, and I believe it is not true of the Chinese mystics: but we can certainly say of the Western mystical tradition that it has been predominantly ascetic and contemptuous of visual aids to perfection. Blake saw in art the great symbolic interpretation of the eternal world; and, more than that, he saw the vision of the artist as identical with the vision of the seer, and the activity of the artist as identical with the worship of the saint.

This attitude has seemed exaggerated even to Blake's warmest admirers. Samuel Palmer, himself an artist of genius, comments in the very appreciative letter on Blake that he wrote to Gilchrist: 'He saw everything through art, and, in matters beyond its range, exalted it from a witness into a judge.' Allan Cunningham, also a sympathetic observer, remarks:

Blake's misfortune was that of possessing this precious gift [imagination] in excess. His fancy overmastered him—until he at length confounded 'the mind's eye' with the corporeal organ, and dreamed himself out of the sympathies of actual life. . . . *Painting like poetry, has followers the body of whose genius is light compared to the length of its wings*,[1] and who, rising above the ordinary sympathies of our nature, are, like Napoleon, betrayed by a star which no eye can see save their own. To this rare class belonged William Blake.

We know, however, that to confound the corporeal with the mind's eye is precisely what Blake did not do: he emphasised the distinction. And the star which he saw he really did see, and wanted to teach others to see—through art, through meditation, through renouncing the illusory pleasures of the world.

The vision which Blake substituted for the material universe was an inspiring one, for it removed the heartbreaking chasm between Man and his environment, it broke down the alienness of the universe —an alienness which has become more impressive and more painful as Man has grown more self-conscious. For the savage this cleavage, as Lévy-Bruhl tells us, does not exist. Nor does it exist for the mystic. He feels his one-ness with all things and is happy. Blake believed that this happiness was open to all. This was the at-one-ment that Christ brought: the sense of being at home in the universe.

O what wonders are the Children of Men! Would to God that they would consider it,—that they would consider their Spiritual Life, regardless of that faint Shadow called Natural Life. [*L.* 1120]

Even the natural life itself, Blake believed, depends on vision, on the spiritual life: not a hair grows except by miracle. For him, 'the

[1] My italics. The quotation comes from Gilchrist's *Life*. Curiously, Blake uses almost the same metaphor about himself in the letter to Thomas Butts of 11 September 1801.

painted veil which those who live call Life' was very thin; and he could not understand how it was that others could not see the reality as clearly as he could. Under his eye the solid rocks disintegrated into patterns of pulsating energy, the internal structure of the tree was laid bare, and 'the green grass sprang in joy'. This is the living unity, so different from the abstract uniformity of the Newtonian world-diagram. And it is bliss to see it, for it leaves no gaps in experience. We understand that reality is not dualistic, nor is it a great 'chain of being', as the Elizabethans and Augustans liked to think: it is the human soul itself, though sadly disintegrated and deformed in its fallen state.

The wise man can have such experience in an ever-increasing degree as he widens his imagination and 'cleanses' the senses by intensified enjoyment. As he passes from a life-ideal which is static to one which is dialectic, as he eschews both rigidity and balance in favour of impulse and excess, he lives more and more in the spontaneous world of the spirit. But we must never forget that the vision itself is *momentary*. It cannot be otherwise, since it is a participation in Eternity and Eternity is out of time; even the word momentary, chosen to give the idea of a *flash*, can be nothing but a metaphor. In the West, we are so accustomed to think of Eternity (following Locke) as an infinite stretch of time that we find it hard to grasp Blake's thought here.

Again and again Blake tries to make it clear that the consciousness of Eternity slips in, as it were, through the cracks in time—percolates through the shell of the mundane egg. This is how he expresses the eternal moment in the second book of *Milton*:

> There is a Moment in each Day that Satan cannot find,
> Nor can his Watch Fiends find it; but the Industrious find
> This Moment & it multiply, & when it once is found
> It renovates every Moment of the Day if rightly placed.[1] [*M.* 535]

[1] The idea is remarkably like Wordsworth's in Book XIV of *The Prelude*: 'There are in our existence spots of time That with distinct pre-eminence retain A renovating virtue whence our minds...Are nourished and invisibly repaired.' *Milton* was written in part during Blake's Felpham period (1800–3) and finished about 1808; *The Prelude* was written between 1799 and 1805, but not published until 1850, after Wordsworth's death. The 'spots of time' passage comes near the end of the poem. It is not impossible that Crabb Robinson read parts of Blake's poem to Wordsworth, and that Wordsworth was impressed by the coincidence of Blake's 'renovating moment' and his own doctrine of recollection.

To find it, then, we must be industrious, eagerly engaged in prayer and the practice of art; and then we must seek to 'multiply' it, to extend its value and its influence to the remaining moments of the day. This description suggests a real technique, but again we are baffled as to its precise nature.

A 'moment', we are told in *Milton*, equals 'a pulsation of the artery': it is the creative unit from which the great events of time are produced—a storehouse of energy. The poet, or imaginative artist, conceives his work in this moment:

> For in this Period the Poet's Work is Done, and all the Great
> Events of Time start forth & are conciev'd in such a Period,
> Within a Moment, a Pulsation of the Artery. [*M.* 521]

We note once again how Blake *energises* his conceptions. Vision, understanding, contemplation, are for him dynamic ideas. This is the characteristically Western note that Blake introduces into concepts which recall the East.

We cannot hope to extend the experience of ecstasy *in time*; and that is why 'binding to oneself a joy Does the winged life destroy'. The moment of understanding comes and is gone. It is the fruits of the moment which can be garnered through the day, if we have known how to 'place the moment' rightly in its relation to our every activity. For this is what Blake means: that the actions of the rest of the day must be considered *sub specie æternitatis*, our thoughts and actions must be brought to the judgement bar of the revelation that we received in that moment.

Thus Blake's technique of the good life is radically different from that practised by the orthodox. They try to be good in order to gain the vision; Blake learns what goodness is from the vision (though the vision itself, of course, has nothing to do with goodness) and orders his life accordingly, without effort and without fuss. And he does not seek to extend the 'moment' in time. The moment is creative, because it is the point at which a possibility is being realised; once it is realised, it slips on to another plane and adds a new cell to our organism. But if we strive consciously to realise the possibility on the material plane (and this is the temptation) what had been freedom becomes petrified and adds yet another shape to the 'universe of death'. This is the mistake of religious people who even when they have a mystical experience try to realise their bliss in moral willed activities. Gerard Manley Hopkins felt that he had to 'pay' in prayers, vows, austerities, for the sense of ecstasy he was given by the hawthorn bloom and the stars and clouds. This attitude, however disguised, is subtly materialistic, and has its origin in fear.

Yet another implication may be found in the four lines quoted from *Milton*. Blake tells us that 'if rightly placed' the vision will 'renovate every Moment of the Day'. To be able to do that, it must clearly occur early in the day. And in suggesting this, Blake again agrees with universal mystical tradition.[1] 'Think in the morning. Act in the noon. Eat in the evening. Sleep in the night.' This aphorism from *The Proverbs of Hell* holds a deeper than surface truth. *Thought* for Blake is what he called 'the burning fire of thought', the practice of vision. *Activity* is the practice of art. *Eating* is the study of art and of ancient wisdom, in books and pictures. *Sleep* is the absorption of such wisdom during the repose of the conscious mind.[2]

The early morning, then, is a peculiarly propitious time for experiencing the eternal moment. There must be few who have not been visited by 'thoughts beyond the reaches of our souls' at dawn, when the freshness of the air and the sense of newness and wonder have more than a physical significance. Mencius knew it when he said 'The great man is he who does not lose the child's heart', thus connecting the dawn of life with the dawn of day, and pointed to the need for daily 'renovation':

> The way in which a man loses the proper goodness of his mind is like the way in which trees are denuded by axes and bills. Hewn down day after day, can it retain its excellence? But there is some growth of its life day and night, and in the calm air of the morning, just between night and day, the mind feels in a degree those desires and aversions which are proper to humanity; but the feeling is not strong; and then it is fettered and destroyed by what the man does during the day.

---

[1] Cf. *The Following of Christ*, I, 33, formerly ascribed to Tauler. 'In regard to time, in the morning a man ought to take special heed of his heart, and not cumber himself much about external works, unless a great necessity intervene. For things are easier to a man in the morning, and at that season he can more effectually turn to God than at any other time.'

[2] This kind of exegesis is not as far-fetched as it may seem. It is in fact an aspect of the symbolic tradition within which Blake worked and on which his interpretation of the Bible and other writers was based. Much valuable work might be done in examining not only Blake's symbolism, but his terminology.

The problem, as Mr Lin Yutang points out in the introduction to his selections from Mencius,[1] is to know 'how to save and keep that air, or spirit, of the early dawn through the day, or how to guard the warm and good heart of the child through life'.

It is at dawn, Blake tells us, that the Saviour bends over him and inspires the writing of *Jerusalem*:

> This theme calls me in sleep night after night, & ev'ry morn
> Awakes me at sun-rise; then I see the Saviour over me
> Spreading his beams of love & dictating the words of this mild song.
> [*J.* 552]

It is at dawn, he tells us again in *Milton* in a passage immediately following the four key lines which I have analysed, that the eternal moment occurs:

> Just in this Moment, when the morning odours rise abroad
> And first from the Wild Thyme, stands a Fountain in a rock
> Of crystal flowing into two Streams: one flows thro' Golgonooza
> And thro' Beulah to Eden beneath Los's western wall:
> The other flows thro' the Aerial Void & all the Churches,
> Meeting again in Golgonooza beyond Satan's Seat. [*M.* 535]

We note that the 'Fountain in a rock'[2] (the cleansing fountain of vision which renovates the senses) stands 'in this Moment'; and that Blake does not despise the power of natural odours to induce the state of mind appropriate to vision.[3] There are two streams from the fountain: the one flows through the practice of art and through sexual love direct to Eden, the other finds its way through the wastes of materialism and ceremonial religion before it joins the first stream in the study of art. The first stream is of course the more direct. We have seen earlier how Blake always connects sexual enjoyment with the dawn.

Milton was conceived and partly written at Felpham, where Blake must often have known the scent of the thyme at dawn. 'The Wild Thyme is Los's Messenger to Eden, a mighty Demon.' The two

---

[1] *The Wisdom of China and India*, p. 744.

[2] The rock may be identified with the alchemical 'lapis', which is Christ.

[3] Cf. letter of 23 September 1800: 'The sweet air & the voices of winds, trees & birds, & the odours of the happy ground, makes it a dwelling for immortals.' His sensibility to odour is a point which marks Blake off from Wordsworth, in whom the tyranny of the eye was well developed.

poems relating mystical experiences which we find in the letters of 2 October 1800 and 22 November 1802, both belong to this period, and in both cases the experiences take place in the early morning. These poems are our clearest evidence for the immediate nature of Blake's vision. We may well consider them in some detail. Blake was sitting on the yellow sands when he received his 'first Vision of Light'. The word 'light' is important: throughout Blake's work the sun is present in his triple aspect of light, heat and motion, the trinity of energy. On this autumn day in 1800 the sun is shining in 'jewels of Light', distinct and clear. The vision of the minute particulars follows:

> Over Sea, over Land
> My Eyes did Expand
> Into regions of air
> Away from all Care,
> Into regions of fire
> Remote from Desire;
> The Light of the Morning
> Heaven's Mountains adorning:
> In particles bright
> The jewels of Light
> Distinct shone & clear.[1] [*L.* 1051–2]

Everything seen in vision appears as human. But now the imaginative eyes see the whole as a single man, a unity:

> My Eyes more and more
> Like a Sea without shore
> Continue Expanding,
> The Heavens commanding,
> Till the Jewels of Light,
> Heavenly Men beaming bright,
> Appear'd as One Man,
> Who complacent began
> My limbs to infold
> In his beams of bright gold;
> Like dross purg'd away
> All my mire & my clay.
> Soft consum'd in delight
> In his bosom Sun bright
> I remain'd. [*L.* 1052–3]

[1] The next fifteen lines of this passage are quoted above, pp. 226–7.

The sun is thus identified with Jesus, the God of Fire, as in *Jerusalem*. The mystical experience is one of ecstasy—the infolding of the body in golden beams; and of purgation through fire, leaving only the spiritual being. Blake surrenders himself to the experience with delight, and he is rewarded with a charge to be a keeper of Christ's fold and taught that the sea and the cliffs are fellow-protectors with him. The fold is all humanity, but Blake would not be 'English Blake' if he did not identify it mystically with England, the isle of Albion.[1]

Soft he smil'd,
And I heard his voice Mild
Saying: "This is My Fold,
O thou Ram horn'd with gold,
Who awakest from Sleep
On the Sides of the Deep.
On the Mountains around
The roarings resound
Of the lion & wolf,
The loud Sea & deep gulf.
These are guards of My Fold,
O thou Ram horn'd with gold"!
And the voice faded mild.
I remain'd as a Child;
All I ever had known
Before me bright Shone.
I saw you & your wife
By the fountains of Life.
Such the Vision to me
Appear'd on the sea. [*L.* 1053]

The second vision, related in the letter of 1802, was seen in 1801 while Blake was walking over the fields from Felpham to Lavant. He conveys the sense of morning freshness and happiness in a few lines:

With happiness stretch'd across the hills
In a cloud that dewy sweetness distills,
With a blue sky spread over with wings
And a mild sun that mounts & sings....
With Angels planted in Hawthorn bowers
And God himself in the passing hours,
With Silver Angels across my way
And Golden Demons that none can stay.... [*L.* 1066]

[1] Cf. his dedication *To the Queen*: 'O Shepherdess of England's Fold!' [*M.P.* 124]

He sees a thistle standing by the side of the path in front of him; and with his double vision he perceives its human lineaments:

> What to others a trifle appears
> Fills me full of smiles or tears;
> For double the vision my Eyes do see,
> And a double vision is always with me.
> With my inward Eye 'tis an old Man grey;
> With my outward, a Thistle across my way. [*L.* 1067]

The thistle, or old man, warns him never to go back in the path that has been appointed him. It is clear that there has been a temptation to shrink from the labour and scorn which Blake knew would follow if he continued his mission of interpreting the eternal world to his age. He is filled with conflict, and uproots the thistle with his foot. Then Los appears in the Sun:

> Then Los appear'd in all his power:
> In the Sun he appear'd, descending before
> My face in fierce flames; in my double sight
> 'Twas outward a Sun, inward Los in his might. [*L.* 1067]

Blake defies the sun in its material aspect, and asserts the dependence of his life on spiritual energy:

> "My hands are labour'd day & night,
> And Ease comes never in my sight.
> My Wife has no indulgence given
> Except what comes to her from heaven.
> We eat little, we drink less;
> This Earth breeds not our happiness.
> Another Sun feeds our life's streams,
> We are not warmed with thy beams;
> Thou measurest not the Time to me,
> Nor yet the Space that I do see;
> My Mind is not with thy light array'd,
> Thy terrors shall not make me afraid." [*L.* 1067–8]

As a result of his defiance of the material world, the sun trembles in heaven and the moon becomes leprous. But Blake himself is rewarded with the fourfold vision (the beatific vision of Eternity), the threefold vision (through sex), 'and twofold Always'.

> May God us keep
> From Single vision & Newton's sleep! [*L.* 1068]

The value of these two vision-poems lies in their transcription of an immediate personal experience: we are able to see more clearly into what the mystical state meant for Blake the man than we can by a simple reading of the symbolic books. We note that there is nothing of the Dionysian *via negativa* in Blake's experience. Blake belongs to the order of mystics, which includes Boehme, who have had to plan out their own way of approach to the divine reality. He was not able to rely for guidance on any traditional system. This fact, of course, has no relevance to Blake's greatness as a mystic. We cannot reduce the variety of religious experience to any one type. Certain mystics have approached truth through the preponderantly emotional avenue, through extreme devotion to a Divine Person; others, like Dionysius and Eckhart, have found self-losing in the Divine Dark the only possible formula which did not distort—it could not indeed *express*—their experience; yet others, like Blake, have found the immediate moment of union translating itself into visionary terms, and have been impelled to elaborate a symbolism.

Blake expressed his apprehension of the soul's drama, as we have seen, under the imagery of a disintegration and a reintegration. He borrowed much from the Bible, from the Cabbala, from Milton, from Boehme; archetypal figures arose from the depths of his unconscious mind; and he gave dramatic unity to his conceptions through the symbolism of a pilgrimage, and of losing and finding again.[1] The lost soul has lain down among the husks and the swine; she awakens to the call of God, and begins to retrace her steps from the world of illusion to the world of reality. That is the simplest analysis, and it is too simple for Blake. The soul itself is disintegrated, and has to reconcile every element of her being on the road back to Eternity.

Miss Evelyn Underhill describes three categories of mystical symbolism:[2] the pilgrimage, the marriage, and the 'Great Work'

---

[1] Cf. the dominant theme of the *Songs of Innocence and Experience* and this illuminating 'fragment of memory' from Samuel Palmer's letter to Gilchrist (*Life*, p. 302): 'I can yet recall it when, on one occasion, dwelling upon the exquisite beauty of the parable of the Prodigal, he began to repeat a part of it; but at the words, "When he was yet a great way off, his father saw him", could go no further; his voice faltered, and he was in tears.' All that this theme meant for Blake is conveyed in the awe-inspiring design on the penultimate page of his *Jerusalem*.

[2] Evelyn Underhill, *Mysticism*, 5th edition, p. 153.

of the spiritual alchemists. Blake is perhaps unique in that he combines all these modes of apprehension and description. No single one was sufficient to convey his subtle and all-inclusive vision. Jerusalem is not only the goal of the mystic quest; she is also the Bride of the Lamb, and she is the pure gold into which 'the noble precious Stone (*Lapis Philosophorum*) which tinctureth nature'[1] transmutes the base metal of the fleshly heart. It is impossible to say that one mode of symbolism preponderates over the others. The pilgrimage is there from first to last: but it is a pilgrimage *inwards*, away from the delusive world of the senses and away from the view of God as 'afar off', as transcendent. The marriage is there too—how could it not be in the great apostle of love?—but how far removed from the sensual is the bliss which transfigures the face of God as he embraces Jerusalem in the great engraving at the end of the epic.[2] Then, lastly, the alchemical *opus*. Here Blake borrows largely from Boehme; and like Boehme, and like the Cabbalists in general, he shows the transmutation of the inner world and the outer world going on side by side. Nature 'untinctured' is dross; transmuted, she is Eternity itself; a tree moves him to tears of joy, and the sun rising is 'an Innumerable company of the Heavenly host crying, "Holy, Holy, Holy is the Lord God Almighty"'.

And thus it was that 'the spirit said to him: "Blake be an artist & nothing else. In this there is felicity."'[3] Only through art—through words and lines and colours—could his extraordinarily complex experience be conveyed. Blake's work stands unique in its fusion of the highest mystical insight and the greatest mastery of art. It is now within the synthesis of art that we shall have to pursue our study of his vision.

---

[1] Jakob Boehme, quoted by Evelyn Underhill, *op. cit.* p. 171.

[2] See Plate VIII.

[3] Henry Crabb Robinson (*Selections from the Remains*, ed. Edith J. Morley, 1932): 'Diary Account of Blake', p. 4.

CHAPTER XXIII

Art

The Whole Business of Man Is The Arts, & All Things Common.
[*L.G.* 766]

THE Industrial Revolution, which during the period of Blake's lifetime was actively enslaving the people of England and reversing the traditional values of Europe, had also commenced its task of turning England's green and pleasant land into a rubbish heap. Blake was acutely aware of what was going on. He had not seen the sordid horrors of the northern factory towns, but clearly he knew all about them: his poems are full of dark Satanic mills, and furnaces, and clinkers, and slag. As a child he must have walked out of London for a little way and noted the 'chain of brick-kilns' that surrounded the city 'like the scars of the small-pox'.[1] In London itself there was the ugly bulk of the Albion flour-mill, plain for anyone to see and compare with the architecture of a past civilisation. Blake realised at once that the triumph of the machine meant the end of art.[2]

And the end of art, in his view, meant the end of civilisation. Blake really believed that the quality of a nation's art, which depended on the encouragement the nation gave to the artist, was the measure of that nation's greatness. Not commerce, as was beginning to be the orthodox opinion. Commerce is the enemy of art:

> Commerce is so far from being beneficial to Arts, or to Empires, that it is destructive of both, as all their History shews, for the above Reason of Individual Merit being its Great hatred.[3] Empires flourish till they become Commercial, & then they are scatter'd abroad to the four winds.
> [*P.A.* 811]

---

[1] See above, Ch. 1, p. 4n.

[2] 'A Machine is not a Man nor a Work of Art; it is destructive of Humanity & of Art; the word Machination' [*P.A.* 823].

[3] Alluding to an acute remark on mass-production a few lines back: 'Commerce Cannot endure Individual Merit; its insatiable Maw must be fed by What all can do Equally well.'

Well, it has taken a long time to see Blake's prognostic on the fate of an empire fulfilled, but his belief that the machine destroys art was fully verified in his own century. Victorian commercial prosperity ushered in the eclipse of beauty and the death of taste in England. We became a nation of barbarians almost overnight.

But quite apart from the indirect effect of the machine and the commercial spirit on beauty and art, there is the growth of what Blake defined as the machine spirit in art itself: the increasing popularity of realism or imitative art. He traces the evil back to the painters of the Venetian and Flemish schools, Titian and Correggio and Rubens, whose skill seemed to him to be artifice, technique for its own sake without the breath of inspiration. 'The cause that every thing in art shall become a Machine.' Their great error is to suppose that art is a copying of Nature, and not, as it should be, the plastic representation of imaginative form, visions of Eternity.

> Men think they can Copy Nature as Correctly as I copy Imagination; this they will find Impossible, & all the Copie[r]s or Pretended Copiers of Nature, from Rembrandt to Reynolds, Prove that Nature becomes to its Victim nothing but Blots & Blurs. Why are Copiers of Nature Incorrect, while Copiers of Imagination are Correct? this is manifest to all.
>
> [*P.A.* 813]

And a little later in the *Public Address* the condemnation of naturalism is taken up again even more incisively:

> No Man of Sense can think that an Imitation of the Objects of Nature is The Art of Painting, or that such Imitation, which any one may easily perform, is worthy of Notice, much less that such an Art should be the Glory & Pride of a Nation. The Italians laugh at English Connoisseurs, who are most of them such silly Fellows as to believe this.
>
> A Man sets himself down with Colours & with all the Articles of Painting; he puts a Model before him & he copies that so neat as to make it a deception: now let any Man of Sense ask himself one Question: Is this Art? can it be worthy of admiration to any body of Understanding? Who could not do this? what man who has eyes and an ordinary share of patience cannot do this neatly? Is this Art? Or is it glorious to a Nation to produce such contemptible Copies? Countrymen, Countrymen, do not suffer yourselves to be disgraced! [*P.A.* 815–6]

Alas! the Man of Sense, had he deigned to give his ear to Blake's question, would only too surely have answered, Yes; this is art; and been quite incapable of understanding what the queer fellow was getting at; and by the end of the century Blake's countrymen had suffered themselves to be disgraced in perfect tranquillity. The photographic representation view of art reigned supreme.

Blake was, in fact, a kind of throw-back in the history of art. He does not really belong in the industrial age. He was unable to conceive of painting as primarily a commercial transaction, in which the artist simply produced what the public liked; he thought of art, on the contrary, as the worship of God. The commercial aspect was secondary.

Blake is probably our last example of the artist-craftsman, working under his own conditions but in obedience to a principle higher than his own will. I think we can say he was the last, for in the career of William Morris we already have a good deal of the precious and the commercial. Blake has much in common with the craftsman of medieval Europe, for whom the higher principle operated in the shape of the Church, or the community, or the patron. In the case of Blake the principle operated immediately, as it did with Dante and Milton, in the shape of inspiration or 'dictation'. With Blake, hand and eye and mind worked together, so that what he saw in his mind's eye he conveyed at once without the intermediary of printing-press or outside illustrator. His method of 'illuminated printing' freed him from the bondage of the commercial system, and in this he is in a stronger position than are those present-day medievalists whose philippics against machinery come to us through the printing-press. Blake's choice of a medium meant complete control over the presentation of the idea, and was fully in accordance with his known integrity of purpose. In the lines of script, in the individualities of colouring, in the designs and in marginal comments he could give adequate expression to his vision. Moreover, the device of 'printing in the infernal method, by corrosives, which in Hell are salutary and medicinal, melting apparent surfaces away, and displaying the infinite which was hid', had a symbolic value for him.

The modern idea of art as the expression of an interesting personality was as meaningless to Blake as it would have been to a medieval artist. If we find him more vociferous, more eccentric and 'prouder' than the medieval artist would have been, the fault lies with his age, which forced him into a violent defence of the truths it did not wish to hear. Blake's pride was the pride of a son of God bent on asserting that sonship not for himself alone but for all mankind, and especially for the downcast and oppressed. He tells us repeatedly that his message, the content of his art, is not from himself but from Eternity. Like Dante and like Milton he uses the uncompromising word 'dictation'. We smile at this enthusiasm just as the eighteenth century did, and the nineteenth, or try to explain it away as figurative language because we have lost all conception of art as a mode of cognition.[1] For us art is aesthetics, the occasion for delicious emotions; and when we come across art which (as all ancient art does) tells us something about the ultimate verities we are at pains to distinguish the content from the form and concentrate on the latter. Or if we consider the doctrinal content we do so clinically, as psycho-analysts and not as philosophers or theologians.

If, again, we try to escape from the dilemma that art tells us nothing and yet has a supreme value, we have recourse to a kind of abstract art that we call 'significant form' and which is supposed to convey meaning through its sheer abstraction. The uninitiated's 'What does it mean?' is greeted with shocked hush-hushes by the illuminati. But we forget that this brings us no nearer to the symbolic perfection of that primitive art which the moderns so much admire. Primitive symbolism is founded not on individual eccentricities but on a common body of metaphysical belief: in short, on a faith and a ritual. It spoke to the believing community and not to a coterie or a single individual. It is the solution to this dilemma that a serious artist like Mr T. S. Eliot thinks he has found in communion with the Christian Church. And indeed, outside the religious community there seems to be no other solution for artists who do not cultivate visionary powers like Blake's. Abstraction is not symbolism, but its antithesis. Abstraction is an operation of the logical reason, issuing mainly in mathematical forms. Symbolism is the fruit of understanding vivified by emotion and issuing chiefly in the concrete forms

---

[1] 'The Ancients did not mean to Impose when they affirm'd their belief in Vision & Revelation. Plato was in Earnest: Milton was in Earnest. They believ'd that God did Visit Man Really & Truly & not as Reynolds pretends' [*R.D.* 1007].

of common life. The simplicity of these forms—the wheel, the egg, the candle, and so on—may be suggestive of a mathematical diagram but has quite another origin. These forms are rooted in the everyday life of common man, and their 'abstraction' is evoked by their becoming vehicles for metaphysical truth. The word of God is like a refiner's fire. It purges art of excess.

Blake was workman and artist. He saw in his own age the division which these two words now express, and hated it from his heart, for he saw that it meant slavery and distortion of the human personality. That work should be other than a joyous activity, and that art should be other than the motive of work, is a heresy peculiar to our machine age. For the medieval craftsman as for the Indian peasant and the North American savage, work truly done *is* art; and what we to-day preserve in museums as the art of past ages and peoples were things made for use in the ordinary course of the day's work. That they are beautiful is a necessary consequence of their being made conscientiously, by skilled workers, within a tradition which was rooted in a metaphysics. The further we go back the more we become conscious that the most ordinary articles of use have a symbolic and metaphysical significance bound up with their function. 'Every thing that lives is holy', said Blake; and everything through which Man expresses his urge to live is holy too. The modern idea of work as a drudgery from which the worker escapes to enjoy, at the highest, the pleasures of art, is a disruption of traditional unity. This daily shifting from plane to plane of living is so unnatural that one can only wonder how men are willing to endure it.

By Blake's time European art was already well on the downward path. Neither rooted in common life nor owning a metaphysical allegiance, the poetry, painting, music and architecture of the late eighteenth century were the diversions of a moneyed class whose main attentions were directed to getting rich quick, in England at least, through the golden opportunities held out to them by the Industrial Revolution. John Locke and his school had completed the whole tendency of post-Renaissance thought in degrading poetry to the level of entertainment, a position which it was well content to hold throughout the Augustan Age, with some feeble protests from Collins and Cowper. It was, therefore, against the Renaissance conception of art as a whole that Blake first directed his attack. And this attack led him, from the very beginning, to draw a distinction between the spirit of classical and that of Gothic art. As a boy he worked for Basire the engraver, who sent him to draw the monuments and figures in the Abbey; and during five years' steady work there Blake gained a love and understanding of the Gothic spirit which remained with him through life. Here was no naturalism, he felt, here was no expression of the balance and perfection of this-worldly living: here, on the contrary, were aspiration and vision translated into terms of stone. 'Grecian is Mathematic Form: Gothic is Living Form. Mathematic Form is Eternal in the Reasoning Memory: Living Form is Eternal Existence', he was to write near the close of his life. His deep study of the Gothic and his understanding of its spirit are central in his thought. In his great painting of *The Last Judgment* 'a Gothic Church is representative of true Art, Call'd Gothic in All Ages by those who follow'd the Fashion'.[1]

Blake's picture of life, as we have seen, is one of tension, of the interaction of contraries. Man has fallen into division: he strives always towards reunion. Los and Urizen are for ever at war in history which is the exteriorisation of the human conflict. This tension receives its supreme expression in the Incarnation and its resolution is Calvary. No one can avoid this tension and to seek to escape from it is spiritual death. But we must be careful that we read the tension aright. It is Urizen's cleverest ruse to confuse the issue: to divert Man's attention from the real struggle, which is between reason and vision, to an imaginary conflict between good and evil. He raises the moral screen between us and reality. He gives us the idea that we can enter Heaven by being good, when we can only enter it by being wise. He calls our energies by the name of sin. The pullulation of wars, laws and ceremonies is a consequence of this Satanic mystification. So are the neuroses from which we all suffer. This is our Original Sin: the eating of the fruit of the Tree of the Knowledge of Good and Evil.

Christ was made flesh and became as we are in order to destroy this false Satanic doctrine and free us from our neurotic selves into

[1] The word Gothic was used by the Augustans as a term of abuse, with the general meaning of 'uncouth', 'barbarous', 'savage'.

the kingdom of our true selves. He came to teach the gospel of the forgiveness of sins, our own and others'. We are not to expect holiness from one another. We are to 'expand' into mutual friendships and understandings. We can do this through the imagination; we can do it through the practice of art. 'Christ and his disciples were all artists.' For art is the perfect expression of significance, of a metaphysical truth: which truth is that *good and evil do not exist*, they are a device of exploiters bent on making the defenceless conform to their pattern.

It is the primal sin of the educationalist to teach children this Satanic rule of good and evil. All conventional education is a crime, in Blake's eyes; and it is after a discussion with him on good and evil that Crabb Robinson reports (17 Dec. 1825): 'Nor would he admit that any education should be attempted except that of cultivation of the imagination & fine arts.' The cultivation of the imagination (i.e. the technique of contemplation) and the fine arts (painting, music, architecture, sculpture): here there is no moralising about good and evil, no coercing of the vital creative energies, but an intelligent guidance of those energies through the plastic power of form and rhythm. No energy is suppressed, no impulse inhibited, no inner conflict initiated—with what dismal fruits in after years, Blake has already suggested in his *The Schoolboy*[1]—but the whole personality is quietly allowed to mature through creative activity. Blake told Dr Trusler that children were the best interpreters of his pictures. That is because they take easily to symbolic art, are ready to learn from it, and prompt to practise it themselves.

Christ's code of forgiveness, then, the rejection of the rigid dualism of good and evil, is also the code of art. In so much as Christ is the ἀνακεφαλαίωσις, in St Paul's term, the summing-up of *all* significance, He *is* Art, the Creative Word by which all things are made. Since, moreover, He came to show that vice is quite other than Urizen and the law picture it—that it is really the negation of energy and not all the loves and graces springing from joy—Blake rightly says that art is the forgiveness of sins. Even in the art of deluded Man we find the spirit of reconciliation: within the sphere

---

[1] See above, pp. 309–12.

of art good and evil no longer exist; all that matters is the greater or lesser perfection of the achievement.

> in Eternity the Four Arts, Poetry, Painting, Music
> And Architecture, which is Science, are the Four Faces of Man.[1]
> [*M.* 518]

Imprisoned in this mortal body, divided Man still beholds the divine humanity by means of the arts; and this vision is their reason for existence. In his 'fresco' *The Vision of the Last Judgment* Blake pictures Albion the Ancient Man surrounded by the blessed who after the labour of ages are ascending into Eternity:

> The Persons who ascend to Meet the Lord, coming in the Clouds with power & great Glory, are representations of those States described in the Bible under the Names of the Fathers before & after the Flood. Noah is seen in the Midst of these, canopied by a Rainbow, on his right hand Shem & on his Left Japhet; these three Persons represent Poetry, Painting & Music, the three Powers in Man of conversing with Paradise, which the flood did not Sweep away. [*V.L.J.* 835]

The problem of representational, abstract and symbolic types of art is not only a corollary of Blake's teaching: it is expressly brought up in his marginal notes on Sir Joshua Reynolds' *Discourses*, notes in which a whole aesthetics is conveyed.[2] If, as Blake held, art is the manifestation of truth, its use of natural forms will be strictly subservient to the prime object of showing forth the secret things of God. It will not be a naturalistic but a symbolic art. And we note, in actual fact, the tendency towards simplification or distortion of natural forms in early painting, as in poetry we note a characteristic disregard for the laws of Nature. It is not enough to say pityingly that the Italian primitives knew nothing of anatomy or perspective or they would have done better. For the purpose they had in view,

---

[1] The next three lines run: 'Not so in Time & Space: there Three are shut out, and only / Science remains thro' Mercy, & by means of Science the Three / Become apparent in Time & Space....' This becomes clear when we remember that in Eternity we 'enter into one another's bosoms'; and architecture remains in this world *the only three-dimensional art*: we can walk into a cathedral and look round, but painting is flat, and music fleeting, and poetry a chain of words. The three other arts take on significance when wedded to architecture. Blake was especially interested in the idea of painting pictures for churches.

[2] See below, pp. 430–8.

which was the visible representation of a heavenly truth or vision, anatomy and perspective were worse than useless. Naturalism merely obscured the supernatural fact which they were at pains to express. So too, we learn, Blake was heard to complain that Nature 'put him out'.

In so far as God has wished to express His truth through the visual language of Nature (to take Berkeley's position for a moment) He has done so in the living objects themselves. The artist does not need to do *that* over again! He can use these forms for his own purposes, he is free to modify and simplify and combine them as he pleases. It is an historic fact that the decay of religion and spiritual insight came precisely with the cult of naturalism in painting and the other arts. We do not feel the inexpressible essence of faith in Raphael's chubby bambini and Botticelli's sensuous Madonnas as we felt it in Fra Angelico and the primitive masters. A Renaissance church-building, too, is plainly adapted to the discourses of reason and not to the discoveries of faith. With music, the most archetypal of the arts since by its nature it can properly represent nothing earthly, there is a decline the more it is separated from the dance, as it is after Bach and Handel. The dance movements of these great masters guarantee their closeness to communal tradition, and we know that their art is not personal. The further back we go the more evident this is.

Nor indeed, could we expect things to be otherwise. The external world has such a pull on us from the moment we enter it that the effort to direct the mind to the eternal world is a life-long struggle. We are drawn down to the earth physically by the force of gravitation; we are dependent upon it for our food and clothing and shelter; our bodies are made up of its elements; our senses are constantly assailed by its colours and sounds and scents. As Wordsworth uncharacteristically admits,

> Earth fills her lap with pleasures of her own;
> Yearnings she hath in her own natural kind,
> And, even with something of a Mother's mind,
> And no unworthy aim,
> The homely Nurse doth all she can
> To make her Foster-child, her Inmate Man,
> Forget the glories he hath known,
> And that imperial palace whence he came.

The great majority of mystics have felt that the beauty of the natural world was an impediment in their path towards divine union. They failed to develop Blake's technique of seeing Nature not with but through the eye. So they clung only to the celestial vision. Renaissance man, on the other hand, turned from the vision of that other and inner world to celebrate the glory of this world. He revelled in the sensuous beauty of flesh and in the intricacy of anatomical detail; he forgot the other-worldly origin of art. He set out, with the Renaissance philosophers, on the road which led to materialism and scepticism.

We are now in a position to see why Gothic art should have made so strong an appeal to Blake. The medieval cathedral is 'living form' first and foremost because it does express the tension which Blake felt to be at the heart of life. It expresses this tension in its upthrust of pillars, in its vaults and its spires, in the stress and strain of the arch, in complexity of forms. Here we have matter which is not content to be matter, solid stone which for all its solidity is ever soaring and striving upwards. In the anonymity of the cathedral, again, Blake felt the strength and comfort of a community united by faith. And this sense of community was vastly increased by the three-dimensionality of the cathedral, the fact that one could penetrate into its marvels. Again, Blake felt the artistic genius of the common man revealed in the gargoyles and finials, the misericords and rood-screens carved by unknown craftsmen; his love of pure and unmerging colours was satisfied by the blues and reds and greens of the great windows. Blake lived with these things intimately, we are told, for five years, at an impressionable period of his life; and he knew that the Augustan critics were taking too limited a view of art when they sneered at Gothic. They would not open their eyes. 'Let them look at Gothic Figures & Gothic Buildings & not talk of Dark Ages or of any Age.' Blake saw quite clearly a fact which was invisible to the men of his time, and has not been entirely assimilated even to-day. He saw that art is not progressive. 'If Art was Progressive We should have had Mich Angelos & Rafaels to Succeed & to Improve upon each other. But it is not so. Genius dies with its Possessor & comes not again till Another is Born with It.' And knowing this, he opened his mind to a great world of delight which was closed to the pundits like Sir Joshua Reynolds and Sir Thomas

Lawrence. He found the medieval delight in simple work honestly and faithfully done.

I say medieval, because the Middle Ages were the only period which Blake knew (and he knew them only through their relics), which embodied a community of faith producing artists of the kind he meant when he said: 'A Poet, a Painter, a Musician: the man who is not one of these is not a Christian.' If he had known more about Eastern communities, or about primitive peoples, he might possibly have found there examples better fitted to his mind. For the medieval Church, 'living form' though it was through its embodiment of true principles of belief and through its artistic integrity, was also the setting for a priestly and ceremonial worship which he hated—though not as much as he hated Natural Religion and science.

We do not know what he felt about other forms of medieval art—about the drama, for example. We have, however, his very interesting comments on Chaucer, in elucidation primarily of the figures in his big painting of *The Canterbury Pilgrims*. At first glance no two writers seem less akin than Chaucer and Blake—Chaucer the great humanist, his shrewd tolerant mocking eyes fixed so happily on the pageant of this world, and Blake the mystic, lost in vision. Yet Blake had an extraordinary understanding of Chaucer's genius, and his comments on the characters of the *Prologue* show critical insight of the first order. He felt that Chaucer, nurtured in the Christian tradition, was despite his irony and worldly wisdom no mocker of vision and inspiration. He was not of the tribe of Hayley and Reynolds. 'It appears in all the writings of Chaucer, and particularly in his Canterbury Tales, that he was very devout, and paid respect to true enthusiastic superstition.' He saw, that is, beyond the fleeting symbol, imperfectly apprehended, to the divine truth, and did not fall into scepticism. Moreover, Chaucer, as 'the great poetical observer of men', could not fulfil a critical function. His duty was to observe and create, not to condemn and apply moral standards. Blake catches the essence of Chaucer's genius, which was the delight in life for its own sake and in all its manifestations.

Blake saw beyond the individual characters of Chaucer's pilgrims to the archetypal characters which are those of humanity in every age:

The characters of Chaucer's Pilgrims are the characters which compose all ages and nations: as one age falls, another rises, different to mortal

PLATE IX

A GROUP FROM 'THE CANTERBURY PILGRIMS'

PLATE X

JOSEPH OF ARIMATHEA PREACHING TO THE INHABITANTS OF BRITAIN

sight, but to immortals only the same; for we see the same characters repeated again and again, in animals, vegetables, minerals, and in men; nothing new occurs in identical existence; Accident ever varies, Substance can never suffer change nor decay. [*D.C.* 783]

As I have said above, it is the function of the artist to express the unchanging truth; though he may express it through natural symbols, yet the principle of Eternity must not be obscured by the temporal dress. This does not mean, as the post-Renaissance writers and critics thought, that universality lies in generalisation. On the contrary: abstraction is of all things destructive of universality, being a construction in the individual's mind which does not correspond with *what is* on the natural plane, much less on the supernatural—but only with *what ought to be.* Vision is not vagueness, as Blake never tires of pointing out: it is apprehended only in the clearest and most determined outlines. Thus Chaucer's characters are able to stand as universal types precisely because they are living individuals with the physical and mental peculiarities and idiosyncrasies pertaining to them as such. A thing must first *live* before it can become *eternal*: a generalisation or an abstraction has not even begun to live.

In the Knight, Chaucer gives a character which even in his own day was becoming extinct in English thought and literature. This idea, the idea of the *hero*, has become progressively more unreal with the modern centuries; for it is intimately connected with metaphysical truth, the hero always embodying a virtuous principle and his adventures being a continued allegory:

The Knight is a true Hero, a good, great, and wise man; his whole length portrait on horseback, as written by Chaucer, cannot be surpassed. He has spent his life in the field; has ever been a conqueror, and is that species of character which in every age stands as the guardian of man against the oppressor. His son is like him with the germ of perhaps greater perfection still, as he blends literature and the arts with his warlike studies. [*D.C.* 783–4]

But for the modern commentator the heroic character, with its dry light shining on a single virtue, is 'pasteboard' in the same sense that primitive art, with its absence of perspective and anatomy, is poverty-stricken. We seek from Roland, from Arthur or Hector a psychological depth that the writer had no intention of giving. Only the supreme genius of Chaucer can carry the weight of intimate detail *and* the metaphysical content; and already, with him, we feel the latter beginning to evaporate. He is just slipping over the boundary which separates the Middle Ages from the Renaissance.

A last point in which we may note the affinity of Chaucer and Blake is their notion of tragedy. The great world-tragedy for Blake is the Fall; and for Chaucer, too, tragedy is a fall from great prosperity to wretchedness. This conception is, of course, that of the whole Middle Ages and not Chaucer's alone: but it has never been put more clearly than in the five lines which Blake quotes from the Prologue to the *Monk's Tale*:

> Tragedie is to seyn a certeyn storie,
> As olde bokes maken us memorie,
> Of him that stood in greet prosperitee
> And is y-fallen out of heigh degree
> Into miserie, and ended wrecchedly.

That is the history of Albion.

When we turn from primitive art and the Gothic achievement to consider classical sculpture and architecture, we find Blake highly critical. He saw in these things the antithesis of true art. He was bold enough to say so. He saw that if Gothic is the expression of a tension between the human and divine, the material and the spiritual, classic art is the formulation of an equilibrium achieved on the human plane. In Gothic we have the hierarchy of soul, mind and body; in 'Grecian' we have a *schema* from which soul is excluded. Gothic, moreover, is the art of a free community; 'Grecian' is the art of an aristocracy based on slavery. Blake was convinced that classical art lacks even the merit of originality. He asserts and re-asserts that its principles were stolen from the archetypal art of the East and then deformed into humanism:

The Artist [Blake] having been taken in vision into the ancient republics, monarchies, and patriarchates of Asia has seen those wonderful originals, called in the Sacred Scriptures the Cherubim, which were sculptured and painted on walls of Temples, Towers, Cities, Palaces, and erected in the highly cultivated states of Egypt, Moab, Edom, Aram, among the Rivers of Paradise, being originals from which the Greeks and Hetrurians copied Hercules Farnese, Venus of Medicis, Apollo Belvidere, and all the grand works of ancient art. They were executed in a very superior style to those justly admired copies, being with their accompaniments terrific and grand in the highest degree....

No man can believe that either Homer's Mythology, or Ovid's, were the production of Greece or of Latium; neither will any one believe, that the Greek statues, as they are called, were the invention of Greek Artists; perhaps the Torso is the only original work remaining; all the rest are evidently copies, though fine ones, from greater works of the Asiatic Patriarchs. The Greek Muses are daughters of Mnemosyne, or Memory, and not of Inspiration or Imagination, therefore not authors of such sublime conceptions. Those wonderful originals seen in my visions, were some of them one hundred feet in height; some were painted as pictures, and some carved as basso relievos, and some as groupes of statues, all containing mythological and recondite meaning, where more is meant than meets the eye.[1] [*D.C.* 780–1]

I have quoted this passage at length because it illustrates Blake's grasp of the ruling principle of traditional art: its archetypal and metaphysical nature, a principle which is perhaps more striking (though not more fundamental) in an unfamiliar art like that of the East than in a European art whose appeal is blurred by familiarity and which has evolved into the naturalistic patterns of post-Renaissance times. At the Royal Academy where he studied as a youth, and by all the pundits of the time, Blake's attention was called to the necessity of studying and imitating the classical perfection. The complexity of Gothic architecture was held to be rude and barbarous in comparison with the majestic simplicity of Greek temples. But Blake saw in these, no less than in the Renaissance palaces which imitated them, an assertion of human self-sufficiency and a denial of vision. In classical art the mind rests in a formal perfection; in Gothic, it is carried on and on in a restless quest for truth and goodness.

In classical art, again, Blake saw an enslavement of the human mind to mathematics which reminded him only too strongly of his old enemies, Bacon, Newton and Locke. I have remarked in an earlier chapter on the logical and grammatical nature of Greek thought; Blake saw this expressed in art too. 'The Gods of Greece

[1] Illustrations of such massive sculpture, perhaps designed and engraved by Blake himself though signed with the name of his master Basire, are to be found in Jacob Bryant's *New System, or an Analysis of Ancient Mythology* (3 vols., 1774–6)—a source-book for Blake's mythology.

& Egypt were Mathematical Diagrams—See Plato's Works', he says. Here he includes Egyptian art (which in the previous quotation he classes with inspired art) along with that of Greece: no doubt remembering the mathematical form of the pyramids. In the symbolic books mathematical expression is characteristic of Urizen as he constructs the physical universe; a Greek temple is an image of this construction. But for Blake art is not an image of Nature, but of Supernature. 'We become what we behold'; and if we constantly behold mathematic form, our human nature is stultified instead of being conformed to the Divine Image. Art thus cuts itself off from its original and special purpose.

Let us remember once more that 'Art is the Forgiveness of sins'. The Gothic church is an expression of this truth. There is a recognition, in its very complexity, of the tangle of human strivings and failings, and a welcome, in its sheltering vastness, for all sorts and conditions of men. But the Greek denied sin: he knew only a nearer or farther approach to mental and physical perfection; he knew the service of the State and its laws, and he identified those laws with religion. If a man came, like Socrates, to point beyond this sphere of earth, he put him to death. The one artistic desire of the Greek was, in Sidney's phrase, 'to make the much-loved earth more lovely'. Greek art contains an implicit denial of the fact of the Fall which was so central for Blake. The Greeks shrank from suffering and delighted in the representation of youth and physical health; but in spite of their cult of euphoria there is a deep pessimism at the heart of classical literature, a longing turned back upon itself which is more terrible than any medieval dance of death because it is without hope.

It was only gradually that Blake turned against Greek art; at first he shared, unthinkingly, the general admiration. But there was no field of human thought in which he did not come, sooner or later, to think things out for himself. We can trace the change in his letters and other writings. The *Imitation of Spenser* in *Poetical Sketches* (1769–78) employs a conventional classical mythology. He pokes fun at Phoebus in *An Island in the Moon* (1789); but Isaiah, in *The Marriage of Heaven and Hell* (1793) speaks of "our friend Diogenes, the Grecian". In this same work, however, there is a slighting reference to Aristotle's 'Analytics' which shows us that Blake will come to reject Greek art through a realisation of the insufficiency of

Greek philosophy. This realisation is explicit in *The Song of Los* (1795) with its condemnation of abstraction:

> To Trismegistus, Palamabron gave an abstract Law:
> To Pythagoras, Socrates & Plato. [*S.L.* 273]

In 1798 he can still appeal to the evidence of the classics when he wishes to rebut the myth of progress. Bishop Watson had stated that 'Human kind . . . is in a far more distinguished situation, as to the powers of the mind, than it was in the childhood of the world.' Blake comments: 'That mankind are in a less distinguished Situation with regard to mind than they were in the time of Homer, Socrates, Phidias, Glycon, Aristotle, etc., let all their works witness.' In his letter to Dr Trusler of 23 August 1799 he puts Aesop, Homer and Plato with Moses and Solomon as the 'wisest of the Ancients', and mentions Homer and Virgil in the same breath with Milton and the Bible as 'addressed to the Imagination, which is Spiritual Sensation, & but mediately to the Understanding or Reason. Such is true Painting, and such was alone valued by the Greeks & the best modern Artists.' In a letter of 26 August in the same year he exhorts George Cumberland not to 'throw aside for any long time the honour intended you by Nature to revive the Greek workmanship'.

Then, for three years, there is silence about the classical artists. During this period Blake is deeply engaged with his first great symbolic book, *The Four Zoas*; he is almost continually in a visionary state, and in that state many things become clear to him that he had not fully realised before. The nature of *reason* is progressively opened to him as the terrible figure of Urizen grows in his mind. This is a time of crisis for Blake—a judgement—in which the nature of error becomes apparent and has to be cast out. 'Whenever any Individual Rejects Error & Embraces Truth, a Last Judgment passes upon that Individual. . . . No Man can Embrace true Art till he has Explor'd & cast out False Art.' In 1802 we find him writing to Butts:

> One thing of real consequence I have accomplish'd by coming into the country, which is to me consolation enough: namely, I have recollected all my scatter'd thoughts on Art & resumed my primitive & original ways of Execution in both painting & engraving, which in the confusion of London I had very much lost & obliterated from my mind. [*L.* 1060]

What were these primitive views? We know them because he had expressed them in 1773 when engraving Michelangelo's print of Joseph of Arimathea:

> Joseph of Arimathea among the Rocks of Albion.
> This is One of the Gothic Artists who Built the Cathedrals in what we call the Dark Ages, Wandering about in sheep skins & goat skins, of whom the World was not worthy; such were the Christians in all Ages. [*M.Pr.* 861]

And we hear no more praise of the Greeks from now on.

The anti-classical storm which rages through Blake's later writings breaks with *Milton* (1804–8). A thunder-clap opens the *Preface*:

> The Stolen and Perverted Writings of Homer & Ovid, of Plato & Cicero, which all men ought to contemn, are set up by artifice against the Sublime of the Bible; but when the New Age is at leisure to Pronounce, all will be set right, & those Grand Works of the more ancient & consciously & professedly Inspired Men will hold their proper rank, & the Daughters of Memory shall become the Daughters of Inspiration. Shakspeare & Milton were both curb'd by the general malady & infection from the silly Greek & Latin slaves of the Sword. [*M.* 464]

From 1804 onwards he never altered his opinion of the classics. 'This is only Grecian, or rather Trojan, worship', he remarks in a letter of 24 May 1804, to Hayley (it was prudent not to be too anti-classical in dealing with *him*!), commenting on the Americans' veneration for Washington; 'I have the happiness of seeing the Divine countenance in such men as Cowper and Milton more distinctly than in any prince or hero.' In another letter of the same year he records his sudden illumination at the Truchsessian exhibition:

> For now! O Glory! and O Delight! I have entirely reduced that spectrous fiend to his station, whose annoyance has been the ruin of my labours for the last passed twenty years of my life. He is the enemy of conjugal love and is the Jupiter of the Greeks, an iron-hearted tyrant, the ruiner of ancient Greece. [*L.* 1108]

It would hardly be profitable to list all his later references to the classics. 'The Greek & Roman Classics is the Antichrist' is his last word, in the last year of his life. We may note however that occasionally he has a good word to say, rather grudgingly, for Plato and

Socrates. He could not but be aware of a spirit in Plato which breaks away from Greek perfectionism, which is other-worldly, and which brought Plato's master Socrates to martyrdom. Plato's doctrine of ideas, too, has much in common with his own mysticism. But he did not realise how fully Plato was with him in his views on art and education. Plato also looks back from the humanistic art of his time to the archaic period, and gives it high praise for its presentation of archetypal forms. Or he looks outside Greece altogether for a more metaphysical art. The function of art for Plato is 'to attune our own distorted modes of thought to cosmic harmonies, "so that by an assimilation of the knower to the to-be-known, the archetypal nature, and coming to be in that likeness, we may attain at last to a part in that 'life's best' that has been appointed by the gods to man for this time being and hereafter"'.[1] Or, in Blake's mode of expression, we become what we behold, we enjoy eternal life on this side of the grave.

If Blake's final word on classical art is condemnatory, his attitude to Renaissance and post-Renaissance art is still more so. If classical art is an imitation of Nature, if the Greek muses are the daughters of memory and not of inspiration, Renaissance art is the imitation of an imitation. Blake saw quite clearly, too, how the other-worldly factor had been eliminated to make way for the cult of the patron and the kindling of the purely human lusts of pride and concupiscence. We may be sure that the admirable object-lesson afforded by Westminster Abbey and St Paul's was not lost upon him. The glory of Gothic and the grandeur of baroque were set visibly side by side for comparison; the one, created by anonymous hands through centuries of faith; the other, the masterpiece of the Savilian professor of astronomy at Oxford, the friend of Newton. Living form and mathematical form were everywhere at hand in London for him to compare and contrast.

The three post-Renaissance centuries in England are the record of a growing deterioration of artistic values if we place value, as Blake did, in adequate symbolisation of metaphysical truth. In the fairies and witches of Shakespeare he was still able to see some relics

[1] Ananda K. Coomaraswamy, *Why Exhibit Works of Art?* (Luzac and Co.). I have been deeply indebted to this little book, which has a value out of all proportion to its size, in writing the present chapter.

of a traditional mythology: the witches are intended as 'the Goddesses of Destiny', and the fairies are 'the rulers of the vegetable world'. In the next century comes Milton with his magnificent attempt to justify the ways of God to men. But alas! both these great writers are infected with the disease of their time, 'curb'd by the general malady & infection from the silly Greek and Latin slaves of the Sword'. It is hard to keep the Divine Vision in times of trouble. Shakespeare was a contemporary of Bacon, Milton of Hobbes and Locke. The other writers succumbed completely. Apart from a few references to Cowper and Chatterton, Blake's picture of eighteenth-century literature is dark indeed. For Dryden, with his fatuous pretensions to civilise Milton by making *Paradise Lost* rhyme, and for Pope's society verses, he has nothing but contempt. As for his own day, the weary decline of the Age of Reason, we need only point to the general acceptance of the Bard of Sussex to indicate its lack of standards.

The implicit flattery of riches which the early Renaissance artists had expressed in the building of pompous mansions and palaces became a more direct adulation in the eighteenth-century school of English portrait-painting. The climax and glory of this school was Sir Joshua Reynolds. Blake came into close contact with Reynolds early in his career; he disliked him violently, and everything that he stood for; and his own theory and practice of painting were evolved in direct opposition to those of Sir Joshua. In his marginal notes on the *Discourses* we have our clearest data for Blake's ideas on the various styles, schools and techniques of art; and I cannot do better than close this chapter with a consideration of the *Discourses* together with Blake's notes on them.

When George III gave his blessing to the foundation of the Royal Academy in 1768 there was only one possibility for the office of president: Reynolds. The King, for some reason, did not like Reynolds; he gave him a knighthood, but he did not sit for a portrait until ten years later. But he could not ignore Reynolds' position as the undoubted leader of the English portrait school. Reynolds was forty-five at the time, the most successful portrait artist of his day, earning an annual income of what would to-day be about £20,000 free of income-tax from an average of three commissions a week. He was a prominent social figure; his circle of friends included Dr Johnson and Goldsmith, and it was he who founded the famous literary club at which the Great Cham held forth. He was by no means an original thinker, but his writings on art are valuable as reflecting the current attitudes of the day with a precision we do not find elsewhere. In fact, the *Discourses* are almost as useful a mirror of what the average educated man thought at the end of the eighteenth century as the *Spectator* papers are for the first decades. It is particularly interesting to note that the influence of Locke is as strong as ever. The main positions of the *Essay concerning Human Understanding* are faithfully applied, in the *Discourses*, to the principles of art. Correct education and not that will-o'-the-wisp, genius, is the foundation of excellence; ideas for subjects come by amassing a stock of common notions and not from innate vision; abstraction is the special mark of the grand style. Above all, avoid 'mere enthusiasm'!

We will not be surprised, then, at the violence of Blake's comments on the *Discourses*. In Reynolds he found a fourth 'sinewy neck' to set by Bacon, Newton and Locke on his rational hydra. 'This Man was Hired to Depress Art', he explodes on the title-page. 'This is the Opinion of Will Blake: my Proofs of this Opinion are given in the following Notes.'

Blake's annotations to the *Discourses* were written about 1808; the text had been published in 1798 and there is an amicable reference to them in a letter of 1820 to Thomas Butts. The last of the discourses he annotates (No. VIII) he must have heard delivered at the close of his first year at the Academy. They were all delivered from the Presidential chair at the annual prize-givings, and they have the defects of occasional utterances. In the last discourse (10 December 1790) Reynolds admits their great fault, which is lack of order: 'to put those ideas into something like order was, to my inexperience, no easy task', and a lesser fault, which is repetitiveness. But, he maintains,

> in reviewing my discourses, it is no small satisfaction to be assured that I have, in no part of them, lent my assistance to foster *newly-hatched unfledged* opinions, or endeavoured to support paradoxes....I have pursued a plain and *honest method*; I have taken up the art simply as I found it exemplified in the practice of the most approved painters.

To this practice, he might have added, 'I have applied the universally accepted conclusions of Mr Locke, and with some assistance from

Mr Burke's *Enquiry into the Sublime and the Beautiful* I have contributed something towards a philosophy of art.' It is with this philosophy that we are now concerned. I might have considered the discourses under the various topics which they raise: the function of painting, the meaning of genius and taste, Nature and Imagination, the materials of art, and so on; but this would have destroyed the cumulative effect of Blake's indignant comments. I have chosen, therefore, to go straight through the discourses, bringing out the important points.

Perhaps the first point that strikes a reader of the *Discourses* is an element of contradiction, not only between what Reynolds says in one place and what he says in another, but still more between his principles and his practice. His written words condemn the great Venetian colourists as an inferior school, unworthy of imitation; only Michelangelo and Raphael are the masters of the grand style. In his actual practice as a painter he stands historically as the introducer of the technique of the Venetian colourists into English portrait-painting. And in the *Discourses* we constantly find him slipping into an admiring reference to Titian or Veronese only to leap back, quickly, into safety. For the consideration of *safety* is, I think, at the bottom of Reynolds' inconsistencies. He was safe in praising the Roman and Florentine schools; he had been taught to admire them himself, and it was academically respectable to go on admiring them, and to teach the young pupils at the Academy to admire them. But his own instincts were all for opulence in colouring and against precision of line. He admits that when he visited Italy in 1749 he was quite unable to appreciate the Raphaels in the Vatican until he forced himself to do so. But his visit to Venice produced an immediate effect. For the rest of his life he went on praising Raphael and denigrating Veronese and Titian in words, but with his brush he paid the Venetians the greatest of compliments. Reynolds had a timid mind, and he was quite capable of saying one thing and practising another.

For a long time it was thought that Reynolds was not the author of his *Discourses*; and even a casual reading will show great variations in style. Some of his sentences have the solidity and penetration of Dr Johnson; others are quite vague and meaningless. Blake notes that

> The contradictions in Reynolds's Discourses are Strong Presumptions that they are the Work of Several Hands, But this is no Proof that

> Reynolds did not Write them. The Man, Either Painter or Philosopher, who Learns or Acquires all he knows from Others, Must be full of Contradictions. [*R.D.* 975]

And this is probably the truth of the matter. Reynolds picked up his ideas where he could get them, in the intervals of a busy life as a painter: from Burke, from Goldsmith, from Johnson, and from the Lockean psychology which was the common property of the age.

The first discourse was delivered at the opening of the Royal Academy on 2 January 1769. It is largely concerned with the attitude of obedience and docility which will be expected from the young students. A note is soon struck which Reynolds maintains throughout the *Discourses*: the discouragement of 'minute accidental discriminations of particular and individual objects' and the praise of 'that grand style of painting, which improves partial representation by the general and invariable ideas of nature'. Blake comments: 'Minute Discrimination is Not Accidental. All Sublimity is founded on Minute Discrimination.' And in reply to Reynolds' assertion that Michelangelo's works turned Raphael from 'a dry, Gothick' manner to the grand style, Blake expresses his entire disbelief

> that Rafael taught Mich. Angelo, or that Mich. Angelo taught Rafael, any more than I believe that the Rose teaches the Lilly how to grow, or the Apple tree teaches the Pear tree how to bear Fruit. I do not believe the tales of Anecdote writers when they militate against Individual Character. [*R.D.* 980]

It is rather a strange experience to read through the *Discourses* to the accompaniment of Blake's comments, the frigid formal sentiments and phrases contrasting oddly with Blake's 'burning fire of thought' and the organic beauty of style which appears as fresh as ever in these indignant asides.

From the young students Reynolds demands an implicit obedience to the rules of art; and 'a Premature Disposition to a Masterly Dexterity is to be repressed'. They must advance step by step, not making 'the mechanical felicity the chief excellence of the art, which is only an ornament'. Blake remarks on this: 'Mechanical Excellence is the Only Vehicle of Genius'—a truth which Reynolds should have been able to see, one would think.

The second discourse (Dec. 1769) is more important. It raises the questions of genius and application, the acquirement of ideas and the imitation of Nature. After gaining facility in drawing and the management of colours, the next stage is to 'endeavour to collect subjects for expression; to amass a stock of ideas, to be combined and varied as occasion may require'. It is only in the third stage that the student is emancipated from submission to authority. He can now examine art itself by the standard of Nature. In conclusion Reynolds gives the following counsel:

There is one precept in which I shall only be opposed by the vain, the ignorant, and the idle. I am not afraid that I shall repeat it too often. You must have no dependence on your own genius. If you have great talents, industry will improve them; if you have but moderate talents, industry will supply their deficiency. Nothing is denied to well-directed labour: nothing is to be obtained without it. Not to enter into metaphysical discussions on the nature or essence of genius, I will venture to assert, that assiduity unabated by difficulty, and a disposition eagerly directed to the object of its pursuit, will produce effects similar to those which some call the result of *natural powers*.

Blake saw that this was Lockean psychology applied to art criticism:

Reynolds's Opinion was that Genius May be Taught & that all Pretence to Inspiration is a Lie & a Deceit, to say the least of it. For if it is a Deceit, the whole Bible is Madness. This Opinion originates in the Greeks' calling the Muses Daughters of Memory. [*R.D.* 980]

The third discourse (Dec. 1770) carries on the attack against innate genius. While there are no precise rules for the acquisition of taste and genius, we see that they are always proportionate to

our attention in observing the works of nature, to our skill in selecting, and to our care in digesting, methodising, and comparing our observations. ... This great ideal perfection and beauty are not to be sought in the heavens, but upon the earth.... [The wise student] examines his own mind, and perceives there nothing of that divine inspiration, with which, he is told, so many others have been favoured. He never travelled to heaven to gather new ideas; and he finds himself possessed of no other qualifications than what mere common observation and a plain understanding can confer.

This is the apotheosis of common sense in art. We may expect Blake to hit back violently:

> The Man who on Examining his own Mind finds nothing of Inspiration ought not to dare to be an Artist, & he is a Fool & a Cunning Knave suited to the Purposes of Evil Demons
>
> The Man who never in his Mind & Thoughts travel'd to Heaven Is No Artist.
>
> Artists who are above a plain Understanding are Mock'd & Destroy'd by this President of Fools. [*R.D.* 987]

There is no doubt, indeed, as we have seen in the affair of Dr Trusler, that it was this view of art which barred Blake in his lifetime from recognition.

If not by inspiration, how does the painter arrive at this ideal beauty? By abstraction, Reynolds replies. Natural forms are full of blemishes; the part of the artist is to observe what is lacking in every particular form, and to correct Nature by herself. Thus he arrives at the perfect state of Nature, which is the Ideal Beauty. This is, of course, the standard neo-Classic formula. Blake in reply asserts the existence of innate ideas:

> Knowledge of Ideal Beauty is Not to be Acquired. It is Born with us. Innate Ideas are in Every Man, Born with him; they are truly Himself. The Man who says that we have No Innate Ideas must be a Fool & Knave, Having No Con-Science or Innate Science. [*R.D.* 989]

The fourth and fifth discourses (Dec. 1771 and 1772) are concerned with the grand style, of which the acknowledged masters are Michelangelo and Raphael, and the ornamental style, originated by the Venetian school. Students must not attempt to portray the passions if they wish to succeed in the grand style. Art has its boundaries.

> If you mean to preserve the most perfect beauty *in its most perfect state*, you cannot express the passions, all of which produce distortion and deformity, more or less, in the most beautiful faces.

Blake reacts fiercely to this waxwork idea of ideal beauty:

> What Nonsense!
>
> Passion & Expression is Beauty Itself. The Face that is Incapable of Passion & Expression is deformity Itself. Let it be Painted & Patch'd & Praised & Advertised for Ever, it will only be admired by Fools. [*R.D.* 997]

The sixth discourse (Dec. 1774) renews the assault on inspiration. Reynolds blames certain artists who, though they well know how their skill was acquired, and that 'our art, being intrinsically imitative, rejects this idea of inspiration, more perhaps than any other', feel it is to their advantage not to undeceive the public on this point. They prefer the mysterious reputation of magicians. Here Blake interjects:

> Reynolds Thinks that Man Learns all that he knows. I say on the Contrary that Man Brings All that he has or can have Into the World with him. Man is Born Like a Garden ready Planted & Sown. This World is too poor to produce one Seed. [*R.D.* 1004]

And when Reynolds goes on: 'The mind is but a barren soil; a soil which is soon exhausted, and will produce no crop, or only one, unless it be constantly fertilized and enriched with foreign matter', Blake's indignation reaches its climax:

> The mind that could have produced this Sentence must have been a Pitiful, a Pitiable Imbecillity. I always thought that the Human Mind was the most Prolific of All Things & Inexhaustible. I certainly do Thank God that I am not like Reynolds. [*R.D.* 1004]

Imitation, Reynolds continues, may be of Nature, which 'is, and must be the fountain which alone is inexhaustible; and from which all excellences must originally flow'. But 'the sagacious imitator' also turns to the work of acknowledged masters; he will borrow

> a particular thought, an action, attitude or figure, and transplant it into his own work; this will either come under the charge of plagiarism, or be warrantable, and deserve commendation, according to the address with which it is performed.

Sir Joshua quotes the example of the Spartans, who did not punish theft, 'but the want of artifice to conceal it'. Albert Dürer, Van Leyden and others 'afford a rich mass of genuine materials, which wrought up and polished to elegance, will add copiousness to what, perhaps, without such aid, would have aspired only to justness and propriety'. Blake's comment on this cool piece of effrontery is concise: 'A Polish'd Villain who Robs & Murders!'

The purpose of Discourse VII (Dec. 1776) is, in Blake's view,

> to Prove That Taste & Genius are not of Heavenly Origin & that all who have supposed that they Are so, are to be Consider'd as Weak headed Fanatics.
>
> The Obligations Reynolds has laid on Bad Artists of all Classes will at all times make them his Admirers, but most especially for this discourse, in which it is proved that the Stupid are born with Faculties Equal to other Men, Only they have not Cultivated them because they thought it not worth the trouble. [*R.D.* 1006–7]

Reynolds enquires into the culture necessary to the painter. It should include an acquaintance with poetry, 'that he may imbibe a poetical spirit, and enlarge his stock of ideas'. Then there is philosophy, which he can get partly from desultory reading, and partly from the conversation of 'learned and ingenious men'. Thus, without formal study, he will lay the foundations of a solid taste. The rest of the discourse is taken up with a consideration of what taste is and how it operates.

The eighth discourse is the last on which Blake comments; it was delivered in December 1778, the year Blake entered the Royal Academy. Here Reynolds traces the progress of the art from simplicity to complexity. Reynolds was no admirer of the Italian primitives; it is significant that though he travelled through Perugia, Assisi and Arezzo in 1752 his Notebooks have no reference to the masterpieces of early painting there. He held, in common with the age in which he lived, the dogma that primitive art was bare and thin for lack of knowledge—'too simple and too inartificial'.

> The art in its infancy, like the first work of a Student, was dry, hard and simple. But this kind of barbarous simplicity would be better named penury, as it proceeds from mere want; from want of knowledge, want of resources, want of abilities to be otherwise: their simplicity was the offspring, not of choice, but of necessity.

'A Lie!' is Blake's laconic comment. He well knew the reasons for which the devotional artists suppressed realism in favour of conventional forms.

It will be unnecessary to go on to analyse those remaining discourses on which Blake did not comment. Reynolds, as we have seen, lacks originality, and his addresses are full of repetition; but he has the great merit of summing-up the attitude of his age, and he makes an excellent foil for the flashes of Blake's insight and indignation. Without Reynolds, and the opposition of Reynolds' disciples, we should never have had the magnificent *Descriptive Catalogue* of the 1809 exhibition (the year following Blake's annotations to the discourses).

The themes of the *Catalogue* take us to the very heart of Blake's ideas on aesthetics; and I have made full use of it to illustrate other chapters of this book. The spirit is precisely that of the Reynolds' annotations:

> shall Painting be confined to the sordid drudgery of fac-simile representations of merely mortal and perishing substances, and not be as poetry and music are, elevated into its own proper sphere of invention and visionary conception? [*D.C.* 794]

But in the *Descriptive Catalogue* we are conscious of a new turn to the argument: an insistence on the *clarity* of visionary perception. Some critics had objected to Blake's representing spirits with material bodies. He retorts that the Greek statues of Apollo and Minerva, which *they* so much admire, are all representations of spiritual existences. All spiritual essences are seen as men, whether by artists, apostles, or prophets. And spirits are not vague or shadowy things, but the most clearly defined of all objects:

> A Spirit and a Vision are not, as the modern philosophy supposes, a cloudy vapour, or a nothing: they are organized and minutely articulated beyond all that the mortal and perishing nature can produce. He who does not imagine in stronger and better lineaments, and in stronger and better light than his perishing and mortal eye can see, does not imagine at all. The painter of this work asserts that all his imaginations appear to him infinitely more perfect and more minutely organized than any thing seen by his mortal eye. Spirits are organized men. [*D.C.* 795]

We understand, then, what Blake meant when he said that the physical world became shadowy to him. He actually lived in a world of vision in comparison with which the concrete things around him were wavering and ill-defined. And here Blake has the unanimous testimony of the mystics to support him. Either what is seen is *nothing* (not *a nothing*), 'darkness, call it solitude or blank desertion', a complete deprivation of sense; or there are perfectly clear visual forms.[1] The great spiritual classics, from the Vedas to the Book of Revelation and the writings of St Teresa, are quite matter-of-fact in their descriptions. Mistiness is always the sign of a false mysticism: one which, through lack of expression in art, has sunk into corruption. That which is most real must evidently be seen with most clarity. It is in the 'low dream', not the 'high dream', that the sheeted ghost and vaporous spectre appear. The Angel of the Annunciation manifests himself with every feather in his wings distinct.

Precision is the master-word of the *Catalogue* and of the *Public Address* which followed in 1810. Precision in vision, in ideas, in expression:

> I have heard many People say, 'Give me the Ideas. It is no matter what Words you put them into,' & others say, 'Give me the Design, it is no matter for the Execution'. These People know Enough of Artifice, but Nothing Of Art. Ideas cannot be Given but in their minutely Appropriate Words, nor Can a Design be made without its minutely Appropriate Execution. [*P.A.* 814]

Again we see the remarkable unifying faculty of Blake's mind at work. His intuition of the organic relation of 'theme' and 'expression' is a commonplace now, though we still almost invariably *act* on the belief that it is the 'idea' that matters and not the 'way it is put'.

The firmness of outline in ancient art is probably the chief point which attracted Blake. As in his annotations to the *Discourses*, he defends the primitives and again states his belief that there is no progress in art. Concerning his own designs he writes:

> He knows what he does is not inferior to the grandest Antiques. Superior they cannot be, for human power cannot go beyond either what he does, or what they have done; it is the gift of God, it is inspiration and vision....Poetry as it exists now on earth, in the various remains of ancient authors, Music as it exists in old tunes or melodies, Painting and Sculpture as it exists in the remains of Antiquity and in the works of more modern genius, is Inspiration, and cannot be surpassed; it is perfect and eternal....The human mind cannot go beyond the gift of God, the Holy

---

[1] More accurately, perhaps, there is *first* the experience of nothingness—the moment of union; then *secondly*, and only in the case of visualisers like Blake, the perception of forms as the moment of union becomes mediated to the understanding.

Ghost. To suppose that Art can go beyond the finest specimens of Art that are now in the world, is not knowing what Art is; it is being blind to the gifts of the spirit. [*D.C.* 798]

This belief in the non-progressiveness of art shows how firmly Blake, perhaps alone in his time, had grasped the principles I have outlined in the first paragraphs of the present chapter: the archetypal nature of art, its roots in metaphysics, and its adaptation of the means to the end. Where art is successful in what it sets out to do, the means are irrelevant. If the primitives produce an effect which even to-day can move us devotionally as the later painters cannot, they have done perfectly what they attempted to do. There is no other criterion.

CHAPTER XXIV

The New Man

O what wonders are the Children of Men! Would to God that they would consider it! [*L.* 1120]

THE remarkable and heartening thing about Blake is that, in spite of all the buffets he got from life, he never fell away from his early emotion of awe at the wonder of Man's existence. He never tried to escape into a Manless universe, as Wordsworth and Byron did. Man is his proper study every time and all the time. All his efforts are directed towards raising Man towards a perception of his infinite potentialities. His aim is to *untwist* the human spirit: and that is why his own longer poems go through such extraordinary convolutions. He is tracing the dark labyrinths of the human brain. He is analysing and assessing the twists and distortions men and women receive in their childhood and carry with them through life. And he is trying to show a way out of the labyrinth.

We have seen the therapy he suggests. First, self-consciousness, self-exploration. 'Thy own eternal lineaments explore' in order to find out 'what is annihilable and what is not'.

"Learn therefore, O Sisters, to distinguish the Eternal Human
That walks about among the stones of fire in bliss & woe
Alternate, from those States or Worlds in which the Spirit travels.
This is the only means to Forgiveness of Enemies.
Therefore remove from Albion these terrible Surfaces.... [*J.* 645]

These terrible surfaces, these masks with which the true Self is hidden, are formed by the neuroses of fear and anxiety and blindness to vision. First we must recognise these neuroses for what they are—see them in all their ramifications, poisoning the springs of our life. Then we must deal with them, by a determined turning away from the selfhood to the non-self, to God who is to be loved in the service of humanity as well as in the act of pure contemplation.

It matters little which of these phases comes first—the love of God 'without' the soul or the love of God 'within'. For these are merely two aspects of the same thing. Which comes first will depend largely on temperament. There are some men, as Blake says, who see God most clearly in the faces of their fellow-men. There are others who find God in silent contemplation and then, when they turn back to the world, see their fellows' faces irradiated by the same divine light that has shone upon their own minds in ecstasy. What matters is that we *connect.* We must avoid the great temptation to separate Man and God in the manner of those tight-lipped pseudo-Christians who are so assiduous in devotion and exploitation alike.

If we really get down to understanding our weaknesses, and really seek the presence of God, we shall begin to find in us the urge to create. Now comes the rôle of art, by practising which in some form or other we save our aspirations from becoming vague, and give a form to energies which have been long suppressed. We learn to see into the spiritual forms of Nature, and we convey our new insight through rhythmic patterns of line and mass and colour and sound. And by so doing, we open a way into understanding for our fellows who may still be struggling with ignorance.

By all these means the New Man that Blake envisaged is liberated from the shell of custom and fears and anxieties which beset him hitherto. In Blake many of his friends sensed the emergence of this New Man, without quite understanding his nature. They were puzzled, shocked, indignant, pitying—but fascinated. He vibrated with energy, and in his presence they began to feel the contagion of vision too. To their astonishment he made them see things they had never seen before. They experienced a new kind of life. 'Blake's mind warmed his listener's, kindled his imagination; almost creating in him a new sense', says Gilchrist, who knew the men who had walked and talked with Blake in his latter days. Samuel Palmer and Francis Oliver Finch were among these young friends. Palmer wrote, in a letter to Gilchrist: 'Blake, once known, could never be forgotten.... In him you saw at once the Maker, the Inventor; one of the few in any age....He was energy itself, and shed around him a kindling influence; an atmosphere of life, full of the ideal. To walk with him in the country was to perceive the soul of beauty through the forms of matter....He was one of the few to be met with in our passage through life, who are not in some way or other, 'double-minded' and inconsistent with themselves....He was a man without a mask....'

And Oliver Finch, in the decisive phrase: 'He struck me as *a new kind of man*.'

A new kind of man—not double-minded—a man without a mask—creating a new sense. . . . The evidence is conclusive. Blake's influence was not lost in his own day, there were a few who listened to him and learned from him: and who knows through what devious ways their insight has come down to us to-day, creating here and there in modern England little oases of understanding and freedom. But Blake's influence must not rest there. He has left behind in his writings and his designs treasures of insight and wisdom, and the imaginative outline of a technique of inner liberation which must form part of our system of education if we are to escape, in this new age that is upon us, from the limitations and frustrations which up to now have barred humanity's progress towards happiness. At the beginning of this book I gave it as my opinion that Blake was the great teacher of the modern Western world; and I hold to that opinion. But Blake pointed away from himself to Christ as the Lord and Master of whom he was but the disciple: the works of Blake provide us with a new interpretation of the Everlasting Gospel, but that Gospel as delivered by Jesus is primary. And with that Gospel we must correlate every other aspect of wisdom: especially those which come to us from the East which taught 'the first principles of human perception'. Every system of thought which teaches Man to advance in self-consciousness must be brought under contribution for the new synthesis.

Advancing along a different line the art or science of psychology has come to the same position as Blake's. In the latest thinkers there seems to be a move away from the Freudian emphasis on the libido towards a stressing of the importance of environmental conditions in childhood. Writers like Karen Horney[1] and Erich Fromm believe that neuroses have their origin in the frustration of a child's growth of personality by its environment, and particularly by hostile or over-

[1] I cannot, however, agree with Karen Horney's assertion that 'the individual in our culture is as a rule not prepared for the hostilities and struggles that are in store for him. He is taught that people are well-intentioned toward him, that it is a virtue to confide in others, and that to be on one's guard is almost a moral defect' (*New Ways in Psycho-analysis*). I should say that the opposite is true: that he is taught to be suspicious and hostile, and that his suspicion and hostility engender the same reactions in others.

demonstrative parents. Thwarted in its personal relationships, the child has no other line of defence than to retire into itself. Hence in later life the neurotic's incapacity for normal relations with other human beings, and the pervasive anxiety which regards any intrusion upon his isolation as a threat to security. The story of this process is written large on the pages of the *Songs of Innocence and Experience* and in the *Miscellaneous Poems*. The trend to safety *away from* the pleasure urge is traced in, for example, *The Angel*, *My Pretty Rose Tree*, and '*An Old Maid Early*', and in all the retreats and refusals of Enitharmon in the symbolic books. The thwarting of growth which leads up to this fugitive trend is shown in *The Little Boy Lost*, *The Schoolboy*, *The Clod and the Pebble*, *Nurse's Song* [II], the full version of *Infant Sorrow* in the *Miscellaneous Poems*, *A Little Boy Lost*, and *A Little Girl Lost*. And the consequences of these thwartings and resultant inhibitions in adult life are made plain in *London*, *A Poison Tree*, '*Never seek to tell thy Love*', '*I laid me down upon a Bank*', '*I asked a thief to steal me a peach*', '*I fear'd the fury of my wind*', and the whole course of the longer poems.

Blake's great advantage over the psychologists has been indicated earlier in this book. It is his genius as poet and artist. The psychologists are the grammarians of the new age, the psychiatrists are the doctors: both fulfil an indispensable if temporary function. But Blake is the interpreter and the educator. The group of young men who surrounded him in his old age were right to call his rooms in Fountain Court 'the House of the Interpreter'. For this is Blake's great and abiding function—to interpret the eternal world to the minds of men. The study of his poems and designs will form an important part of any scheme of education which envisages the creation of the New Man, the man freed from fear. There will be room for an intelligent grading of Blake's writings and drawings from this point of view: the 'innocent' ones to be studied first, those which describe conflict later, and the 'indignant pages' later still. The child's visionary powers will be drawn out and supported by Blake's visions, his delight in song and dance will be sustained through the medium of Blake's lyrics set to suitable music. Thus the study of Blake's work may become a living reality in the life and education of the future.

INDEX

[NOTE. The more important references are given in heavy type. Titles of written works are given in italics. Titles of paintings, engravings and other designs are given between double inverted commas.]